General Lifestyle Survey

Results for 2009

CONTENTS

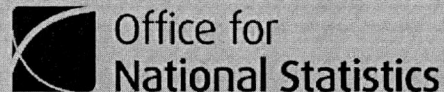
Manual workers smoke more but drink less than professionals

General Lifestyle Survey 2009

Date: 27 January 2011.
Coverage: Great Britain **Theme:** Health

Smoking is nearly twice as common among adults in routine and manual occupation groups as it is in managerial and professional groups. In households classified as routine and manual, 29 per cent of adults smoked cigarettes, compared to 15 per cent of adults in managerial and professional households. (Table 1.8)

In contrast, when it comes to drinking, managers and professionals have a higher weekly alcohol intake than routine and manual workers. Average weekly alcohol consumption was 13.5 units for adults in households classified as managerial and professional and 10.7 units for adults in routine and manual households. (Table 2.6)

These facts are set out in *Smoking and drinking among adults, 2009,* published today by the Office for National Statistics as part of the General Lifestyle Survey (See Background Note 1).
Other facts revealed on smoking habits in 2009 were:

- For the third year running, 21 per cent of the adult population in Great Britain were cigarette smokers, compared to 45 per cent in 1974 when the smoking data were first collected (Table 1.1)
- The smoking prevalence difference between men and women has substantially dropped, to 22 per cent (men) and 20 per cent (women) in 2009, from the 1974 level of 51 per cent (men) and 41 per cent (women) (Table 1.1)
- In the regions of England, prevalence was highest in the North West, where 23 per cent of adults were smokers and lowest in the South West (18 per cent) (Table 1.11)
- Nearly two thirds of smokers said they would like to give up. The proportion wanting to give up has decreased from 72 per cent in 2000 to 63 per cent in 2009 (Table 1.28)

Although filter-tipped cigarettes continue to be the most widely smoked type of cigarette, especially among women, there has been a substantial increase in the proportion of smokers who smoke

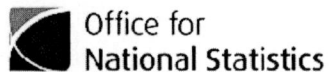
mainly hand-rolled tobacco. In 2009 21 per cent of women smokers said they rolled their own, compared to only 2 per cent in 1990. In 2009 37 per cent of men smokers rolled their own compared with 18 per cent in 1990. (Table 1.17)

Other facts revealed on drinking habits in 2009 were:

- In managerial and professional households, 41 per cent of men exceeded 4 units and 35 per cent of women exceeded 3 units on at least one day in the week before interview, compared to 34 per cent of men and 23 per cent of women in routine and manual households (Table 2.14)

- In managerial and professional households, 23 per cent of men and 15 per cent of women drank heavily (more than 8 units for men, more than 6 units for women) on at least one day in the previous week, compared to 19 per cent of men and 11 per cent of women in routine and manual households (Table 2.14)

- Average weekly consumption was similar in all age groups from 16 to 64 years but was much lower in the 65 and over group (Table 2.1)

- Older age groups tended to drink more often than younger age groups. The proportions drinking on 5 or more days in the week before interview were: 4 per cent (16-24 years), 10 per cent (25-44), 18 per cent (45-64) and 20 per cent (65 and over). The proportions drinking every day in the previous week were: 1 per cent (16-24 years), 4 per cent (25-44), 10 per cent (45-64) and 14 per cent (65 and over) (Table 2.11)

- When they did drink, however, young people were more likely to drink heavily than older people. Of those that drank alcohol in the week before interview, the proportions who drank heavily on at least one day were: 46 per cent (16-24 years), 35 per cent (25-44), 25 per cent (45-64), 6 per cent (65 and over) (Table 2.12b)

The current recommendations for daily alcohol intake are that it should not regularly exceed three to four units for men and two to three units for women.

Smoking and drinking among adults, 2009 can be found at
www.statistics.gov.uk/statbase/Product.asp?vlnk=5756

Today, ONS also releases alcohol-related death rates for the UK, England, Wales and Government Office Regions for 2009 (and revised rates for 2002 to 2008 due to revisions in the mid-year population estimates). Data and a Statistical Bulletin can be found at
www.statistics.gov.uk/statbase/Product.asp?vlnk=14496

Background Notes

1.   Smoking and drinking among adults, 2009 is based on information provided by 13,488 respondents aged over 16. The data were collected as part of the General Lifestyle Survey (GLF). An overview report on other findings from the GLF is also published today.

2.   The General Lifestyle Survey (GLF) is a multi-purpose continuous survey carried out by the Office for National Statistics. It collects information on a range of topics from people living in private households in Great Britain. The survey presents a picture of households, families and people living in Great Britain. This information is used by government departments and other organisations, such as educational establishments, businesses and charities to contribute to policy decisions and for planning and monitoring purposes.

3.   Classifications such as 'routine and manual' and 'managerial and professional' are based on the National Statistics Socio-economic Classification (NS-SEC). The 3 class version of NS-SEC also includes an intermediate group. Occupations classified as routine and manual include call centre worker, electrician, train driver, HGV driver, postal worker, shop assistant. Occupations classified as intermediate include secretary, fireman, self-employed with fewer than 25 employees, e.g. self-employed builder, hairdresser, car dealer, shop-owner. Occupations classified as managerial and professional include doctors, nurses, teachers, lawyers, actors and those usually responsible for planning, organising and co-ordinating work or finance.   Further information is available at:
http://www.ons.gov.uk/about-statistics/classifications/current/ns-sec/index.html

4.   A standard unit is the equivalent of 10ml of ethyl alcohol. A single 25 ml measure of spirits with an ABV (alcohol by volume) of 40 per cent contains one unit of alcohol.

5.   An article titled 'Social inequalities in alcohol related adult mortality by National Statistics Socio-Economic Classification, England and Wales, 2001-03' will be published in *Health Statistics Quarterly* No 50 (Summer 2011) on 24 May 2011.

6.   Details of the policy governing the release of new data are available from the media office.

7.   National Statistics are produced to high professional standards set out in the Code of Practice for Official Statistics. They undergo regular quality assurance reviews to ensure that they meet customer needs. They are produced free from any political interference.
© Crown copyright 2011.

....

Issued by: Office for National Statistics, Government Buildings, Cardiff Road, Newport NP10 8XG

Media contact:
Tel   **Jim Campbell   0845 6041858**
           Emergency on-call   07867 906553
E-mail   **press.office@ons.gsi.gov.uk**

Statistical contact:

Tel   **Steven Dunstan 01633 455628**

E-mail   **socialsurveys@ons.gsi.gov.uk**

Website:

www.ons.gov.uk

General Lifestyle Survey Overview

A report on the 2009 General Lifestyle Survey

Editor: **Steven Dunstan**

Office for National Statistics

A National Statistics publication

National Statistics are produced to high professional standards set out in the Code of Practice for Official Statistics. They are produced free from political influence.

About us

The Office for National Statistics

The Office for National Statistics (ONS) is the executive office of the UK Statistics Authority, a non-ministerial department which reports directly to Parliament. ONS is the UK government's single largest statistical producer. It compiles information about the UK's society and economy, and provides the evidence-base for policy and decision-making, the allocation of resources, and public accountability. The Director-General of ONS reports directly to the National Statistician who is the Authority's Chief Executive and the Head of the Government Statistical Service.

The Government Statistical Service

The Government Statistical Service (GSS) is a network of professional statisticians and their staff operating both within the Office for National Statistics and across more than 30 other government departments and agencies.

Contacts

This publication

For information about the content of this publication, contact the General Lifestyle Survey
Tel: 01633 455678
Email: socialsurveys@ons.gsi.gov.uk

Principal Research Officer: Steven Dunstan

Other customer enquiries

ONS Customer Contact Centre
Tel: 0845 601 3034
International: +44 (0)845 601 3034
Minicom: 01633 815044
Email: info@statistics.gsi.gov.uk
Fax: 01633 652747
Post: Room 1.101, Government Buildings, Cardiff Road, Newport, South Wales NP10 8XG
www.ons.gov.uk

Media enquiries

Tel: 0845 604 1858
Email: press.office@ons.gsi.gov.uk

Copyright and reproduction

Contents

1: Overview

2: Overview tables

3: Reference to technical appendices

Introduction

This report presents the latest information from the General LiFestyle Survey (GLF) for the 2009 calendar year (January to December). The report comprises a basic overview, covering the main topics of the survey, and tabular output for the Smoking; Drinking; Housing and consumer durables; Marriage and cohabitation; Pensions; and General health and use of health services topic areas. The tabular output is provided in the form of Microsoft Excel tables that can be downloaded by clicking on the table references within the report.

The GLF was previously known as the General Household Survey (GHS), but was renamed in 2008 to coincide with the survey's inclusion in the Integrated Household Survey (www.statistics.gov.uk/StatBase/Product.asp?vlnk=15381&Pos=&ColRank=1&Rank=422).

Survey background

The GLF is a multi-purpose continuous survey carried out by the Office for National Statistics (ONS). It collects information on a range of topics from people living in private households in Great Britain. The survey started as the GHS in 1971 and has been carried out continuously since then, except for breaks to review it in 1997/1998 and to redevelop it in 1999/2000.

The survey presents a picture of households, families and people living in Great Britain. This information is used by government departments and other organisations, such as educational establishments, businesses and charities, to contribute to policy decisions and for planning and monitoring purposes.

The interview consists of questions relating to the household, answered by a household reference person or spouse, and an individual questionnaire, asked of all resident adults aged 16 and over. Demographic and health information is also collected about children in the household. The GLF collects data on a wide range of core topics which are included on the survey every year. These are:

- demographic information about households, families and people
- housing tenure and household accommodation
- access to and ownership of consumer durables, including vehicles
- employment
- education
- health and use of health services
- smoking
- drinking
- family information, including marriage, cohabitation and fertility

- income

The 2009 GLF was sponsored by ONS, the NHS Information Centre for Health and Social Care, Department for Work and Pensions, HM Revenue & Customs and Scottish Government.

From 1994-95 to 2004-05 the GHS was conducted on a financial year basis, with fieldwork spread evenly across the year April to March. However, in 2005 the survey period reverted to a calendar year and the whole of the annual sample (which was increased to 16,560), was dealt with in the nine months April to December 2005. From January 2006, the survey runs from January to December each year.

Since the 2005 survey did not cover the January to March quarter, this affected annual estimates for topics which are subject to seasonal variation. To rectify this, where the questions were the same in 2005 as in 2004-05, the final quarter of the 2004-05 survey was added (weighted in the correct proportion) to the nine months of the 2005 survey.

Another change in 2005 was that, in line with European requirements, GHS adopted a longitudinal sample design in which people remain in the sample for four years (waves) with one quarter of the sample being replaced each year. Thus approximately three quarters of the 2005 sample were re-interviewed in 2006. More details are given in Appendix B.

The 2009 survey

In 2009, 8,206 households in Great Britain took part in the GLF and around 15,000 interviews were conducted with adults aged 16 and older. The household response rate was 73 per cent. Further details about the sample design and response are given in Appendix B.

A glossary of definitions and terms used throughout the report and notes on how these have changed over time is provided in Appendix A.

The survey results (from 1998) have been adjusted to account for non-response to the survey and to control for differences between the sample and population. Details of the weighting process are given in Appendix D.

The GLF is a survey of a sample of the population and is therefore subject to sampling error, where the estimates inferred from the sample are not the same as if a census of the population was taken. A measure of this error is provided by the standard error estimates, which are published against certain statistics in Appendix C.

The questionnaire that was used to collect the 2009 survey data is given in Appendix E; and a list of the main topics covered by the survey since it began in 1971 is provided in Appendix F.

Related links

A separate report on the 2009 GLF smoking and drinking results can be found on the ONS website at www.statistics.gov.uk/StatBase/Product.asp?vlnk=5756.

GLF 2009 results will be combined with those from other sources in the ONS *Social Trends, Pension Trends and Health Statistics Quarterly* releases that will be published later in 2011.

Social Trends:
www.statistics.gov.uk/StatBase/Product.asp?vlnk=13675&Pos=&ColRank=1&Rank=422

Pension Trends:
www.statistics.gov.uk/StatBase/Product.asp?vlnk=14173&Pos=&ColRank=1&Rank=422

Health Statistics Quarterly:
www.statistics.gov.uk/StatBase/Product.asp?vlnk=6725&Pos=&ColRank=2&Rank=448

The GLF results are for private households in Great Britain; however, a similar survey called the Continuous Household Survey (CHS) is carried out in Northern Ireland. The survey is designed, conducted and analysed by the Central Survey Unit of the Northern Ireland Statistics and Research Agency (NISRA): www.csu.nisra.gov.uk/survey.asp29.htm

Additional tabulations

This report gives a broad overview of the results of the survey, including tabular output. However, many users of GLF data have very specific data requirements that may not appear in the desired form in this report. The ONS can provide more detailed analysis of the tables in this report, and can also provide additional tabulations to meet specific requests. A charge will be made to cover the cost of providing additional information.

Anonymised microdata from the GLF and GHS surveys are available from the United Kingdom Data Archive. Details on access arrangements and associated costs can be found at www.data-archive.ac.uk or by telephoning 01206 872143.

List of Contributors

Authors:	Riaz Ali
	Steven Dunstan
General Lifestyle Survey team:	Deborah Curtis
	Simon Robinson
	Sian-Elin Wyatt
	Jayne White
	Vicky Darke
	Mike Tom
	Paul Horton
	Teresa McCloy
Reviewers:	NHS Information Centre for Health and Social Care
	Department for Work and Pensions
	Department for Communities and Local Government
	Scottish Government
	HM Revenue & Customs
	Department for Culture, Media and Sport
	ONS Centre for Demography
	ONS Centre for Health Analysis and Life Events
	ONS Economic Labour and Social Analysis
Other contributors:	Steven Maurice

Acknowledgements

A large scale survey is a collaborative effort and the authors wish to thank the interviewers and other ONS staff who contributed to the study. The authors would also like to thank the sponsors for both their contribution and ongoing commitment to the survey. Also, the help of respondents who gave up their time to be interviewed is gratefully appreciated, without their co-operation the survey would not be possible.

Overview

This overview provides a brief summary of some of the key findings from the General LiFestyle Survey (GLF), and the General Household Survey (GHS). There is separate report for the smoking and drinking survey topics: http://www.statistics.gov.uk/StatBase/Product.asp?vlnk=5756.

All of the tables referred to in the overview can be accessed by clicking on the links in the *List of tables* section of the report.

Households, families and people

Between 1971 and 1991 the average size of a household in Great Britain declined from 2.91 persons to 2.48. It continued to decline, though at a slower rate, throughout the 1990s falling to 2.32 by 1998, since then it has changed little. In 2009 the average number of persons per household was 2.35. (*Table 3.1*)

The proportion of people that live alone has increased considerably since the 1970s. In 1973, 9 per cent of adults lived alone, compared with 16 per cent of adults in 2009. There were also marked differences between the age groups. For example, adults aged 25 to 44 were five times more likely to live alone in 2009 (10 per cent) than in 1973 (2 per cent). (*Table 3.3*)

In 2009, 77 per cent of families with dependent children in Great Britain were headed by a married or cohabiting couple, no change since 2007. This proportion fell markedly in the 1970s, 1980s and 1990s, (92 per cent of families were of this type in 1971) but has changed little since the late 1990s. The percentage of families that are headed by a lone mother increased from 7 per cent in 1971 to 22 per cent in 1998 and has changed little since then. In 2009, 20 per cent of families were headed by a lone mother. The proportion headed by a lone father has increased marginally since the early 1970s, but since the mid-1990s has remained at about 2 to 3 per cent. In total, the proportion of families headed by a lone parent was 8 per cent in 1971, but is nearly three times higher in 2009 at 23 per cent. (*Table 3.6*)

In 2009, 51 per cent of families with dependent children headed by a lone parent, had a usual weekly gross income of £300 or less; compared with only 11 per cent of families headed by a married couple and 15 per cent of those headed by a cohabiting couple. (*Table 3.11*)

Housing and consumer durables

Between 1971 and 2009 the proportion of households owning their home rose from 49 per cent to 69 per cent. Most of the increase occurred during the 1980s and was due to a marked increase in the proportion of households owning with a mortgage. (*Table 4.1*)

The percentage of households renting council homes increased from 31 per cent in 1971 to 34 per cent in 1981, but since then has declined steadily to 10 per cent in 2009. (*Table 4.1*)

The percentage of households renting from a housing association increased from 1 per cent in 1971 to 3 per cent in 1991 with the increase continuing since then to 8 per cent in 2009. (*Table 4.1*)

The percentage of households renting privately fell from 20 per cent in 1971 to 10 per cent in 1995. Between 1995 and 2008 the proportion remained between 9 and 11 per cent, but increased to 13 per cent in 2009. This increase was offset by a decrease in the proportion of owner occupiers with a mortgage from 39 per cent in 2008 to 37 per cent in 2009. (*Table 4.1*)

The shift between owner occupiers with a mortgage and private renters is most evident for households where the household reference person (HRP) had been resident for less than 2 years. For example, the proportion of owner-occupiers with a mortgage decreased from 43 per cent in 2008 to 27 per cent in 2009, but the proportion of private renters increased from 31 per cent to 50 per cent for the group where length of residency of the HRP was 12 months but less than 2 years. (*Table 4.13*)

Since the early 1970s the survey has recorded a significant increase in the ownership of many consumer durables and household amenities. For example, 97 per cent of households had central heating in 2009, compared with only 37 per cent in 1972. Access to a car or van has also risen since the survey began (at least one car or van was available to 52 per cent of households in 1972, this increased to 77 per cent in 2009). (*Table 4.19*)

Just over half (54 per cent) of all households had a telephone in 1975. In 2009 over 99 per cent had a phone (either fixed or mobile). In 2000, when the GHS first asked about mobile phones, the proportion of households in which at least one person had a mobile phone was 58 per cent; this increased to 84 per cent in 2009. (*Table 4.19*)

The proportion of households with a home computer increased from 13 per cent in 1985 to 76 per cent of all households in 2009. (*Table 4.19*)

Marriage and cohabitation

In the 1970s the GHS asked women aged 18 to 49 about their current marriage, since then the questions have been developed and extended from time to time to reflect changes taking place in society. The survey now obtains information about marital history and periods of cohabitation from all adults aged 16 to 59.

In 2009, 13 per cent of both men and women aged 16 to 59 were cohabiting. Among men aged 16 to 59, those in the 25 to 34 age groups were more likely to cohabit than any other age group (25 per cent of men aged 25 to 29 and 28 per cent of men aged 30 to 34, compared with fewer than 18 per cent in all other age groups). Among women, 28 per cent of those aged 25 to 29 were cohabiting compared with 3 to 23 per cent in the other age groups. However the difference between the 25 to 29 and 30 to 34 age groups was not statistically significant in 2009. (*Table 5.3*)

Among women aged 18 to 49, the longest time series for which data are available, the proportion of women who were married at the time of interview declined from 74 per cent in 1979 to 47 per cent in 2009. The proportion of women who were single (i.e. who had never been married) more than doubled from 18 per cent in 1979 to 38 per cent in 2002. In 2009, 43 per cent of women aged 18 to 49 were single. (*Table 5.7*)

The proportion of non-married women aged 18 to 49 who were cohabiting at the time of interview, has increased from 11 per cent in 1979 to 32 per cent in 2009. (*Table 5.8*)

Occupational and personal pension schemes

The GHS has included questions on occupational pensions on a regular basis since 1981 and on personal pensions since 1987. The GLF continues to include these questions.

Occupational pension schemes are schemes provided by employers. They do not include group personal pensions, group stakeholder pensions or group self-invested personal pensions. Since 1989, trends in participation in occupational pension schemes have differed for men and women and for those working part-time and full-time.

The proportion of men working full-time who were members of their current employer's occupational pension scheme decreased from 64 per cent in 1989 to 54 per cent in 2000 and has remained at between 53 and 55 per cent every year since then. In 2009, 54 per cent of men working full-time were members of their current employer's occupational pension scheme. The percentage of women working full-time who were members of their current employer's occupational pension scheme showed a different pattern, rising from 55 per cent in 1989 to 60 per cent in 2002. In 2009, 58 per cent of women working full-time were members of their current employer's occupational pension scheme. (*Table 6.3*)

Among women working part-time, the proportions who were members of their current employer's occupational pension scheme has increased from 15 per cent in 1989 to 40 per cent in 2009. (*Table 6.3*)

Since 1991 the survey has provided trend data on personal pension arrangements among self-employed men. The possession of a current personal pension among self-employed men working full-time remained fairly stable between 1991 and 1998 at around two thirds. Between 1998 and 2009 the proportion with a current personal pension decreased from 64 per cent to 38 per cent. (*Table 6.13*)

For full-time and part-time combined, self-employed men were more likely than self-employed women to have a current personal pension arrangements (35 per cent of self-employed men compared with 22 per cent of self-employed women were contributing to a personal pension scheme in 2009). Over a third (39 per cent) of self-employed men had never had a personal pension compared with over a half (58 per cent) of women. (*Table 6.12*)

General health and use of health services

The GLF provides information about the self-reported health of adults and, by proxy, children including their use of health services.

In 2008 the question relating to health over the previous 12 months, that had three possible responses; 'good', 'fairly good' or 'not good', was replaced by a question relating to health in general with five possible responses; 'very good', 'good', 'fair', 'bad' or 'very bad'. This new question, harmonised with national surveys across the European Union, was originally added to the GHS in 2005 and a time series from 2005 to 2009 is provided in table 7.1. In 2009, 40 per cent of adults said their general health was very good, 39 per cent reported good health, 15 per cent reported they had fair health, 5 per cent reported they had bad health and 1 per cent said their health was very bad. (*Table 7.1*)

To allow comparisons between the two general health questions, both were included on the GHS (and asked of all adults) between 2005 and 2007, with the three-category question asked first. This means that responses during this period may be subject to bias caused by question exposure/order effects, for example, where adults who might have otherwise responded 'very good' to the five-category question could have responded 'good' in line with the highest category of the three-category question. This might explain the notable change in the percentages between the 'very good' and 'good' categories between 2007 and 2008. Therefore care should be taken if drawing conclusions concerning this change. (*Table 7.1*)

Thirty per cent of people (averaged over all age groups) reported a long standing illness or disability in 2009. Just over half of those with long standing illness or disability, 18 per cent of all respondents, said that it limited their activities. (*Table 7.2*)

In 2009, 15 per cent of adults and children had consulted an NHS GP in the 14 days before interview. This proportion has changed little in the previous 30 years. Females had an average of six NHS GP consultations per year, whereas males had four. (*Table 7.17 and Table 7.18*)

The proportion of respondents who had attended an outpatient or casualty department in the three months before interview increased from 10 per cent in 1972 to 16 per cent in 1998 and then fell to 14 per cent in 2001. In 2009, 13 per cent of all respondents had attended an outpatient or casualty department in the three months before interview. (*Table 7.26*)

The proportion of people attending hospitals as day patients in the twelve months before interview increased since this question was first asked in 1992, from 4 per cent to 8 per cent in 2009. A similar proportion of respondents, 7 per cent, reported an inpatient stay in the twelve months before interview, this has stayed the same since 2006. (*Table 7.27 and Table 7.28*)

Overview tables

List of tables

2.4	Maximum drunk on any one day last week by sex and age: 1998 to 2009
2.5	Average weekly alcohol consumption (units), by sex and age
2.6	Average weekly alcohol consumption (units), by sex and socio-economic class based on the current or last job of the household reference person
2.7	Average weekly alcohol consumption (units), by sex and usual gross weekly household income (£)
2.8	Average weekly alcohol consumption (units), by sex and economic activity status
2.9	Average weekly alcohol consumption (units), by sex and usual gross weekly earnings (£)
2.10	Average weekly alcohol consumption (units), by sex and Government Office Region
2.11	Whether drank last week and number of drinking days by sex and age
2.12	Maximum drunk on any one day last week, by sex and age
2.12b	Maximum drunk by those who consumed alcohol on any one day last week, by sex and age
2.13	Drinking last week, by sex, and socio-economic classification based on the current or last job of the household reference person
2.14	Maximum number of units drunk on at least one day last week, by sex and socio-economic classification based on the current or last job of the household reference person
2.15	Drinking last week, by sex and usual gross weekly household income
2.16	Maximum drunk on any one day last week by sex and usual gross weekly household income
2.17	Drinking last week, by sex and economic activity status
2.18	Maximum drunk on any one day last week, by sex and economic activity status
2.19	Drinking last week, by sex and usual gross weekly earnings
2.20	Maximum drunk on any one day last week, by sex and usual gross weekly earnings
2.21	Drinking last week, by sex and Government Office Region
2.22	Maximum drunk on any one day last week, by sex and Government Office Region

3	**Households, families and people**
3.1	Trends in household size: 1971 to 2009
3.2	Trends in household type: 1971 to 2009
3.3	Percentage living alone by age: 1973 to 2009
3.4	Percentage of men and women living alone by age
3.5	Type of household: 1979 to 2009
3.6	Family type and marital status of lone parents: 1971 to 2009
3.7	Families with dependent children: 1972 to 2009
3.8	Average (mean) number of dependent children by family type: 1971 to 2009
3.9	Age of youngest dependent child by family type
3.10	Stepfamilies with dependent children by family type
3.11	Usual gross weekly household income of families with dependent children by family type
3.12	The distribution of the population by sex and age: 1971 to 2009
3.13	Percentage of males and females by age
3.14	Socio-economic classification based on own current or last job by sex and age
3.15	Ethnic group of GHS/GLF respondents: 2001 to 2009
3.16	GLF respondents: age by ethnic group
3.17	GLF respondents: sex by ethnic group
3.18	GLF respondents: Ethnic group by Government Office Region
3.19	GLF respondents: average household size by ethnic group of household reference person
3.20	GLF respondents: percentage born in the UK by age and ethnic group
3.21	Weighted bases for Tables 3.3 and 3.8

4	**Housing and consumer durables**
4.1	Tenure: 1971 to 2009
4.2	Type of accommodation: 1971 to 2009
4.3	Type of accommodation occupied by households renting from a council compared with other households: 1981 to 2009
4.4	(a) Type of accommodation by tenure
	(b) Tenure by type of accommodation
4.5	(a) Household type by tenure
	(b) Tenure by household type
4.6	Housing profile by family type: lone parent families compared with other families

4.7	Type of accommodation by household type
4.8	Usual gross weekly income by tenure
4.9	(a) Age of household reference person by tenure
	(b) Tenure by age of household reference person
4.10	Tenure by sex and marital status of household reference person
4.11	Housing tenure by ethnic group of household reference person
4.12	(a) Socio-economic classification and economic activity status of household reference person by tenure
	(b) Tenure by socio-economic classification and economic activity status of household reference person
4.13	(a) Length of residence of household reference person by tenure
	(b) Tenure by length of residence of household reference person
4.14	Persons per room: 1971 to 2009
4.15	Persons per room and mean household size by tenure
4.16	Closeness of fit relative to the bedroom standard by tenure
4.17	Cars or vans: 1972 to 2009
4.18	Availability of a car or van by socio-economic classification of household reference person
4.19	Consumer durables, central heating and cars: 1972 to 2009
4.20	Consumer durables, central heating and cars by socio-economic classification of household reference person
4.21	Consumer durables, central heating and cars by usual gross weekly household income
4.22	Consumer durables, central heating and cars by household type
4.23	Consumer durables, central heating and cars: lone parent families compared with other families

5	**Marriage and cohabitation**
5.1	Sex by marital status
5.2	(a) Age by sex and marital status
	(b) Marital status by sex and age
5.3	Percentage currently cohabiting by sex and age
5.4	Percentage currently cohabiting by legal marital status and age
5.5	Cohabitees: age by legal marital status
5.6	Cohabitees: age by sex
5.7	Legal marital status of women aged 18-49: 1979 to 2009
5.8	Percentage of women aged 18-49 cohabiting by legal marital status: 1979 to 2009
5.9	Women aged 16-59:
	(a) Whether has dependent children in the household by marital status
	(b) Marital status by whether has dependent children in the household
5.10	Women aged 16-59: percentage cohabiting by legal marital status and whether has dependent children in the household
5.11	Cohabiting women aged 16-59: whether has dependent children in the household by legal marital status
5.12	Number of past cohabitations not ending in marriage by sex and age
5.13	Number of past cohabitations not ending in marriage by current marital status and sex
5.14	Age at first cohabitation which did not end in marriage by year cohabitation began and sex
5.15	Duration of past cohabitations which did not end in marriage by number of past cohabitations and sex

6	**Occupational and personal pension schemes**
6.1	Current pension scheme membership by age and sex
6.2	Membership of current employer's occupational pension scheme by sex and whether working full time or part time
6.3	Membership of current employer's occupational pension scheme by sex: 1983 to 2009
6.4	Current pension scheme membership by sex and socio-economic classification
6.5	Membership of current employer's occupational pension scheme by sex and socio-economic classification
6.6	Current pension scheme membership by sex and usual gross weekly earnings
6.7	Current pension scheme membership by sex and length of time with current employer, 2007
6.8	Whether or not current employer has a occupational pension scheme by sex and length of time with current employer, 2007
6.9	Current pension scheme membership by sex and number of employees in the establishment
6.10	Membership of current employer's occupational pension scheme by sex and number of employees at the establishment
6.11	Membership of current employer's occupational pension scheme by sex and industry group, 2006 - 2008

Notes to tables

1. **Harmonised outputs**: where appropriate, tables including marital status, living arrangements, ethnic groups, tenure, economic activity, accommodation type, length of residence and general health have adopted the harmonised output categories described on the Office for National Statistics website. However, where long established time series are shown, harmonised outputs may not have been used.

2. **Classification variables**: variables such as age and income, are not presented in a standard form throughout the report partly because the groupings of interest depend on the subject matter of the chapter, and partly because many of the trend series were started when the results used in the report had to be extracted from tabulations prepared to meet different departmental requirements.

3. **Non-response and missing information**: the information from a household which co-operates in the survey may be incomplete, either because of a partial refusal (for example, to income), or because information was collected by proxy and certain questions omitted if considered inappropriate for proxy interviews (for example, marriage and cohabitation data), or because a particular item was missed because of lack of understanding or an error.

    Households that did not co-operate at all are omitted from all the analyses; those who omitted whole sections (for example, marriages) because they were partial refusals or interviewed by proxy are omitted from the analyses of that section. The 'no answers' arising from the omission of particular items have been excluded from the base numbers shown in the tables and from the bases used for percentages. Socio-economic classification and income variables are the most common variables which have too many missing answers to ignore.

4. **Base numbers**: The reliability of estimates with a small base were investigated. Shaded figures indicate the estimates are unreliable and any analysis using these figures may be invalid. Any use of these shaded figures must be accompanied by this disclaimer.

5. **Percentages**: A percentage may be quoted in the text for a single category that is identifiable in the tables only by summing two or more component percentages. In order to avoid rounding errors, the percentage has been recalculated for the single category and therefore may differ by one percentage point from the sum of the percentages derived from the tables.

    The row or column percentages may add to 99% or 101% because of rounding.

6. **Conventions**: The following conventions have been used within tables:
    .. data not available
    - category not applicable
    0 less than 0.5% or no observations

7. **Statistical significance**: Unless otherwise stated, changes and differences mentioned in the text have been found to be statistically significant at the 95 per cent confidence level.

8. **Mean**: Throughout the report the arithmetic term 'mean' is used rather than 'average'. The mean is a measure of the central tendency for continuous variables, calculated as the sum of all scores in a distribution, divided by the total number of scores.

9. **Weighting**: All percentages and means presented in the tables in the substantive chapters are based on data weighted to compensate for differential non-response. Both the unweighted and weighted bases are given. The unweighted base represents the number of people / households interviewed in the specified group. The weighted base gives an estimate in thousands.

    Trend tables show unweighted and weighted figures for 1998 to give an indication of the effect of the weighting.

    Missing answers are excluded from the tables and in some cases this is reflected in the weighted bases, that is, these numbers vary between tables. For this reason, the bases themselves are not recommended as a source for population estimates.

Reference to technical appendices

The General Lifestyle Survey is supported by a number of technical appendices that provide information about the methodology that is used on the survey. The appendices can be accessed by clicking on the references below.

A. Definitions and Terms

B. Sample Design and Response

C. Sampling Errors

D. Weighting

E. Household and Individual Questionnaires

F. Summary of main topics included in GHS/GLF questionnaires: 1971 to 2009

General Lifestyle Survey

Technical Appendices 2009

Editor   **Steven Dunstan**

Office for National Statistics

A National Statistics publication

National Statistics are produced to high professional standards set out in the Code of Practice for Official Statistics. They are produced free from political influence.

About us

The Office for National Statistics

The Office for National Statistics (ONS) is the executive office of the UK Statistics Authority, a non-ministerial department which reports directly to Parliament. ONS is the UK government's single largest statistical producer. It compiles information about the UK's society and economy, and provides the evidence-base for policy and decision-making, the allocation of resources, and public accountability. The Director-General of ONS reports directly to the National Statistician who is the Authority's Chief Executive and the Head of the Government Statistical Service.

The Government Statistical Service

The Government Statistical Service (GSS) is a network of professional statisticians and their staff operating both within the Office for National Statistics and across more than 30 other government departments and agencies.

Contacts

This publication

For information about the content of this publication, contact the General Lifestyle Survey
Tel: 01633 455678
Email: socialsurveys@ons.gsi.gov.uk

Principal Research Officer: Steven Dunstan

Other customer enquiries

ONS Customer Contact Centre
Tel: 0845 601 3034
International: +44 (0)845 601 3034
Minicom: 01633 815044
Email: info@statistics.gsi.gov.uk
Fax: 01633 652747
Post: Room 1.101, Government Buildings,
Cardiff Road, Newport, South Wales NP10 8XG
www.ons.gov.uk

Media enquiries

Tel: 0845 604 1858
Email: press.office@ons.gsi.gov.uk

Copyright and reproduction

Any enquiries regarding this publication should be sent to: info@statistics.gsi.gov.uk

This publication is available for download at:
www.ons.gov.uk

Definitions and terms

Appendix A

Definitions and terms used are listed in alphabetical order

Acute sickness

See Sickness

Adults

Adults are defined as persons aged 16 or over in all tables except those showing dependent children where single persons aged 16 to 18 who are in full-time education are counted as dependent children. The GLF interviews all people aged 16 and over in private households.

Bedroom standard

This concept is used to estimate occupation density by allocating a standard number of bedrooms to each household in accordance with its age/sex/marital status composition and the relationship of the members to one another. A separate bedroom is allocated to each married couple, any other person aged 21 or over, each pair of adolescents aged 10 to 20 of the same sex and each pair of children under 10. Any unpaired person aged 10 to 20 is paired if possible, with a child under 10 of the same sex or if that is not possible, is given a separate bedroom as is any unpaired child under 10. This standard is then compared with the actual number of bedrooms (including bedsitters) available for the sole use of the household, and deficiencies or excesses are tabulated. Bedrooms converted to other uses are not counted as available, unless they have been denoted as bedrooms by the informants; bedrooms not actually in use are counted unless uninhabitable.

Central Heating

Central heating is defined as any system whereby two or more rooms (including kitchens, halls, landings, bathrooms and WCs) are heated from a central source, such as a boiler and a back boiler to an open fire or the electricity supply. This definition includes a system where the boiler or back boiler heats one room and also supplies the power to heat at least one other room.

Under-floor heating systems, electric air systems and night storage heaters are included. Where a household has only one room in the accommodation it is treated as having central heating if that room is heated from a central source along with other rooms in the house or building.

Chronic sickness

See **Sickness**

Cohabitation

See **Marital status**

Co-ownership or equity sharing schemes

Co-ownership or equity sharing schemes are those where a share in the property is bought by the occupier under an agreement with the housing association. The monthly charges paid for the accommodation include an amount towards the repayment of the collective mortgage on the scheme. The co-owner never becomes the sole owner of the property, but on leaving the scheme usually receives a cash sum.

See also **Tenure**

Dependent children

Dependent children are persons aged under 16 or single persons aged 16 to 18 and in full-time education, in the family unit and living in the household.

Doctor consultations

Data on doctor consultations presented in this report relate to consultations with National Health Service general medical practitioners during the two weeks before interview. Visits to the surgery, home visits and telephone conversations are included, but contacts only with a receptionist are excluded. Consultations with practice nurses were excluded prior to 2000, but since then are identified separately. The GLF also collects information about consultations paid for privately.

The average number of consultations per person per year is calculated by multiplying the total number of consultations within the reference period, for any particular group, by 26 (the number of two-week periods in a year) and dividing the product by the total number of persons in the sample of that group.

Drinking

Questions about drinking alcohol were included in the General Household Survey every two years from 1978 to 1998. Following the review of the GHS they have been included every year from 2000 onwards.

Since 1998 the GHS has measured the maximum daily amount drunk last week. This is in line with the Government's advice on sensible drinking which is now based on daily benchmarks rather than weekly consumption. Regular consumption of between three and four units a day for men and two to three units a day for women does not carry a significant health risk, but consistently drinking above these levels is not advised.

The questions are asked of all people aged 16 and over in the household with a self-completion form offered to those aged 16 or 17. Respondents are asked on how many days they drank alcohol during the previous week. They are then asked how much of each of six different types of drink they drank on their heaviest drinking day during the previous week. These amounts are added to give an estimate of the maximum the respondent had drunk on any one day.

Economic activity

Economically active

People over the minimum school-leaving age of 16, who were working or unemployed (as defined below) in the week before the week of interview. These persons constitute the labour force.

Working persons

This category includes persons aged 16 and over who, in the week before the week of interview worked for wages, salary or other form of cash payment such as commission or tips for any number of hours. It covers persons absent from work in the reference week because of holiday, sickness, strike, or temporary lay-off, provided they had a job to return to with the same employer. It also includes persons attending an educational establishment during the specified week if they were paid by their employer while attending it, people on Government training schemes and unpaid family workers.

Persons are excluded if they worked in a voluntary capacity for expenses only or for payment in kind, unless they worked for a business, firm or professional practice owned by a relative. Full-time students are classified as 'working', 'unemployed' or 'inactive' according to their own reports of what they were doing during the reference week.

Unemployed persons

The GLF uses the International Labour Organisation (ILO) definition of unemployment. This classifies anyone as unemployed if he or she was out of work and had looked for work in the four weeks before interview or would have but for temporary sickness or injury and was available to start work in the two weeks after interview.

The treatment of all categories on the GLF is in line with that used on the Labour Force Survey (LFS).

Economically inactive

People who are neither working nor unemployed by the ILO measure. For example, this would include those who were looking after a home or retired.

Ethnic group

The GHS introduced the current National Statistics ethnic classification in 2001. The classification has a separate category for people from mixed ethnic backgrounds. In the previous system people with these backgrounds had to select a specific ethnic group or categorise themselves as 'other'.

Household members are classified by the person answering the Household Schedule as:

- British or other White background
- White and Black Caribbean, White and Black African, White and Asian, Other Mixed background
- Indian, Pakistani, Bangladeshi, Other Asian background
- Black Caribbean, Black African, Other Black background
- Chinese
- Other ethnic group

Family

A GLF family unit is defined as:

a) a married or opposite sex cohabiting couple on their own; or

b) married or opposite sex cohabiting couple, a lone parent and their never-married children (who may be adult), provided these children have no children of their own.; or

c) a same sex couple in a legally recognised civil partnership.

Persons who cannot be allocated to a family as defined above are said to be persons not in the family – i.e. as 'non-family units'. In general GLF family units cannot span more than two generations, i.e. grandparents and grandchildren cannot belong to the same family unit. The exception to this is where it is established that the grandparents are responsible for looking after the grandchildren (e.g. while the parents are abroad). Adopted and stepchildren belong to the same family unit as their adoptive/step-parents. Foster-children however are not part of their foster-parents' family (since they are not related to their foster-parents) and are counted as separate non-family units. See also **Lone-parent family**.

Full-time working

Full-time working is defined as more than 30 hours a week with the exception of occupations in education where more than 26 hours a week was included as full time.

Government Office Region (GOR)

Government Office Regions came into force in 1998. They replaced the Standard Statistical Regions as the primary classification for the presentation of English regional statistics. Standard Statistical Region was retained for some long term trend tables up to 2000. See also NHS Regional Office.

GP consultations

See Doctor consultations

Hospital visits

Inpatient stays

Inpatient data relate to stays overnight or longer (in a twelve month reference period) in NHS or private hospitals. All types of cases are counted including psychiatric and maternity except babies born in hospital who are included only if they remained in hospital after their mother was discharged.

Outpatient attendances

Outpatient data relate to attendances (in a reference period of three calendar months) at NHS or private hospitals, other than as an inpatient. Consultative outpatient attendances, casualty attendances and attendances at ancillary departments are all included and a separate count is made of attendances at a casualty department.

Day patient

Day patients are defined as patients admitted to a hospital bed during the course of a day or to a day ward where a bed, couch or trolley is available for the patient's use. They are admitted with the intention of receiving care or treatment which can be completed in a few hours so that they do not require a stay in hospital overnight. If a patient admitted as a day patient then stays overnight they are counted as an in-patient.

Household

A household is defined as:

a single person or a group of people who have the address as their only or main residence and who either share one meal a day or share the living accommodation. (See L McCrossan, A Handbook for Interviewers. HMSO, London 1991.)

A group of people is not counted as a household solely on the basis of a shared kitchen or bathroom.

A person is in general regarded as living at the address if he or she (or the informant) considers the address to be his or her main residence. There are however certain rules which take priority over this criterion.

From 2008 students who are living in halls of residence are also included as residents of the household sampled even If they are not *in situ* at the time for the interview.

Children of any age away from home in a temporary job and children under 16 at boarding school are *always* included in the parental household.

Anyone who has been away from the address *continuously* for six months or longer is excluded.

Anyone who has been living continuously at the address for six months or longer is included even if he or she has his or her main residence elsewhere.

Addresses used only as second homes are never counted as a main residence.

Household Reference Person (HRP)

For some topics it is necessary to select one person in the household to indicate the characteristics of the household more generally. In common with other Government surveys, in 2000, the GHS replaced the Head of Household with the Household Reference Person for this purpose.

The household reference person is defined as follows:

* in households with a *sole* householder that person is the household reference person
* in households with *joint* householders the person with the *highest income* is taken as the household reference person

- if both householders have exactly the same income the *older* is taken as the household reference person

Note that this definition does not require a question about people's actual incomes; only a question about who has the highest income. The main changes from the HOH definition are described in Appendix A in 'Living in Britain 2000'.

Household type

There are many ways of grouping or classifying households into household types, most are based on the age, sex and number of household members.

The main classification of household type as used in Chapter 4 tables uses the following categories:

- 1 adult aged 16-59
- 2 adults aged 16-59
- small family - 1 or 2 persons aged 16 or over and 1 or 2 persons aged under 16
- large family - 1 or more persons aged 16 or over and 3 or more persons aged under 16 or 3 or more persons aged 16 or over and 2 persons aged under 16
- large adult household - 3 or more persons aged 16 or over with or without 1 person aged under 16
- 2 adults, 1 or both aged 60 or over
- 1 adult aged 60 or over.

The term 'family' in this context does not necessarily imply any relationship.

GLF tables covering Chapter 3 also use a modified version of household type which takes account of the age of the youngest household member. 'Small family', 'large family' and 'large adult household' are replaced by the following:

- 1 adult aged 16-59
- 2 adults aged 16-59
- Youngest person aged 0-4
- youngest person aged 5-15
- 3 or more adults
- 2 adults, 1 or both aged 60 or over
- 1 adult aged 60 or over

The first two categories above are combined in some tables.

Households are also classified according to the family units they contain (see Family for definition), into the following categories:

- One family households* containing:
  - o   married couple with dependent children
  - o   married couple with non-dependent children only
  - o   married couple with no children
  - o   cohabiting couple with dependent children
  - o   cohabiting couple with non-dependent children only
  - o   cohabiting couple with no children
  - o   lone parent with dependent children
  - o   lone parent with non-dependent children only.

- Households containing two or more families

- Non-family households containing
  - o   lone parent with dependent children
  - o   lone parent with non-dependent children only
  - o   1 person only
  - o   2 or more non-family† adults

Some of the above categories are combined for certain tables and figures.

Other individuals who were not family members may also have been present

† Individuals may, of course be related without constituting a GLF family unit. A household consisting of a brother and sister, for example, is a non-family household of two or more non-family adults.

Income

Usual gross weekly income

Total income for an individual refers to income at the time of the interview and is obtained by summing the components of earnings, benefits, pensions, dividends, interest and other regular payments. Gross weekly income of employees and those on benefits is calculated if interest and dividends are the only components missing.

If the last pay packet/cheque was unusual, for example in including holiday pay in advance or a tax refund, the respondent is asked for usual pay. No account is taken of whether a job is temporary or permanent. Payments made less than weekly are divided by the number of weeks covered to obtain a weekly figure.

Usual gross weekly household income is the sum of usual gross weekly income for all adults in the household. Those interviewed by proxy are also included.

Lone-parent family

A lone-parent family consists of one parent, irrespective of sex, living with his or her never-married dependent children, provided these children have no children of their own.

Married or cohabiting women with dependent children, whose partners are not defined as resident in the household are not classified as one-parent families. It is known that the majority of them are only temporarily separated from their husbands for a reason that does not imply the breakdown of the marriage (for example: the husband usually works away from home). (See the GHS 1980 Report p.9 for further details.)

Longstanding conditions and complaints

See Sickness

Marriage and cohabitation

From 1971 to 1978 the Family Information section was addressed only to married women aged under 45 who were asked questions on their present marriage and birth expectations. In 1979 the section was expanded to include questions on cohabitation prior to marriage, previous marriages and all live births was addressed to all women aged 16 to 49 except non-married women aged 16 and 17. In 1986 the section was extended to cover all women and men aged 16 to 59. In 1998 all adults aged 16 to 59 were asked about any periods of cohabitation not leading to marriage. This section was extended in 2000 to include the length of past cohabitations not ending in marriage and what people perceived to be the end of the cohabitation (the end of the relationship, the end of sharing the accommodation or both).

Marital status

Since 1996 separate questions have been asked at the beginning of the questionnaire to identify the legal marital status and living arrangements of respondents in the household. The latter includes a category for cohabiting.

Before 1996 unrelated adults of the opposite sex were classified as cohabiting if they considered themselves to be living together as a couple. From 1996 this has included a small number of same sex couples, unless otherwise stated in the table. From 2006 those in a legally recognised civil partnership have been presented separately from those in non-legal same sex relationships.

Married/non-married

In this dichotomy 'married ' generally includes cohabiting and 'non-married' covers those who are single, widowed, separated, divorced or not cohabiting.

Living arrangements (de facto marital status)

Before 1996 additional information from the Family Information section of the individuals' questionnaire was used to determine living arrangements (previously known as 'defacto marital status') and the classification only applied to those aged 16 to 59 who answered the marital history questions. For this population it only differed from the main marital status for those who revealed in the Family Information section that they were cohabiting rather than having the marital status given at the beginning of the interview. 'Cohabiting' took priority over other categories. Since 1996 information on legal marital status and living arrangements has been taken from the beginning of the interview where both are now asked.

Legal marital status

This classification applies to persons aged 16 to 59 who answer the marital history questions. Cohabiting people are categorised according to formal marital status. The classification differs from strict legal marital status in accepting the respondents' opinion of whether their marriage has terminated in separation rather than applying the criterion of legal separation.

Median

See Quantiles

National Statistics Socio-economic classification (NS-SEC)

From April 2001 the National Statistics Socio-economic Classification (NS-SEC) was introduced for all official statistics and surveys. It replaced Social Class based on occupation and Socio-economic Groups (SEG). Full details can be found in 'The National Statistics Socio-economic Classification User Manual 2002' ONS 2002.

Descriptive definition	NS-SEC categories
Large employers and higher managerial occupations	L1, L2
Higher professional occupations	L3
Lower managerial and professional occupations	L4, L5, L6
Intermediate occupations	L7
Small employers and own account workers	L8, L9
Lower supervisory and technical occupations	L10, L11
Semi-routine occupations	L12
Routine occupations	L13
Never worked and long-term unemployed	L14

The three residual categories: L15 (full time students); L16 (occupation not stated or inadequately described) and L17 (not classifiable for other reasons) are excluded when the classification is collapsed into its analytical classes.

The categories can be further grouped into:

Managerial and professional occupations	L1-L6
Intermediate occupations	L7-L9
Routine + manual occupations	L10-L13

This results in the exclusion of those who have never worked and the long term unemployed, in addition to the groups mentioned above.

The main differences users need to be aware of are:

- the introduction of SOC2000 which includes various new technology occupations not previously defined in SOC90
- definitional variations in employment status in particular with reference to the term 'supervisor'
- the inclusion of armed forces personnel in the appropriate occupation group
- the separate classification of full-time students, whether or not they have been or are presently in paid employment and
- the separate classification of long term unemployed who previously were classified by their most recent occupation.

This change has resulted in a discontinuity in time series data. The operational categories of NS-SEC can be aggregated to produce an approximated version of the previous Socio-economic Group. These approximations have been shown to achieve an overall continuity level of 87%. Some tables on smoking have used this approximation.

Pensions

The GLF asks questions about any pension scheme, either occupational or personal, that the respondent belonged to on the date of interview. It is quite possible that some respondents may have held entitlement in the occupational pension scheme of a previous employer or a personal pension scheme in the past. The GLF measures current membership and not the percentage of respondents who will get an occupational or personal pension when they retire.

In April 2002 the State Second Pension (S2P) was introduced. This new pension reformed the State Earnings Related Pension Scheme (SERPS) to provide a more generous additional pension for low and moderate earners, certain groups of carers and people with a longstanding illness or disability. Since 1988 individual employees have had the option of contracting out of the S2P (formerly SERPS) by starting their own personal pension plan. Some respondents may be contributing to both an occupational and personal pension scheme.

From 2001 to 2002 the GHS asked employees whether or not they had arranged their own personal/stakeholder pension. If they answered 'yes' they were asked a supplementary question to establish whether it was a personal or stakeholder pension. In 2003 these two questions were replaced with a multiple response question that allowed the respondent to select one or more of the following answers:

- A personal or private pension or retirement annuity
- A Group Personal Pension (this is a collection of personal pensions arranged by an employer for a group of employees)
- A Stakeholder Pension arranged for yourself
- A Stakeholder Pension arranged through your employer (who may or may not contribute to such a pension)
- None of these
- Don't know

Some of the change in the proportion of employees with a personal pension in 2002 and 2003 may be due to the different ways respondents were asked about personal pension arrangements.

Questions on personal pension arrangements for self-employed persons did not change.

The majority of tables show data for men working full-time. This is because the sample sizes for male employees working part-time and self-employed men working part-time are too small to give reliable estimates.

Qualification levels

Degree or Degree equivalent, and above
Higher degree and postgraduate qualifications
First degree (including B.Ed.)
Postgraduate Diplomas and Certificates (including PGCE)
Professional qualifications at degree level e.g. graduate member of professional institute, chartered accountant or surveyor
NVQ or SVQ level 4 or 5

Other Higher Education below degree level
Diplomas in higher education & other higher education qualifications
HNC, HND, Higher level BTEC
Teaching qualifications for schools or further education (below Degree level standard)
Nursing, or other medical qualifications not covered above (below Degree level standard)
RSA higher diploma

A levels, vocational level 3 & equivalents

A level or equivalent
AS level
SCE Higher, Scottish Certificate Sixth Year Studies or equivalent
NVQ or SVQ level 3
GNVQ Advanced or GSVQ level 3
OND, ONC, BTEC National, SCOTVEC National Certificate
City & Guilds advanced craft, Part III (& other names)
RSA advanced diploma

Trade Apprenticeships
GCSE/O Level grade A*-C, vocational level 2 & equivalents
NVQ or SVQ level 2
GNVQ intermediate or GSVQ level 2
RSA Diploma
City & Guilds Craft or Part II (& other names)
BTEC, SCOTVEC first or general diploma etc.
O level or GCSE grade A-C, SCE Standard or Ordinary grades 1-3

Qualifications at level 1 and below
NVQ or SVQ level 1
GNVQ Foundation level, GSVQ level 1
GCSE or O level below grade C, SCE Standard or Ordinary below grade 3
CSE below grade 1
BTEC, SCOTVEC first or general certificate
SCOTVEC modules
RSA Stage I, II, or III
City and Guilds part 1
Junior certificate
YT Certificate/ YTP

Other qualifications: level unknown
Other vocational or professional or foreign qualifications

No qualifications
Excludes those who never went to school (omitted from the classification altogether).

This is not a complete listing of all qualifications. In particular, it does not give all the names which have been used by BTEC or City and Guilds. Neither does it give names for vocational qualifications from other awarding bodies besides BTEC, City and Guilds, RSA and SCOTVEC, although it should cover the majority of vocational qualifications awarded.
The qualification levels do not in all cases correspond to those used in statistics published by the Department for Education.

Quantiles

The quantiles of a distribution, eg of household income, divide it into equal parts.

Median: the median of a distribution divides it into two equal parts. Thus half the households in a distribution of household income have an income higher than the median and the other half have an income lower than the median.

Quartiles: the quartiles of a distribution divide it into quarters. Thus the upper quartile of a distribution of household income is the level of income that is expected by 25% of the households in the distribution; 25% of the households have an income less than the lower quartile. It follows that 50% of the households have an income between the upper and lower quartiles.

Quintiles: the quintiles of a distribution divide it into fifths. Thus the upper quintile of a distribution of household income is the level of income that is expected by 20% of the households in the distribution; 20% of the households have an income less than the lower quintile. It follows that 60% of the households have an income between the upper and lower quintiles.

Relatives in the household

The term 'relative' includes any household member related to the household reference person by blood, marriage or adoption. Foster-children are therefore not regarded as relatives.

Rooms

These are defined as habitable rooms, including (unless otherwise specified) kitchens, whether eaten in or not but excluding rooms used solely for business purposes, those not usable throughout the year (eg conservatories) and those not normally used for living purposes such as toilets, cloakrooms, store rooms, pantries, cellars and garages.

Sickness

Acute sickness

Acute sickness is defined as restriction of the level of normal activity, because of illness or injury, at any time during the two weeks before interview. Since the two-week reference period covers weekends, normal activities include leisure activities as well as school attendance, going to work or doing housework. Anyone with a chronic condition that caused additional restriction during the reference period is counted among those with acute sickness.

The average number of restricted activity days per person per year is calculated in the same way as the average number of doctor consultations.

Chronic sickness

Information on chronic sickness was obtained from the following two-part question:

'Do you have any longstanding illness, disability or infirmity? By longstanding I mean anything that has troubled you over a period of time or that is likely to affect you over a period of time.

IF YES
Does this illness or disability limit your activities in any way?'

'Longstanding illness' is defined as a positive answer to the first part of the question and 'limiting longstanding illness' as a positive answer to both parts of the question.

The data collected are based on people's subjective assessment of their health and therefore changes over time may reflect changes in people's expectations of their health as well as changes in incidence or duration of chronic sickness. In addition, different sub-groups of the population may have varying expectations, activities and capacities of adaptation.

Longstanding conditions and complaints

The GLF collects information about the nature of longstanding illness. Respondents who report a longstanding illness are asked 'What is the matter with you?' and details of the illness or disability are recorded by the interviewers and coded into a number of broad categories. Interviewers are instructed to focus on the symptoms of the illness rather than the cause and code what the respondent said was currently the matter without probing for cause. This approach has been used in 1988, 1989, 1994 to 1996, 1998 and 2000 to 2009.

The categories used when coding the conditions correspond broadly to the chapter headings of the International Classification of Diseases (ICD). However, the ICD is used mostly for coding conditions and diseases according to cause whereas the GLF coding is based only on the symptoms reported. This gives rise to discrepancies in some areas between the two classifications.

Smoking

Questions about smoking behaviour have been included on the GHS in alternate years from 1974 to 1998, and every year from 2000 onwards. The questions are asked of all people aged 16 and over in the household with a self-completion form offered to those aged 16 or 17, where appropriate.

Information on tar yields is only collected for manufactured cigarettes. Tar yields are provided by the laboratory of the Government Chemist.

Socio-economic classification

See National Statistics Socio-economic classification

Step-family

See Family

Tenure

From 1981 households who were buying a share in the property from a housing association or co-operative through a shared ownership (equity sharing) or co-ownership scheme are included in the category of owner-occupiers. In earlier years such households were included with those renting from a housing association or co-operative.

Renting from a council includes renting from a local authority or New Town corporation or commissions or Scottish Homes (formerly the Scottish Special Housing Association).

Renting from a housing association also includes co-operatives and charitable trusts. It also covers fair rent schemes. Since 1996 housing associations are more correctly described as Registered Social Landlords (RSLs). RSLs are not-for-profit organisations which include: charitable housing associations, industrial and provident societies and companies registered under the Companies Act 1985.

Social sector renters includes households renting from a local authority or New Town corporation or commission or Scottish Homes and those renting from housing associations, cooperatives and charitable trusts.

Private renters include those who rent from a private individual or organisation and those whose accommodation is tied to their job even if the landlord is a local authority, housing association or Housing Action Trust, or if the accommodation is rent free. Squatters are also included in this category.

Unemployed

See Economic activity

Weighting

All percentages and means presented in the tables in the substantive chapters are based on data weighted to compensate for differential non-response. Both the unweighted and weighted bases are given. The unweighted base represents the number of people / households interviewed in the specified group. The weighted base gives an estimate in thousands.

Trend tables show unweighted and weighted figures for 1998 to give an indication of the effect of the weighting.

Missing answers are excluded from the tables and in some cases this is reflected in the weighted bases, that is, these numbers vary between tables. For this reason, the bases themselves are not recommended as a source for population estimates.

A full description of the method of weighting and the effects on data are in Appendix D.

Working

See **Economic activity**

Sample Design and Response

Appendix B

Sample design and response

In 2009, 11,958 addresses were sampled. The GLF aims to interview all adults aged 16 or over at every household at the sampled address[1]. From 2008 students who are living in halls of residence are also included as residents of the household sampled even if they are not *in situ* at the time of the interview. The survey uses a probability, stratified two-stage sample design. The Primary Sampling Units (PSUs) are postcode sectors, which are similar in size to wards and the secondary sampling units are addresses within those sectors.

Sample design

The revised 2000 survey design introduced new stratifiers[2]. Stratification involves the division of the population into sub-groups, or strata, from which independent samples are taken. This ensures that a representative sample will be drawn with respect to the stratifiers (i.e. the proportion of units sampled from any particular stratum will equal the proportion in the population with that characteristic). Stratification of a sample can lead to substantial improvements in the precision of survey estimators. Optimal precision is achieved where the factors used as strata are those that correlate most highly with the survey variables. From 2000, the stratification factors were based on an area classifier and selected indicators from the 1991 Census. Details of how these were selected were reported in the January 2000 edition of the ONS Survey Methodology bulletin[3]. In 2005 the indicators were updated using the 2001 Census.

Initially, postcode sectors were allocated to 30 major strata. These were based on the 10 Government Office Regions in England, 5 subdivisions in Scotland and 2 in Wales. The English regions were divided between the former Metropolitan and non-Metropolitan counties. In addition London was subdivided into quadrants (Northwest, Northeast, Southwest and Southeast) with each quadrant being divided into inner and outer areas[4]. Using a finer division of London in the regional stratifier had a large effect on the increase in precision.

Within each major stratum, postcode sectors were then stratified according to the selected indicators taken from the Census. Sectors were initially ranked according to the proportion of households with no car, and then divided into three bands containing approximately the same number of households. Within each band, sectors were re-ranked according to the proportion of households with household reference person in socio-economic groups 1 to 5 and 13, and these bands were then sub-divided into three further bands of approximately equal size. Finally, within each of these bands, sectors were re-ranked according to the proportion of people who were pensioners. In order to minimise the difference between one band and the next, the ranking by the pensioners and socio-economic group criteria were in the reverse order in consecutive bands, as shown in Figure B.A.

Major strata were then divided into minor strata with equal numbers of addresses, the number of minor strata per major strata being proportionate to the size of the major stratum. Since 1984, the frame has been divided into 576 minor strata and one PSU has been selected from each per year. Of the 576 PSUs selected, 48 are randomly allocated to each month of the year. Each PSU forms a quota of work for an interviewer. Within each PSU, 23 addresses are randomly selected.

In 2005 the frame was divided into 720 strata. In 2006, 588 of these were rolled forward to the next wave in the longitudinal design. There were 132 pseudo wave 4 strata which were replaced and an additional 96 strata added, giving 816 for 2006. In 2007, 648 of these were again rolled forward to the next wave in the longitudinal design. There were 168 pseudo wave 4 strata which were replaced and an additional 60 strata added, giving 876 for 2007. In 2008, 684 of these were rolled forward to the next wave in the longitudinal design. There were 192 pseudo wave 4 strata which were replaced and an additional 36 strata added, giving 912 for 2008. In 2009, 684 of these were rolled forward to the next wave in the longitudinal design. There were 228 pseudo wave 4 strata which were replaced, giving 912 for 2009.

The expansion to the number of strata was in preparation for the launch of the Integrated Household Survey (IHS). More information on the IHS can be found on the Office for National Statistics website at:

http://www.statistics.gov.uk/statbase/Product.asp?vlnk=15381

Figure B.A

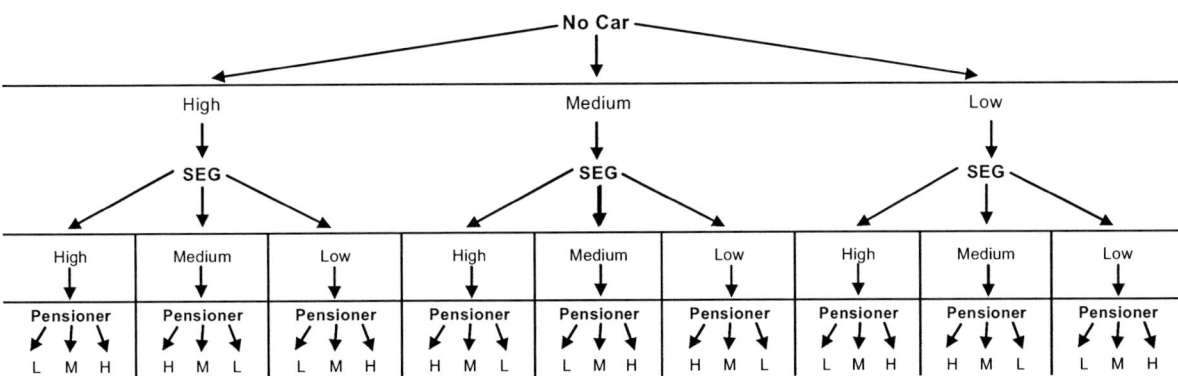

Sample design for the longitudinal component

In 2005, the survey adopted a new sample design in line with European requirements, changing from a cross-sectional to a longitudinal format.

The GHS/GLF sample design follows a four-year sample rotation in which people remain in the sample for four years (waves) with one quarter of the sample being replaced each year. Each quarter of the sample is known as a replication, and each replication is representative of the target population. Figure B-B illustrates how the design operates. From 2008 the system is fully established where the sample for any one year consists of four replications which have been in the survey for 1, 2, 3 or 4 years. Each year one of the four replications is dropped and a new one added, giving an overlap of up to 75 per cent between successive years. This has been implemented to avoid high attrition rates due to repeated interviewing.

At the end of the interview, we ask the wave 1, wave 2 and wave 3 respondents for their agreement to be re-interviewed in the following year. Table B1a shows the percentage of respondents that agreed to be re-interviewed in the following year (i.e. agreed to recall). Agree to recall rate for wave 1, 2 and 3 adults in 2009 was 85%. Only 3% (343) didn't agree to recall for the next wave interview. Out of these 343 respondents, 218 were wave 1, 78 wave 2 and 47 wave 3 interviews. Thirteen per cent (1,584) were coded as 'don't know' (including refusals & proxies that weren't asked for recall question). Out of these 1,584 'don't knows', only 23 were full interviews 1,346 proxy interviews and 215 no interviews.

Table B1a

Table **B1a** Agree to recall rate for the next wave interview

All persons

	Great Britain 2009	
	Recall status	
Agree to recall for the next wave interview		
	%	
Yes	85	10,607
No	3	343
Don t know (Code for non contacts, refusals and proxies)	13	1,584
Unweighted sample		*12,534*

A major advantage of the longitudinal component of the design is that it is more efficient at detecting statistically significant estimates of change over time than a design utilising independently selected cross-sections. This is because peoples' responses to the same question at different points in time tend to be positively correlated and this has the effect of reducing the estimated standard errors of change. Consequently, year on year comparisons will give the most efficient method of detecting changes over time, i.e. when overlap between the two time points is at its highest. This approach was adopted on the Labour Force Survey to give more efficient measures of employment/unemployment.

The longitudinal design (as illustrated in figure B-B) means that GHS/GLF datasets from 2006 are not independent, with approximately three quarters of the sample from the previous year being re-interviewed during the current year.

Figure B-B

Sample replication	Year 1	Year 2	Year 3	Year 4	Year 5	Year 6	
1	1st						
2	1st	2nd					
3	1st	2nd	3rd				
4	1st	2nd	3rd	4th			
5		1st	2nd	3rd	4th		
6			1st	2nd	3rd	4th	
7				1st	2nd	3rd	etc.
8					1st	2nd	etc.
9						1st	etc.

	New sample
	Follow-up sample

Conversion of multi-occupancy addresses to households

Most addresses contain just one private household, a few - such as institutions and purely business addresses[5] - contain no private households, while others contain more than one private household. For addresses containing more than one household, set procedures are laid down in order to give each household only one chance of selection.

As the Postcode Address File (PAF) does not give names of occupants of addresses, it is not possible to use the number of different surnames at an address as an indicator of the number of households living there. A rough guide to the number of households at an address is provided on the PAF by the multi-occupancy (MO) count. The MO count is a fairly accurate indicator in Scotland but is less accurate in England and Wales, so it is used only when sampling at addresses in Scotland.

All addresses in England and Wales, and those in Scotland with an MO count of two or less, are given only one chance of selection for the sample. At such addresses, interviewers interview all the households they find up to a maximum of three. If there are more than three households at the address, the interviewer selects the households for interview by listing all households at the address systematically then making a random choice by referring to a household selection table.

Addresses in Scotland with an MO count of three or more, where the probability that there is more than one household is fairly high, are given as many chances of selection as the value of the MO count. When the interviewer arrives at such an address, he or she checks the actual number of households and interviews a proportion of them according to instructions. The proportion is set originally by the MO count and adjusted according to the number of households actually found, with a maximum of three households being interviewed at any address. The interviewer selects the households for interview by listing all households at the address systematically and making a random choice, as above, by means of a table.

No addresses are deleted from the sample to compensate for the extra interviews that may result from these multi-household addresses, but a maximum of four extra interviews per quota of addresses is allowed. Once four extra interviews have been carried out in an interviewer's quota, only the first household selected at each multi-occupancy address is included. As a result of the limits on additional interviews, households in concealed multi-occupied addresses may be slightly under-represented in the GLF sample.

Data collection

Information for the GLF is collected week by week throughout the year[6] by personal interview. From 2006 onwards, interviews took place from January to December each year. In 2005, the field period changed from financial year to calendar year. As the 2004/5 survey finished in March 2005, interviewing for the 2005 survey started in April 2005 and ended in December 2005. However, data from the 2005 January to March period of the 2004/5 survey was included in the analyses of the 2005 data in order to prevent seasonal bias. Since 1994 the survey has been carried out using Computer Assisted Personal Interviewing (CAPI) on laptop computers and Blaise software by face-to-face interviewers. Since 2000, telephone interviewers have converted GHS proxy interviews to full interviews using Computer Assisted Telephone Interviewing (CATI) from a central unit. However, there were no proxy conversions in 2009. Interviews are sought with all adult members (aged 16 or over) of the sample of private households and some information about children in the household is also collected.

A letter is sent in advance of an interviewer calling at an address. The letter briefly describes the purpose and nature of the survey and prepares the recipient for a visit by an interviewer. Since 2001, postage stamps have been included in the advance letter (see 'Improving response').

Data quality

The face-to-face and telephone interviewers who work on the GLF are recruited only after careful selection procedures after which they take part in an initial training course. Before working on the GLF they attend a briefing and new recruits are always supervised either by being accompanied in the field by a Field Manager or monitored by a Telephone Interviewing Unit (TIU) supervisor. All interviewers who continue to work on the GLF are observed regularly in their work.

Proxy interviews and the proxy conversion exercise

On occasion it may prove impossible, despite repeated calls, to contact a particular member of a household in person and, in strictly controlled circumstances, interviewers are permitted to conduct a proxy interview with a close household member. In these cases certain opinion-type questions and some questions on smoking and drinking behaviour, qualifications, health and family information are omitted.

During the review of the GHS[7] the conversion of proxy interviews to full interviews was examined in order to improve the quality of data (a full interview is one in which the respondent has answered all sections of the questionnaire in person, either face-to-face or by telephone). This was achieved by re-contacting the household member, who was unavailable during the initial face-to-face interview, to answer the questions that were not asked of the proxy respondent on his/her behalf. The most efficient way of re-contacting these respondents was by employing Telephone Interviewing Unit (TIU) interviewers who could contact a widely dispersed population more efficiently than would be possible by conducting face-to-face interviews. Table B.1 shows the percentages of the types of interview taken for all persons in the co-operating households since 2000 before and after the proxy conversion exercise. In 2008 due to a technical problem in the questionnaire, the information on proxy conversion rates is not available. In 2009 there were no proxy conversions completed, which has increased the percentage of proxy interviews.

Table B1 –Table B1b

Table **B1** Type of interview taken by proxy conversion status

All persons   *Great Britain*

	Proxy Conversion Status									
	2004		2005[1]		2006[2]		2007[2]		2008[2,3]	2009[2,3]
	Before	After	Before	After	Before	After	Before	After		
	%	%	%	%	%	%	%	%	%	%
Full interview	71	73	70	72	71	73	71	73	71	71
Proxy	7	5	8	6	8	6	7	5	8	8
Child/Other	21	21	22	22	22	22	22	22	21	21
Unweighted sample	20,421	20,421	30,069	30,069	22,924	22,924	21,472	21,472	20,503	18,988

1 2005 data includes last quarter of 2004/5 data due to survey change from financial year to calendar year.
2 Results from 2006 onwards include longitudinal data.
3 Figures are not available on the percentage of proxies converted in 2008 and 2009.

Table **B1b** Type of interview taken by wave

All persons   *Great Britain 2009*

	Proxy conversion status	
	Wave1	Wave 2+
	%	%
Full interview	68	73
Proxy	11	7
Child/Other	22	20
Unweighted sample	6,578	12,410

Response

The GLF is conducted with people who volunteer their time to answer questions about themselves. The voluntary nature of the survey means that people who do not wish to take part in the survey can refuse to do so. Reasons for not participating in the survey vary from a dislike of surveys to poor health that prevents them from taking part. The sample is designed to ensure that the results of the survey represent the population of Great Britain. The risk of the survey not being representative is likely to increase with every refusal or non-contact with a sampled household (survey non-response). One measure of the quality of survey results is therefore the response rate.

Harmonised outcome codes and survey response rates

Harmonised outcome codes and definitions of response rates[8] were introduced for the first time on the 2002/3 GHS and other large household surveys, following recommendations from National Statistics and the National Centre for Social Research joint working group on standard survey outcomes. The harmonised outcome codes are categorised as complete and partial interviews, non-contact, refusals and other non-responders, and unknown and known ineligibility.

The joint working group also recommended that surveys include an estimate of the proportion of cases of unknown eligibility that are eligible from 2002 onwards. It is assumed that the proportion of eligible cases amongst those cases where eligibility is unknown is the same as that amongst cases where eligibility has been established.

Four response rates are now calculated for the GLF on the basis of these outcome codes (full interviews also include cases where the complete interview has been partly completed by the selected person and partly by proxy):

Overall response rate

This indicates how many full and partial interviews were achieved as a proportion of those eligible for the survey. In order to obtain the most conservative response rate measures, the denominator includes an estimate of the proportion of cases of unknown eligibility that would in fact be eligible for interview. In 2009 the overall response rate was 73 per cent.

Full response rate

This is similar to the overall response rate calculated above, but only full interviews are included in the numerator. The full response rate for the GLF in 2009 was 60 per cent.

Co-operation rate

This indicates the number of achieved interviews as a proportion of those contacted during the fieldwork period. The co-operation rate for the GLF in 2009 was 76 per cent.

Contact rate

The contact rate measures the proportion of cases in which some household members were reached by the interviewer even though they might then have refused or been unable to give further information about the household or to participate in the survey. In 2009 the contact rate for the GLF was 93 per cent.

Table B2 shows the outcome of visits to the addresses selected for the 2009 sample and the resultant number of households interviewed. Out of the 11,958 addresses that were selected, 11,006 were eligible and this yielded a sample of 11,086 eligible households. In 8,004 households, interviews (including proxies) were achieved with every member of the household. In a further 202 households interviews were achieved with some but not all members of the household. This produced a total of 8,206 full or partial interviews.

In total, 22 per cent of households selected for interview in 2009 were not interviewed because they did not wish to take part (17 per cent) or because they could not be contacted (5 per cent) (table not shown). Table B3 shows annual response by interview outcome category.

Tables B2-B3

Table **B2** The sample of addresses and households

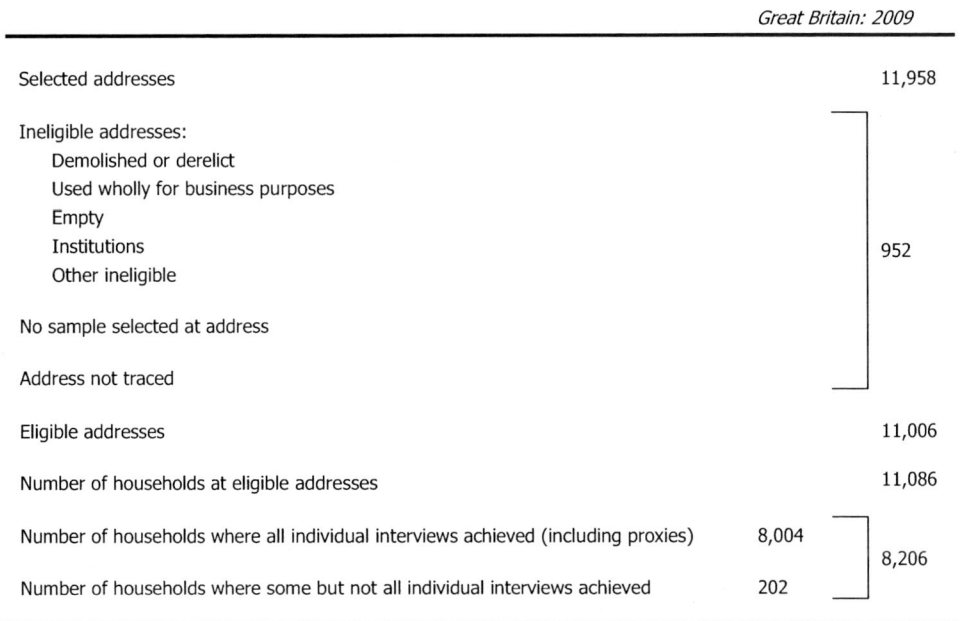

	Great Britain: 2009
Selected addresses	11,958
Ineligible addresses:	
Demolished or derelict	
Used wholly for business purposes	
Empty	
Institutions	952
Other ineligible	
No sample selected at address	
Address not traced	
Eligible addresses	11,006
Number of households at eligible addresses	11,086
Number of households where all individual interviews achieved (including proxies)	8,004
Number of households where some but not all individual interviews achieved	202
	8,206

Table **B3** Annual Response

Households   *Great Britain: 2009*

Outcome category		No.	%
1	Complete household co-operation	6,769	61.1
2	Non-interview with one of more household members, proxy taken	1,235	11.1
3	Non-contact with one or more household members	76	0.7
4	Refusal by at least one household member	126	1.1
5	Non-contact with household/resident	753	6.8
6	HQ refusal	491	4.4
7	Other refusal	1,631	14.7
8	Other non-response	5	0.0
Unweighted sample base = 100%		*11,086*	

Trends in response

In order to continue to measure the response to the survey over time, a 'middle' response rate has been calculated since 1971. The middle response rate includes full interviews and accepts some of the partial household interviews as response – that is, it includes households where information has been collected by proxy and is therefore missing certain sections (category 2 in Table B3), but does not include those where information is missing altogether for one or more household members (categories 3 and 4 in Table B3). In other words, this middle rate can be thought of as the proportion of the sample of households known to be eligible from whom all or nearly all the information was obtained.

For the purposes of comparison, the middle response rate has been calculated, although it is not in itself a classification of the harmonised response rates. In 2009, full interviews also included complete interviews completed partly by the selected person and partly by proxy.

In 2009 the middle response rate was 70.8 per cent. Table B4 shows middle response rates by Government Office Region. Trends in the middle response rate are shown in Table B5. Since 1971, the middle response rate has shown some fluctuation. The decline in response rate since the early 1990s is due to an increase in the proportion of households refusing to participate (12 per cent in 1991 rising to 17 per cent in 2009) rather than failure to contact people. This decline reflects a general trend in decreasing response experienced by all survey organisations.

Table **B4** Middle response rates by wave and Government Office Region

Households				Great Britain: 2009
Government Office Region	Wave 1 %	Wave 2 + %	%	Rank
North East	59.9	84.3	74.4	4
North West	63.8	79.7	73.0	5
Yorkshire and the Humber	64.1	83.4	75.4	2
East Midlands	65.2	85.4	77.1	1
West Midlands	57.6	77.4	68.9	9
East of England	57.1	81.0	72.0	6
London	49.3	74.9	62.2	11
South East (excluding Greater London)	53.3	76.2	66.5	10
South West	50.9	83.3	70.3	7
Wales	57.0	79.5	70.3	8
Scotland	64.8	81.9	74.5	3
Great Britain	58.0	80.2	70.8	

Full interviews include complete interviews partly completed by selected person and partly by proxy.

Table **B5** Trends in the middle response rate: 1971 to 2009

Households	Great Britain
Year	Response rate
	%
1971	83
1972	81
1973	81
1974	83
1975	84
1976	84
1977	83
1978	82
1979	83
1980	82
1981	84
1982	84
1983	82
1984	81
1985	82
1986	84
1987	85
1988	85
1989	84
1990	81
1991	84
1992	83
1993	82
1994	80
1995	80
1996	76
1998	72
2000	67
2001	72
2002	69
2003	70
2004	69
2005[1,2]	72
2006	76
2007	73
2008	73
2009	71

[1] 2005 data includes last quarter of 2004/5 data due to survey change from financial year to calendar year.
[2] **From 2005 full interviews include complete interviews partly completed by selected person and partly by proxy.**

Improving response

The GLF uses a number of methods to try to improve response. One ongoing method of improving response has been to reissue addresses to interviewers where there is a possibility of obtaining a better outcome, for example if there was initially a non-contact or a circumstantial refusal.

During the 2001/2 survey the advance letter was changed to mention that the survey had been running for 30 years. This change shows respondents how important the survey is and how many people take part. For subsequent years a similar advance letter has been produced informing respondents that the survey has been running for over 30 years.

Another method was introduced in 2002 following the findings of the Response Working Group of the Office for National Statistics. The Group found that response was higher among households who received postage stamps with their advance letters. Since August 2002, stamps have been included in all advance letters.

Respondents receive a £10 gift voucher for each full follow-up interview they complete. Where a follow-up interview is taken by proxy, a voucher is only issued if the TIU converts the proxy interview to a full interview.

Sample sizes

Tables B6 and B7 show the numbers of households and individuals interviewed on the 2009 GLF by age, sex, region and country.

Table **B6** Unweighted bases: number of household reference persons in GLF 2009 by age, sex, region and country

Household reference persons								Great Britain: 2009
	Age							All
	16-24	25-34	35-44	45-54	55-64	65-74	75+	
Sex								
Male	70	470	906	943	1018	926	647	4980
Female	105	384	585	545	576	442	581	3218
Government Office Region								
North East	7	33	42	58	86	76	68	370
North West	17	97	183	191	192	150	140	970
Yorkshire and the Humber	29	106	144	144	149	117	105	794
East Midlands	19	71	117	114	130	124	112	687
West Midlands	10	68	125	139	134	120	104	700
East of England	15	84	152	160	152	150	138	851
London	18	92	166	156	131	84	89	736
South East	16	105	217	198	218	192	162	1108
South West	13	66	137	108	156	141	127	748
Country								
England	144	722	1283	1268	1348	1154	1045	6964
Wales	9	55	75	82	93	85	60	459
Scotland	22	77	133	138	153	129	123	775
Total	175	854	1491	1488	1594	1368	1228	8198

Shaded figures also show the number of households in each region and country.

Table **B7** unweighted bases: number of people in GLF by age, sex, region and country

All persons										*Great Britain: 2009*
	Age									All
	0-4	5-15	16-24	25-34	35-44	45-54	55-64	65-74	75+	
Sex										
Male	580	1,329	904	888	1,222	1,223	1,275	1,078	701	9,200
Female	549	1,205	889	1,022	1,386	1,334	1,378	1,098	927	9,788
Government Office Region										
North East	43	74	59	64	76	98	145	117	84	760
North West	130	301	224	209	306	316	304	231	188	2,209
Yorkshire and the Humber	107	262	176	207	249	257	255	186	138	1,837
East Midlands	96	189	140	167	212	194	221	205	145	1,569
West Midlands	92	240	161	158	214	248	227	203	147	1,690
East of England	122	281	182	199	266	278	269	239	187	2,023
London	133	283	214	222	308	253	204	134	116	1,867
South East	171	313	219	255	373	346	355	303	213	2,548
South West	93	214	132	153	246	198	261	223	176	1,696
Country										
England	987	2,157	1,507	1,634	2,250	2,188	2,241	1,841	1,394	16,199
Wales	67	163	108	111	136	141	153	138	82	1,099
Scotland	75	214	178	165	222	228	259	197	152	1,690
Total	1,129	2,534	1,793	1,910	2,608	2,557	2,653	2,176	1,628	18,988

Notes and references

1. A limit is put on the number of households that are contacted per address. This is explained in detail at the 'Conversion of multi-occupancy addresses to households' section of Appendix B.

2. From 1984 to 1998, the stratifiers used were a regional variable (based on the standard statistical region until 1996 and on the Government Office Region in 1998) and variables that measured the prevalence of privately rented accommodation, local authority accommodation and people in professional and managerial socio-economic groups.

3. Insalaco F Choosing stratifiers for the General Household Survey *ONS Social Survey Division, Survey Methodology Bulletin*, No. 46, January 2000.

4. The GOR regional stratifier:

1.   North East Met
2.   North East Non Met
3.   North West Met
4.   North West Non Met
5.   Merseyside
6.   Yorks and Humberside Met
7.   Yorks and Humberside Non Met
8.   East Midlands
9.   West Midlands Met
10.   West Midlands Non Met
11.   Eastern Outer Met
12.   Eastern Other
13.   Inner London North-East
14.   Inner London North-West
15.   Inner London South-East
16.   Inner London South-West
17.   Outer London North-East
18.   Outer London North-West
19.   Outer London South-East
20.   Outer London South-West
21.   South East Outer Met
22.   South East Other
23.   South West
24.   Wales 1 – Glamorgan, Gwent
25.   Wales 2 – Clwyd, Gwynedd, Dyfed, Powys
26.   Highlands, Grampian, Tayside
27.   Fife, Central, Lothian
28.   Glasgow Met
29.   Strathclyde (excl. Glasgow)
30.   Borders, Dumfries, Galloway

5. Most institutions and business addresses are not listed on the small-user PAF. If an address was found in the field to be non-private (e.g. boarding house containing four or more boarders at the time the interviewer calls), the interviewer was instructed not to take an interview. However, a household member in hospital at the time of interview was included in the sample provided that he or she had not been away from home for more than six months and was expected to return. In this case a proxy interview was taken.

6. In 1988, the GHS interviewing year was changed from a calendar year to a financial year basis. From 2005, the GHS interviewing year was changed back from financial year to calendar year.

7. Walker A et al *Living in Britain Results from the 2002 General Household Survey: Appendix E.* TSO London 2002. Also available on the web: http://www.statistics.gov.uk/lib2000/index.html

8. Lynn P, Beerten R, Laiho J and Martin J. Recommended Standard Final Outcome Categories and Standard Definition of Response Rate for Social Surveys. ISER Working Papers. Number 2001 – 23. http://ideas.repec.org/p/ese/iserwp/2001-23.html

Sampling Errors

Appendix C

Tables in this appendix present estimated standard errors for some of the main variables used in this report, taking into account the complex sample design of the survey.

Sources of error in surveys

Survey results are subject to various sources of error. The total error in a survey estimate is the difference between the estimate derived from the sample data collected and the true value for the population. The total error is made up of two main types: systematic and random error.

Systematic error

Systematic error occurs when data are consistently biased in a certain way, such that the variation from the true values for the population will not average to zero over repeats of the survey. For example, if a certain section of the population is excluded from the sampling frame, estimates may be biased because non-respondents to the survey have different characteristics to respondents. Another cause of bias may be that interviewers systematically influence responses in one way or another. Substantial efforts have been made to avoid systematic errors, for example, through extensive interviewer training and by weighting the data collected for non-response.

Random error

Random error, or bias, is the variation in sample data from the true values for the population, which occurs by chance. This type of error is expected to average to zero over a number of repeats of the survey. Random error may result from sources such as variation in respondents' interpretation of the survey questions, or interviewer variation. Efforts are made to minimise these effects through pilot work and consistent interviewer training.

Sampling errors

An important component of random error is sampling error, which arises because the variable estimates are based on a sample rather than a full census of the population. The results obtained for any single sample would be likely to vary slightly from the true values for the population. The difference between the estimates derived from the sample and the true population values is referred to as the sampling error. The amount of variation can generally be reduced by increasing the size of the sample, and by improving the sample design. Standard errors have been measured for estimates derived from the General LiFestyle Survey (GLF), and these may be used to assess the accuracy of the estimates presented in this report.

Calculating standard errors

Unlike non-sampling errors, it is possible to estimate the size of the sampling error, by calculating the standard error of the survey estimators. The standard error (se) of a percentage p, based on a simple random sample of size n is calculated by the formula,

$$se(p)_{srs} = \sqrt{\frac{p(100-p)}{n}}$$

The GLF uses a multi-stage sample design, which involves both clustering and stratification (see Appendix B). The complexity of the design means that sampling errors calculated on the basis of a simple random sample design will not reflect the true variance in the survey estimates. Clustering can lead to a substantial increase in sampling error if the households or individuals within the primary sampling units (PSUs) are relatively homogenous but the PSUs differ from one another. By contrast, stratification tends to reduce sampling error and is particularly effective when the stratification factor is related to the characteristics of interest on the survey.

The GLF adopts a complex sample design and therefore the size of the standard error depends on how the characteristic of interest is spread within and between the PSUs and strata. The method used to calculate the standard errors for the survey takes this into account. It explicitly allows for the fact that the estimated values (percentages and means) are ratios of two survey estimates: the number with the characteristic of interest is the numerator (y) and the sample size is the denominator (x), both of which are subject to random error.

The standard error of a survey estimate is found by calculating the positive square root of the estimated variance of the ratio. The formula used to estimate the variance of a ratio estimator r (where $r = y/x$) is shown below.

$$\text{var}(r) = \frac{1}{x^2}\left[\text{var}(y) + r^2\,\text{var}(x) - 2r\,\text{cov}(y,x)\right]$$

Var(r) is the estimate of the variance of the ratio, r, expressed in terms of *var(y)* and *var(x)* which are the estimated variances of y and x, and *cov(y,x)* which is their estimated covariance. The resulting estimate is only valid if the denominator (x) does not vary too greatly. The method compares the differences between totals for adjacent PSUs (postal sectors) in the characteristic of interest. The ordering of PSUs reflects the ranking of postal sectors on the stratifiers used in the sample design.

Design factors

The design factor, or deft, of an estimate p is the ratio of the complex standard error of p to the standard error of p that would have resulted had the survey design been a simple random sample of the same size.

$$deft(p) = \frac{se(p)}{se_{srs}(p)}$$

This is often used to give a broad indication of the effect of the clustering on the reliability of estimates. The size of the design factor varies between survey variables reflecting the degree to which a characteristic of interest is clustered within PSUs, or is distributed between strata. For a single variable the size of the design factor also varies according to the size of the subgroup on which the estimate is based, and on the distribution of that subgroup between PSUs and strata. Design factors below 1.0 show that the complex sample design improved on the estimate that we would have expected from a simple random sample, probably due to the benefits of stratification. Design factors greater than 1.0 show less reliable estimates than might be gained from a simple random sample, due to the effects of clustering. Design factors equal to 1.0 indicate no difference in the survey design on the reliability of the estimate.

The formula to calculate the standard error of the difference between two percentages for a complex sample design is:

$$se(p_1 - p_2) = \sqrt{\left[deft_1^2\left(\frac{p_1(100 - p_1)}{n_1} \right) + deft_2^2\left(\frac{p_2(100 - p_2)}{n_2} \right) \right]}$$

Where p_1 and p_2 are observed percentages for the two sub-samples and n_1 and n_2 are the sub-sample sizes.

Confidence intervals

The estimate produced from a sample survey will rarely be identical to the population value, but statistical theory allows us to measure precision. A confidence interval can be calculated around the estimated value, which gives a range in which the true value for the population is likely to fall. The standard error measures the precision with which the estimates from the sample approximate to the true population values and is used to construct the confidence interval for each survey estimate.

The 95 per cent confidence intervals have been calculated for each estimated value presented. These are known as such, because if it were possible to repeat the survey under the same conditions a number of times, we would expect 95 per cent of the confidence intervals calculated in this way to contain the true population value for that estimate. When assessing the results of a single survey, it is usual to assume that there is only a 5 per cent chance that the true population value falls outside the 95 per cent confidence interval calculated for each survey estimate. To construct the bounds of the confidence interval, 1.96 times the standard error is subtracted from, and added to, the estimated value, since under a normal distribution, 95 per cent of values lie within 1.96 standard errors of the mean value. The confidence interval is then given by:

$$p \pm 1.96se(p)$$

The 95 per cent confidence interval for the difference between two percentages is given by:

$$(p_1 - p_2) \pm 1.96se(p_1 - p_2)$$

If this confidence interval includes zero then the observed difference is considered to be a result of chance variation in the sample. If the interval does not include zero then it is unlikely (less than 5 per cent probability) that the observed difference could have occurred by chance.

Standard errors for the 2009 GLF

The standard errors were calculated on weighted data using STATA[1]. Weighting for different sampling probabilities results in larger sampling errors than for an equal-probability sample without weights. However, weighting which uses population totals to control for differential non-response tends to lead to a reduction in the errors. The method used to calculate the sampling errors correctly allows for the inflation in the sampling errors caused by the first type of weighting but, in treating the second type of weighting in the same way as the first, incorrectly inflates the estimates further. Therefore the standard errors and defts presented are likely to be slight over-estimates. Weighted data were used so that the values of the percentages and means were the same as those in the substantive chapters of the report.

Tables C.1 to C.12 show the standard error, the 95 per cent confidence interval and the deft for selected survey estimates. The tables do not cover all the topics discussed in the report but show a selection of estimates.

For the design factors of household based estimators, 3 per cent were below 1.1, 27 per cent were less than 1.2 and 60 per cent of the defts were less than 1.3. There were six cases (20 per cent of the household-based estimates) where the deft was 1.5 or greater. The higher defts were mostly for tenure and accommodation type (Table C.1) where the effects of clustering lead to a loss of precision compared with that of a simple random sample.

For the design factors of person based estimators, 6 per cent were below 1, 19 per cent were below 1.1, 36 per cent were less than 1.2, and 62 per cent of the defts were less than 1.3. 11 per cent of the defts were 1.5 or greater, including many of those for estimates of ethnicity, shown in Table C.6. As well as clustering in the same sectors, people from the same ethnic backgrounds will generally cluster within the same households, and so estimates have high sampling errors and high defts. In contrast, estimates broken down by gender will generally have lower sampling errors because there is often one man and one woman in a household; for example, the estimates of males and females in the population have defts of 0.9 (Table C.4).

Estimating standard errors for other survey measures

The standard errors of survey measures, which are not presented in the tables and for sample subgroups may be estimated by applying an appropriate value of deft to the sampling error. The choice of an appropriate value of deft will vary according to whether the basic survey measure is included in the tables. Since most deft values are relatively small (1.3 or less) the absolute effect of adjusting sampling errors to take account of the survey's complex design will be small. In most cases it will result in an increase of less than 30 per cent over the standard error assuming a simple random sample. Whether it is considered necessary to use deft or to use the basic estimates of standard errors assuming a simple random sample is a matter of judgement and depends chiefly on the use of the survey results.

Significance of year on year changes

In 2005, the GHS adopted a new sample design in line with European requirements, changing from a cross-sectional to a longitudinal format (see Appendix B for details). Therefore, when looking to see if a year on year change is significant you need to take account of the fact that the samples are not independent, that is, a proportion of the people interviewed the previous year will be re-interviewed in the current year. As stated above, the 95 per cent confidence interval for the difference between two percentages is given by:

$$(p_t - p_{t-1}) \pm 1.96 se(p_t - p_{t-1})$$

And if this confidence interval includes zero then the observed difference is considered to be a result of chance variation in the sample. If the interval does not include zero then it is unlikely (less than 5 per cent probability) that the observed difference could have occurred by chance. However, where the samples are not independent, the variance for the estimate of change, p_t - p_t-1, includes an additional term to take account of the correlation, giving:

$$se(p_t - p_{t-1}) = \sqrt{\mathrm{var}(p_t) + \mathrm{var}(p_{t-1}) - 2\,\mathrm{cov}(p_t, p_{t-1})}$$

Because the covariance cannot be calculated from the data provided, we have provided the complete standard errors of change for p_t - p_t-1 for some key estimates. These can be found in tables C5a, C9a, C10a and C11a.

Where significance tests are required for other estimates, assuming independent samples would be a suitable conservative approach. That is to say any significant change found using this method would still be significant taking the overlap into account.

Notes and references

1. STATA is a statistical analysis software package. For further details of the method of calculation see: Elliot D. A comparison of software for producing sampling errors on social surveys. *SSD Survey Methodology Bulletin 1999*; 44: 27-36.

Table C.1 Standard errors and 95% confidence intervals for household tenure, household type and accommodation type

Base	Characteristic	%(p)	Unweighted sample size	Standard error of p	95% confidence intervals		Deft
All households							
	Household type						
	1 adult aged 16-59	13.4	8,203	0.52	12.4	- 14.4	1.4
	2 adults aged 16-59	15.5	8,203	0.47	14.6	- 16.4	1.2
	Youngest person aged 0-4	10.4	8,203	0.39	9.6	- 11.2	1.2
	Youngest person aged 5-15	14.8	8,203	0.44	13.9	- 15.7	1.1
	3 or more adults	11.9	8,203	0.44	11.0	- 12.8	1.2
	2 adults, 1 or both aged 60 or over	16.4	8,203	0.41	15.6	- 17.2	1.0
	1 adult aged 60 or over	17.6	8,203	0.47	16.7	- 18.5	1.1
	Tenure						
	Owner occupied, owned outright	31.8	8,203	0.64	30.5	- 33.1	1.2
	Owner occupied, with mortgage	37.2	8,203	0.66	35.9	- 38.5	1.2
	Rented from council	9.9	8,203	0.49	8.9	- 10.9	1.5
	Rented from housing association	8.2	8,203	0.44	7.3	- 9.1	1.5
	Rented privately, unfurnished	10.8	8,203	0.49	9.8	- 11.8	1.5
	Rented privately, furnished	2.0	8,203	0.23	1.5	- 2.5	1.4
	Accommodation type						
	Detached house	23.3	8,203	0.67	22.0	- 24.6	1.4
	Semi-detached house	30.6	8,203	0.71	29.2	- 32.0	1.4
	Terraced house	27.2	8,203	0.74	25.7	- 28.7	1.5
	Purpose-built flat or maisonette	15.0	8,203	0.61	13.8	- 16.2	1.5
	Converted flat or maisonette/rooms	3.8	8,203	0.38	3.1	- 4.5	1.8
	With business premises/other	0.0	8,203	0.03	-0.1	- 0.1	1.1

Table C.2 Standard errors and 95% confidence intervals for number of persons and cars at each household

Base	Characteristic	%(p)	Unweighted sample size	Standard error of p	95% confidence intervals		Deft
All households							
	Number of persons						
	1	30.9	8,203	0.60	29.7 -	32.1	1.2
	2	33.0	8,203	0.55	31.9 -	34.1	1.1
	3	15.3	8,203	0.47	14.4 -	16.2	1.2
	4	14.3	8,203	0.44	13.4 -	15.2	1.1
	5	4.7	8,203	0.28	4.2 -	5.2	1.2
	6 or more	1.8	8,203	0.17	1.5 -	2.1	1.2
	Number of cars/light vans						
	1	45.0	8,203	0.66	43.7 -	46.3	1.2
	2 or more	32.1	8,203	0.65	30.8 -	33.4	1.3
	none	22.9	8,203	0.58	21.8 -	24.0	1.3

Table C.3 Standard errors and 95% confidence intervals for households' ownership of selected consumer durables

Base	Characteristic	%(p)	Unweighted sample size	Standard error of p	95% confidence intervals		Deft
All households							
	Selected consumer durables						
	Home computer	76.4	8,203	0.53	75.4 -	77.4	1.1
	Washing machine	96.3	8,203	0.23	95.8 -	96.8	1.1

Table C.4 Standard errors and 95% confidence intervals for age and sex

Base	Characteristic	%(*p*)	Unweighted sample size	Standard error of *p*	95% confidence intervals		Deft
	Sex						
All persons	Male	49.4	18,988	0.31	48.8 -	50.0	0.9
	Female	50.6	18,988	0.31	50.0 -	51.2	0.9
	Age						
All persons	0-4	6.1	18,988	0.21	5.7 -	6.5	1.2
	5-15	12.7	18,988	0.29	12.1 -	13.3	1.2
	16-44	39.7	18,988	0.46	38.8 -	40.6	1.3
	45-64	25.6	18,988	0.40	24.8 -	26.4	1.3
	65-74	8.6	18,988	0.24	8.1 -	9.1	1.2
	75 and over	7.3	18,988	0.24	6.8 -	7.8	1.3
All males	0-4	6.4	9,200	0.30	5.8 -	7.0	1.2
	5-15	13.5	9,200	0.40	12.7 -	14.3	1.1
	16-44	40.4	9,200	0.58	39.3 -	41.5	1.1
	45-64	25.4	9,200	0.47	24.5 -	26.3	1.0
	65-74	8.3	9,200	0.27	7.8 -	8.8	1.0
	75 and over	6.0	9,200	0.26	5.5 -	6.5	1.1
All females	0-4	5.9	9,788	0.28	5.4 -	6.4	1.2
	5-15	11.9	9,788	0.37	11.2 -	12.6	1.1
	16-44	39.1	9,788	0.58	38.0 -	40.2	1.2
	45-64	25.7	9,788	0.50	24.7 -	26.7	1.1
	65-74	8.9	9,788	0.30	8.3 -	9.5	1.0
	75 and over	8.5	9,788	0.32	7.9 -	9.1	1.1

C.5 Standard errors and 95% confidence intervals for marital status

Base	Characteristic	%(*p*)	Unweighted sample size	Standard error of *p*	95% confidence intervals		Deft
	Marital status						
All persons aged 16 and over	Married	50.3	15,325	0.57	49.2 -	51.4	1.4
	Cohabiting	9.9	15,325	0.44	9.0 -	10.8	1.8
	Single	24.7	15,325	0.49	23.7 -	25.7	1.4
	Widowed	6.9	15,325	0.23	6.4 -	7.4	1.1
	Divorced	6.0	15,325	0.21	5.6 -	6.4	1.1
	Separated	1.6	15,325	0.12	1.4 -	1.8	1.2
Men aged 16 and over	Married	51.6	7,291	0.66	50.3 -	52.9	1.2
	Cohabiting	10.2	7,291	0.46	9.3 -	11.1	1.3
	Single	28.0	7,291	0.68	26.7 -	29.3	1.3
	Widowed	3.7	7,291	0.22	3.3 -	4.1	1.0
	Divorced	4.4	7,291	0.28	3.9 -	4.9	1.2
	Separated	1.6	7,291	0.17	1.3 -	1.9	1.2
Women aged 16 and over	Married	49.0	8,034	0.64	47.7 -	50.3	1.1
	Cohabiting	9.7	8,034	0.43	8.9 -	10.5	1.3
	Single	21.7	8,034	0.59	20.5 -	22.9	1.3
	Widowed	10.0	8,034	0.37	9.3 -	10.7	1.1
	Divorced	7.6	8,034	0.33	7.0 -	8.2	1.1
	Separated	1.7	8,034	0.16	1.4 -	2.0	1.1
All persons aged 16 to 24	Married	5.1	1,793	0.88	0.3 -	6.8	1.9
	Cohabiting	7.5	1,793	0.85	5.8 -	9.2	1.6
	Single	86.8	1,793	1.24	84.4 -	89.2	1.8
	Widowed	0.0	1,793	0.00	0.0 -	0.0	0.0
	Divorced	0.3	1,793	0.32	-0.3 -	0.9	0.9
	Separated	0.2	1,793	0.09	0.0 -	0.4	1.1
All persons aged 25 to 34	Married	40.1	1,910	1.55	37.1 -	43.1	1.5
	Cohabiting	24.5	1,910	1.51	21.5 -	27.5	1.7
	Single	32.8	1,910	1.49	29.9 -	35.7	1.5
	Widowed	0.0	1,910	0.0	0.0 -	0.0	0.0
	Divorced	0.8	1,910	0.19	0.4 -	1.2	1.0
	Separated	1.0	1,910	0.25	0.5 -	1.5	1.2
All persons aged 35 to 44	Married	58.8	2,608	1.30	56.3 -	61.3	1.4
	Cohabiting	15.4	2,608	0.95	13.5 -	17.3	1.4
	Single	16.6	2,608	0.98	14.7 -	18.5	1.4
	Widowed	0.4	2,608	0.13	0.1 -	0.7	1.1
	Divorced	5.4	2,608	0.49	4.4 -	6.4	1.2
	Separated	2.5	2,608	0.33	1.9 -	3.1	1.2
All persons aged 45 to 54	Married	68.4	2,557	1.31	65.8 -	71.0	1.4
	Cohabiting	7.0	2,557	0.68	5.7 -	8.3	1.4
	Single	10.4	2,557	0.77	8.9 -	11.9	1.3
	Widowed	0.8	2,557	0.20	0.4 -	1.2	1.1
	Divorced	10.4	2,557	0.73	9.0 -	11.8	1.2
	Separated	2.3	2,557	0.36	1.6 -	3.0	1.2
All persons aged 55 to 64	Married	68.7	2,653	1.06	66.6 -	70.8	1.1
	Cohabiting	4.9	2,653	0.54	3.8 -	6.0	1.2
	Single	6.3	2,653	0.56	5.2 -	7.4	1.1
	Widowed	5.5	2,653	0.48	4.6 -	6.4	1.0
	Divorced	11.9	2,653	0.67	10.6 -	13.2	1.0
	Separated	2.2	2,653	0.30	1.6 -	2.8	1.0
All persons aged 65 to 74	Married	65.2	2,176	1.22	62.8 -	67.6	1.0
	Cohabiting	2.0	2,176	0.33	1.4 -	2.6	1.0
	Single	6.1	2,176	0.60	4.9 -	7.3	1.0
	Widowed	15.9	2,176	0.88	14.2 -	17.6	1.0
	Divorced	9.2	2,176	0.72	7.8 -	10.6	1.0
	Separated	1.5	2,176	0.30	0.9 -	2.1	1.0
All persons aged 75 and over	Married	41.8	1,628	1.49	38.9 -	44.7	1.1
	Cohabiting	0.7	1,628	0.25	0.2 -	1.2	1.1
	Single	5.2	1,628	0.57	4.1 -	6.3	1.0
	Widowed	46.9	1,628	1.53	43.9 -	49.9	1.1
	Divorced	4.3	1,628	0.58	3.2 -	5.4	1.1
	Separated	1.1	1,628	0.27	0.6 -	1.6	1.0

C5a Standard errors of change for marital status

Base	Characteristic	%(*diff_p*)	Standard error of *diff_p*
	Marital status		
All persons aged 16 and over	Married	-0.4	0.80
	Cohabiting	-0.5	0.60
	Single	0.4	0.73
	Widowed	0.1	0.33
	Divorced	0.3	0.30
	Separated	0.0	0.17
Men aged 16 and over	Married	-0.5	0.94
	Cohabiting	-0.6	0.62
	Single	0.2	0.99
	Widowed	0.3	0.31
	Divorced	0.1	0.38
	Separated	0.3	0.23
Women aged 16 and over	Married	-0.4	0.87
	Cohabiting	-0.5	0.59
	Single	0.7	0.83
	Widowed	-0.1	0.52
	Divorced	0.5	0.44
	Separated	-0.2	0.25
All persons aged 16 to 24	Married	2.0	1.08
	Cohabiting	-2.4	1.39
	Single	0.2	1.78
	Widowed	0.0	0.00
	Divorced	0.0	0.03
	Separated	0.0	0.20
All persons aged 25 to 34	Married	1.3	2.22
	Cohabiting	-1.5	2.00
	Single	0.6	2.15
	Widowed	0.0	0.03
	Divorced	-0.4	0.30
	Separated	-0.2	0.35
All persons aged 35 to 44	Married	-1.4	1.82
	Cohabiting	-0.2	1.31
	Single	0.8	1.31
	Widowed	0.1	0.17
	Divorced	0.7	0.65
	Separated	-0.2	0.52
All persons aged 45 to 54	Married	-0.6	1.73
	Cohabiting	-0.2	0.92
	Single	1.1	1.03
	Widowed	0.0	0.26
	Divorced	-0.3	1.00
	Separated	-0.2	0.50
All persons aged 55 to 64	Married	-3.1	1.46
	Cohabiting	0.9	0.70
	Single	0.6	0.73
	Widowed	0.2	0.67
	Divorced	0.6	0.98
	Separated	0.6	0.40
All persons aged 65 to 74	Married	-2.8	1.71
	Cohabiting	0.4	0.46
	Single	0.8	0.83
	Widowed	0.3	1.23
	Divorced	1.3	0.98
	Separated	-0.1	0.43
All persons aged 75 and over	Married	1.2	2.09
	Cohabiting	0.1	0.33
	Single	-1.1	0.91
	Widowed	-0.5	2.12
	Divorced	0.1	0.76
	Separated	0.3	0.36

Table C.6 Standard errors and 95% confidence intervals for ethnic origin

Base	Characteristic	%(*p*)	Unweighted sample size	Standard error of *p*	95% confidence intervals		Deft
All persons aged 16 and over							
	Ethnic origin						
	White	91.3	15,069	0.58	90.2 -	92.4	2.5
	Mixed race	0.7	15,069	0.11	0.5 -	0.9	1.7
	Asian-Indian	1.8	15,069	0.27	1.3 -	2.3	2.5
	Asian-Pakistani, Bangladeshi, Other	2.1	15,069	0.29	1.5 -	2.7	2.5
	Black Caribbean	1.1	15,069	0.18	0.7 -	1.5	2.1
	Black African	1.3	15,069	0.20	0.9 -	1.7	2.3
	Other	1.7	15,069	0.21	1.3 -	2.1	2.1

Table C.7 Standard errors and 95% confidence intervals for education level

Base	Characteristic	%(*p*)	Unweighted sample size	Standard error of *p*	95% confidence intervals		Deft
	Education level						
All persons aged 16 to 69	Higher education	29.8	13,457	0.63	28.6 -	31.0	1.6
	Other qualifications	50.9	13,457	0.60	49.7 -	52.1	1.4
	None	19.3	13,457	0.50	18.3 -	20.3	1.5
All men aged 16 to 69	Higher education	30.5	6,182	0.85	28.8 -	32.2	1.5
	Other qualifications	53.1	6,182	0.85	51.4 -	54.8	1.4
	None	16.4	6,182	0.58	15.3 -	17.5	1.2
All women aged 16 to 69	Higher education	29.2	7,275	0.71	27.8 -	30.6	1.3
	Other qualifications	49.0	7,275	0.69	47.6 -	50.4	1.2
	None	21.9	7,275	0.60	20.7 -	23.1	1.2

Table C.8 Standard errors and 95% confidence intervals for socio-economic classification and employment status of adults

Base	Characteristic	%(*p*)	Unweighted sample size	Standard error of *p*	95% confidence intervals		Deft
	Socio-economic classification						
All persons aged 16 and over	Higher managerial and professional	11.9	14,128	0.38	11.2 -	12.6	1.4
	Lower managerial and professional	24.0	14,128	0.47	23.1 -	24.9	1.3
	Intermediate	12.3	14,128	0.34	11.6 -	13.0	1.2
	Small employers and own account	7.6	14,128	0.28	7.1 -	8.1	1.3
	Lower supervisory and technical	9.4	14,128	0.29	8.8 -	10.0	1.2
	Semi-routine	16.6	14,128	0.38	15.9 -	17.3	1.2
	Routine	11.8	14,128	0.36	11.1 -	12.5	1.3
	Never worked and long-term unemployed	6.4	14,128	0.32	5.8 -	7.0	1.5
All men aged 16 and over	Higher managerial and professional	16.6	6,692	0.59	15.4 -	17.8	1.3
	Lower managerial and professional	22.3	6,692	0.64	21.0 -	23.6	1.3
	Intermediate	5.7	6,692	0.34	5.0 -	6.4	1.2
	Small employers and own account	11.0	6,692	0.47	10.1 -	11.9	1.2
	Lower supervisory and technical	13.7	6,692	0.49	12.7 -	14.7	1.2
	Semi-routine	11.9	6,692	0.51	10.9 -	12.9	1.3
	Routine	12.9	6,692	0.48	12.0 -	13.8	1.2
	Never worked and long-term unemployed	6.0	6,692	0.41	5.2 -	6.8	1.4
All women aged 16 and over	Higher managerial and professional	7.4	7,436	0.35	6.7 -	8.1	1.1
	Lower managerial and professional	25.6	7,436	0.59	24.4 -	26.8	1.2
	Intermediate	18.5	7,436	0.55	17.4 -	19.6	1.2
	Small employers and own account	4.5	7,436	0.26	4.0 -	5.0	1.1
	Lower supervisory and technical	5.3	7,436	0.31	4.7 -	5.9	1.2
	Semi-routine	21.1	7,436	0.55	20.0 -	22.2	1.2
	Routine	10.8	7,436	0.43	10.0 -	11.6	1.2
	Never worked and long-term unemployed	6.8	7,436	0.39	6.0 -	7.6	1.3
All persons aged 16 to 44	Higher managerial and professional	13.0	5,373	0.60	11.8 -	14.2	1.4
	Lower managerial and professional	24.3	5,373	0.70	22.9 -	25.7	1.3
	Intermediate	11.8	5,373	0.50	10.8 -	12.8	1.3
	Small employers and own account	6.0	5,373	0.40	5.2 -	6.8	1.3
	Lower supervisory and technical	8.5	5,373	0.41	7.7 -	9.3	1.2
	Semi-routine	16.8	5,373	0.62	15.6 -	18.0	1.3
	Routine	10.4	5,373	0.50	9.4 -	11.4	1.3
	Never worked and long-term unemployed	9.2	5,373	0.53	8.2 -	10.2	1.5
All persons aged 45 to 64	Higher managerial and professional	12.8	5,033	0.60	11.6 -	14.0	1.2
	Lower managerial and professional	26.0	5,033	0.76	24.5 -	27.5	1.2
	Intermediate	11.9	5,033	0.52	10.9 -	12.9	1.1
	Small employers and own account	9.6	5,033	0.51	8.6 -	10.6	1.2
	Lower supervisory and technical	9.4	5,033	0.49	8.4 -	10.4	1.1
	Semi-routine	15.9	5,033	0.61	14.7 -	17.1	1.2
	Routine	11.2	5,033	0.55	10.1 -	12.3	1.2
	Never worked and long-term unemployed	3.1	5,033	0.33	2.5 -	3.7	1.3
All persons aged 65 to 74	Higher managerial and professional	8.3	2,124	0.61	7.1 -	9.5	0.9
	Lower managerial and professional	19.2	2,124	0.98	17.3 -	21.1	1.0
	Intermediate	13.1	2,124	0.77	11.6 -	14.6	0.9
	Small employers and own account	9.4	2,124	0.65	8.1 -	10.7	0.9
	Lower supervisory and technical	10.5	2,124	0.72	9.1 -	11.9	0.9
	Semi-routine	17.9	2,124	0.88	16.2 -	19.6	0.9
	Routine	17.0	2,124	0.88	15.3 -	18.7	0.9
	Never worked and long-term unemployed	4.5	2,124	0.71	3.1 -	5.9	1.4
All persons aged 75 and over	Higher managerial and professional	7.5	1,598	0.70	6.1 -	8.9	0.9
	Lower managerial and professional	21.0	1,598	1.10	18.8 -	23.2	1.0
	Intermediate	14.7	1,598	0.95	12.8 -	16.6	1.0
	Small employers and own account	6.6	1,598	0.64	5.3 -	7.9	0.9
	Lower supervisory and technical	11.6	1,598	0.83	10.0 -	13.2	1.0
	Semi-routine	17.0	1,598	1.00	15.0 -	19.0	1.0
	Routine	14.8	1,598	1.06	12.7 -	16.9	1.1
	Never worked and long-term unemployed	6.7	1,598	0.92	4.9 -	8.5	1.4
	Employment status						
All persons aged 16 and over	In employment	58.6	15,068	0.55	57.5 -	59.7	1.4
	Unemployed	5.6	15,068	0.26	5.1 -	6.1	1.4
	Economically inactive	35.8	15,068	0.53	34.8 -	36.8	1.3
All men aged 16 and over	In employment	63.0	7,144	0.71	61.6 -	64.4	1.3
	Unemployed	7.1	7,144	0.42	6.3 -	7.9	1.4
	Economically inactive	29.9	7,144	0.66	28.6 -	31.2	1.2

Table C.9 Standard errors and 95% confidence intervals for health measures

Base	Characteristic	%(*p*)	Unweighted sample size	Standard error of *p*	95% confidence intervals		Deft
	Self-reported sickness						
All persons	Long-standing illness or disability	29.4	18,689	0.49	28.4 -	30.4	1.5
	Limiting long-standing illness or disability	17.5	18,685	0.36	16.8 -	18.2	1.3
	Restricted activity in the last 14 days due to illness or injury (acute sickness)	10.8	17,142	0.30	10.2 -	11.4	1.2
All males	Long-standing illness or disability	28.5	9,029	0.61	27.3 -	29.7	1.3
	Limiting long-standing illness or disability	16.4	9,027	0.47	15.5 -	17.3	1.2
	Restricted activity in the last 14 days due to illness or injury (acute sickness)	9.6	8,085	0.39	8.8 -	10.4	1.2
All females	Long-standing illness or disability	30.3	9,660	0.59	29.1 -	31.5	1.3
	Limiting long-standing illness or disability	18.5	9,658	0.45	17.6 -	19.4	1.1
	Restricted activity in the last 14 days due to illness or injury (acute sickness)	11.9	9,057	0.42	11.1 -	12.7	1.2
All persons aged 0 to 4	Long-standing illness or disability	8.0	1,122	0.92	6.2 -	9.8	1.2
	Limiting long-standing illness or disability	3.3	1,122	0.57	2.2 -	4.4	1.1
	Restricted activity in the last 14 days due to illness or injury (acute sickness)	6.5	1,123	0.95	4.6 -	8.4	1.3
All persons aged 5 to 15	Long-standing illness or disability	12.2	2,508	0.76	10.7 -	13.7	1.1
	Limiting long-standing illness or disability	6.1	2,508	0.53	5.1 -	7.1	1.1
	Restricted activity in the last 14 days due to illness or injury (acute sickness)	5.7	2,508	0.55	4.6 -	6.8	1.2
All persons aged 16 to 44	Long-standing illness or disability	18.4	6,121	0.64	17.1 -	19.7	1.4
	Limiting long-standing illness or disability	9.8	6,120	0.43	9.0 -	10.6	1.2
	Restricted activity in the last 14 days due to illness or injury (acute sickness)	9.2	5,110	0.46	8.3 -	10.1	1.2
All persons aged 45 to 64	Long-standing illness or disability	39.6	5,153	0.91	37.8 -	41.4	1.3
	Limiting long-standing illness or disability	23.4	5,150	0.77	21.9 -	24.9	1.3
	Restricted activity in the last 14 days due to illness or injury (acute sickness)	13.2	4,748	0.58	12.1 -	14.3	1.1
All persons aged 65 to 74	Long-standing illness or disability	57.8	2,164	1.17	55.5 -	60.1	1.0
	Limiting long-standing illness or disability	35.6	2,164	1.07	33.5 -	37.7	0.9
	Restricted activity in the last 14 days due to illness or injury (acute sickness)	15.9	2,088	0.87	14.2 -	17.6	0.9
All persons aged 75+	Long-standing illness or disability	66.7	1,621	1.29	64.2 -	69.2	1.0
	Limiting long-standing illness or disability	47.6	1,621	1.33	45.0 -	50.2	1.0
	Restricted activity in the last 14 days due to illness or injury (acute sickness)	17.6	1,565	1.02	15.6 -	19.6	1.0

Table C.9a Standard errors of change for health measures

Base	Characteristic	%(*diff_p*)	Standard error of *diff_p*
	Self-reported sickness		
All persons	Long-standing illness or disability	0.7	0.70
	Limiting long-standing illness or disability	0.7	0.51
	Restricted activity in the last 14 days due to illness or injury (acute sickness)	-0.5	0.43
All males	Long-standing illness or disability	0.5	0.86
	Limiting long-standing illness or disability	0.7	0.64
	Restricted activity in the last 14 days due to illness or injury (acute sickness)	-0.7	0.56
All females	Long-standing illness or disability	1.0	0.84
	Limiting long-standing illness or disability	0.7	0.65
	Restricted activity in the last 14 days due to illness or injury (acute sickness)	-0.3	0.58
All persons aged 0 to 4	Long-standing illness or disability	-0.4	1.36
	Limiting long-standing illness or disability	0.5	0.82
	Restricted activity in the last 14 days due to illness or injury (acute sickness)	-0.1	1.25
All persons aged 5 to 15	Long-standing illness or disability	-0.1	1.04
	Limiting long-standing illness or disability	0.6	0.72
	Restricted activity in the last 14 days due to illness or injury (acute sickness)	-0.3	0.73
All persons aged 16 to 44	Long-standing illness or disability	0.3	0.92
	Limiting long-standing illness or disability	0.0	0.63
	Restricted activity in the last 14 days due to illness or injury (acute sickness)	-0.3	0.66
All persons aged 45 to 64	Long-standing illness or disability	1.3	1.22
	Limiting long-standing illness or disability	1.1	1.04
	Restricted activity in the last 14 days due to illness or injury (acute sickness)	-0.6	0.79
All persons aged 65 to 74	Long-standing illness or disability	2.3	1.64
	Limiting long-standing illness or disability	2.4	1.51
	Restricted activity in the last 14 days due to illness or injury (acute sickness)	-1.9	1.26
All persons aged 75+	Long-standing illness or disability	0.1	1.85
	Limiting long-standing illness or disability	0.8	1.91
	Restricted activity in the last 14 days due to illness or injury (acute sickness)	-0.6	1.46

Table C.10 Standard errors and 95% confidence intervals for cigarette smoking

Base	Characteristic	%(p)	Unweighted sample size	Standard error of p	95% confidence intervals		Deft
	Cigarette smoking						
All persons aged 16 and over	Current cigarette smoker	21.0	13,446	0.54	19.9 -	22.1	1.5
	Ex-regular cigarette smoker	25.3	13,446	0.47	24.4 -	26.2	1.3
	Never regularly smoked cigarettes	53.7	13,446	0.62	52.5 -	54.9	1.4
All men aged 16 and over	Current cigarette smoker	21.9	6,157	0.72	20.5 -	23.3	1.4
	Ex-regular cigarette smoker	28.5	6,157	0.68	27.2 -	29.8	1.2
	Never regularly smoked cigarettes	49.6	6,157	0.79	48.1 -	51.1	1.3
All women aged 16 and over	Current cigarette smoker	20.2	7,289	0.60	19.1 -	21.4	1.3
	Ex-regular cigarette smoker	22.5	7,289	0.55	21.4 -	23.6	1.1
	Never regularly smoked cigarettes	57.3	7,289	0.71	55.9 -	58.7	1.2

Table C.10a Standard errors of change for cigarette smoking

Base	Characteristic	%(*diff_p*)	Standard error of *diff_p*
	Cigarette smoking		
All persons aged 16 and over	Current cigarette smoker	0.0	0.73
	Ex-regular cigarette smoker	-0.2	0.65
	Never regularly smoked cigarettes	0.2	0.83
All men aged 16 and over	Current cigarette smoker	0.4	0.96
	Ex-regular cigarette smoker	-1.3	0.95
	Never regularly smoked cigarettes	0.9	1.09
All women aged 16 and over	Current cigarette smoker	-0.3	0.84
	Ex-regular cigarette smoker	0.8	0.75
	Never regularly smoked cigarettes	-0.5	0.97

Table C.11 Standard errors and 95% confidence intervals for alcohol consumption (maximum daily amount)

Base	Characteristic	%(*p*)	Unweighted sample size	Standard error of *p*	95% confidence intervals		Deft
	Alcohol consumption (maximum daily amount)						
All men aged 16 and over	Drank nothing last week	32.0	6,158	0.76	30.5 -	33.5	1.3
	Drank up to 4 units	30.9	6,158	0.69	29.5 -	32.3	1.2
	Drank more than 4 and up to 8 units	16.8	6,158	0.54	15.7 -	17.9	1.1
	Drank more than 8 units	20.4	6,158	0.64	19.1 -	21.6	1.3
All women aged 16 and over	Drank nothing last week	45.8	7,288	0.73	44.4 -	47.2	1.2
	Drank up to 3 units	25.2	7,288	0.58	24.1 -	26.3	1.1
	Drank more than 3 and up to 6 units	16.0	7,288	0.47	15.1 -	16.9	1.1
	Drank more than 6 units	13.1	7,288	0.48	12.2 -	14.0	1.2
All aged 16 to 24	Drank nothing last week	47.7	1,194	1.93	43.9 -	51.5	1.5
	Drank up to 4/3 units	16.0	1,194	1.28	13.5 -	18.5	1.4
	Drank more than 4/3 and up to 8/6 units	12.0	1,194	1.13	9.8 -	14.2	1.4
	Drank more than 8/6 units	24.3	1,194	1.61	21.1 -	27.5	1.5
All aged 25 to 44	Drank nothing last week	35.9	3,688	1.07	33.8 -	38.0	1.5
	Drank up to 4/3 units	24.6	3,688	0.87	22.9 -	26.3	1.4
	Drank more than 4/3 and up to 8/6 units	16.9	3,688	0.68	15.6 -	18.2	1.2
	Drank more than 8/6 units	22.6	3,688	0.92	20.8 -	24.4	1.5
All aged 45 to 64	Drank nothing last week	34.7	4,736	0.94	32.9 -	36.5	1.3
	Drank up to 4/3 units	29.0	4,736	0.80	27.4 -	30.6	1.2
	Drank more than 4/3 and up to 8/6 units	20.2	4,736	0.71	18.8 -	21.6	1.2
	Drank more than 8/6 units	16.1	4,736	0.64	14.8 -	17.4	1.2
All aged 65 and over	Drank nothing last week	47.1	3,650	0.93	45.3 -	48.9	1.0
	Drank up to 4/3 units	37.7	3,650	0.87	36.0 -	39.4	1.0
	Drank more than 4/3 and up to 8/6 units	11.8	3,650	0.58	10.7 -	12.9	1.0
	Drank more than 8/6 units	3.4	3,650	0.30	2.8 -	4.0	1.0
All aged 16 and over	Drank nothing last week	39.3	13,446	0.63	38.1 -	40.5	1.5
	Drank up to 4/3 units	27.9	13,446	0.48	27.0 -	28.8	1.2
	Drank more than 4/3 and up to 8/6 units	16.3	13,446	0.38	15.6 -	17.0	1.2
	Drank more than 8/6 units	16.5	13,446	0.46	15.6 -	17.4	1.4

Table C11a Standard errors of change for alcohol consumption (maximum daily amount)

Base	Characteristic	%(*diff_p*)	Standard error of *diff_p*
	Alcohol consumption (maximum daily amount)		
All men aged 16 and over	Drank nothing last week	2.2	1.05
	Drank up to 4 units	-2.0	0.98
	Drank more than 4 and up to 8 units	0.8	0.73
	Drank more than 8 units	-1.0	0.94
All women aged 16 and over	Drank nothing last week	0.5	1.06
	Drank up to 3 units	-0.5	0.81
	Drank more than 3 and up to 6 units	1.2	0.65
	Drank more than 6 units	-1.2	0.69
All aged 16 to 24	Drank nothing last week	4.5	2.72
	Drank up to 4/3 units	-2.2	1.80
	Drank more than 4/3 and up to 8/6 units	0.1	1.48
	Drank more than 8/6 units	-2.4	2.22
All aged 25 to 44	Drank nothing last week	0.6	1.44
	Drank up to 4/3 units	-1.1	1.21
	Drank more than 4/3 and up to 8/6 units	1.3	0.92
	Drank more than 8/6 units	-0.8	1.24
All aged 45 to 64	Drank nothing last week	1.5	1.28
	Drank up to 4/3 units	-1.7	1.11
	Drank more than 4/3 and up to 8/6 units	1.0	0.94
	Drank more than 8/6 units	-0.8	0.91
All aged 65 and over	Drank nothing last week	0.2	1.31
	Drank up to 4/3 units	-0.5	1.26
	Drank more than 4/3 and up to 8/6 units	1.2	0.81
	Drank more than 8/6 units	-0.8	0.50
All aged 16 and over	Drank nothing last week	1.3	0.90
	Drank up to 4/3 units	-1.2	0.70
	Drank more than 4/3 and up to 8/6 units	1.0	0.53
	Drank more than 8/6 units	-1.1	0.67

Table C.12 Standard errors and 95% confidence intervals for number of cohabitations

Base	Characteristic	%(p)	Unweighted sample size	Standard error of p	95% confidence intervals		Deft
	Number of cohabitations						
All women aged 16 to 59	None	83.5	4,310	0.63	82.3	- 84.7	1.1
	One	12.1	4,310	0.53	11.1	- 13.1	1.1
	Two or more	4.4	4,310	0.33	3.8	- 5.0	1.1
All men aged 16 to 59	None	83.2	3,453	0.79	81.7	- 84.7	1.3
	One	10.7	3,453	0.61	9.5	- 11.9	1.2
	Two or more	6.1	3,453	0.52	5.1	- 7.1	1.4
All people aged 16 to 24	None	93.6	960	0.81	92.0	- 95.2	1.2
	One	5.0	960	0.74	3.5	- 6.5	1.2
	Two or more	1.4	960	0.35	0.7	- 2.1	1.0
All people aged 25 to 34	None	79.9	1,487	1.11	77.7	- 82.1	1.2
	One	15.1	1,487	0.94	13.3	- 16.9	1.1
	Two or more	5.0	1,487	0.71	3.6	- 6.4	1.4
All people aged 35 to 44	None	76.0	2,156	1.13	73.8	- 78.2	1.3
	One	15.9	2,156	1.00	13.9	- 17.9	1.3
	Two or more	8.0	2,156	0.68	6.7	- 9.3	1.2
All people aged 45 to 54	None	85.5	2,117	0.88	83.8	- 87.2	1.2
	One	9.3	2,117	0.70	7.9	- 10.7	1.1
	Two or more	5.2	2,117	0.57	4.1	- 6.3	1.2
All people aged 55 to 59	None	91.0	1,041	1.01	89.0	- 93.0	1.1
	One	5.6	1,041	0.75	4.1	- 7.1	1.0
	Two or more	3.5	1,041	0.65	2.2	- 4.8	1.1
All people aged 16 to 59	None	83.4	7,761	0.52	82.4	- 84.4	1.3
	One	11.4	7,761	0.43	10.6	- 12.2	1.3
	Two or more	5.2	7,761	0.30	4.6	- 5.8	1.2

Weighting

Appendix D

All surveys accept that there will be some degree of non-response, although great efforts are made to keep it to a minimum[1]. The General LiFestyle Survey (GLF) compensates for **unit non-response** (where all survey information for a sampled household is missing) through weighting, which is described in this appendix.. The method adopted to reduce **item non-response** (where information for particular questions is missing as the result of conducting proxy interviews) is discussed in *Appendix B Sample design and response*.

Longitudinal surveys like the GLF experience two forms of non-response: non-participation to wave one and non-participation to later waves of the survey (also known as attrition). The term non-response will be used to refer to the former and attrition to refer to the latter.

The 2009 GLF is weighted using a two-step approach. The first step uses sample-based weighting to compensate for non-response and attrition. The second step uses population-based weighting to match the sample distribution to the population distribution in terms of age group, gender and region[2].

Weighting for non-response and attrition

Weighting for non-response and attrition can be seen as giving each respondent a weight so that they represent non-respondents who are similar to them in terms of survey characteristics. To be able to use this method consistent information about both respondents and non-respondents is needed to model the likelihood of response for different groups. In the case of non-response, little information is available on non-responding households directly from the survey[3], so an external data source is required. For attrition, we are able to match back to previous years of the survey where longitudinal households have provided information.

The sample-based procedure for determining weighting characteristics is considered separately below for those sampled households in wave one and those in waves other than one.

Sample-based weighting for non-response using the 2001 Census

Although we have no direct data on non-responding households to the GLF we use information from the Census to indirectly estimate the likelihood of response. Unlike the GLF, which relies upon voluntary co-operation from respondents, the Census is mandatory and therefore non-response is kept to an absolute minimum.

After the 2001 Census, methodological work was conducted to match Census addresses with the sampled addresses for some of the large household surveys, which included the GHS. Therefore, it was possible to match GHS respondents and non-respondents with corresponding information from the Census for the same address. We could then model and calculate response rates for types of household that were being under-represented in the survey. A combination of household variables available on an annual basis, such as household type, social class, region and car ownership were analysed using the software package AnswerTree (which uses chi-squared statistics to group households with similar response patterns)[4]. These chosen characteristics were used to produce the weighting classes shown in Figure D.A.

The weighting classes and weights determined from the work described above are then applied to weight the GLF data (for wave one respondents) on an annual basis.

Figure D.A

Figure D.A 2001 Weighting classes formed in the AnswerTree analysis

LEVEL 1 SPLIT	LEVEL 2 SPLIT	LEVEL 3 SPLIT	LEVEL 4 SPLIT	WEIGHT CLASS
Region	Number of Rooms	Number of Pensioners in the household	Sex of the Household Reference Person	
West Midlands London	More than three	All pensioners	Female	1
			Male	2
		Two or two or more persons in the household but only 1 pensioner		3
		Two or two or more persons in the household where more than one person is a pensioner No pensioners in the household		4
	Three or fewer			5
Yorkshire & Humberside East Midlands South West Wales	**Household size**			
	More than two			6
	Two			7
	One	**Adults not employed**		
		One		8
		Zero		9
North East North West & Merseyside East of England South East Scotland	**Number of Adults**			
	More than two			10
	Two	**Accommodation Type**		
		Purpose built flat Part of a converted or shared house Other		11
		Detached Semi-detached Terraced		12
	One			13

Sample-based weighting for attrition using the 2008 GLF

As mentioned earlier, attrition is a form of non-response found on longitudinal surveys between waves. The longitudinal implementation of the GLF means that approximately three-quarters of sampled households had been surveyed in 2008. As these sampled households had previously participated in the survey, details of respondents and non-respondents were linked back to their corresponding information at the previous wave. Logistic regression was used to model the likelihood of response in the current wave against the characteristics of households at their interview in the previous wave. A variety of household variables such as household type, socio-economic class, region and car ownership were tested for inclusion. Characteristics determined as significant by the logistic regression model (at the five per cent significance level) were used to weight for this attrition[5]. The variables reaching significance are listed in Figure D.B below.

Figure D.B

Figure D.B Significant weighting variables formed in the logistic regression analysis

Variables
When household reference person arrived in UK
Ethnicity of household reference person
Number of partial interviews in household
Dwelling type
Tenure
Number of household who smoke nowadays
Drinking amount of the household reference person
Government Office Region
Age of household reference person
Number of people in the household who checked their payslip during interview
Any qualifications (any resident)
Number of people in the household who refused or answered 'don't know' to a known sensitive question
Household composition
Current wave
Number of calls made to the household to arrange the interview

Population-based weighting

Population-based weighting schemes address deficiencies in the data due to sample-non coverage. They can also further reduce non-response bias and reduce the variance (sampling error) of survey estimates.

The population-based method

The GLF sample is weighted to population totals based on Mid-Year Estimates, Quarterly Population Estimates and National Population Projections. The population totals are consistent with those used to weight ONS' Labour Force Survey.

The population information and GLF data were grouped into twelve age by gender categories and six region categories to form weighting classes as shown in Figure D.C. The population-based weighting consists of adjusting the existing weights (including factors for design and non-response) so that the final weights ensure that weighted totals for the above demographic categories match the population totals.

This procedure, also known as calibration, was carried out using the GES SAS macro. This was implemented in such a way as to ensure that all individuals within a household were given the same final weights[6].

Figure D.C

Figure D.C Weighting classes used for GES analysis

Age/sex	Region
0-4	London
5-15	Scotland
16-24 male	Wales
16-24 female	Other Metropolitan
25-44 male	Other Non-metropolitan
25-44 female	South East
45-64 male	
45-64 female	
65-74 male	
65-74 female	
75+ male	
75+ female	

Presentation and interpretation of weighted data

Weighted data cannot be meaningfully compared to unweighted data from previous years without knowledge of how the weighting changes the estimates. In the GHS trend tables, weighted and unweighted data are presented for 1998 and weighted data are shown only from 2000 to 2009. Care should be taken when interpreting trend data or individual tables compared with other years as part of a time series.

It should be noted that the weighted bases used in this report are not recommended as a source for population estimates. They are the denominator for the percentages shown in tables and should not be regarded as estimates of population size[7].

Effects of weighting on data

Tables D.1 and D.2 identify the effects of weighting by comparing unweighted and weighted data for 2009. They also show the differences between the weighted and unweighted estimates 2001 to 2009, on a selection of household and individual level variables.

Tables D.1 and D.2

For the 2009 estimates, the weighting had a noticeable effect on the following variables.

Increase in value of estimate

- Households that are buying with a mortgage from 34.2% to 37.3%.
- 4 or more adult households from 4.4% to 6.3%.
- Households with home computer van from 74.8% to 76.4%.

Decrease in value of estimate

- 2 or more adult households from 51.6% to 47.6%
- Households that are owned outright from 37.6% to 31.9%.
- Households containing a married couple and no children from 27.2% to 22.2%.

The differences between the weighted and unweighted data for 2002 to 2009 are also shown in Tables D.1 and D.2. It can be seen that the differences produced by weighting in 2009 were similar to those in previous years for the same variables.

Notes and references

1. Appendix B describes the variation in response for the GHS since it began in 1971.

2. Barton, J. Developing a Weighting and Grossing System for the General Household Survey: *Social Survey Methodology Bulletin* (Issue 49 July 2001).

3. Some surveys collect information about the characteristics of non-responding households although this is not routinely the case on the GLF.

4. AnswerTree uses the CHAID (Chi-squared Automatic Interaction Detection) algorithm, which uses chi-squared statistics to identify optimal splits or groupings of independent variables in terms of predicting the outcome of a dependent variable, in this case response.

5. The attrition weights build on the weights calculated for when these longitudinal cases were in their first wave. This means both non-response and attrition are covered within this weight.

6. GES, or *Generalized Estimation System*, is a SAS macro produced by Statistics Canada. The weights are formed using a form of calibration called Generalized Regression, or GREG estimation. The macro allows bounds to be set on the adjustment factors in the calibration.

7. Missing answers are excluded from the tables and in some cases this is reflected in the weighted bases, i.e. these numbers vary between tables. For this reason, the bases themselves are not recommended as a source for population estimates.

Table D1 Weighted compared with unweighted data for years 2002 to 2009 – household level

Household level variables

% of households		2009		Effect of weighting							
		Unweighted	Weighted	Weighted 2002 - Unweighted 2002	Weighted 2003 - Unweighted 2003	Weighted 2004 - Unweighted 2004	Weighted 2005 - Unweighted 2005	Weighted 2006 - Unweighted 2006	Weighted 2007 - Unweighted 2007	Weighted 2008 - Unweighted 2008	Weighted 2009 - Unweighted 2009
		(a)	(b)								
											(b-a)
Household size											
1 person		12.7	13.2	2.0	2.3	2.3	2.4	1.1	1.1	0.7	0.5
2 persons		32.1	28.1	-1.7	-1.0	-1.4	-1.3	-2.6	-2.8	-3.3	-4.0
3 persons		18.9	19.5	0.1	0.0	0.0	0.0	1.2	1.3	0.9	0.6
4 persons		22.4	24.3	-0.3	-0.8	-0.5	-0.7	0.3	0.1	0.5	1.9
5 persons		9.2	10.0	-0.1	-0.4	-0.2	-0.4	-0.2	-0.1	0.3	0.8
6 or more persons		4.7	4.9	0.0	-0.1	-0.1	-0.1	0.2	0.4	0.8	0.2
	Base	18,988	59,191,698								
Number of adults											
1 adult		33.6	34.8	2.1	2.2	2.2	2.3	2.2	2.4	1.5	1.2
2 adults		51.6	47.6	-2.5	-3.2	-3.0	-3.2	-4.9	-4.8	-4.3	-4.0
3 adults		10.4	11.3	0.1	0.4	0.3	0.4	1.5	1.1	0.9	0.9
4 or more adults		4.4	6.3	0.5	0.6	0.5	0.5	1.1	1.3	1.9	1.9
	Base	8,203	25,190,143								
Number of children											
No children		74.3	73.8	0.6	2.1	1.3	1.8	1.0	0.8	0.2	-0.5
1 child		12.8	13.7	0.3	0.1	0.1	0.0	0.8	0.8	0.9	0.9
2 children		9.5	9.6	-0.6	-1.4	-0.9	-1.2	-1.1	-1.0	-0.6	0.1
3 or more children		3.3	3.0	-0.4	-0.8	-0.5	-0.6	-0.6	-0.6	-0.7	-0.3
	Base	8,203	25,190,143								
Household type											
1 person only		29.4	30.9	2.0	2.3	2.3	2.4	2.4	2.6	1.9	1.5
2 or more unrelated adults		1.9	2.1	0.3	0.3	0.4	0.4	0.1	0.0	0.4	0.2
Married couple, dependent children		16.6	17.8	-0.6	-1.4	-1.0	-1.4	-0.5	-0.3	0.1	1.2
Married couple, independent children		5.6	6.5	0.1	0.3	0.1	0.2	0.9	1.0	1.1	0.9
Married couple, no children		27.2	22.2	-2.0	-1.7	-1.8	-2.0	-3.8	-4.4	-4.7	-5.0
Lone parent, dependent children		6.5	6.3	0.0	-0.1	0.0	0.0	0.0	0.0	-0.3	-0.2
Lone parent, independent children		3.0	3.4	0.1	0.2	0.2	0.1	0.4	0.3	0.4	0.4
2 or more families (inc. same sex cohab)		0.9	1.0	0.0	0.0	0.0	-0.1	0.2	0.3	0.3	0.1
Cohabiting couple, with children		4.2	4.4	0.1	-0.3	-0.1	-0.3	0.0	0.1	0.2	0.2
Cohabiting couple, no children		4.3	4.8	0.1	0.2	0.0	0.3	0.1	0.3	0.7	0.5
	Base	8,164	25,190,143								
Tenure - harmonised											
Owns outright		37.6	31.9	-1.6	-1.5	-1.1	-1.6	-3.4	-3.9	-4.6	-5.7
Buying on mortgage		34.2	37.3	0.0	-0.1	-0.7	-0.4	0.4	1.2	2.2	3.1
Rents from Council/Local Authority		9.4	9.9	0.7	0.6	0.7	0.8	0.9	0.9	0.8	0.5
Rents from HA/Reg. Social Landlord		7.7	8.1	0.2	0.1	0.3	0.1	0.5	0.6	0.5	0.4
Rents privately - unfurnished/nk		9.5	10.8	0.4	0.6	0.4	0.5	0.6	0.7	0.8	1.3
Rents privately - furnished		1.6	2.0	0.5	0.4	0.5	0.5	0.7	0.4	0.5	0.4
	Base	8,199	25,132,487								
Ownership of consumer durables											
Washing machine		96.5	96.3	-0.5	-0.6	-0.5	-0.4	-0.5	-0.4	-0.3	-0.2
Telephone		99.6	99.7	0.0	-0.1	0.0	-0.1	0.0	0.0	-0.1	0.1
Home computer		74.8	76.4	-0.4	-0.3	-0.7	-0.6	0.2	0.5	0.6	1.6
	Base	8,200	25,142,684								
Central heating		97.0	97.0	-0.3	-0.1	-0.2	-0.3	-0.3	-0.3	-0.4	0.0
	Base	8,201	25,142,684								
Car or van ownership											
No car or van		22.2	22.8	1.4	1.4	1.7	1.7	2.0	2.0	1.9	0.6
One car or van		45.9	45.1	0.5	0.3	0.5	0.6	-0.2	-0.4	-1.2	-0.8
Two cars or vans		26.1	25.5	-1.7	-1.7	-2.0	-2.0	-2.1	-2.0	-1.3	-0.6
Three or more cars or vans		5.9	6.6	-0.2	-0.1	-0.2	-0.2	0.3	0.4	0.6	0.7
	Base	8,203	25,142,684								

Table D2   Weighted compared with unweighted data for years 2002 to 2009 – individual level

Table D2   Weighted versus unweighted data for years 2002 to 2009 - individual level

Individual level variables

% of individuals	2009 Unweighted (a)	2009 Weighted (b)	Weighted 2002 - Unweighted 2002	Weighted 2003 - Unweighted 2003	Weighted 2004 - Unweighted 2004	Weighted 2005 - Unweighted 2005	Weighted 2006 - Unweighted 2006	Weighted 2007 - Unweighted 2007	Weighted 2008 - Unweighted 2008	Weighted 2009 - Unweighted 2009 (b-a)
Limiting long-standing illness or disability										
Male	18.8	17.3	-0.4	-0.1	-0.1	-0.5	-0.6	0.8	-1.1	-1.5
Female	20.0	18.8	0.1	0.3	0.3	0.3	-0.2	0.6	-0.7	-1.2
Total	19.4	18.0	-0.2	0.1	0.2	-0.1	-0.3	0.7	-0.9	-1.4
Non-limiting long-standing illness or disability										
Male	13.8	12.5	-0.4	-0.2	-0.3	0	-0.7	-0.1	-1.2	-1.3
Female	12.6	12.0	-0.2	-0.1	0.0	0.4	-0.4	0.6	-0.5	-0.6
Total	13.1	12.2	-0.3	-0.2	-0.2	0.2	-0.5	0.3	-0.8	-0.9
No long-standing illness or disability										
Male	67.5	70.3	0.8	0.4	0.3	0.5	1.3	-0.7	1.4	2.8
Female	67.4	69.2	0.1	-0.1	-0.2	-0.3	0.5	-1.2	0.9	1.8
Total	67.4	69.7	0.4	0.1	0.0	0.1	0.9	-1.0	0.1	2.3
Health										
Very good										
Male	37.7	40.8	-	-	-	0.3	0.8	-0.1	1.7	3.1
Female	37.9	39.6	-	-	-	0	0.0	-0.7	0.6	1.7
Total	37.8	40.2	-	-	-	0.1	0.4	-0.4	1.1	2.4
Good			-	-	-					
Male	39.8	38.7	-	-	-	0	0.1	0.6	0.1	-1.1
Female	39.2	38.7	-	-	-	-0.2	0.1	0.1	0.1	-0.5
Total	39.5	38.7	-	-	-	-0.1	0.1	0.4	0.1	-0.8
Fair			-	-	-					
Male	16.0	14.5	-	-	-	-0.3	-0.6	-0.2	-1.2	-1.5
Female	17.1	16.3	-	-	-	0.2	-0.3	-0.3	-0.4	-0.8
Total	16.6	15.4	-	-	-	-0.1	-0.4	-0.3	-0.8	-1.2
BAD			-	-	-					
Male	5.2	4.9	-	-	-	0	-0.3	-0.4	-0.4	-0.3
Female	4.8	4.4	-	-	-	0.1	0.2	0.5	-0.1	-0.4
Total	5.0	4.6	-	-	-	0	0.0	0.1	-0.2	-0.4
Very bad			-	-	-					
Male	1.3	1.1	-	-	-	0	-0.1	0.0	-0.1	-0.2
Female	1.0	1.0	-	-	-	0	0.0	0.4	-0.1	0.0
Total	1.2	1.0	-	-	-	0	-0.1	0.1	-0.1	-0.2
Restricted activity in the last 14 days due to illness or injury (acute sickness)										
Male	10.1	9.6	-0.1	-0.3	0.0	0.1	-0.2	-0.3	-0.3	-0.5
Female	12.1	11.9	0.1	-0.1	0.1	0.3	0.1	-0.3	-0.3	-0.2
Total	11.2	10.8	0.0	-0.2	0.0	0.3	0.0	-0.3	-0.3	-0.4
Cigarette smoking by sex										
Men										
Current cigarette smokers	20.2	21.9	1.0	1.2	0.9	1.3	1.6	1.8	1.7	1.7
Ex-regular cigarette smokers	31.8	28.5	-1.5	-1.2	-1.1	-1.5	-2.5	-3.0	-2.7	-3.3
Never or (only occasionally) smoked	48.0	49.6	0.5	0.0	0.1	0.3	1.0	1.2	1.0	1.6
Women										
Current cigarette smokers	19.3	20.3	0.4	0.3	0.2	0.5	0.7	0.6	1.2	1.0
Ex-regular cigarette smokers	23.7	22.5	-0.2	-0.1	-0.4	-0.4	-0.8	-1.1	-1.2	-1.2
Never or (only occasionally) smoked	57.0	57.3	-0.2	-0.2	0.1	-0.1	0.1	0.5	0.0	0.3
Total										
Current cigarette smokers	19.7	21	0.7	0.8	0.6	0.9	1.1	1.3	1.4	1.3
Ex-regular cigarette smokers	27.4	25.3	-0.7	-0.7	-0.6	-0.9	-1.5	-2.0	-1.8	-2.1
Never or (only occasionally) smoked	52.9	53.7	0.1	-0.1	0.1	0.1	0.4	0.8	0.4	0.8
Maximum daily amount of alcohol drank last week by sex										
Men										
Drank nothing last week	30.5	32.0	0.4	0.1	0.6	0.4	1.5	1.6	1.2	1.5
Up to 4 units	33.4	30.9	-1.2	-1.1	-1.3	-1.5	4.7	-2.0	-1.9	-2.5
More than 4 units and up to 8	17.5	16.8	-0.1	0.2	-0.1	-0.1	-2.6	-0.7	-0.7	-0.7
More than 8 units	18.6	20.4	1.0	0.8	0.8	1.2	-3.7	1.1	1.4	1.8
Women										
Drank nothing last week	45.5	45.8	0.5	0.4	0.7	0.4	1.5	2.2	1.6	0.3
Up to 3 units	26.6	25.2	-0.8	-0.7	-0.8	-0.7	12.0	-1.5	-1.5	-1.4
More than 3 units and up to 6	16.1	16.0	-0.1	-0.1	-0.1	0	-7.0	-1.0	-1.0	-0.1
More than 6 units	11.8	13.1	0.3	0.4	0.1	0.3	-6.5	0.3	0.9	1.3

- Data was not collected before 2005.

Household and Individual Questionnaires

Appendix E

2009

GENERAL LIFESTYLE SURVEY

HOUSEHOLD SECTION

Area   Information already entered.

Address   Information already entered.
             1..30

HHold   Information already entered.
             1..4

StartDat   ENTER DATE INTERVIEW WITH THIS HOUSEHOLD WAS
             STARTED.

DateChk   IS THIS...

             The first time you've opened this questionnaire...1
             or the second or later time?..2
             EMERGENCY CODE IF COMPUTER'S DATE IS WRONG AT LATER CHECK......5

IntEdit   CODE WHETHER THIS IS THE INTERVIEW STAGE, A PROXY
             CONVERSION, OR THE EDIT STAGE.

             Interview... 1
             Proxy Conversion by telephone (TELEPHONE INTERVIEW UNIT ONLY)............2
             OFFICE ONLY – EDIT..7

HOUSEHOLD INFORMATION

Information to be collected for all persons in all households

1.   Name   Who normally lives at this address?

RECORD A NAME / IDENTIFIER FOR EACH MEMBER OF THE HOUSEHOLD

ENTER TEXT OF AT MOST 12 CHARACTERS

2.   Curstat   Code the appropriate current status for each household member for this wave.

Resident at this household..1
Under the age of 16..2
Moved, now resident locally details known can interview.........................3
Moved, resident elsewhere in GB, details known, reallocate....................4
Moved, resident at unknown address..5
Was resident here but has died since last call.......................................6
Was resident here but since last call now moved to an institution (for 6 months or more)...7
Was resident here but since last call now resident abroad (for 6 months or more)..8
Ineligible. Mover at GSK, new case created/ no orig. samp. Members........9

3.   NewPerson   Does anyone else normally live at this address?
(Record any additional people who joined the household since last wave)

Yes...1
No...2

4.   NewName   Record the names for each new member of the household.
(If NewPerson = 1)

5.   Sex   Record sex.
Male..1
Female...2

6.   Birth   What is your date of birth?

FOR DAY NOT GIVEN...........ENTER 15 FOR DAY.
FOR MONTH NOT GIVEN.....ENTER 6 FOR MONTH

**Ask those who did not know, or refused to give their date of birth
(Birth = DK OR REFUSAL)**

7.   AgeIf   What was your age last birthday?

98 or more = CODE 97
0..97

8.   DVAge   (Computed in Blaise)
Age for whole sample, from Birth and AgeIf
00..120

9.   HallRes   Is this person living in halls of residence or at a boarding school? Student nurses living in NHS accommodation elsewhere in Great Britain should not be included in this household.

Yes..1
No..2

**Ask if respondent is aged 16 or over
(DVAge > 15)**

10.   xMarSta   ASK OR RECORD
CODE FIRST THAT APPLIES
Are you currently....
single, that is, never married?...1
married and living with your husband/wife?..2
a civil partner in a legally-recognised Civil Partnership............................3
married and separated from your husband/wife?..4
divorced?...5
or widowed?...6
SPONTANEOUS ONLY – In a legally-recognised Civil Partnership and separated his/her civil partner..7
SPONTANEOUS ONLY – Formerly a civil partner, the Civil Partnership now legally dissolved..8
SPONTANEOUS ONLY – A surviving civil partner: his/her partner having since died...9

Ask if there is more than one person in the household AND respondent is aged 16 or over AND is single, separated, divorced or widowed
(Household size > 1   &   DVAge > 15   &   Marstat = 1, 3, 4 or 5)

11.   LiveWth   ASK OR RECORD

May I just check, are you living with someone in the household as a couple?
Yes...1
No...2
SPONTANEOUS ONLY - same sex couple (but not in a formal registered Civil Partnership)...3

Ask if respondent is aged 16 or over
(DVAge > 15)

12.   HRPId   Record if Name is the person in whose name this accommodation is owned or rented

Yes...1
No...2

Ask if there is more than one person in the household, AND the respondent is aged 16 or over
(Household size > 1   &   DVAge > 15)

13.   Hhldr   In whose name is the accommodation owned or rented?
ASK OR RECORD

This person alone...1
This person jointly..3
NOT owner/renter 5

Ask if there is more than one person in the household, AND the accommodation is jointly owned
(Household size > 1 & Hhldr = 3)

14.   HiHNum   You have told me that...jointly own or rent the accommodation. Which of them who has the highest income (from earnings, benefits, pensions and any other sources)?

INTERVIEWER: THESE ARE THE JOINT HOUSEHOLDERS

ENTER PERSON NUMBER - IF TWO OR MORE HAVE SAME INCOME, ENTER 17
1..17

Ask if there is more than one person in the household, AND the joint householders have the same income
(Household size > 1 & HiHNum = 17)

15.   JntEldA   ENTER PERSON NUMBER OF THE ELDEST JOINT HOUSEHOLDER FROM THOSE WITH THE SAME HIGHEST INCOME

ASK OR RECORD
1..17

Ask if household size is greater than one, AND the joint householders do not know, or refuse to say who has the greatest income
(Household size > 1 & HiHNum = Don't know or Refusal)

16.   JntEldB   ENTER PERSON NUMBER OF THE ELDEST JOINT HOUSEHOLDER

ASK OR RECORD
1..16

Ask all households

17.   DVHRPnum   PERSON NUMBER OF HRP. (Computed in Blaise)
Ask if the HRP is married or cohabiting
(HRPnum = 1..14 & MarStat = 2 or LiveWith = 1)

18.   HRPPart   THE HRP IS (HRP's NAME)

ENTER THE PERSON NUMBER OF THE HRP's SPOUSE/PARTNER
NO SPOUSE/PARTNER = 17
1..17

Ask all households

19.   R   I would now like to ask how the people in your household are related to each other.

CODE RELATIONSHIP - ... IS ...'S ....

Spouse..1
Cohabitee..2
Son/daughter (inc. adopted)...3
Step-son/daughter..4
Foster child...5
Son- in -law/daughter - in –law...6
Parent/Guardian...7
Step-parent...8
Foster parent...9
Parent- In – law..10
Brother/sister (inc. adopted)..11
Step-brother/sister.. 12
Foster brother/sister...13
Brother/sister-in-law...14
Grand-child..15
Grand-parent..16
Other relative...17
Other non-relative...18
Civil Partner...20

20.   CheckAdd   Is this your correct address?
Yes..1
No...2

ACCOMMODATION TYPE

All households

21.   Accom   IS THE ACCOMMODATION:

N.B. MUST BE SPACE USED BY HOUSEHOLD

a house or bungalow...1
a flat or maisonette...2
a room/rooms...3
other...4

Ask if respondents live in a house or bungalow
(Accom = 1)

22.   HseType   IS IT (THE HOUSE/BUNGALOW)

detached..1
semi-detached..2
or terraced/end of terrace?..3

Ask if respondents live in a flat or maisonette
(Accom = 2)

23.   FltTyp   IS IT (THE FLAT/MAISONETTE)

a purpose-built block..1
a converted house/some other kind of building?...........................2

Ask if respondents live in a room/rooms
(Accom = 3)

24.   DwellNo   Is the apartment or flat....

A building is an independent structure with one or more dwellings enclosed by a roof and external walls.

Each house in a row of terraced houses counts as one building.

Flats with more than one entrance count as one building only if all flats are accessible from each entrance.

In a building with less than 10 dwellings..1
Or in a building with 10 or more dwellings?..2

Ask if respondents said their accommodation was 'something else'
(Accom = 4)

25.   AccOth   IS IT (THE ACCOMMODATION)

caravan, mobile home or houseboat...1
or some other kind of accommodation?..2

Ask if respondents live in a flat/maisonette or rooms
(Accom = 2 or 3)

26.   DwellNo   IS IT (THE APPARTMENT OR FLAT):

(BUILDING DEFINITION: A BUILDING IS AN INDEPENDENT STRUCTURE WITH ONE OR MORE DWELLINGS ENCLOSED BY A ROOF AND EXTERNAL WALLS. EACH HOUSE IN A ROW OF TERRACED HOUSES COUNTS AS ONE BUILDING. FLATS WITH MORE THAN ONE ENTRANCE COUNT AS ONE BUILDING ONLY IF ALL FLATS ACCESSIBLE FROM EACH ENTRANCE.)

in a building with less than 10 dwellings..1
or in a building with 10 or more dwellings?..2

Ask all households

27.   AcProb   Do you have any of the following problems with your accommodation or the area you live in?

IF ASKED: BY 'AREA' I MEAN WITHIN ABOUT A 15-20 MINUTES WALK OR 5-10 MINUTES DRIVE FROM YOUR HOME.

28.   Damp   Damp Do you have this problem with your accommodation...
Leaking roof, damp walls/floors, damp foundations, or rotten floorboards or window frames?

Yes...1
No..2

IF ASKED: BY 'AREA' I MEAN WITHIN ABOUT A 15-20 MINUTES WALK OR 5-10 MINUTES DRIVE FROM YOUR HOME.

29.   TooDark   Too dark, or not enough light?

THIS QUESTION ASKS ABOUT PROBLEMS WITH ANY OF THE ROOMS BEING TOO DARK/NOT HAVING ENOUGH LIGHT (ON A SUNNY DAY). NOT NECESSARILY ALL OF THE ROOMS IN THE ACCOMMODATION HAVE TO BE DARK.

Yes...1
No..2

IF ASKED: BY 'AREA' I MEAN WITHIN ABOUT A 15-20 MINUTES WALK OR 5 – 10 MINUTES DRIVE FROM YOUR HOME.

30.   Noisy   Noise from neighbours or noise from the street (traffic, business, factories etc.)?

Yes...1
No..2

IF ASKED: BY 'AREA' I MEAN WITHIN ABOUT A 15-20 MINUTES WALK OR 5 – 10 MINUTES DRIVE FROM YOUR HOME.

31.   Pollut   Pollution, grime or other environmental problems in the area caused by traffic or industry?

IF ASKED: BY 'AREA' I MEAN WITHIN ABOUT A 15-20 MINUTES WALK OR 5-10 MINUTES DRIVE FROM YOUR HOME.

Yes.. 1
No..2

32.   Crime   Crime, violence or vandalism in the area?

IF ASKED: BY 'AREA' I MEAN WITHIN ABOUT A 15-20 MINUTES WALK OR 5-10 MINUTES DRIVE FROM YOUR HOME.

Yes...1
No..2

33.   Rooms2   I want to ask you about all the rooms you have in your household's accommodation including any rooms you sublet to other people.

How many of the following rooms do you have in this house/flat?

A COMBINED ROOM COUNTS AS ONE ROOM

34.   Bedrooms   How many bedrooms do you have?

INCLUDE BEDSITTERS, BOXROOMS OR ATTIC BEDROOMS

0..20

35.   KitOver   How many kitchens over 6.5 feet wide do you have?

NARROWEST SIDE MUST BE 6.5 FEET FROM WALL TO WALL

0..20

36.   KitUnder   How many kitchens under 6.5 feet wide do you have?

0..20

37.   Living   How many living rooms do you have?

INCLUDE DINING ROOMS, SUNLOUNGE OR CONSERVATORY USED
ALL YEAR ROUND

0..20

38.   BathShow   Have you got either a bath or a shower?

Yes for sole use of the household..1
Yes, shared...2
No..3

39.   Bathroom   How many bathrooms do you have with plumbed in bath/shower?

0..20

40.   FlshToil   Do you have an inside flushing toilet for sole use of the household?

Yes...1
No...2

41.   Utility   How many utility and other rooms do you have?

0..20

42.   GHSCentH   ASK OR RECORD
                         Do you have any form of central heating, including electric storage heaters,
                         in your (part of the) accommodation?

Yes...1
No...2

43.   Garage   Can I just check, do you have a garage or parking space that is part of the
                            property?

                            Yes...1
                            No..2

                            INCLUDE:
                            ACCESS/USE OF GARAGE TO PROVIDE PARKING IN CONNECTION
                            WITH THE ACCOMMODATION (FOR EXAMPLE, ACCESS TO A SHARED
                            GARAGE WITH A PARKING SPACE ALLOCATED TO THE
                            FLAT/APARTMENT).

44.   GaragPy   Do you pay a separate fee for this garage or parking space?

                            Yes...1
                            No (included in rent or part of property)..2

45.   CTBand   Could you please tell me which Council Tax band the accommodation is in;
                            Is it in ?

                            RUNNING PROMPT

                            THIS MUST BE THE BAND SET BY THE COUNCIL - DO NOT ACCEPT
                            RESPONDENT'S OWN ESTIMATE OF THE BAND OF THE PROPERTY.
                            IF THIS HOUSEHOLD'S ACCOMMODATION IS NOT VALUED
                            SEPARATELY (EG BECAUSE IT IS RENTED AS PART OF LARGER
                            PREMISES) THEN USE CODE <10>

                            Band A...1
                            Band B...2
                            Band C...3
                            Band D...4
                            Band E...5
                            Band F...6
                            Band G...7
                            Band H...8
                            Or
                            Band I..9

Household accommodation not valued separately................................10

46.   CTBen   Some people qualify for Council Tax Benefit or rebate
Do you or does anyone else in your household receive Council Tax Benefit
or rebate either directly or by having it paid to your landlord on your behalf?

Yes.. 1
No...2

Ask if CTBen =1

47.   AmtCTB   How much Council Tax Benefit or rebate did you receive?
ENTER AMOUNT TO NEAREST £1

0..9997

48.   PerCTB   How long did this cover?

one week...1
two weeks..2
three weeks..3
four weeks... 4
calendar month...5
two calendar months.. 7
eight times a year...8
nine times a year..9
ten times a year..10
three months/13 weeks.. 13
six months/26 weeks... 26
one year/12 months/52 weeks..52
less than one week...90
one off/lump sum..95
None of these: Explain in a note <Ctrl> + <M>......................97

CONSUMER DURABLES

Ask all households

49.   IntroDur   Now I'd like to ask you about various household items you may have - this gives us an indication of how living standards are changing.

50.   HasDur   Does your household have any of the following items in your (part of the) accommodation?

INCLUDE ITEMS STORED OR UNDER REPAIR.
INCLUDE ITEMS OWNED, RENTED OR ON LOAN.
IF ANY MEMBER POSSESSES AN ITEM, THE HOUSEHOLD POSSESSES IT.

51.   TVcol   Colour TV set?

Yes..1
No...2

Ask if household does not have a colour tv
(TVcol = 2)

52.   TVwhy   (You said your household doesn't have a Colour TV). Is that because you...

don't want one...1
would like one but cannot afford it.......................................2
or is there some other reason?...3

Ask all households

53.   WashMach   Washing Machine?

Yes..1
No...2

Ask if household does not have a washing machine
(WashMach = 2)

54.   WashWhy

You said your household doesn't have a washing machine). Is that because you don't want one...1

would like one but cannot afford it..2

or is there some other reason?...3

Ask all households

55.   Telephon   Telephone?

SHARED TELEPHONES LOCATED IN PUBLIC HALLWAYS TO BE INCLUDED ONLY IF THIS HOUSEHOLD IS RESPONSIBLE FOR PAYING THE ACCOUNT.
INCLUDE MOBILE PHONES.
PROMPT AS NECESSARY

Yes, fixed telephone..1
Yes, mobile telephone..2
Yes, fixed and mobile telephone...3
No...4

Ask if household does not have a telephone
(Telephon = 4)

56.   TelWhy   (You said your household doesn't have a telephone). Is that because you...

RUNNING PROMPT

don't want one..1
would like one but cannot afford it..2
or is there some other reason?...3

Ask all households

57.   Computer   Home computer?

EXCLUDE: VIDEO GAMES

Yes...1

No...2

Ask if household does not have a home computer
(Computer = 2)

58. CompWhy You said your household doesn't have a computer). Is that because you

don't want one... 1

would like one but cannot afford it...2

or is there some other reason?..3

Ask all households

59. UseVcl Do you, or any members of your household, at present own or have continuous use of motor vehicle?

INCLUDE COMPANY CARS/VANS IF AVAILABLE FOR PRIVATE USE
EXCLUDE COMPANY CARS/VANS IF PROVIDED ONLY FOR WORK
PURPOSES

Yes...1

No...2

Ask if the household has use of motor vehicles(s)
(If UseVcl =1)

For each vehicle in turn

60. TypeVcl FOR EACH VEHICLE IN TURN:
I would now like to ask about the (Nth) vehicle. Is it...

a car..1

a light van...2

a motor cycle..3

or some other motor vehicle?..4

61. PrivVcl FOR EACH VEHICLE IN TURN:
Is the vehicle...

privately owned...1

or is it a company vehicle?...2

Ask if it is a company vehicle
(UseVcl = 1 & PrivVcl = 2)

62. WhoCar Enter the person number of whose company car it is

1..16

63. ListPr What was the manufacturer's list price of this vehicle when new, to the nearest £1,000?

IF A PRECISE FIGURE IS NOT AVAILABLE, KEY D/K.

1..99997

Ask list price is unknown
(UseVcl = 1 & PrivVcl = 2 & ListPr = DK)

64. Band SHOWCARD 1

Could you tell me in which of these bands was the list price of this vehicle when new?

Up to £10,000...1
£10,001 to £13,000...2
£13,001 to £16,000...3
£16,001 to £19,000...4
£19,001 to £22,000...5
£22,001 to £25,000...6
£25,001 to £30,000...7
£30,001 to £40,000...8
£40,001 and over..9

Ask if price band is unknown
(UseVcl = 1 & PrivVcl = 2 & ListPr = DK & Band = DK)

65.   Model   Could you tell me the make and model and engine size of this vehicle?

IF NO INFORMATION ON MAKE/MODEL IS AVAILABLE, TRY TO RECORD AT LEAST THE ENGINE SIZE.

TYPE IN VEHICLE INFO
NO MORE THAN 80 CHARACTERS

Ask if the household has use of motor vehicles(s)
(If UseVcl =1)

66.   AnyMore   Do you, or any members of your household, at present own or have continuous use of any more motor vehicles?

INCLUDE COMPANY CARS (IF AVAILABLE FOR PRIVATE USE)

Yes...1
No..2

Ask if household does have a vehicle but not a car or light van
(UseVcl = 1 & DVNumCar = 0)

67.   NoCar   This household doesn't have a car or light van. Is that because...

RUNNING PROMPT

don't want one...1
would like one but cannot afford it..2
or is there some other reason?...3

Ask if household does not have continuous use of a vehicle
(UseVcl = 2)

68.   CarWhy   This household doesn't have a vehicle. Is that because...

RUNNING PROMPT

don't want one...1
would like one but cannot afford it...2
or is there some other reason?...3

TENURE

Ask all households

69.   Ten1   SHOWCARD 1

In which of these ways do you occupy this accommodation?

MAKE SURE ANSWER APPLIES TO HRP

Own outright...1
Buying it with the help of a mortgage or loan..2
Pay part rent and part mortgage (shared ownership)...............................3
Rent it..4
Live here rent-free (including rent-free in relative's/friend's property;
excluding squatting)..5
Squatting..6

**Ask if household rents the accommodation, or lives there rent-free
(Ten1 = 4 or 5)**

70.   Tied   Does the accommodation go with the job of anyone in the household?

IF THE ACCOMMODATION GOES WITH THE JOB OF SOMEBODY WHO
IS TEMPORARILY NOT A MEMBER OF THE HOUSEHOLD, CODE YES.
IF THE ACCOMMODATION USED TO GO WITH THE JOB OF SOMEONE
IN THE HOUSEHOLD, BUT THIS IS NO LONGER THE CASE, CODE NO.
Yes..1
No...2

71.   LLord   Who is your landlord?

CODE FIRST THAT APPLIES

the local authority/council/Scottish Homes...1
a housing association, charitable trust or Local Housing Company............2

employer (organisation) of a household member.....................................3
another organisation...4
relative/friend (before you lived here) of a
household member...5
employer (individual) of a household member.......................................6
another individual private landlord?..7

72.   Furn   Is the accommodation provided: ...

RUNNING PROMPT

Furnished...1
partly furnished (e.g. carpets and curtains only)...................................2
or unfurnished?...3

Ask all households

73.   YearBuy   In which year did you (buy this accommodation / sign the first contract to
                       rent this accommodation / move to this address)?

AN ESTIMATE IS ACCEPTABLE
ENTER YEAR IN 4 DIGIT FORMAT, E.G. 2000

1900...2009

HOUSING COSTS

Ask if household rents the accommodation

(Ten1 = 4)

74. RentAmt How much rent did your household actually pay last time it was due,

after deducting any housing benefit (rent rebate)?

ENTER TO THE NEAREST £1 (AFTER HOUSING BENEFIT).

INCLUDE COUNCIL TAX, COUNCIL WATER CHARGE, WATER RATES IF PAID AS PART OF RENT

0.00..9997.00

If RentAmt > 0

75. RentPer How long did this cover?
one week...1
two weeks...2
three weeks...3
four weeks...4
calendar month...5
two calendar months...7
eight times a year..8
nine times a year...9
ten times a year...10
three months/13 weeks..13
six months/26 weeks..26
one year/12 months/52 weeks...52
less than one week...90
one off/lump sum..95
none of these: EXPLAIN IN A NOTE <Ctrl> + <M>...............................97

76. RentHol Do you have a rent holiday?
Yes...1
No...2

If answered yes to rent holiday

(Ten1 = 4 & RentHol = 1)

77.   RentHoWk   For how many weeks a year do you have a rent holiday?

0..52

Ask if household rents the accommodation

(Ten1 = 4)

78.   HBen   Some people qualify for Housing Benefit, that is, a rent rebate or allowance.

Do you or anyone else in your household receive Housing Benefit either directly or by having it paid to your landlord on your behalf?

Yes..1
No...2

Ask if receiving Housing Benefit

(Ten1 = 4 & HBen = 1)

79.   AmtHB   How much Housing Benefit was allowed for the last rent?

ENTER AMOUNT TO THE NEAREST £1

0..1000

80.   PerHB   How long did this cover?

one week...1

two weeks...2

three weeks...3

four weeks...4

calendar month..5

two calendar months..7

eight times a year...8

nine times a year..9

ten times a year..10

three months/13 weeks...13

six months/26 weeks...26

one year/12 months/52 weeks...52

less than one week..90

one off/lump sum...95

none of these: EXPLAIN IN A NOTE <Ctrl> + <M>...............97

Ask if household rents the accommodation

(Ten1 = 4)

81.   Servic   SHOWCARD 6

Do you pay for any of the services shown on this card? Exclude any which

are included as part of your rent.

ENTER AT MOST 9 VALUES

Water..1

Electricity..2

Gas...3

Liquid or solid fuel (e.g. oil, coke, etc.)....................................4

Heating, hot water..5

Structural (building) insurance...6

Sewage removal...7

Other service charges..8

Regular maintenance and repairs..9

None of these...10

If household pays extra for services

(Servic = 1-9)

82.   ServInc   Could you give me an estimate of how much you pay each month for these

services (water, electricity, gas etc)?

A TOTAL FOR ALL SERVICES TOGETHER.

A ROUGH ESTIMATE IS SUFFICIENT, IN POUNDS.

0..9997

Ask if household have a mortgage/loan or part mortgage (shared ownership)

(Ten1 = 2,3)

83.   MorgYr   In which year did your present mortgage begin?

1900..2009

84.   MorgTyp   SHOWCARD 7

Looking at this card, which one of these options best describes your

mortgage?

an endowment mortgage (where your mortgage payments cover interest only),...1
a repayment mortgage (where your mortgage payments cover interest and part of the original 2
a pension mortgage (where your mortgage payments cover interest only),..3
or a PEP mortgage, ISA mortgage or Unit Trust mortgage,......................4
or both an endowment (or any interest only) mortgage and a repayment mortgage..5
an interest only mortgage with more than one linked investment (e.g. pension and unit trust , endowment and ISA).................................6
an interest only mortgage with no linked investment (e.g. no endowment, pension, PEP or 7
or another type (not listed above)...8

85.   MorgPayL   How much was your last payment on this mortgage/loan?

ENTER THIS AMOUNT TO THIS NEAREST POUND

0..9997

86.   MorgPerL   How long did this cover?

one week..1
two weeks..2
three weeks..3
four weeks..4
calendar month...5
two calendar months..7
eight times a year...8
nine times a year..9
ten times a year..10
three months/13 weeks..13
six months/26 weeks...26
one year/12 months/52 weeks...52
less than one week..90
one off/lump sum...95
none of these: EXPLAIN IN A NOTE <Ctrl> + <M>..............................97

Ask all households

87.   AffIntro   I'd like you to think about your total housing cost. By that I mean all the

bills to do with running a house. That includes your mortgage or rent

payments, bills such as gas, electricity, water and refuse removal charges.

88.   Burden   To what extent are the total housing costs a financial burden or struggle for

your household ?

Would you say it is ...

RUNNING PROMPT

a heavy burden/ struggle,...1
a slight burden/ struggle,...2
or not a burden/ struggle at all?...3

TRAILER MODULE

MATERIAL DEPRIVATION

Ask all households

89.   IntroHH   The following set of questions ask about your home and neighbourhood

90.   WatHot   Does your accommodation have hot running water?

Yes..1
No... 2

91.   MovHse   Do you think that your household may move from your present
accommodation in the next 6 months?
If respondent is unsure code 'Yes'

Yes..1
No..2

Ask if household may move house from their present accommodation

(MovHse = 1)

92.   MvHsReas   What is the main reason that your household may move from your present
accommodation in the next 6 months

landlord has given/will give notice to end the tenancy............................1
there is no formal tenancy and landlord has given/will give notice..............2
eviction (or other legal reasons)...3
financial difficulties 4
family related reason..5
employment related reason..6
other reason...7

93.   NoSpace   Do you have a shortage of space in your accommodation?

Respondent's opinion/perception about shortage of space
can be living space and/or storage space

Yes...1
No..2

94.   Litter   How often is there litter lying around in your neighbourhood?

Very frequently..1
Frequently..2
Sometimes..3
Rarely or never...4

95.   Damaged   How often is there damaged public property (bus stops, lamp posts,
pavements, playgrounds etc.) in your neighbourhood?
damage can be deliberate, accidental or due to wear and tear"

Very frequently..1
Frequently..2
Sometimes..3
Rarely or never...4

96.   UseTrans   Does any member of your household use public transport?

Bus, train, metro, tram and similar

If would like to use but doesn't because service is unavailable code 'Yes'
here and 'very difficult' at next screen

Yes...1
No..2

Ask if any member in household uses public transport

(UseTrans = 1)

97.   PbTrans   How easy is it for members of your household to access public transport?

Very difficult...1
Difficult...2
Easy...3
Very easy...4

98.   UsePost   Does any member of your household send and receive both parcels and

letters?
Yes..1
No..2

Ask if any member in household sends and receive both parcels and letters

(UsePost = 1)

99.   PostalS   How easy is it for members of your household to access these postal services?

Very difficult...1
Difficult...2
Easy...3
Very easy...4

100.   UseBank   Does any member of your household use banking services such as
withdrawing and transferring money and paying bills?
include telephone or internet banking if used

Yes..1
No..2

Ask if any member in household uses banking services such as withdrawing and transferring money and paying bills

(UseBank = 1)

101. BankinS   How easy is it for members of your household to access these
banking services?
withdrawing money, transferring money, paying bills

Very difficult...1
Difficult...2
Easy..3
Very easy...4

102. NetCnect   Does your household have an internet connection?

Yes..1
No because can't afford it...2
No for some other reason...3

103. FurnRep   Would your household replace furniture if it became worn out?

Yes..1
No because can't afford it...2
No for some other reason...3

END OF HOUSEHOLD QUESTIONNAIRE

2009

GENERAL HOUSEHOLD SURVEY

INDIVIDUAL SECTION

Ask this section of all adults

1.   Iswitch   THIS IS WHERE YOU START RECORDING ANSWERS FOR INDIVIDUALS.
DO YOU WANT TO RECORD ANSWERS FOR (name) NOW OR LATER?

Yes, now..1
Later...2
or is there no interview with this person?................................3

Ask if answers are to be recorded now
(Iswitch = 1)

2.   PersProx   INTERVIEWER: IS THE INTERVIEW ABOUT (name) BEING GIVEN:

In person..1
or by someone else?..2

Ask if answers are to be recorded now, but are being answered by someone else
(Iswitch = 1 & PersProx = 2)

3.   ProxyNum   ENTER PERSON NUMBER OF PERSON GIVING THE INFORMATION

1..16
MIGRATION, CITIZENSHIP, NATIONAL IDENTITY, ETHNICITY

All persons (adult and children) individually

4.   Ntnlty   What is your/(..)'s nationality?

COMMON CODES:

UK,British..926
Irish Republic..372
Hong Kong..344
China...156
Other...997

Ask if nationality was 'other'
(Ntnlty = 997)

5.   NatSpec   TYPE IN MAIN NATIONALITY

ENTER TEXT OF AT MOST 40 CHARACTERS

6.   Nltyspc   PRESS <SPACE BAR> TO ENTER THE CODING FRAME

PRESS ENTER TO SELECT A CODE AND ENTER AGAIN TO
CONTINUE
4..992

7.   Cry01   And in which country were you/was (...) born?

IF RESPONDENT SAYS BRITAIN, PROBE FOR COUNTRY
<HELP F9>

COMMON CODES:

England...921
Wales 924
Scotland..923
Northern Ireland..922
UK...926
Republic of Ireland..372
Hong Kong..344
China...156
Other...997

Ask if country of birth was 'other'
(Cry01 = 997)

8.   CrySpec   TYPE IN COUNTRY

ENTER TEXT OF AT MOST 40 CHARACTERS

9.   CryO   PRESS <SPACE BAR> TO ENTER THE CODING FRAME

PRESS ENTER TO SELECT A CODE AND ENTER AGAIN TO
CONTINUE
4..992

Ask if not born in the UK
(Cry01 = 372) or (Cry01 = 344) or (Cry01 = 156) or (Cry01 = 997)

10.   CameYr   Which year did you/(...) first arrive in the United Kingdom?

ENTER IN 4 DIGIT FORMAT E.G.: 2000

1900..2009

11.   CONTUK   Apart from holidays and short visits abroad have you/has (…) lived in the
UK continuously since then?

Yes...1
No..2

Ask if CONTUK=2

12.   CameY2   Which year did you/(..) last arrive in the UK?

ENTER IN 4 DIGIT FORMAT E.G.: 2000

1900..2009

Ask if CameY2 or CameYr is in survey year or previous year

13. CameMt   In which month did you/(..) arrive in the UK?

January...1
February..2
March..3
April..4
May...5
June..6
July...7
August...8
September..9
October..10
November...11
December...12

All persons

14. CtzIntro   I've got some questions now about citizenship.

15. CkCtz   Last time you told us that you were eligible to hold a Passport for [Citizen].

Yes, still the case...1
No, not the case...2

16.   Citizen   For what country or countries do you hold, or are entitled to hold, a
                    Wave 1 or Passport?
                    CkCtz = 2)

                    "EU PASSPORT": CHECK IF ISSUED IN THE UK OR PROBE 'IN
                    WHAT COUNTRY WAS THE PASSPORT ISSUED?'

                    CODE FIRST COUNTRY
                    COMMON CODES:

                    United Kingdom..926
                    Republic of Ireland..372
                    Ghana..288
                    Nigeria...566
                    Jamaica...388
                    India..356
                    South Africa...710
                    Pakistan...586
                    Poland 616
                    Other...997

                    Ask if country of citizenship is 'other'
                    (Citizen = 997)

17.   CtzSp1   TYPE IN COUNTRY

                    ENTER TEXT OF AT MOST 40 CHARACTERS

18.   CtzCode   PRESS <SPACE BAR> AND CHOOSE COUNTRY FROM CODING
                    FRAME

                    PRESS ENTER TO SELECT A CODE AND ENTER AGAIN TO
                    CONTINUE

                    CODE FIRST COUNTRY

                    4..992

19. OthPass Do you hold or are you entitled to hold a Passport for any other country?

Yes..1
No..2

20. Citiz2 For what other country or countries do you hold, or are entitled to hold, a (OthPass = 1) Passport?

"EU PASSPORT": CHECK IF ISSUED IN THE UK OR PROBE 'IN WHAT COUNTRY WAS THE PASSPORT ISSUED?'

COMMON CODES:

United Kingdom..926
Republic of Ireland...372
Ghana..288
Nigeria...566
Jamaica..388
India...356
South Africa..710
Pakistan..586
Poland...616
Other...997

**Ask if second country of citizenship is 'other'
(Citiz2 = 997)**

21. CtzSp2 Type in country

ENTER TEXT OF AT MOST 40 CHARACTERS

22. CtzCode2 PRESS <SPACE BAR> AND CHOOSE COUNTRY FROM CODING FRAME
PRESS ENTER TO SELECT A CODE AND ENTER AGAIN TO CONTINUE

CODE SECOND COUNTRY

4..992

All persons

23.   FatCob   And in which country was your / (...'s) father born?

IF RESPONDENT SAYS BRITAIN, PROBE FOR COUNTRY
<HELP F9>

COMMON CODES:

England	921
Northern Ireland	922
Scotland	923
Wales	924
Irish Republic	372
Kenya	404
Ghana	288
Nigeria	566
Jamaica	388
Bangladesh	50
India	356
Pakistan	586
Other	997

Ask if father's country of birth was 'other'
(FatCob = 997)

24.   CrySp1   TYPE IN COUNTRY

ENTER TEXT OF AT MOST 40 CHARACTERS

25.   CryCd1   PRESS <SPACE BAR> TO ENTER THE CODING FRAME
PRESS ENTER TO SELECT A CODE AND ENTER AGAIN TO CONTINUE

4..992

Ask all persons

26.   MotCob   And in which country was your/ (...'s) mother born?

IF RESPONDENT SAYS BRITAIN, PROBE FOR COUNTRY
<HELP F9>

COMMON CODES:

England..921
Northern Ireland...922
Scotland...923
Wales...924
Irish Republic...372
Kenya...404
Ghana...288
Nigeria..566
Jamaica..388
Bangladesh...50
India..356
Pakistan...586
Other..997

Ask if mother's country of birth was 'other'
(MotCob = 997)

27.   CrySp2   TYPE IN COUNTRY

ENTER TEXT OF AT MOST 40 CHARACTERS

28.   CryCd2   PRESS <SPACE BAR> TO ENTER THE CODING FRAME
PRESS ENTER TO SELECT CODE AND ENTER AGAIN TO CONTINUE

4..992

All persons aged 16 and over
Ask if household is in England

SHOWCARD 2-E

29.   NatldE   What do you/does (..) consider your/his/her national identity to be, you may choose as many as apply, is it...

English...1
Scottish...2
Welsh..3
Irish...4
British..5
Other...6

Ask if household is in Scotland

SHOWCARD 2-S

30.   NatldS   What do you/does (..) consider your/his/her national identity to be, you may choose as many as apply, is it...

Scottish...1
English...2
Welsh..3
Irish...4
British..5
Other...6

Ask if household is in Wales

SHOWCARD 2-W

31.   NatldW   What do you/does (..) consider your/his/her national identity to be, you may choose as many as apply, is it...

Welsh..1
English...2
Scottish...3
Irish...4
British..5
Other...6

If answered other
(NatIdE=6 or NatIdS=6 or NatIdW=6)

32.   NatIdo   How would you describe your national identity?

ENTER DESCRIPTION OF NATIONAL IDENTITY

ENTER TEXT OF AT MOST 40 CHARACTERS

All persons

SHOWCARD 3

33.   Eth01   To which of these ethnic groups do you consider you belong?

White...1
Mixed..2
Asian or Asian British...3
Black or Black British..4
Chinese...5
Other ethnic group..6

Ask if Eth01=1

34.   EthWh   And to which of these groups do you/does (..) consider you/he/she belongs...

British...1
Another White Background...2

Ask if Eth01=2

35.   EthMx   And to which of these groups do you/does (..) consider you/he/she belongs....

White and Black Caribbean..1

White and Black African...2
White and Asian...3
Another Mixed background...4

Ask if Eth01=3

36.   EthAs   And to which of these groups do you/does (..) consider you/he/she belongs........

Indian..1
Pakistani...2
Bangladeshi...3
Another Asian background..4

Ask if Eth01=4

37.   EthBl   And to which of these groups do you/does (..) consider you/he/she belongs....

Caribbean..1
African..2
or
Another Black background...3

Ask if EthWh=2 or EthMx=4 or EthAs=4 or EthBl=3

38.   EthOth   Please can you describe your ethnic group?

ENTER DESCRIPTION OF ETHNIC GROUP

ENTER TEXT OF AT MOST 150 CHARACTERS

39.   Eth02   PRESS <SPACE BAR> TO ENTER THE CODING FRAME

PRESS ENTER TO SELECT CODE AND ENTER AGAIN TO CONTINUE

RELIGION

All persons

40.   Relig   What is your/(..) religion, even if you/he/she is/are not currently practising?

PROMPT AS NECESSARY

Christian..1
Buddhist..2
Hindu..3
Jewish...4
Muslim...5
Sikh..6
Any other religion..7
No religion at all...8

LENGTH OF RESIDENCY

41. RestMe2   How many years have you lived at this address?

0..99

Ask if RestMe2=0

42. ResMth   How many months have you/has (..) lived here?
1..11

Ask if RestMth<3

43. ResBby   Is (..) a baby born in the last three months?

Yes...1
No...2

Ask if RestMth<3 and ResBby=2

44. M3Cry   Three months ago, were you/was (..) living in...

The UK...1
Or somewhere else...2

Ask if M3Cry=2

45. M3CrySpec   Which country was that?

TYPE IN COUNTRY

ENTER TEXT OF AT MOST 40 CHARACTERS

46. M3CryO   PRESS <SPACE BAR> TO ENTER THE CODING FRAME

4..992

Ask if RestMth<3 and ResBby=2 and M3Cry=1

47.   M3Area   ASK OR RECORD

Which town or village were you/was (..) living in then?

TAKE NEAREST

ENTER TEXT OF AT MOST 20 CHARACTERS

48.   M3Cty   ASK OR RECORD

Which county or borough is that in?

TAKE NEAREST

ENTER TEXT OF AT MOST 20 CHARACTERS

49.   M3ResC   PRESS <SPACE BAR> TO ENTER CODING FRAME

If there is more than one code for the place, enter the first listed
code

1..999999

50.   OYEqM3   May I just check, were you/was (..) also living at that address 12 months
Ago, that is on ([day], [month],[year]?

Yes, same place,...1
No...2
Baby, under 1 year old..3

Ask if (ResMth > 2) AND (ResMth <= 11) OR (OYEqM3 = 2)

51.   OYCry   Twelve months ago were you/was (..) living in...
The UK..1
Yes..2
Somewhere else...3

Ask if OYCry=2

52.   OYCrySpec   Which country was that?

TYPE IN COUNTRY

ENTER TEXT OF AT MOST 40 CHARACTERS

53.   OYCryO   PRESS <SPACE BAR> TO ENTER THE CODING FRAME

4..992

Ask if (ResMth > 2) AND (ResMth <= 11) OR (OYEqM3 = 2) AND (OYCry=1)

54.   OYArea   ASK OR RECORD

Which town or village were you/was (..) living in then?

TAKE NEAREST

ENTER TEXT OF AT MOST 20 CHARACTERS

55.   OYCty   ASK OR RECORD

Which county or borough is that in?

TAKE NEAREST

ENTER TEXT OF AT MOST 20 CHARACTERS

56.   OYResC   PRESS <SPACE BAR> TO ENTER CODING FRAME

If there is more than one code for the place, enter the first listed code

1..999999

EMPLOYMENT

Ask this section of all adults

Ask if respondent is a man aged 16-64, or a woman aged 16-62

57.   Schm08   Last week, that is in the seven days ending Sunday the [RefDay] of [RefMnth], were you/was (..) on any of the following schemes...

RUNNING PROMPT

Work Based Learning for Young People (GB only)................................1
New Deal..2
Work-Based Learning for Adults/Training for work................................3
Job Skills (NI only)..10
Worktrack (NI only)..15
Entry to employment..21
Any other training scheme...50
Or none of these...66
Just 16 and non-response this time...97

Ask if respondent is a man aged 65+, or a woman aged 63+ or schm08=66 or TecLec4=3

58.   Wrking   Did you/he/she[i] do any paid work in the 7 days ending Sunday the [RefDay] of [RefMnth], either as an employee or as self-employed?

Yes..1
No..2

Ask if on New Deal scheme
(Schm08 = 2)

59.   NDType4   May I just ask...
                      Were you /was he/she on the...

INDIVIDUAL PROMPT - CODE FIRST THAT APPLIES

New Deal for Disabled People..1
New Deal for Lone Parents..3
New Deal for Young People..4
New Deal for 25+..5
New Deal for 50+..6
New Deal for Partners..7
None of these..8
Don't know..9

Ask if on New Deal scheme and more than 17
(Schm08 = 2 andDVage>17)

60.   NewDea4   Can I ask, which of the following New Deal options were you/was he/she on (in that week)

RUNNING PROMPT

Still on the Gateway or having advisory interviews................................1
Working for an employer in the Public or Private Sector.........................3
Working for the voluntary sector..4
Working for an environmental task force..5
In full-time study on an approved course..6
Receiving help setting up as self employed.....................................7
Basic Employment Training (BET)..8
Education and Training Opportunities (ETO) 9
Or on the Follow Through scheme..10
Don't know..97

Ask if on any other training
(Schm08 = 50)

61.   TecLec4   May I just check, was that...

A programme funded by the Learning and Skills Councils (England) or the
National Council for Education and Learning in Wales............................1
A scheme in Scotland run by a Local Enterprise Company (LEC)...............2
Or was it some other scheme..3

Ask if (Schm08 = 1 or Schm08=3 or TecLec4=1 or TecLec4=2 or Schm08=10 or Schm08=50 or NewDea4=97 or Schm08=15)

62.   YTEtMp   In the week ending Sunday the [RefDay] of [RefMnth] on that government scheme were you / was he / she

INDIVIDUAL PROMPT - CODE FIRST THAT APPLIES

With an employer providing work experience or practical training...............1
On a project providing work experience or practical training.....................2
At a college or training centre..3
Temporarily away from an employer or project....................................4
Temporarily away from a college or training centre...............................5

Ask if (YTEtMp= 3 or YTEtMp=5 or NewDea4=1 or NewDea4=6 or NewDea4=19 or NewDea4=8 or NewDea4=9)

63.   YTEtJb   In the week ending Sunday the.[RefDay] of [RefMnth], did you/he/she do any paid work or have any other paid job or business in addition to the government scheme you have just told me about?

Yes...1
No...2

Ask if didn't do any paid work in the last week
(Wrking=2)

64.   JbAway   Even though you were/(..) was not doing paid work, did you/he/she have a job or business that you/he/she were/was away from in the week ending Sunday the [RefDay] of [RefMnth] (and that you/he/she expect to return to)

Yes...1
No...2
Waiting to take up a new job/business already obtained..........................3

Ask if respondent was not away from a job or waiting to take up a new job
(JbAway=2 or 3)

65.   OwnBus   Did you/he/she do any unpaid work in the week (ending Sunday the [RefDay] of [RefMnth]) for any business that you/he/she owns?

Yes...1

No..2

Ask if respondent did not do unpaid work for own business (Ownbus=2)

66.   RelBus   or (any unpaid work for a business) that a relative owns?

Yes...1

No..2

Ask if respondent did not do any paid or unpaid work in the last week (Relbus=2 or YTEtJb=2)

67.   EverWk   (And) have you/has (..) ever (in your/his/her life) had paid work, apart from casual or holiday work (or the job you/he/she is/are waiting to begin)? Please include self-employment or a government scheme.

Yes...1

No..2

Ask if respondent has ever worked (EverWk=1)

68.   LeftYr   Which year did you/he/she leave your/his/her last paid job?

Exclude casual/holiday work
If left last job before 1900, enter 1900.

1900..2009

69.   LeftM   Which month in that year did you/he/she leave?

January...1
February..2
March..3
April..4
May..5
June...6
July..7
August..8
September...9
October...10
November..11
December..12

Ask those who are in current employment or have had a job in the past

70.   IndD   What did the firm/organisation you worked for mainly make or do (at the place where you worked)?

DESCRIBE FULLY - PROBE MANUFACTURING or PROCESSING or DISTRIBUTING ETC. AND MAIN GOODS PRODUCED, MATERIALS USED, WHOLESALE or RETAIL ETC.

ENTER TEXT AT MOST 80 CHARACTERS

71.   OccT   CURRENT OR LAST JOB

What was your (main) job (in the week ending Sunday the (n))?

ENTER TEXT AT MOST 30 CHARACTERS

72.   OccD   CURRENT OR LAST JOB

What did you mainly do in your job?
RECORD SPECIAL QUALIFICATIONS/TRAINING NEEDED TO DO THE JOB

ENTER TEXT AT MOST 80 CHARACTERS

Ask those who are in current employment
(Wrking=1)

73.   Sector   And was that...

RUNNING PROMPT
PUBLIC LIMITED COMPANY (PLC) = CODE 1
OTHER LIMITED COMPANY = CODE 1
SELF-EMPLOYED = CODE 1

A private firm or business, a limited company.....................................1
Or some other kind of organisation..2

Ask if working for some other kind organisation
(Sector=2)

74.   Sectro03   ASK OR RECORD

What kind of non-private organisation was it...

INDIVIDUAL PROMPT - CODE FIRST THAT APPLIES

A public limited company (plc)? Check it is not code 2...........................1
A nationalised industry/state corporation? Check it is not code 1..............2
Central government or civil service?..3
Local government or council (including police, fire services and local
authority controlled schools/colleges)?...4
A university, or other grant funded education establishment (include opted-
out schools)?..5
A health authority or NHS Trust?...6
A charity, voluntary organisation or trust?...7
The armed forces?..8
Some other kind of organisation?..9

75.   Stat   Were you working as an employee or were you self-employed?
Ask (or record if on government scheme or doing unpaid
work)

Employee...1
Self-employed...2
Government Scheme..3
Unpaid family worker...4

Ask if employee
(Stat = 1)

76.   PdWage   May I just check, ...
were you/was he/she paid either a salary or a wage by an employer?

Yes...1
No..2

Ask if not paid a wage
(PdWage=2)

77.   Self   May I just check, ..
were you/was he/she...

INDIVIDUAL PROMPT - CODE ALL THAT APPLY (UP TO 4)

Paid a salary or wage by an agency...1
A sole director of your own limited business..2
Running a business or professional practice...3
A partner in a business or professional practice......................................4
Working for yourself...5
A sub-contractor..6
Or doing free-lance work..7
None of the above...8

Ask if employee
(Stat = 1)

78.   Supvis   In your job, did you have formal responsibility for supervising the work of
other employees?
DO NOT INCLUDE PEOPLE WHO ONLY SUPERVISE:
- CHILDREN, E.G. TEACHERS, NANNIES, CHILDMINDERS
- ANIMALS
- SECURITY OF BUILDINGS, E.G. CARETAKERS, SECURITY GUARDS

Yes...1
No..2

79.   Manage   ASK OR RECORD

(And) do you have any managerial duties?

Manager...1

Foreman/supervisor..2

Not manager/supervisor..3

Ask if not self-employed
(Stat = 1,3 or 4)

80.   MpnE02   How many people worked for your employer at the place where you worked?

1-10..1

11-19..2

20-24..3

Don't know but under 25..4

25-49..5

50-249 6

250-499..7

Don't know between 50 and 499...8

500 or more..9

Ask if self-employed
(Stat = 2)

81.   Solo   Were you working on your own or did you have employees?

on own/with partner(s) but no employees..1

with employees..2

Ask if self-employed with employees
(Solo = 2)

82.   MpNS02   How many people did you employ at the place where you ?

1-10..1

11-19..2

20-24..3

Don't know but under 25..4

25-49..5

50-249..6

250-499..7

Don't know between 50 and 499...8

500 or more..9

Ask if 1-10 people work for/with respondent
(MpnE02 = 1 or MpnS02=1)

83.   OneTen   May I just check what the exact number was?

1..10

Ask if 50-249 people at respondent's workplace
(MpnE02 = 6)

84.   emp50to249   May I just check whether this was between...

50-99 or...1
100-249...2

Ask if 500+ people at respondent's workplace
(MpnE02= 9)

85.   emp500plus   May I just check whether this was between...

500-999 or...1
1000 or more...2

Ask all those who have ever worked

86.   FtPtWk   In your (main) job were you working...

full-time...1
or part-time...2

Ask if work part-time
(FtPtWk=2)

87.   YPtJob   I would like to ask you why you took a part-time rather than a full-time job. Was it because......

INDIVIDUAL PROMPT - CODE FIRST THAT APPLIES.

You were a student/you were at school..1
You were ill or disabled...2
You could not find a full-time job...3
You did not want a full-time job...4

Ask if in paid work, currently away from a job or business or on a government scheme
(Wrking=1 or JbAway=1 or Stat=3)
(not asked of proxy respondents)

88.   EverOT   Do you ever do any work which you would regard as paid or unpaid overtime?

HOURS IN MAIN JOB ONLY

Yes...1
No..2

Ask if respondent never does any overtime or does unpaid work for own business or relative's business
(EverOT=2 or OwnBus=1 or RelBus=1)

89.   Totus1   How many hours per week do you usually work in your (main) job/business – please exclude meal breaks?

THE HOURS SHOULD BE ROUNDED TO THE NEAREST 15 MINUTES, WITH PART HOURS AS DECIMALS, FOR EXAMPLE 36 HOURS 30 MINUTES WOULD BE RECORDED AS 36.5, 40 HOURS 45 MINUTES WOULD BE RECORDED AS 40.75. 97 OR MORE = 97

0.00..97.00

Ask if respondent sometimes works overtime
(EverOT=1)

90.   Usuhr   Thinking of your (main) job/business, how many hours per week do you usually work – please exclude meal breaks?

THE HOURS SHOULD BE ROUNDED TO THE NEAREST 15 MINUTES, WITH PART HOURS AS DECIMALS, FOR EXAMPLE 36 HOURS 30 MINUTES WOULD BE RECORDED AS 36.5, 40 HOURS 45 MINUTES WOULD BE RECORDED AS 40.75.
97 OR MORE = 97

0.00..97.00

91.   PotHr   How many hours paid overtime do you usually work per week?

THE HOURS SHOULD BE ROUNDED TO THE NEAREST 15 MINUTES, WITH PART HOURS AS DECIMALS, FOR EXAMPLE 36 HOURS 30 MINUTES WOULD BE RECORDED AS 36.5, 40 HOURS 45 MINUTES WOULD BE RECORDED AS 40.75.
97 OR MORE = 97

0.00..97.00

92.   UotHr   How many hours unpaid overtime do you usually work per week?

THE HOURS SHOULD BE ROUNDED TO THE NEAREST 15 MINUTES, WITH PART HOURS AS DECIMALS, FOR EXAMPLE 36 HOURS 30 MINUTES WOULD BE RECORDED AS 36.5, 40 HOURS 45 MINUTES WOULD BE RECORDED AS 40.75.
97 OR MORE = 97

0.00..97.00

93.   AgreeHrs   Your total usual hours come to …. Is that about right or not?
97 OR MORE = 97

Yes..1
No..2

Ask if did unpaid work for own/relatives business
(OwnBus = 1 OR RelBus = 1)

94.   UnPaidHr   Thinking of the business that you did unpaid work for, how many hours per week unpaid work do you usually do for that business?

1..97

Ask if YTEtJb=1

95.   MoreJbs   Do you normally have more than one paid job in addition to the one you have just told me about?

EXCLUDE WORK AS BABY-SITTERS OR MAIL ORDER AGENTS

Yes..1
No..2

Ask if respondent has more than one paid job
(MoreJbs = 1)

96.   SecondJb   What is your second job?

ENTER JOB TITLE

ENTER A TEXT OF AT MOST 80 CHARACTERS

97.   EmpSE2nd   Were you working as an employee or were you self-employed?

Employee..1
Self-employed...2

98.   OthJbs   Do you have any other paid jobs?

Yes...1
No..2

Ask if respondent has a third paid job
(OthJbs = 1)

99.   ThirdJb   What is your third job?

ENTER JOB TITLE

ENTER A TEXT OF AT MOST 80 CHARACTERS

100.   EmpSE3rd   Were you working as an employee or were you self-employed?

Employee...1
Self-employed..2

Ask if respondent has more than one job
(MoreJbs = 1)

101.   TotHrOth   How many hours per week do you usually work in your second
(and third) jobs - please exclude meals breaks?

97 OR MORE = 97

0.00..97.00

**Ask if respondent works but, in total, less than 30 hours a week
((YTEtJb=1) & Totus1 + Usuhr + PotHr + Uothr + UnpaidHr
+ TotHrOth < 30))**

102.   LThan30   The total number of hours you work per week on average is less
than 30 hours.
What is your main reason for working less than 30 hours a week?

Undergoing education or training...1
Personal illness or disability...2
Want to work more hours but cannot find a job or work for more hours........3
Do not want to work more hours...4
Considers number of hours in job(s) as full-time..................................5
Housework, looking after children or other dependant............................6
Other reason..7

Ask all respondents, except proxy

SHOWCARD 5

103.   EcStatus   I'm going to ask you about what you've been doing over the past 12 months,
but first, can I just check, which of these categories best describes you at
present?

Working full-time...1
Working part-time..2
Unemployed...3
Student (incl. pupil at school, those in training)....................................4
Looking after family home..5
Long-term sick or disabled...6
Retired from paid work..7
Not in paid work for some other reason..8

104.   SameSit   Can I just check, has your situation changed in the last 12 months (that is
since (date))?

Yes..1
No...2

If situation has changed
(SameSit = 1)

SHOWCARD 5

105.   Mths12   What were you doing 12 months ago, that is in (month) last year?

Working full-time   1
Working part-time   2
Unemployed   3
Student (incl. pupil at school, those in training)   4
Looking after family home   5
Long-term sick or disabled   6
Retired from paid work   7
Not in paid work for some other reason   8

SHOWCARD 5

106.   Mths11   What were you doing 11 months ago, that is in (month)?

Working full-time..1
Working part-time..2
Unemployed..3
Student (incl. pupil at school, those in training)....................................4
Looking after family home..5
Long-term sick or disabled..6
Retired from paid work..7
Not in paid work for some other reason..8

SHOWCARD 5

107.   Mths10   What were you doing 10 months ago, that is in (month)?

Working full-time..1
Working part-time..2
Unemployed..3
Student (incl. pupil at school, those in training)....................................4
Looking after family home..5
Long-term sick or disabled..6
Retired from paid work..7
Not in paid work for some other reason..8

SHOWCARD 5

108. Mths9   What were you doing 9 months ago, that is in (month)?

Working full-time..1
Working part-time...2
Unemployed..3
Student (incl. pupil at school, those in training)...................................4
Looking after family home..5
Long-term sick or disabled..6
Retired from paid work...7
Not in paid work for some other reason..8

SHOWCARD 5

109. Mths8   What were you doing 8 months ago, that is in (month)?

Working full-time..1
Working part-time...2
Unemployed..3
Student (incl. pupil at school, those in training)...................................4
Looking after family home..5
Long-term sick or disabled..6
Retired from paid work...7
Not in paid work for some other reason..8

SHOWCARD 5

110. Mths7   What were you doing 7 months ago, that is in (month)?

Working full-time..1
Working part-time...2
Unemployed..3
Student (incl. pupil at school, those in training)...................................4
Looking after family home..5
Long-term sick or disabled..6
Retired from paid work...7
Not in paid work for some other reason..8

SHOWCARD 5

111.   Mths6   What were you doing 6 months ago, that is in (month)?

Working full-time...1
Working part-time..2
Unemployed...3
Student (incl. pupil at school, those in training)....................................4
Looking after family home...5
Long-term sick or disabled..6
Retired from paid work..7
Not in paid work for some other reason..8

SHOWCARD 5

112.   Mths5   What were you doing 5 months ago, that is in (month)?

Working full-time...1
Working part-time..2
Unemployed...3
Student (incl. pupil at school, those in training)....................................4
Looking after family home...5
Long-term sick or disabled..6
Retired from paid work..7
Not in paid work for some other reason..8

SHOWCARD 5

113.   Mths4   What were you doing 4 months ago, that is in (month)?

Working full-time...1
Working part-time..2
Unemployed...3
Student (incl. pupil at school, those in training)....................................4
Looking after family home...5
Long-term sick or disabled..6
Retired from paid work..7
Not in paid work for some other reason..8

SHOWCARD 5

114. Mths3 What were you doing 3 months ago, that is in (month)?

Working full-time...1
Working part-time..2
Unemployed..3
Student (incl. pupil at school, those in training).....................................4
Looking after family home...5
Long-term sick or disabled...6
Retired from paid work...7
Not in paid work for some other reason..8

SHOWCARD 5

115. Mths2 What were you doing 2 months ago, that is in (month)?

Working full-time...1
Working part-time..2
Unemployed..3
Student (incl. pupil at school, those in training).....................................4
Looking after family home...5
Long-term sick or disabled...6
Retired from paid work...7
Not in paid work for some other reason..8

SHOWCARD 5

116. Mths1 What were you doing 1 month ago, that is in (month)?

Working full-time...1
Working part-time..2
Unemployed..3
Student (incl. pupil at school, those in training).....................................4
Looking after family home...5
Long-term sick or disabled...6
Retired from paid work...7
Not in paid work for some other reason..8

Ask if respondent did not do any paid or unpaid work in the last week or worked for own business or a business owned by a relative ((Everwk=1 or 2) or RelBus=1 or OwnBus=1

117.   Look4   Thinking of the 4 weeks ending Sunday the [RefDay],... were you/was(..) looking for any kind of paid work at any time in those 4 weeks?

Yes...1
No..2

Ask if respondent did not look for paid work in the past 4 weeks and is aged between 16 and 59 (Look4=2 and DVAge>15 and DVAge <60)

118.   LkYt4   or were you/was he/she looking in those 4 weeks for a place on a government scheme?

Yes...1
No..2

Ask if respondent is less than 70 and didn't look for paid work or a place on a government scheme (Look4=2 and DVAge>59 and DVAge <70 or (LkYt4=2)

119.   Wait   (And) were you/was he/she waiting to take up a job that you/he/she had already obtained?

Yes...1
No..2

Ask if was not waiting to take up a job already obtained (Wait=2)

120.   LikeWk   Even though you were/he/she was not looking for work in the 4 weeks ending Sunday the [RefDay], would you/he/she like to have a regular paid job at the moment, either a full- or part-time job?

Yes...1
No..2

121.   NoLoWa   May I just check, ...
                      what were the reasons you/he/she did not look for work in the last 4 weeks?

CODE ALL THAT APPLY

Waiting for the results of an application for a job/ being assessed by a
training agent...1
Student...2
Looking after the family/home...3
Temporarily sick or injured...4
Long-term sick or disabled..5
Believes no jobs available..6
Not yet started looking..7
Doesn't need employment..8
Retired from paid work..9
Any other reason..10

**Ask if more than one reason given for not looking for work in the last 4
weeks**
(More than one answer to NoLoWa)

122.   NoLWM   May I just check, ...
                      what was the main reason you/he/she did not look for work in the last 4
                      weeks?

CODE ALL THAT APPLY
Waiting for the results of an application for a job/being assessed by a
training agent...1
Student...2
Looking after the family/home...3
Temporarily sick or injured...4
Long-term sick or disabled..5
Believes no jobs available..6
Not yet started looking..7
Doesn't need employment..8
Retired from paid work..9
Any other reason..10

Ask if looking for paid work/government scheme in last 4 weeks, would like work or waiting to take up a new job
(Look4 = 1) OR (LkYt4 = 1) OR (LikeWk = 1) OR (JbAway = 3)) OR (Wait = 1)

123.   Start

If a job or a place on a government scheme had been available in the week ending Sunday the [RefDay], would you/he/she have been able to start within 2 weeks?

Yes..1
No...2

Ask if not able to take up job within 2 weeks
(Start=2)

124.   YStart

Why would you/he/she not have been able to start within 2 weeks?

CODE MAIN REASON ONLY

Must complete education...1
Cannot leave present job within 2 weeks...2
Looking after the family/home...3
Temporarily sick or injured...4
Long-term sick or disabled...5
Other reason...6

Ask if looking after the family/home
(YStart=3)

125.   YStrtF

May I just check, ...
Was the main reason you/he/she could not start work because...

RUNNING PROMPT

You were caring for children below school age.................................1
You were caring for other children...2
You were caring for a dependent adult relative................................3
Some other reason...4

Ask if looking for a paid job or a place on a government scheme and not waiting to take up a job
(Look4=1 or LkYt4 and JbAway ≠3)

126.   LkTimA   How long have you/has he/she been looking for paid work/a place on a government scheme/an additional or replacement job?

Not yet started..1
Less than 1 month..2
1 month but less than 3 months...3
3 months but less than 6 months...4
6 months but less than 12 months...5
12 months but less than 18 months...6
18 months but less than 2 years...7
2 years but less than 3 years...8
3 years but less than 4 years...9
4 years but less than 5 years...10
5 years or more...11

Ask if waiting to take up a job
(Wait=1 or JbAway =3)

127.   LkTimB   How long have you/has he/she been looking for paid work/an additional or replacement job?

Not yet started..1
Less than 1 month..2
1 month but less than 3 months...3
3 months but less than 6 months...4
6 months but less than 12 months...5
12 months but less than 18 months...6
18 months but less than 2 years...7
2 years but less than 3 years...8
3 years but less than 4 years...9
4 years but less than 5 years...10
5 years or more...11

PENSIONS

The whole section on pensions (apart from the last question) is only asked of those in paid work, (including those temporarily away from job or on a government scheme), but excluding unpaid family workers.
((Wrking = 1   OR   JbAway = 1   OR   Stat = 1 or 3)   &   (OwnBus = 2   &   RelBus = 2))
The routing instructions above each question apply only to those who meet the above criteria.

If employee or on a government scheme
(Stat = 1   OR   Stat =3)

128.   PenSchm   (Thinking now of your present job,) some people (will) receive a pension from their employer when they retire, as well as the state pension.
Does your present employer run an occupational pension scheme or superannuation scheme for any employees?

INCLUDE CONTRIBUTORY AND NON-CONTRIBUTORY SCHEMES
EXCLUDE EMPLOYER SPONSORED GROUP PERSONAL PENSION AND STAKEHOLDER PENSIONS

Yes..1
No...2

Ask if employer runs an occupational pension scheme
(PenSchm = 1)

129.   Eligible   Are you eligible to belong to your employer's occupational pension scheme?

Yes..1
No...2

Ask if eligible for employer's pension scheme
(Eligible = 1)

130.   EmPenShm   Do you belong to your employer's occupational pension scheme?

Yes..1
No...2

Ask if did not know or refused to say whether the employer offered an occupational pension scheme, or whether they were eligible, or whether they belonged to one
(PenSchm OR Eligible OR EmPenShm = DK / refusal)

131.   PSchPoss   So do you think it's possible that you belong to an occupational pension scheme run by your employer, or do you definitely not belong to one?

Possibly belongs..1
Definitely not..2

Ask if employee OR (under pensionable age and not self-employed) - this is to select those who may have answered don't know, or refused to answer Stat
(Stat = 1 OR (under pensionable age & Stat ≠ 2))

132.   PersPnt1   INTERVIEWER - INTRODUCE IF NECESSARY.
Now I would like to ask you about other types of pension arrangements (rather than employers' occupational pension schemes).

133.   PersPe   SHOWCARD 16

Do you at present have any of the pension arrangements shown on this card?

CODE ALL THAT APPLY

INTERVIEWER: CODE 4 ALSO INCLUDES ARRANGEMENTS WHERE SPOUSE OR SOMEONE OTHER THAN EMPLOYER HAS SET UP THE STAKEHOLDER PENSION.

A personal or private pension or retirement annuity...............................1
A Group Personal Pension (that is a collection of personal pensions
arranged by an employer for a group of employees)..............................2
A Stakeholder Pension arranged through your employer
(who may or may not contribute)...3
A Stakeholder Pension you arranged yourself......................................4
None of these..5
Don't know..6

Ask if has a personal/private pension and if employee (not asked of proxies)
(Stat = 1 AND PersPe = 1)

134.   PPECont   Does your employer contribute to your personal/private pension?

                Yes...1
                No..2

Ask if has a personal/private pension and if employee OR (under pensionable age and not self-employed) (not asked of proxies)
(Stat = 1 OR (under pensionable age AND Stat ≠ 2) & PersPe = 1)

135.   PPPCont   Do you currently make any contributions to your personal/private pension?

                Yes...1
                No..2

136.   PPGov   Since the date of the last interview (DATE) has any money been paid into your personal/private pension by HM Revenue and Customs (formerly the Inland Revenue)?

                Yes...1
                No..2
                Don't know..3

Ask if has a Group Personal Pension and if employee (not asked of proxies)
(Stat = 1 AND PersPe = 2)

137.   GPECont   Does your employer contribute to your Group Personal Pension?

                Yes...1
                No..2

Ask if has a Group Personal Pension and if employee OR (under pensionable age and not self-employed) (not asked of proxies)
(Stat = 1 OR (under pensionable age   AND   Stat ≠ 2) & PersPe = 2)

138. GPPCont   Do you currently make any contributions to your Group Personal Pension?

Yes...1
No...2

139. GPGov   Since the date of the last interview (DATE) has any money been paid into your Group Personal Pension by the HM Revenue and Customs (formerly the Inland Revenue)?

Yes...1
No...2
Don't know...3

Ask if has a Stakeholder Pension arranged through employer and if employee (not asked of proxies)
(Stat = 1   AND   PersPe = 3)

140. SEECont   Does your employer contribute to your Stakeholder Pension arranged through your employer?

Yes...1
No...2

Ask if has a Stakeholder Pension arranged through employer and if employee OR (under pensionable age and not self-employed) (not asked of proxies)
(Stat = 1 OR (under pensionable age   AND   Stat ≠ 2) AND   PersPe = 3)

141. SEPCont   Do you currently make any contributions to your Stakeholder Pension arranged through your employer?

Yes...1

No..2

142. SEGov   Since the date of the last interview (DATE) has any money been paid into Stakeholder Pension arranged through your employer by HM Revenue and Customs (formerly the Inland Revenue)?

Yes...1

No..2

Don't know...3

Ask if has a Stakeholder Pension arranged by self and if employee (not asked of proxies)
(Stat = 1   AND   PersPe = 4)

143. SPECont   Does your employer contribute to your Stakeholder Pension you arranged yourself?

Yes...1

No..2

Ask if has a Stakeholder Pension arranged by self and if employee OR (under pensionable age and not self-employed) (not asked of proxies)
(Stat = 1 OR (under pensionable age AND Stat ≠ 2) AND PersPen = 4)

144. SPPCont   Do you currently make any contributions to your Stakeholder Pension you arranged yourself?

Yes...1

No..2

145. SPGov   Since the date of the last interview (DATE) has any money been paid into your Stakeholder Pension you arranged yourself by HM Revenue & Customs (formerly the Inland Revenue)?

Yes...1

No..2

Don't know...3

Ask if respondent currently makes contributions to Group Personal Pension (not asked of proxies)
(PPPCont = 1)

146.   PenAmnt   In total, how much do you currently contribute each month to your personal/private pension(s)?

IF HAVE MORE THAN ONE POLICY, SUM UP ALL POLICIES

0.00..99997.00

147.   PenPer   What period does this cover?

one week...1
two weeks...2
three weeks...3
four weeks...4
calendar month..5
two calendar months..6
eight times a year...7
nine times a year..8
ten times a year..9
three months/13 weeks..10
six months/26 weeks..11
one year/12 months/52 weeks..12
less than one week...13
one off/lump sum..14
none of these: EXPLAIN IN A NOTE <Ctrl> + <M>.................15

Ask if self-employed
(Stat = 2)

148.   PersPnt2   INTERVIEWER - INTRODUCE IF NECESSARY.
Now I would like to ask you about personal pension schemes.

149.   SePrsPen   Self-employed people may arrange pensions for themselves and get tax relief on their contributions. These schemes include personal pensions, stakeholder pensions and 'self-employed pensions' (sometimes called 'Section 226 Retirement Annuities').

Do you at present contribute to one of these schemes?

Yes..1

No...2

Ask if contributes to one of the schemes and is not a proxy respondent (SePrsPen =1 AND Persprox=1)

150.   SePrsS   Which types of scheme are you contributing to – personal pension, stakeholder pension, or some other scheme?

CODE ALL THAT APPLY

Personal pension...1
Stakeholder pension...2
Other...3

Ask if respondent is contributing to a personal pension or a stakeholder pension (SePrsS = 1 or 2)

151.   SEPPPAmt   In total how much do you contribute each month to this pension scheme?

IF HAVE MORE THAN ONE POLICY, SUM UP ALL POLICIES

0.01..99999.00

152.   SEPPPer   What period does this cover?

one week..1
two weeks...2
three weeks...3
four weeks..4
calendar month...5
two calendar months..7
eight times a year..8
nine times a year...9
ten times a year...10
three months/13 weeks...13
six months/26 weeks..26
one year/12 months/52 weeks...52
less than one week...90
one off/lump sum...95
none of these: EXPLAIN IN A NOTE <Ctrl> + <M>............................97

Ask if does not, or does not know if they contribute to one of the above schemes and is not a proxy respondent
(SePrsPen = 2 or DK AND Persprox=1)

153.   SeEvPers   Have you ever contributed to one of these schemes?

Yes...1
No..2

This question is asked of anyone under pensionable age who is not currently in paid work
(Under pensionable age & Wrking ≠ 1 & JbAway ≠ 1 & Stat ≠ 3 & OwnBus ≠ 1 & RelBus ≠1)

154.   NewShp   Since April 2001, anyone can take out a stakeholder or other personal pension.

Do you at present have one of these types of pension for yourself?

PROMPT AS NECESSARY

Yes, stakeholder..1
Yes, other personal pension...2
No..3

Ask if yes at NewShp and is not a proxy respondent
(NewShp=1 OR 2 AND Persprox =1)

155.   NewShpc   Have you or anyone else made any contributions to (this/either) pension in the last 12 months?

Yes...1
No..2

Ask if yes at NewShpc
(NewShpc = 1)

156.   TotLst12   How much have you or anyone else contributed to your personal pension over the last 12 months?

IF HAVE MORE THAN ONE POLICY, SUM UP ALL POLICIES

0.01..99999.00

157.   PpenPer   What period does this cover?

one week	1
two weeks	2
three weeks	3
four weeks	4
calendar month	5
two calendar months	7
eight times a year	8
nine times a year	9
ten times a year	10
three months/13 weeks	13
six months/26 weeks	26
one year/12 months/52 weeks	52
less than one week	90
one off/lump sum	95
none of these: EXPLAIN IN A NOTE <Ctrl> + <M>	97

EDUCATION

Ask this section of adults 16 and above (it is not asked of proxies)

158.   QualCh   I would now like to ask you about education and work-related training. Do you have any qualifications…

INDIVIDUAL PROMPT – CODE ALL THAT APPLY

from school, college or university..1
connected with work...2
or from government schemes?..3
No qualifications (Spontaneous only)..4
Don't know (Spontaneous only)..5

Ask if respondent has a qualification, or answers don't know (QualCh = 1, 2, 3 or 5)

159. Quals　　　SHOWCARD 10

Which qualifications do (you think) you have, starting with the highest qualifications?

CODE ALL THAT APPLY - PROMPT AS NECESSARY

Degree level qualification including foundation degrees, graduate membership of a professional institute or PGCE or higher.........................1

Diploma in higher education..2

HNC/HND...3

ONC/OND...4

BTEC/ BEC/ TEC / EdExcel...5

SCOTVEC/ SCOTEC/ SCOTBEC (Scotland)......................................6

Teaching qualification (excluding PGCE)..7

Nursing or other medical qualification not yet mentioned.........................8

Other higher education qualification below degree level...........................9

A level / Vocational A-level or equivalent...10

Highers (Scotland)...11

NVQ/SVQ..12

GNVQ/GSVQ..13

AS level /Vocational AS level or equivalent..14

Advanced Highers or
Certificate of Sixth Year Studies (CSYS) (Scotland).............................15

Access to HE...16

O level or equivalent..17

Intermediate 2 NQs (Scotland)..18

Intermediate 1 NQs (Scotland)..19

Standard Grade or O Grade (Scotland)..20

GCSE / Vocational GCSE...21

CSE...22

National Qualifications (including SGA) (Scotland)................................23

RSA/ OCR...24

City and Guilds...25

YT Certificate/YTP...26

Key Skills/ Basic Skills..27

Entry Level Qualifications...28

Any other professional/vocational qualifications/
foreign qualifications...29

Don't know..30

Ask if has NVQ/SVQ
(Quals = 12 AND does NOT have a higher qualification)

160.   NVQlev   What is your highest level of full NVQ/SVQ?

Level 1...1
Level 2...2
Level 3...3
Level 4...4
Level 5...5
Don't know...6

Ask if highest qualification is a degree level qualification
(Quals = 1 AND does NOT have a higher qualification)

161.   Degree   Is your degree...

CODE FIRST THAT APPLIES

a higher degree (including PGCE)..1
a first degree...2
a foundation degree...3
other (e.g. graduate member of a professional institute or chartered
accountant)..4
Don't know...5

Ask if has a higher degree
(Degree = 1)

162.   HighO   ASK OR RECORD

Was your higher degree...

CODE FIRST THAT APPLIES

a Doctorate...1
a Masters..2
a Postgraduate Certificate in Education..3
or some other postgraduate degree or professional qualification..................4
Don't know...5

Ask if highest qualification is a teaching qualification excluding PGCE
(Quals = 7   AND   does NOT have a higher qualification)

163.   Teach   Was your teaching qualification for...

CODE ALL THAT APPLY

Further education...1
Key Stage 4...2
Key Stage 3...3
Key Stage 2...4
Key Stage 1...5
Foundation Stage..6
Don't know..7

Ask if highest qualification is RSA/OCR
(Quals = 24   AND   does NOT have a higher qualification)

164.   RSA   Is your highest RSA...

CODE FIRST THAT APPLIES

a higher diploma..1
an advanced diploma or advanced certificate.......................................2
a diploma...3
or some other RSA (including Stage I,II & III).......................................4
Don't Know..5

Ask if highest qualification is SCOTVEC
(Quals = 6   AND   does NOT have a higher qualification)

165.   SCTVEC   Is your highest SCOTVEC qualification...

CODE FIRST THAT APPLIES

At a higher level (level 4)...1
At full National Certificate (level 3)..2
At a first diploma or general diploma (level 2).....................................3
At a first certificate or general certificate (below level 2).......................4
Modules towards a National Certificate...5
Don't know...6

Ask if highest qualification is BTEC, BEC, TEC or EdExcel
(Quals = 5 AND does NOT have a higher qualification)

166. BTEC

Is your highest BTEC qualification...

CODE FIRST THAT APPLIES

at higher level (level 4)...1
at National Certificate or National Diploma level (level 3)........................2
a first diploma or general diploma (level 2)..3
a first certificate or general certificate (below level 2)..........................4
Don't know...5

Ask if highest qualification is GNVQ\GSVQ
(Quals = 13 AND does NOT have a higher qualification)

167. GNVQ

Is your highest GNVQ/GSVQ at...

CODE FIRST THAT APPLIES
A FULL QUALIFICATION = 6 UNITS
A PART QUALIFICATION = 3 UNITS

Advanced..1
Full Intermediate...2
Part One Intermediate..3
Full Foundation...4
Part One Foundation...5
Don't know..6

Ask if highest qualification is City and Guilds
(Quals = 25 AND does NOT have a higher qualification)

168. CandG

Is your highest City and Guilds qualification....

CODE FIRST THAT APPLIES

advanced craft/part 3..1
craft/part 2...2
foundation/part 1...3
Don't know..4

Ask if highest qualification is A levels / Vocational A-Levels
(Quals = 10　AND　does NOT have a higher qualification)

169.　NumAL　　Do you have...

one A level or equivalent...1
or more than one...2
Don't know..3

Ask if highest qualification is Scottish Highers
(Quals = 11　AND　does NOT have a higher qualification)

170.　NumSCE　　Do you have...

1 or 2 Highers...1
3 or more Highers..2
Don't know..3

Ask if highest qualification is AS levels / Vocational AS levels
(Quals = 14　AND　does NOT have a higher qualification)

171.　NumAS　　Do you have...

one AS level..1
2 or 3 AS levels...2
or 4 or more passes at this level..3
Don't know..4

Ask if highest qualification is GCSE or Standard Grade or O Grade or Intermediate 1 or Intermediate 2)
(Quals = 18, 19, 20　OR 21 AND does NOT have a higher qualification)

172.　GCSE　　Do you have any (GCSEs at grades A-C), (Standard Grades at 1-3 / O Grades
at (A-C), (Intermediate 2 at A-C and/or Intermediate 1 at A)?

Yes...1
No...2
Don't know..3

Ask if highest qualification is CSE
(Quals = 22 AND does NOT have a higher qualification)

173.   CSE   Do you have any CSEs at grade 1?

Yes..1
No...2
Don't know...3

Ask if has O levels, Standard Grades 1-3, O Grades A-C, GCSEs at grade A-C, CSEs at grade 1, Intermediate 2 grade A-C or Intermediate 1 grade A
(Quals = 17 or GCSE = 1 or CSE = 1)

174.   NumOL   ASK OR RECORD

You mentioned that you have passes at (GCSE at Grade A-C) (CSE Grade 1) (O level or equivalent) (Standard Grades at 1-3/O Grade at A-C) (Intermediate 2 at A-C) (Intermediate 1 at A). Do you have...

fewer than 5 passes...1
or 5 or more passes at this level.....................................2
Don't know...3

175.   EngMath   Do you have any (GCSEs at grades A-C), (CSE Grade 1), (Standard Grades at 1-3/ O Grades at A-C), (Intermediate 2 at A-C) or (Intermediate 1 at A) in English or Mathematics?

English...1
Maths..2
Both..3
Neither...4

Ask if respondent has any qualifications
(QualCh = 1, 2 or 3)

176.   AgeHQual   How old were you when you achieved your highest qualification?

1..97
Ask all respondents

177.   QulNow   Are you currently working towards or studying towards any qualifications?

Yes..1
No...2

Ask if respondent is currently working towards qualification
(QulNow = 1)

178.   QulWht   SHOWCARD 10

What qualification are you studying for?

CODE ALL THAT APPLY - PROMPT AS NECESSARY

Degree level qualification including foundation degrees, graduate
membership of a professional institute or PGCE or higher............................1
Diploma in higher education..2
HNC/HND...3
ONC/OND..4
BTEC/ BEC/ TEC / EdExcel...5
SCOTVEC/ SCOTEC/ SCOTBEC (Scotland)...6
Teaching qualification (excluding PGCE)...7
Nursing or other medical qualification not yet mentioned............................8
Other higher education qualification below degree level............................9
A level / Vocational A-level or equivalent..10
Highers (Scotland)...11
NVQ/SVQ...12
GNVQ/GSVQ...13
AS level /Vocational AS level or equivalent...14
Advanced Highers or Certificate of Sixth Year Studies (CSYS) (Scotland). 15
Access to HE..16
O level or equivalent...17
Intermediate 2 NQs (Scotland)..18
Intermediate 1 NQs (Scotland)...19
Standard Grade or O Grade (Scotland)...20
GCSE / Vocational GCSE..21
CSE..22
National Qualifications (including SGA) (Scotland)..............................23
RSA/ OCR..24
City and Guilds..25
YT Certificate/YTP..26
Key Skills/ Basic Skills..27
Entry Level Qualifications..28
Any other professional/vocational qualifications/foreign qualifications........29
Don't know..30

Ask if studying for a degree
(QulWht = 1)

179.   DegNow   Are you studying for...

a higher degree (including PGCE)..1
a first degree..2
a foundation degree...3
other (e.g. graduate member of a professional institute or chartered
accountant)..4
Don't know...5

Ask if studying for a higher degree
(DegNow = 1)

180.   HghNow   Are you studying for...

a Doctorate...1
a Masters..2
a Postgraduate Certificate in Education..3
or some other postgraduate degree or professional qualification...............4
Don't know..5

Ask if studying for a BTEC/BEC/TEC
(QulWht = 5)

181.   TECNow   What level BTEC/BEC/TEC are you studying for?

at higher level (level 4)..1
at National Certificate or National Diploma level (level 3)........................2
a first diploma or general diploma (level 2)...3
a first certificate or general certificate (below level 2)............................4
Don't know..5

Ask if studying for a SCOTVEC/SCOTEC/SCOTBEC
(QulWht = 6)

182.   SCNow   Are you studying for a SCOTVEC/SCOTEC/SCOTBEC...

at higher level (level 4)..1
at full National Certificate (level 3)..2
at a first diploma or general diploma (level 2)..3
at a first certificate or general certificate (below level 2)........................4
modules towards a National Certificate..5
Don't know...6

Ask if studying for an RSA
(QulWht = 24)

183.   RSANow   Are you studying for a RSA at...

higher diploma level...1
advanced diploma or advanced certificate level....................................2
diploma level...3
or some other RSA (including Stage I,II & III)..4
Don't know...5

Ask if studying for an NVQ/SVQ
(QulWht = 12)

184.   NVQLe2   What is the highest level of NVQ/SVQ you are working towards?

Level 1..1
Level 2..2
Level 3..3
Level 4..4
Level 5..5
Don't know...6

Ask if answered other or don't know at quals
(Quals = 29, 30)

185.   Appren   Are you doing, or have you completed, a recognised trade apprenticeship?

INCLUDE ADVANCED AND FOUNDATION MODERN APPRENTICESHIPS (AMA/FMA) AND 'TRADE' APPRENTICESHIPS

Yes, (completed)..1
Yes, (still doing)...2
Yes, has completed one apprenticeship and is now doing a further one......3
No...4

Ask all adults 16 and over (not asked of proxy respondents)

186.   Enroll   Are you at present (at school or at a FE/ sixth form college) enrolled on any full-time or part-time education course excluding leisure classes? (Include correspondence courses and open learning as well as other forms of full-time or part-time education course.)

Yes..1
No..2

Ask if enrolled on an education course
(Enroll = 1)

187.   Attend   And are you …

RUNNING PROMPT
Still attending...1
Waiting for term to (re)start...2
Or have you stopped going...3

Ask if respondent is still attending school or college, or waiting for term to [re]start
(Attend = 1 or 2)

188.   Course   Are you (at school or at a FE/ sixth form college), on a full or part-time course, a medical or nursing course, a sandwich course, or some other kind of course?

CODE FIRST THAT APPLIES

(School/full-time)/(CODE NOT APPLICABLE – AGED 20+).....................1
(School/part-time)/(CODE NOT APPLICABLE – AGED 20+)...................2
Sandwich course...3
Studying at a university or college including FE/ Sixth Form College
FULL-TIME..4
Training for a qualification in nursing, physiotherapy, or a similar
medical subject..5
On a part-time course at university or college
INCLUDING day release and block release..6
On an Open College Course...7
On an Open University Course...8
Any other correspondence course...9
Any other self/open learning course...10

Ask if respondent has stopped attending school or college, AND is NOT under the age of 20
(Attend = 3 & Age > 19)

189.   Course20   Are you (at school or at a FE/ Sixth Form College), on a full or part-time course, a medical or nursing course, a sandwich course, or some other kind of course?

CODE FIRST THAT APPLIES

Sandwich course...3
Studying at a university or college including FE/ Sixth Form College
FULL-TIME..4
Training for a qualification in nursing, physiotherapy, or a similar
medical subject..5
On a part-time course at university or college
INCLUDING day release and block release..6
On an Open College Course...7
On an Open University Course...8
Any other correspondence course...9
Any other self/open learning course...10

Ask all adults 16 and over (not asked of proxy respondents)

190.   EdAge   How old were you when you finished your continuous full-time education?

CODE AS 97 IF NO EDUCATION;
CODE AS 96 IF STILL IN EDUCATION

1..97

ADULT HEALTH

Ask this section of all adults (1(GenHlth) to 14 (ReasDen) and NHSDir and NHSDuse are not asked of proxy respondents)

Ask all (except proxy respondents)

191.   QHealth1   How is your/his/her health in general; would you say it was...

RUNNING PROMPT

Very good...1
Good...2
Fair...3
Bad...4
Or very bad..5

192.   LSIll   (And) do you/does (..) have any long-standing illness, disability or infirmity by long-standing I mean anything that has troubled you/him/her over a period of time or that is likely to affect you/him/her over a period of time?

Yes..1
No..2

Ask if LSIll=1

193.   IllLim   Does this illness or disability (Do any of these illnesses or disabilities) limit your/his/her activities in any way?

Yes..1
No..2

Ask if has a long-standing illness
(LSIll = 1)

194.   LMatter   Earlier you said you had a longstanding illness....
What is the matter with you?

THIS IS TO ENSURE THAT THE RESPONDENT MENTIONS ALL THEIR LONGSTANDING ILLNESSES. YOU DO NOT HAVE TO RECORD VERBATIM – A SUMMARY WILL DO.

ENTER TEXT OF AT MOST 100 CHARACTERS

195. LMatNum   HOW MANY LONGSTANDING ILLNESSES OR INFIRMITIES DOES RESPONDENT HAVE?

ENTER NUMBER OF LONGSTANDING COMPLAINTS MENTIONED IF MORE THAN 6 - TAKE THE SIX THAT THE RESPONDENT CONSIDERS THE MOST IMPORTANT

1..6

For each illness

196. LMat   WHAT IS THE MATTER WITH RESPONDENT?

ENTER THE (FIRST/SECOND/etc.) CONDITION/SYMPTOM RESPONDENT MENTIONED

ENTER TEXT OF AT MOST 55 CHARACTERS

197. ICD   CODE FOR (FIRST/SECOND/etc.)COMPLAINT AT LMAT

ENTER SPACE BAR TO SEE CODES

IF CODE NOT FOUND, CHANGE ILLNESS DESCRIPTION AT BOTTOM OF LOOKUP WINDOW TO 'NONE' AND SELECT CODE FOR 'NONE OF THESE'

PRESS ENTER TO SELECT CODE AND ENTER AGAIN TO CONTINUE

ENTER TEXT OF AT MOST 2 CHARACTERS

Ask if has a long-standing illness
(LSIll = 1)

198. LimitAct   Does this illness or disability (Do any of these illnesses or disabilities) limit your activities in any way?

Yes...1
No..2

Ask if activities are limited
(LimitAct = 1)

199.   LimitL6   Would you say your activities are limited or strongly limited?

Limited...1
Strongly limited...2

Ask all (except proxy respondents)

200.   CutDown   Now I'd like you to think about the 2 weeks ending yesterday. During those 2 weeks, did you have to cut down on any of the things you usually do (about the house/at work or in your free time) because of illness or injury?

Yes...1
No...2

Ask if had to cut down on normal activities because of illness or injury
(CutDown = 1)

201.   NDysCutD   How many days was this in all during these 2 weeks, including Saturdays and Sundays?

1..14

202.   Cmatter   What was the matter with you?

ENTER TEXT OF AT MOST 40 CHARACTERS

Ask all (except proxy respondents)

203.   MedRec   Was there any time since the date of the last interview (date) when, in your opinion, you personally needed a medical examination or treatment for a health problem but you did not receive it?

Yes, there was at least one occasion but did not receive..........................1
No, there was no occasion...2

Ask if answered yes to MedRec
(MedRec = 1)

204.   ReasMed   What was the main reason for not receiving the examination or treatment or (the most recent time)?

DO NOT PROMPT
IF RESPONDENT SAYS CANNOT AFFORD PRESCRIPTION, USE CODE 1

Could not afford to (too expensive)..1
Waiting list...2
Could not take time because of work, care for children or for others............3
Too far to travel/no means of transportation...4
Fear of doctor/hospitals/examination/ treatment....................................5
Wanted to wait and see if problem got better on its own...........................6
Didn't know any good doctor or specialist...7
Other reasons..8

Ask all (except proxy respondents)

205.   DenRec   Was there any time since the date of the last interview (date) when, in your opinion, you personally needed a dental examination or treatment but you did not receive it?
Yes, there was at least one occasion but did not receive.........................1
No, there was no occasion..2

Ask if answered yes to DenRec
(DenRec = 1)

206.   ReasDen   What was the main reason for not receiving the dental examination or treatment (the most recent time)?

SPONTANEOUS

Could not afford to (too expensive)..1
Waiting list...2
Could not take time because of work, care for children or for others...........3
Too far to travel/no means of transportation...4
Fear of dentists/hospitals/examination/ treatment..................................5
Wanted to wait and see if problem got better on its own...........................6
Didn't know any good dentist...7
Can't find NHS dentist willing to take me on as a patient.........................8

Other reasons..9

Ask if answered yes to DenRec
(DenRec = 1)

207. ReasDen   What was the main reason for not receiving the dental examination or treatment (the most recent time)?

SPONTANEOUS

Could not afford to (too expensive)..1
Waiting list...2
Could not take time because of work, care for children or for others...........3
Too far to travel/no means of transportation.......................................4
Fear of dentists/hospitals/examination/ treatment...............................5
Wanted to wait and see if problem got better on its own.........................6
Didn't know any good dentist..7
Can't find NHS dentist willing to take me on as a patient.......................8
Other reasons...9

If respondent can't find NHS dentist
(ReasDen=8)

208. ReasNHS   May I just check, could you afford to go to a private dentist instead?

Yes...1
No...2

Ask all adults

209. DocTalk   During the 2 weeks ending yesterday, apart from any visit to a hospital, did you talk to a doctor for any reason at all, either in person or by telephone?

EXCLUDE: CONSULTATIONS MADE ON BEHALF OF CHILDREN UNDER 16 AND PERSONS OUTSIDE THE HOUSEHOLD.

Yes...1
No...2

Ask if contact with doctor during the last 2 weeks
(DocTalk = 1)

210. NChats   How many times did you talk to a doctor in these 2 weeks?

1..9

For each consultation

211. WhsBhlf   On whose behalf was this consultation made?

Respondent...1
Other member of household 16 or over...2

**Ask if consultation was on the behalf of another member of the
household**
(WhsBhlf = 2)

212. ForPerNo   CODE WHO CONSULTATION WAS MADE FOR

(PERSON NUMBER)

1..16

For each consultation

213. NHS   Was this consultation...

Under the National Health Service...1
or paid for privately..2

214. GP   Was the doctor...

RUNNING PROMPT

A GP (ie a family doctor)..1
or some other kind of doctor...2

215.   DocWhere   Did you talk to the doctor...

RUNNING PROMPT

By telephone..1
at your home...2
in the doctor's surgery..3
at a health centre..4
or elsewhere...5

216.   Presc   Did the doctor give (send) you a prescription?

Yes...1
No...2

Ask all adults

217.   SeeChn   During the last 2 weeks ending yesterday, did you see a practice nurse atthe GP surgery on your own behalf?

Yes...1
No...2

Ask if the respondent saw a nurse
(SeeChn = 1)

218.   NNurse   How many times did you see a practice nurse at the GP surgery in these 2 weeks?

RECORD NUMBER OF TIMES

1..9

Ask all adults

219. OutPatnt   During the months of (LAST 3 COMPLETE CALENDAR MONTHS) did you attend as a patient at the casualty or outpatient department of a hospital (apart from straightforward ante- or post-natal visits)?

INCLUDE - VISITS TO PRIVATE HOSPITALS AND PRIVATE CLINICS, MINOR INJURIES UNITS AND WALK-IN CENTRES

EXCLUDE - DOCTORS SEEN ABROAD UNLESS FORCES DOCTORS
- DAY PATIENTS (THEY ARE COVERED BY DAYPATNT)

Yes..1
No...2

Ask if respondent attended outpatients
(OutPatnt = 1)

220. NTimes1   How many times did you attend in (EARLIEST MONTH IN REFERENCE PERIOD)?

0..97

221. NTimes2   How many times did you attend in (SECOND MONTH IN REFERENCE PERIOD)?

0..97

222. NTimes3   How many times did you attend in (THIRD MONTH IN REFERENCE PERIOD)?

0..97

223. Casualty   Was this visit (were any of these visits) to the Casualty department or was it (were they all) to some other part of the hospital?

At least one visit to Casualty...1
No Casualty visits..2

Ask if respondent visited casualty
(Casualty = 1)

224.   NCasVis   (May I just check) How many times did you go to Casualty altogether?

1..31

Ask if respondent attended outpatients
(OutPatnt = 1)

225.   PrVists   Was your outpatient visit (were any of your outpatient visits) during (REFERENCE PERIOD) made under the NHS, or was it (were any of them) paid for privately?

All under NHS...1
At least one paid for privately..2

Ask if some private visits
(PrVists = 2)

226.   NPrVists   ASK OR RECORD

(May I just check), How many of the visits were paid for privately?

1..31

Ask all adults

227.   DayPatnt   Since the date of the last interview (date), have you been in hospital for treatment as a day patient, i.e. admitted to a hospital bed or day ward, but not required to remain overnight?

Yes...1
No...2

Ask if has been a day patient AND is a women aged between 16-49
(DayPatnt = 1 & Sex = 2 & DVAge = 16-49)

228.   MatDPat   May I just check, was that/were any of those day patient admissions for you to have a baby?

Yes..1
No...2

Ask if respondent was a day patient because she was having a baby
(MatDPat = Yes)

229.   NumMatDP   How many separate days have you had as a day patient for having a baby since (DATE ONE YEAR AGO)?

97 DAYS OR MORE - CODE 97

1..97

230.   PrMatDP   Was this day-patient stay (were any of these day-patient stays) for having a baby under the NHS, or was it (were any of them) paid for privately?

All under NHS..1
At least one paid for privately...2

Ask if day patient stay for having a baby was paid for privately AND
respondent was in hospital for more than one day
(PrMatDP = 2 & NumMatDP > 1)

231.   NPrMatDP   ASK OR RECORD

How many of the visits were paid for privately?

1..31

**Ask if the respondent was a day patient
(DayPatnt = 1)**

232.   NHSPDays   (Apart from those maternity stays) how many separate days in hospital
have you had as a day patient since (DATE ONE YEAR AGO)?

97 DAYS OR MORE - CODE 97

0..97

**Ask if had one or more days in hospital
(NHSPDays > 0)**

233.   PrDptnt   Was this day-patient treatment (were any of these day-patient treatments)
under the NHS, or was it (were any of them) paid for privately?

All under NHS...1
At least one paid for privately...2

**Ask if day patient stay was paid for privately AND they were in hospital
for more than one day
(PrDptnt = 2   &   NHSPDays > 1)**

234.   NPrDpTnt   ASK OR RECORD

How many of the visits were paid for privately?

1..31

Ask all adults

235.   InPatnt   Since the date of the last interview (date), have you been in hospital as an
inpatient, overnight or longer?

Yes...1
No..2

Ask if respondent has been an inpatient AND she is a women aged 16-49
(InPatnt = 1 & Sex = 2 & DVAge = 16-49)

236.   MatInPat   May I just check, was that/were any of those inpatient admissions for you to have a baby?

Yes...1
No...2

Ask if inpatient admission was to have a baby
(MatInPat = 1)

237.   NMtStay   How many separate stays in hospital as an inpatient in order to have a baby have you had since (DATE 1 YEAR AGO)?

1..6

Ask for each maternity stay

238.   MtNights   How many nights altogether were you in hospital on your (no.) stay to have a baby?

1..97

239.   MatNHSTr   Were you treated under the NHS or were you a private patient on that occasion?

NHS...1
Private Patient...2

If private patient
(MatNHSTr = 2)

240.   MtPrvSty   Were you treated in an NHS hospital or in a private one?

NHS hospital..1
Private hospital..2

**Ask if respondent has been an inpatient
(InPatnt = 1)**

241.   NStays   (Apart from those maternity stays) how many separate stays in hospital as an inpatient have you had since (DATE 1 YEAR AGO)?

0..6

Ask for each stay

242.   Nights How many nights altogether were you in hospital on our first/second/...sixth) stay?

1..97

243.   NHSTreat   Were you treated under the NHS or were you a private patient on that occasion?

NHS...1
Private Patient...2

**Ask if a private patient
(NHSTreat = 2)**

244.   PrvStay   Were you treated in an NHS hospital or in a private one?

NHS hospital..1
Private hospital...2

Ask all adults (except proxy respondents)

245.   NHSDir   Have you ever heard of NHS Direct? (In Scotland - NHS24)

Yes..1
No..2

**Ask if respondent has heard of NHS Direct/ NHS24
(NHSDir = 1)**

246.   NHSDuse   During the last year, that is, since (DATE ONE YEAR AGO), have you used NHS Direct? (In Scotland - NHS24)

Yes..1
No..2

CHILD HEALTH

Ask each child under 16 in household (not asked of proxy respondents)

247. AskHlth   THE NEXT SECTION IS ABOUT CHILD HEALTH.
WE ONLY NEED TO COLLECT THIS INFORMATION ONCE FOR EACH CHILD IN THE HOUSEHOLD.
WHO WILL ANSWER THE CHILD HEALTH SECTION FOR (CHILD'S NAME)?

INTERVIEWER ENTER PERSON NUMBER.

1..14

248. AskNowCH   INTERVIEWER: DO YOU WANT TO ASK THIS SECTION FOR (CHILD'S NAME) NOW OR LATER?

IF YOU HAVE ALREADY ASKED THIS SECTION FOR (CHILD'S NAME), DO NOT CHANGE FROM CODE 1.

Yes, now/Already asked...1
Later..2

If the section is to be asked later
(AskNowCH = 2)

249. CStill   REMINDER
THE FOLLOWING ADULTS STILL NEED TO ANSWER THE CHILD HEALTH SECTION ON BEHALF OF SOME OF THE CHILDREN.

If the section is to be asked now
(AskNowCH = 1)

For each child

250. Genhlth2   How is (NAME) health in general? Would you say it was...

Very good...1
Good...2
Fair..3
Bad...4
Very bad...5

251. Illness   Does (NAME) have any long-standing illness, disability or infirmity? By long-standing, I mean anything that has troubled them over a period of time or that is likely to affect them over a period of time?

Yes...1
No..2

Ask if child has a longstanding illness, disability or infirmity (Illness =1)

252. LMatter   What is the matter with (NAME)?

THIS IS TO ENSURE THAT THE RESPONDENT MENTIONS ALL LONGSTANDING ILLNESSES. YOU DO NOT HAVE TO RECORD VERBATIM HERE - A SUMMARY WILL DO.

ENTER TEXT OF AT MOST 40 CHARACTERS

253. LMatNum   HOW MANY LONGSTANDING ILLNESSES OR INFIRMITIES DOES (NAME) HAVE?

ENTER NUMBER OF LONGSTANDING COMPLAINTS MENTIONED IF MORE THAN 6 - TAKE THE SIX THAT THE RESPONDENT CONSIDERS THE MOST IMPORTANT.

1..6

For each illness mentioned at LMatNum

254. LMatCH   WHAT IS THE MATTER WITH (NAME)?

ENTER THE (FIRST/SECOND/etc.) CONDITION/SYMPTOM RESPONDENT MENTIONED

ENTER TEXT OF AT MOST 40 CHARACTERS

255.   ICDCH   CODE FOR EACH COMPLAINT AT LMatCH

ENTER SPACE BAR TO SEE CODES

IF CODE NOT FOUND, CHANGE ILLNESS DESCRIPTION AT BOTTOM OF LOOKUP WINDOW TO 'NONE' AND SELECT CODE FOR 'NONE OF THESE'. PRESS ENTER TO SELECT CODE AND ENTER AGAIN TO CONTINUE.

If child has a longstanding illness, disability or infirmity
(Illness =1)

256.   LimitAct   Does this illness or disability (Do any of these illnesses or disabilities) limit (NAME)'s activities in any way?

Yes...1
No..2

Ask if child's activities are limited by an illness/disability
(LimitAct = 1)

257.   LimitL6C   Would you say their activities are limited or strongly limited?

Limited..1
Strongly limited..2

For each child

258.   CutDown   Now I'd like you to think about the 2 weeks ending yesterday. During those 2 weeks, did (NAME) have to cut down on any of the things he/she usually does (at school or in his/her free time) because of (answer at LMatter or some other) illness or injury?

Yes...1
No..2

Ask if child has had to cut down
(CutDown = 1)

259.   NDysCutD How many days did (NAME) have to cut down in all during these 2 weeks, including Saturdays and Sundays?

1..14

260.   Matter   What was the matter with (NAME)?

ENTER TEXT OF AT MOST 80 CHARACTERS

For each child

261.   DocTalk   During the 2 weeks ending yesterday, apart from visits to a hospital, did (NAME) talk to a doctor for any reason at all, or did you or any other member of the household talk to a doctor on his/her behalf?

Include being seen by a doctor at a school clinic, but exclude visits to a child welfare clinic run by a local authority.

INCLUDE TELEPHONE CONSULTATIONS AND CONSULTATIONS MADE ON BEHALF OF CHILDREN.

Yes...1
No..2

If child consulted a doctor
(DocTalk = 1)

262.   NChats   How many times did (NAME) talk to the doctor (or you or any other member of the household consult the doctor on NAME behalf) in those 2 weeks?

1..9

For each consultation

263.   NHS   Was this consultation...

RUNNING PROMPT

Under the National Health Service...1
or paid for privately...2

264.   GP   Was the doctor...

RUNNING PROMPT

A GP (i.e. a family doctor)..1
or some other kind of doctor..2

265.   DocWhere   Did you or any other member of the household (or NAME) talk to the doctor...

                                    RUNNING PROMPT

                                    By telephone...1
                                    at your home..2
                                    in the doctor's surgery...3
                                    at a health centre...4
                                    or elsewhere..5

266.   Presc   Did the doctor give (send) (NAME) a prescription?

                                    Yes..1
                                    No...2

                                    For each child

267.   Seenurse   During the last 2 weeks ending yesterday did (NAME)...

                                    INDIVIDUAL PROMPT - CODE ALL THAT APPLY

                                    see a practice nurse at the GP surgery...1
                                    see a health visitor at the GP surgery...2
                                    go to child health clinic..3
                                    go to child welfare clinic...4
                                    or did they not go to any of these..5

                                    Ask if child saw a practice nurse
                                    (Seenurse = 1)

268.   Nnurse   How many times did (NAME) see a practice nurse at the GP surgery in these two weeks?

                                    RECORD NUMBER OF TIMES

                                    1..9

For each child

269. OutPatnt   During the months of (LAST 3 COMPLETE CALENDAR MONTHS), did
                   (NAME) attend as a patient the casualty or outpatient department of a
                   hospital?

                   INCLUDE MINOR INJURIES UNITS AND WALK-IN CENTRES

                   Yes...1
                   No..2

Ask if child has been an outpatient
(OutPatnt = 1)

270. NTimes1   How many times did (NAME) attend in (EARLIEST MONTH IN
                   REFERENCE PERIOD)?

                   0..97

271. NTimes2   How many times did (NAME) attend in (SECOND MONTH IN
                   REFERENCE PERIOD)?

                   0..97

272. NTimes3   How many times did (NAME) attend in (THIRD MONTH IN
                   REFERENCE PERIOD)?

                   0..97

273. Casualty   Was the visit (were any of the visits) to the Casualty department or was
                   it (were they) to some other part of the hospital?

                   At least one visit to Casualty...1
                   No Casualty visits...2

Ask if child went to casualty
(Casualty = 1)

274.   NCasVis   (May I just check) How many times did (NAME) go to Casualty altogether?

                1..31

For each child

275.   DayPatnt   Since the date of the last interview, that is since (DATE 1 YEAR AGO) has (NAME) been in hospital for treatment as a day patient, i.e. admitted to a hospital bed or day ward, but not required to remain in hospital overnight?

                Yes...1
                No..2

Ask if child has been a day patient
(DayPatnt = 1)

276.   NHSPDays   How many separate days in hospital has (NAME) had as a day patient since (DATE 1 YEAR AGO)?

                1..97

For each child

277.   InPatnt   During the last year, that is, since (DATE 1 YEAR AGO) has (NAME) been in hospital as an inpatient, overnight or longer?

                EXCLUDE: Births unless baby stayed in hospital after mother had left.

                Yes...1
                No..2

Ask if child has been an inpatient
(InPatnt = 1)

278.   NStays   How many separate stays in hospital as an inpatient has (NAME) had since (DATE 1 YEAR AGO)?

IF 6 OR MORE, CODE 6

1..6

For each stay

279.   Nights   How many nights altogether was (NAME) in hospital during stay number (...)?

1..97

CHILDCARE

Ask this section for each child aged 0 - 12 years inclusive

280.   AskCare   The next section is about your childcare needs.
We are interested in where your child is when neither you (nor your partner) are present, for example, at school, in a crèche, or at some other day care.
We are also interested in a typical term time week, that is, a week of 7 days, and which is outside school (and parents') holidays
Who will answer the childcare section for (NAME)?

ENTER PERSON NUMBER

IF NO TYPICAL WEEK - PICK THE MOST RECENT WEEK WITHOUT HOLIDAYS.
WE ONLY NEED TO COLLECT THIS INFORMATION ONCE FOR EACH CHILD AGED 12 YEARS OR LESS IN THE HOUSEHOLD.

1..14

281.   ChAtt   SHOWCARD 18

At any time during a typical term time week did (NAME) attend any of the following?

Play group or pre-school...1
Day-care centre or workplace crèche...2
Nursery school..3
School (infant to secondary)...4
Breakfast/After school club..5
Children's centres/integrated centres/combined centres.........................6
Boarding school...7
None of these..8

Ask if child attended playgroup/pre-school or nursery school
(ChAtt=1 or 3)

282.   WkKind   How many hours during a typical term time week did (NAME) spend in the playgroup, pre-school or nursery school?

                     INCLUDE:
                     - 'NORMAL' SCHOOL HOURS (I.E. EDUCATIONAL HOURS) AND MEAL-TIMES
                     EXCLUDE:
                     - BEFORE/AFTER SCHOOL CLUBS
                     - TRAVEL TIME ON SCHOOL TRANSPORT
                     0..99

Ask if child attended school
(ChAtt= 4)

283.   WkSchl   How many hours during that typical week did (NAME) spend in school?

                     INCLUDE:
                     - 'NORMAL' SCHOOL HOURS (I.E. EDUCATIONAL HOURS) AND MEAL-TIMES
                     EXCLUDE:
                     - BEFORE/AFTER SCHOOL CLUBS
                     - TRAVEL TIME ON SCHOOL TRANSPORT

                     0..99

Ask if child attended a breakfast or after school club or at an organised children's centre, integrated centre or combined centre
(ChAtt= 5 or 6)

284.   WkBA   How many hours during a typical term time week did (NAME) spend in a Breakfast or After school club or at an organised children's centre, integrated centre or combined centre?

                     INCLUDE:
                     - BREAKFAST/AFTERSCHOOL CLUBS
                     - OUTSIDE SCHOOL HOURS
                     - AT AN ORGANISED CENTRE
                     EXCLUDE:
                     - SPORTING AND CULTURAL ACTIVITIES OUTSIDE SCHOOL HOURS (E.G. MUSIC LESSONS, SPORTS CLUB). NB THESE ARE NOT USED AS A CHILDCARE SERVICE BUT RATHER FOR CHILD LEISURE.

                     0..99

**Ask if child attended a day-care centre or workplace crèche
(ChAtt= 2)**

285. WkDcare

How many hours during a typical term time week did (NAME) spend in a
day-care centre, crèche, family day care (even if for just a few hours)?

- INCLUDES DURING SCHOOL HOURS
- AT AN ORGANISED CENTRE
- IT IS ORGANISED, IN THAT THE CARER WILL BE EMPLOYED BY AN
ORGANISATION
- TYPICALLY IN A CENTRE, THOUGH FAMILY DAY CARE USES
APPROVED CARERS IN THEIR OWN HOMES
INCLUDE SPECIAL DAYCARE FOR CHILDREN WITH SPECIAL NEEDS
EXCLUDE SPORTING AND CULTURAL ACTIVITIES

0..99

Ask for each child

286. ChPeo

SHOWCARD 19

And during that typical term time week did any of the people listed on this
card normally look after (NAME), excluding care for social occasions? (Other
than resident parent(s)/guardian(s) and staff contact whilst at places
previously mentioned)

NANNY REFERS TO AN EMPLOYED NANNY (DOMESTIC HELP TO
LOOK AFTER CHILDREN)

CODE ALL THAT APPLY

Child's grandparents..1
Child's non-resident parent/an ex-spouse/an ex-partner.........................2
Child's brother or sister..3
Other relatives..4
Au Pair/Nanny (includes live-in and day nannies)....................................5
Friends or neighbours..6
Childminder..7
Other non-relatives..8
None of the above..9

Ask if child was looked after by anyone other than resident parent(s)/guardian(s) and staff contact whilst at places previously mentioned
(ChPeo ≠9)

287.   WkPcare   Thinking of these people, how many hours of PAID CARE did they provide for (NAME) during that typical term time week?

- CARER IS PAID DIRECTLY BY PARENT
- AT HOME OR CHILDMINDER'S HOME

0..99

288.   WkUPcare   And how many hours of UNPAID CARE did they provide for (NAME) during that typical term time week?

0..99

SMOKING

Ask this section of all adults, except proxy respondents

Ask if respondent is 18+ and stated they smoked nowadays
(CigNow=1)

289.   SmkIntro   The next section consists of a series of questions about SMOKING (Not asked of proxy respondents)

Ask all 16 and 17 year olds
(DVAge = 16-17)

290.   SelfCom1   RESPONDENT IS AGED 16 OR 17 - OFFER SELF-COMPLETION FORM AND ENTER CODE.

Respondent accepted self-completion...1
Respondent refused self-completion..2
Data now to be keyed by interviewer..3

Ask if respondent is 18+
DVAge > 17

291.   SmokEver   (And) have you/has (..) ever smoked a cigarette, a cigar, or a pipe?

Yes...1
No..2

Ask if respondent has ever smoked
(SmokEver=1)

292.   CigNow   And do you/does he/she smoke cigarettes at all nowadays

Yes...1
No..2

**Ask if respondent smokes cigarettes now
(CigNow = 1 or CigNow2 = 1)**

293.   QtyWkEnd   About how many cigarettes A DAY do you usually smoke at weekends?

IF LESS THAN 1, ENTER 0.

0..97

294.   QtyWkDay   About how many cigarettes A DAY do you usually smoke on weekdays?

IF LESS THAN 1, ENTER 0.

0..97

295.   CigType   Do you mainly smoke.....

RUNNING PROMPT

filter-tipped cigarettes...1
or plain or untipped cigarettes...2
or hand-rolled cigarettes...3

**Ask if cigarette types include plain or filter cigarettes
(CigType = 1 or 2)**

296.   CiglDesc   Which brand of cigarette do you usually smoke?

GIVE 1) FULL BRAND NAME 2) SIZE, e.g. King, luxury, regular.
IF NO REGULAR BRAND THEN TYPE 'no reg.' HERE.
IF RESPONDENT SMOKES TWO BRANDS EQUALLY TYPE 'two' IN
LETTERS HERE.

IF POSSIBLE PLEASE CHECK THE CIGARETTE PACKET

ENTER TEXT OF AT MOST 60 CHARACTERS

297.   CigCODE   Code for brand at CigIDesc

ENTER SPACE BAR TO SEE CODES

PLEASE DO NOT SELECT FIRST EXAMPLE OF NAMED BRAND, BUT
CHECK YOU HAVE CHOSEN THE CORRECT ONE.

IF BRAND NOT FOUND, CHANGE CIGARETTE BRAND DESCRIPTION
AT BOTTOM OF LOOKUP WINDOW TO 'nf' AND SELECT CODE FOR
'BRAND NOT FOUND'. PRESS ENTER TO SELECT CODE AND ENTER
AGAIN TO CONTINUE.

298.   CigPack   INTERVIEWER – CODE WHETHER THE RESPONDENT'S
                         CIGARETTE PACKET WAS CHECKED

Cigarette packet checked by respondent/ interviewer...........................1
Cigarette packet not checked..2

Ask if respondent smokes cigarettes now
(CigNow = 1 or CigNow2 = 1)

299.   NoSmoke   How easy or difficult would you find it to go without smoking for a
                         whole day? Would you find it...

RUNNING PROMPT

Very easy...1
Fairly easy...2
Fairly difficult or...3
Very difficult...4

300.   GiveUp   Would you like to give up smoking altogether?

Yes..1
No..2
Don't know..3

301.   FirstCig   How soon after waking do you USUALLY smoke your first cigarette of the day?

PROMPT AS NECESSARY

Less than 5 minutes..1
5-14 minutes..2
15-29 minutes..3
30 minutes but less than 1 hour...4
1 hour but less than 2 hours..5
2 hours or more..6

Ask if respondent does not smoke cigarettes now but has smoked a cigarette or cigar or pipe *(SmokEver or SmokEver2 = 1 & CigNow or CigNow2 = 2)*

302.   CigEver   Have you ever smoked cigarettes regularly?

Yes..1
No..2

Ask if respondent has ever smoked cigarettes regularly *(CigEver = 1)*

303.   CigUsed   About how many cigarettes did you smoke IN A DAY when you smoked them regularly?

IF LESS THAN 1, ENTER 0.

0..97

304.   CigStop   How long ago did you stop smoking cigarettes regularly?

PROMPT AS NECESSARY

Less than 6 months ago...1
6 months but less than a year ago...2
1 year but less than 2 years ago..3
2 years but less than 5 years ago..4
5 years but less than 10 years ago...5
10 years or more ago...6

**Ask of all respondents who have ever smoked cigarettes
(CigNow or CigNow2 = 1   or   CigEver = 1)**

305.   CigAge   How old were you when you started to smoke cigarettes regularly?

SPONTANEOUS: NEVER SMOKED CIGARETTES REGULARLY -
CODE 0

0..97

**Ask respondents who have ever smoked
(SmokEver = 1 or SmokEver2 = 1)**

306.   CigarReg   Do you smoke at least one cigar of any kind per month nowadays?

Yes...1
No..2

**Ask if respondent smokes at least one cigar per month
(CigarReg = 1)**

307.   CigarsWk   About how many cigars do you usually smoke in a week?

IF LESS THAN 1, ENTER 0.

0..97

**Ask if respondent does not smoke at least one cigar per month
(CigarReg = 2)**

308.   CigarEvr   Have you ever regularly smoked at least one cigar of any kind per month?

Yes...1
No..2

**Ask men who have ever smoked
(SmokEver = 1   AND   Sex = 1)**

309.   PipeNow   Do you smoke a pipe at all nowadays?

Yes...1
No..2

Ask if respondent doesn't currently smoke a pipe
(PipeNow = 2)

310.   PipEver   Have you ever smoked a pipe regularly?

Yes..1

No...2

Ask if CigNow = Yes or CigarReg = Yes or PipeNow = Yes

311.   GiveUpC   Which of the following statements best describes you?

CODE FIRST THAT APPLIES

I intend to give up smoking within the next month..................................1
I intend to give up smoking within the next 6 months.............................2
I intend to give up smoking within the next year.....................................3
I intend to give up smoking but not in the next year..............................4
I intend to give up smoking, but I'm not sure when................................5
I don't intend to give up smoking..6

DRINKING

Ask this section of all adults except proxy respondents

Ask all 16 and 17 year olds
(DVAge = 16-17)

312   Selfcom2   I'm now going to ask you a few questions about what you drink - that is if do drink.

IF RESPONDENT PREFERS TO SELF-COMLPETE, OFFER SELF-COMPLETION FORM AND ENTER CODE.

Interviewer asked section..1
Respondent accepted self-completion form...2
Self-completion now keyed by interviewer...3

Ask all (except proxy respondents)
(DVAge □ 18   or   Selfcom2 = 1 or 3)

313.   DrinkNow   Do you ever drink alcohol nowadays, including drinks you brew or make at home?

Yes...1
No..2

Ask if does not drink nowadays
(DrinkNow = 2)

314.   DrinkAny   Could I just check, does that mean you never have an alcoholic drink nowadays, or do you have an alcoholic drink very occasionally, perhaps for medicinal purposes or on special occasions like Christmas or New Year?

Very occasionally..1
Never..2

Ask if never drinks
(DrinkAny = 2)

315.   TeeTotal   Have you always been a non-drinker, or did you stop drinking for some reason?

Always a non-drinker...1
Used to drink but stopped..2

Ask if respondent has always been a non-drinker
(TeeTotal = 1)

316.   NonDrink   What would you say is the MAIN reason you have always been a non-drinker?

     Religious reasons...1
     Don't like it..2
     Parent's advice/influence...3
     Health reasons...4
     Can't afford it...5
     Other...6

Ask if respondent used to drink but stopped
(TeeTotal = 2)

317.   StopDrin   What would you say was the MAIN reason you stopped drinking?

     Religious reasons...1
     Don't like it..2
     Parent's advice/influence...3
     Health reasons...4
     Can't afford it...5
     Other...6

Ask if respondent drinks at all nowadays
(DrinkNow = 1   or   DrinkAny = 1)

318.   DrinkAmt   I'm going to read out a few descriptions about the amounts of alcohol people drink, and I'd like you to say which one fits you best. Would you say you:

     hardly drink at all...1
     drink a little...2
     drink a moderate amount..3
     drink quite a lot..4
     or drink heavily...5

DRINKING OVER LAST 12 MONTHS (Questions 316 –347)

Ask if respondent drinks at all nowadays
(DrinkNow = 1   or   DrinkAny = 1)

319.   Intro   I'd like to ask you whether you have drunk different types of alcoholic drink in the last 12 months.

I'd like to hear about ALL types of alcoholic drinks you have had.
If you are not sure whether a drink you have had goes into a category, please let me know. I do not need to know about non-alcoholic or low alcohol drinks.

THE HELP KEYS GIVE YOU MORE INFORMATION ABOUT WHAT SHOULD BE INCLUDED AT THE DIFFERENT DRINKS CATEGORIES.

320.   NBeer   SHOWCARD 20

I'd like to ask you first about normal strength beer or cider which has less than 6% alcohol. How often have you had a drink of normal strength beer, lager, stout, cider or shandy (excluding cans and bottles of shandy) during the last 12 months?

NORMAL = LESS THAN 6% ALCOHOL BY VOLUME.
IF RESPONDENT DOES NOT KNOW WHETHER BEER ETC DRUNK IS STRONG OR NORMAL, INCLUDE HERE AS NORMAL.

USE HELP SCREEN FOR OTHER DRINKS TO BE INCLUDED HERE.

Almost every day........1
5 or 6 days a week........2
3 or 4 days a week........3
once or twice a week........4
once or twice a month........5
once every couple of months........6
once or twice a year........7
not at all in last 12 months........8

Ask if respondent drank normal strength beer or cider at all in last 12 months
(NBeer = 1 - 7)

321.　NBeerM　　　How much NORMAL STRENGTH BEER, LAGER, STOUT, CIDER or SHANDY (excluding cans and bottles of shandy) have you usually drunk on any one day during the last 12 months?

CODE MEASURES THAT YOU ARE GOING TO USE.
PROBE IF NECESSARY.
CODE ALL THAT APPLY.

Half pints...1
Small cans...2
Large cans...3
Bottles 4

For each type of measure of normal strength beer

ASK OR RECORD

322.　NBeerQ　　　How many (half pints/ small cans/ large cans/ bottles) of NORMAL STRENGTH BEER, LAGER, STOUT, CIDER or SHANDY (excluding cans and bottles of shandy) have you usually drunk on any one day during the last 12 months?

1..97

Ask if respondent drinks at all nowadays
(Drinknow = 1   or   DrinkAny = 1)

323. SBeer   SHOWCARD 20

Now I'd like to ask you about STRONG BEER OR CIDER which has 6% or more alcohol (e.g. Tennants Extra, Special Brew, Diamond White). How often have you had a drink of strong BEER, LAGER, STOUT or CIDER during the last 12 months?

STRONG=6% AND OVER ALCOHOL BY VOLUME.
IF RESPONDENT DOES NOT KNOW WHETHER BEER ETC DRUNK IS STRONG OR NORMAL, INCLUDE AS NORMAL STRENGTH AT NBEER ABOVE.
USE HELP SCREEN FOR OTHER DRINKS TO BE INCLUDED HERE.

Almost every day...1
5 or 6 days a week...2
3 or 4 days a week...3
once or twice a week..4
once or twice a month...5
once every couple of months..6
once or twice a year..7
not at all in last 12 months...8

Ask if respondent drank strong beer or cider at all in last 12 months
(SBeer = 1 - 7)

324. SBeerM   How much STRONG BEER, LAGER, STOUT or CIDER have you usually drank on any one day during the last 12 months?

CODE MEASURES THAT YOU ARE GOING TO USE.
PROBE IF NECESSARY.
CODE ALL THAT APPLY.

Half pints..1
Small cans..2
Large cans..3
Bottles...4

For each type of measure of strong beer

ASK OR RECORD

325.   SBeerQ   How many (half pints/ small cans/ large cans/ bottles) of STRONG BEER, LAGER, STOUT or CIDER have you usually drunk on any one day during the last 12 months?

1..97

Ask if respondent drinks at all nowadays
(Drinknow = 1   or   DrinkAny = 1)

SHOWCARD 20

326.   Spirits   How often have you had a drink of SPIRITS OR LIQUEURS, such as Gin, Whisky, Brandy, Rum, Vodka, Advocaat or cocktails during the last 12 months?

USE HELP SCREEN FOR OTHER DRINKS TO BE INCLUDED HERE

Almost every day...1
5 or 6 days a week...2
3 or 4 days a week...3
once or twice a week..4
once or twice a month..5
once every couple of months...6
once or twice a year...7
not at all in last 12 months...8

Ask if respondent drank spirits at all in the last 12 months
(Spirits = 1 – 7)

327.   SpritsQ   How much SPIRITS OR LIQUEURS, such as Gin, Whisky, Brandy, Rum, Vodka, Advocaat or cocktails have you usually drunk on any one day during the last 12 months?

CODE THE NUMBER OF SINGLES - COUNT DOUBLES AS TWO SINGLES.

1..97

Ask if respondent drinks at all nowadays
(Drinknow = 1　or　DrinkAny = 1)

SHOWCARD 20

328.　Sherry　　How often have you had a drink of SHERRY OR MARTINI including Port, Vermouth, Cinzano and Dubonnet, during the last 12 months?

USE HELP SCREEN FOR OTHER DRINKS TO BE INCLUDED HERE

Almost every day...1
5 or 6 days a week..2
3 or 4 days a week..3
once or twice a week...4
once or twice a month...5
once every couple of months..6
once or twice a year..7
not at all in last 12 months...8

Ask if respondent drank sherry at all in the last 12 months
(Sherry = 1 –7)

329.　SherryQ　　How much SHERRY OR MARTINI, including Port, Vermouth, Cinzano and Dubonnet have you usually drunk on any one day during the last 12 months?

CODE THE NUMBER OF GLASSES

1..97

Ask if respondent drinks at all nowadays
(Drinknow = 1   or   DrinkAny = 1)

SHOWCARD 20

330.   Wine   How often have you had a drink of WINE, including Babycham and Champagne, during the last 12 months?

USE HELP SCREEN FOR OTHER DRINKS TO BE INCLUDED HERE

Almost every day...1
5 or 6 days a week...2
3 or 4 days a week...3
once or twice a week..4
once or twice a month..5
once every couple of months..6
once or twice a year...7
not at all in last 12 months...8

Ask if respondent drank wine at all in the last 12 months
(Wine = 1 –7)

331.   Wine   How much WINE, including Babycham and Champagne, have you usually drunk on any one day during the last 12 months?

CODE THE NUMBER OF GLASSES.

1..97

332.   BWineQ2   Were those ...

RUNNING PROMPT.

Small Glasses (approx. 125ml)...1
Standard (approx. 175ml)...2
Or Large Glasses (approx. 250ml)..3
Bottles (Spontaneous Only)...4
Don't Know (Spontaneous Only..5

Ask if respondent drinks at all nowadays
(Drinknow = 1 or DrinkAny = 1)

SHOWCARD 20

333. Pops How often have you had a drink of ALCOPOPS (i.e. alcoholic lemonade, alcoholic colas or other alcoholic fruit-or-herb-flavoured drinks for e.g. Smirnoff Ice, Bacardi Breezer, WKD, Metz etc), during the last 12 months?

USE HELP SCREEN FOR OTHER DRINKS TO BE INCLUDED HERE

Almost every day...1
5 or 6 days a week..2
3 or 4 days a week..3
once or twice a week...4
once or twice a month 5
once every couple of months...6
once or twice a year..7
not at all in last 12 months..8

Ask if respondent drank Alcopops at all in the last 12 months
(Pops = 1 – 7)

334. PopsQ How much ALCOPOPS (i.e. alcoholic lemonade, alcoholic colas or other alcoholic fruit-or-herb-flavoured drinks) have you usually drunk on any one day during the last 12 months?

CODE THE NUMBER OF BOTTLES
1..97

Ask if respondent drinks at all nowadays
(Drinknow = 1 or DrinkAny = 1)

SHOWCARD 20

335.   DrinkOft   Thinking now about all kinds of drinks, how often have you had an alcoholic drink of any kind during the last 12 months?

Almost every day..1
5 or 6 days a week...2
3 or 4 days a week..3
once or twice a week...4
once or twice a month...5
once every couple of months...6
once or twice a year..7
not at all in last 12 months..8

End of 12 month drinking section

Ask if respondent drinks at all nowadays
(DrinkNow = 1 or DrinkAny = 1)

336.   DrinkL7   I'd like to ask you whether you have drank different types of alcoholic drink in the last 7 days.

I'd like to hear about ALL types of alcoholic drinks you have had.
I do not need to know about non-alcoholic or low alcohol drinks.

Did you have an alcoholic drink in the seven days ending yesterday?

Yes...1
No...2

Ask if respondent has had an alcoholic drink in the last week
(DrinkL7 = 1)

337.   DrnkDay   On how many days out of the last seven did you have an alcoholic drink?

1..7

Ask if respondent had an alcoholic drink on two or more days last week
(DrnkDay = 2-7)

338. DrnkSame   Did you drink more on some days than others, or did you drink about the same on each of those days?

Drank more on one/some day(s) than other(s)......................................1
Same each day...2

Ask if respondent had an alcoholic drink last week
(DrinkL7 = 1)

339. WhichDay   Which day (last week) did you last have an alcoholic drink?

Sunday...1
Monday..2
Tuesday...3
Wednesday..4
Thursday..5
Friday...6
Saturday...7

Ask if respondent has had an alcoholic drink in the last week
(DrinkL7 = 1)

SHOWCARD 21

340. DrnkTyp   Thinking about last (DAY AT WHICHDAY) what types of drink did you have that day?

If you are not sure whether a drink you have had goes into a category, please let me know.

CODE ALL THAT APPLY

Normal strength beer/lager/cider/shandy..1
Strong beer/lager/cider...2
Spirits or liqueurs..3
Sherry or Martini...4
Wine..5
Alcopops...6

Ask if respondent drank 'normal strength beer/lager/cider/shandy' on that day
(DrnkTyp = 1)

341. NBrL7   Still thinking about last (DAY AT WHICHDAY), how much NORMAL
STRENGTH BEER, LAGER, STOUT, CIDER or SHANDY (excluding
cans and bottles of shandy) did you drink that day?

CODE MEASURES THAT YOU ARE GOING TO USE,
PROBE IF NECESSARY.
CODE ALL THAT APPLY.

Half pints..1
Small cans...2
Large cans...3
Bottles..4

For each measure mentioned at NBrL7

ASK OR RECORD

342. NBrL7Q   How many (Answer AT NBrL7) of NORMAL STRENGTH BEER,
LAGER, STOUT, CIDER OR SHANDY (EXCLUDING CANS AND BOTTLES
OF SHANDY) did you drink that day?
1..97

Ask if respondent drank 'strong beer/lager/cider' on that day
(DrnkTyp = 2)

343. SBrL7   Still thinking about last (DAY AT WHICHDAY), how much STRONG
BEER, LAGER, STOUT OR CIDER did you drink that day?

CODE MEASURES THAT YOU ARE GOING TO USE
PROBE IF NECESSARY.
CODE ALL THAT APPLY.

Half pints..1
Small cans...2
Large cans...3
Bottles..4

For each measure mentioned at SBrL7

ASK OR RECORD

344.   SBrL7Q   How many (Answer AT SBrL7) of STRONG BEER, LAGER, STOUT or CIDER did you drink on that day?

                         1..97

Ask if respondent drank spirits or liqueurs on that day
(DrnkTyp = 3)

345.   SpirL7   Still thinking about last (DAY AT WHICHDAY), how much spirits or liqueurs, such as Whisky, Brandy, Rum, Vodka, Advocaat or cocktails did you drink on that day?

                         CODE THE NUMBER OF SINGLES - COUNT DOUBLES AS TWO SINGLES
                         1..97

Ask if respondent drank Sherry or Martini on that day
(DrnkTyp = 4)

346.   ShryL7   Still thinking about last (DAY AT WHICHDAY), how much Sherry or Martini, including Port, Vermouth, Cinzano and Dubonnet did you drink on that day?

                         CODE THE NUMBER OF GLASSES

                         1..97

Ask if respondent drank wine on that day
(DrnkTyp = 5)

347.   WineL7   Still thinking about last (DAY AT WHICHDAY), how much Wine, including Babycham and Champagne, did you drink on that day?

                         CODE THE NUMBER OF GLASSES
                         1 BOTTLE = 6 GLASSES. 1 LITRE = 8 GLASSES.

                         1..97

348.   BWine2   Were those ...

RUNNING PROMPT.

Small Glasses (approx. 125ml)..1
Standard (approx. 175ml)..2
Or Large Glasses (approx. 250ml)...3
Bottles (Spontaneous Only)...4
Don't Know (Spontaneous Only...5

Ask if respondent drank Alcopops on that day
(DrnkTyp = 6)

349.   PopsL7   Still thinking about last (DAY AT WHICHDAY), how much Alcopops
(i.e. Smirnoff Ice, Bacardi Breezer, WKD, Metz) did you drink on that day?

CODE THE NUMBER OF BOTTLES

1..97

Ask if respondent drinks at all nowadays
(Drinknow = 1 or Drinkany = 1)

350.   DrAmount   Compared to five years ago, would you say that, on the whole, you drink...

RUNNING PROMPT

More...1
about the same...2
or less nowadays..3

FAMILY INFORMATION

Ask this section of all persons aged 16-59 (except proxy respondents)

351.   FamIntro   The next section consists of a series of questions about Family Information. (Not asked of proxy respondents)

To all married couples
(xMarSta = 2 or 4)

352.   ChkFIA   INTERVIEWER CODE

Respondent is married and spouse IS a household member....................1
Respondent is married but their spouse is NOT a household member.........2

Ask if married, but partner NOT a household member
(ChkFIA = 2)

353.   HusbAway   INTRODUCE AS NECESSARY

May I check, is your husband/ wife absent because he/ she usually works away from home, the marriage has broken down or for some other reason?

Usually works away (include Armed Forces, Merchant Navy)...................1
Marriage broken down/ separated...2
Other reason...3

To all

354.   SelfCom3   The next set of questions is about family information, which you may wish to complete on your own.

EXPLAIN THAT THESE QUESTIONS COVER ANY CURRENT AND PREVIOUS MARRIAGES AND PERIODS OF LIVING TOGETHER AND FOR WOMEN THERE ARE QUESTIONS ABOUT ANY CHILDREN THEY HAVE HAD.

-IF YOU HAVE CHOSEN LAPTOP SELF-COMPLETION PLEASE EXPLAIN THAT INSTRUCTIONS WILL APPEAR ON THE SCREEN AND THEN WORK THROUGH THE FIRST 5 QUESTIONS WITH RESPONDENT. REMEMBER TO PRESS <F2> TO SAVE WORK BEFORE HANDING OVER LAPTOP.

-IF YOU HAVE CHOSEN PAPER SELF-COMPLETION OFFER THE FORM TO RESPONDENT.

Respondent accepted self-completion by laptop NOW............................1
Will complete later..2
Respondent accepted self-completion by paper....................................3
Section read and entered by interviewer..4
Interviewer now entering data from paper questionnaire.........................5
Respondent refused whole section...6

Ask if Respondent accepts self-completion by laptop (CASI) (SelfCom3 = 1)

[TestQ1 to TestQ5 are only test questions for the respondent so that they can practice answering different types of questions on the laptop.]

355.   TestQ1   The next section consists of a series of questions for you to go through with the interviewer

356.   TestQ2   How old are you?

Please enter the number of years

00..99

357.   TestQ3   Can you tell me the year in which you were born?

Enter year in a 4 digit format e.g. 2000

1900..2009

358.   TestQ4   Can you tell me the month in which you were born?

Enter the month

January...1
February...2
March...3
April...4
May..5
June...6
July..7
August..8
September...9
October...10
November..11
December..12

359.   TestQ5   Can you tell me your date of birth?

Enter in full e.g. 01/02/1976

360.   TESTEND   The next section consists of questions on family information and are for you to complete alone. If you have any problems please ask the interviewer for help

Ask people who have been married
(xMarsta = 2, 4, 5 or 6)

361.   AreWed   Earlier you said you were married/ separated/ divorced/ widowed. Thinking of this/ your last marriage, are/ were you legally married or are/ were you simply living together as a couple?

Legally married..1
Living together as a couple...2

**Ask if respondent was legally married
(AreWed = 1)**

362.   HowWed   Did you get married with a religious ceremony of some kind, or at a registry office or approved premises?

Religious ceremony of some kind...1
Civil marriage in register office or approved premises.............................2
Both religious ceremony and registry office/ approved premises...............3

**Ask if respondent has been legally married
(AreWed = 1)**

363.   NumMar   How many times have you been legally married?

PLEASE INCLUDE PRESENT MARRIAGE

1..7

**Ask all cohabiting couples, including same sex couples (exc. couples now separated)
(Livewth = 1 or 3   or   AreWed = 2)**

364.   ClYr   THIS QUESTION REFERS TO YOUR CURRENT RELATIONSHIP WHERE YOU ARE LIVING WITH SOMEONE AS A COUPLE BUT ARE NOT LEGALLY MARRIED

ENTER YEAR IN 4 DIGIT FORMAT E.G. 2000

Which year did you and your partner start living together as a couple?

1900..2009

365.   CLMon   THIS QUESTION REFERS TO YOUR CURRENT RELATIONSHIP WHERE YOU ARE LIVING WITH SOMEONE AS A COUPLE BUT ARE NOT LEGALLY MARRIED

ENTER MONTH

Which month did you and your partner start living together as a couple?

1..12

Ask cohabiting couples, including same sex couples, but not separated, divorced or widowed respondents
(Livewth = 1 or 3 OR Arewed = 2 AND is NOT separated, divorced or widowed)

366. ClMar · Have you ever been legally married?

Yes...1
No..2

Ask if respondent has been legally married
(ClMar = 1)

367. ClNumMar How many times have you been legally married altogether?

1..7

Ask of all who are, or have been, legally married
(NumMar >= 1 or ClNumMar >= 1)

368. Intro THE NEXT SCREEN CONSISTS OF A TABLE OF MARRIAGES FOR (NAME).
PLEASE ENTER DETAILS OF MARRIAGES STARTING WITH THE EARLIEST AND ENDING WITH THE CURRENT OR MOST RECENT.

For each marriage

369. YrMar In which year were you married?

ENTER YEAR IN 4 DIGIT FORMAT E.G. 2000

1900..2009

370. MonMar In which month in that year (year) were you married?

ENTER MONTH

1..12

371.   LvTgthr   Before getting married did you and your husband/wife live together as a couple?

Yes...1
No...2

Ask if lived as a couple before getting married
(LvTgthr = 1)

372.   YrLvTg   In which year did you start living together?

ENTER YEAR IN 4 DIGIT FORM E.G.2000

1900..2009

373.   MonLvTg   which month in that year (year) did you start living together?

ENTER MONTH

1..12

Ask all who are or have been legally married
(NumMar >= 1   or   ClNumMar >= 1)

For last marriage entered

374.   Current   Thinking about your present/ most recent/ first marriage, is this marriage current, or has it ended through death, divorce or separation?

Current...1
Ended through death, divorce or separation...2

Ask if marriage ended
(Current = 2   or   marriage number less than total marriages)

375.   HowEnded   ASK OR RECORD

Did your marriage end in ...

RUNNING PROMPT

Death...1
Divorce...2
or separation..3

Ask if marriage ended in death
(HowEnded = 1)

376.   YrDie   in which year did your husband/wife die?

ENTER YEAR IN 4 DIGIT FORMAT E.G. 2000

1900-2009

377.   MonDie   in which month of that year (year) did your husband/wife die?
ENTER MONTH

1..12

Ask if marriage ended in divorce or separation
(HowEnded = 2 or 3)

378.   YrSep   in which year did you stop living together as a couple?

ENTER YEAR IN 4 DIGIT FORMAT E.G. 2000

1900-2009

379.   MonSep   in which month of that year (*year*) did you stop living together?

ENTER MONTH

1..12

**Ask if marriage ended in divorce
(HowEnded =2)**

380. YrDiv

in which year was your decree absolute granted?

ENTER YEAR IN 4 DIGIT FORMAT E.G. 2000

1900-2009

381. MonDiv

in which month of that year (year) was your decree absolute granted?

ENTER MONTH

1..12

**Ask if respondent is aged 16-59
(DVAge = 16-59)**

382. Cohab

Have you had any (other) relationships in which you lived together with someone as a couple but did not get married?

Yes...1
No..2

**Ask if respondent is aged 16-59, and has had previous cohabiting Relationships
DVAge = 16-59 & Cohab = 1)**

383. Numcohab

How many relationships have you had altogether in which you lived together with someone as a couple but did not get married?
(Please exclude your present relationship)

1..7

384. Intro

Now I would like to ask you some questions about (the first three of these relationships/ this relationship/ these relationships).

(RECORD DETAILS OF THE FIRST THREE RELATIONSHIPS, STARTING WITH THE FIRST)

Ask each question for the first, second and third relationship

385.   TimeCoY1   Thinking about the first/second/third relationships where you lived with someone as a couple but did not get married......how long did you live together in terms of years and months?

PLEASE ENTER NUMBER OF YEARS ONLY

0..99

386.   TimecoM1   NOW ENTER NUMBER OF MONTHS

0..11

387.   WhencoY1   Can you tell me the year in which you started or stopped living together as a couple with your partner?

ENTER THE YEAR

1950..2009

388.   WhencoM1   Can you tell me the month in which you started or stopped living together as a couple with your partner?

INTERVIEWER ENTER THE MONTH

1..12

389.   Starten1   INTERVIEWER: IS THIS WHEN THE RESPONDENT AND HIS/HER PARTNER STARTED LIVING TOGETHER OR FINISHED LIVING TOGETHER AS A COUPLE?

Started living together...1
Finished living together...2

390.   Othdate1   If that was the date you started/stopped living together, then you stopped/started living together in ...(month) ...(year)
Does that seem about right?

Yes...1
No...2

Ask if computed start/end date not correct
(Othdate1 = 2)

391.   RghtdtM1   (What is the correct date?)

INTERVIEWER ENTER THE MONTH

1..12

392.   RghtdtY1   What is the correct date?

ENTER THE YEAR

1950..2009

Ask if respondent is aged 16-59, and has had previous cohabiting relationships
(DVAge = 16-59   &   Cohab = 1)

Ask each question for the first, second and third relationship

393.   EndCoh1   You said you stopped living together in …(month) …(year) May I just check was this when you stopped living together in the same accommodation, when the relationship ended or both?

Stopped living in the same accommodation only...................................1
End of the relationship only...2
Both happened at the same time...3
Partner died...4

Ask if date given is when they stopped living together
(EndCoh1 = 1)

394.   EndrelY1   In which year did the relationship end?

ENTER THE YEAR

1950..2009

395.   EndrelM1   In which month did the relationship end?

ENTER THE MONTH

1..12

Ask if the date given is when relationship ended
(EndCoh1 = 2)

396.   EndlivY1   In which year did you stop living in the same accommodation?

ENTER THE YEAR

1950..2009

397.   EndlivM1   In which month did you stop living in the same accommodation?

  INTERVIEWER ENTER THE MONTH

1..12

Ask respondents aged 16-59
(DVAge = 16-59)
***If respondent is female (sex=2) also include ***

398.   Children   ASK OR RECORD

Do you have any children in the household?

(INCLUDES ADULT CHILDREN)
(*AND/OR STEP OR FOSTER CHILDREN.)

(Respondent instruction)
(IF APPROPRIATE PLEASE INCLUDE ANY CHILDREN FROM YOUR PARTNER'S PREVIOUS RELATIONSHIP)

Yes..1
No...2

Ask women who have a child in the household
(Sex = 2   &   Children =1)

399.   StpChldF   (The next questions are about the family.) Do you have any step, foster, or adopted children of any age living with you? (For stepchildren, please include any children of any age from your husband/partner's previous marriage or relationship.)

Yes..1
No...2

Ask men who have a child in the household
(Sex = 1 & Children =1)

400. StpChldM Do you have any stepchildren of any age living with you? (Please include any children of any age from your wife/partner's previous marriage or relationship.)

Yes...1
No..2

Ask women with a step, foster or adopted child
(StpChldF = 1)

401. NumStepF How many step children live with you? (Please include children of any age from your husband/partner's previous marriage or relationship.)

0..7

Ask men with a stepchild living with them
(StpChldM=1)

402. NumStepM How many step children live with you? (Please include children of any age age your husband/partner's previous marriage or relationship.)

1..7

Ask women with a step, foster or adopted child living with them
(StpChldF = 1)

403. NumFost How many foster children have you living with you altogether?

0..7

404. NumAdop How many adopted children have you living with you altogether?

0..7

Ask women with a step, foster or adopted child, or a man with a stepchild living with them
(StpChldF = 1 or StpChldM=1)

405. StepInt THE NEXT SCREEN CONSISTS OF A TABLE FOR THE STEP-CHILDREN (AND ADOPTED AND FOSTER- CHILDREN) OF (NAME) PLEASE ENTER DETAILS FOR EACH CHILD.

Ask for each step/foster/adopted child

406.　ChildNo　　From the list below, please copy the number of the first/second step/foster/adopted child.

INCLUDES ADULT CHILDREN

1..20

407.　ChldType　　Thinking about name. Is name your step-child, your adopted-child or are they your foster-child?

Step...1
Foster..2
Adopted...3

408.　ChLivYr　　Please state the year (CHILDS NAME) started living with you.

ENTER YEAR (IN 4 DIGIT FORMAT, E.G. 2000)

1900..2009

409.　ChLivMon　　Please state the month (CHILDS NAME) started living with you.

ENTER MONTH

1..12

Ask all women
(Sex = 2)

410.　Baby　　ASK OR RECORD
EXCLUDE: ANY STILLBORN.
INCLUDE: ALL CHILDREN RESPONDENT HAS GIVEN BIRTH TO.

Have you ever given birth to a baby - even one who only lived for a short time?

Yes..1
No..2

Ask women who have had a baby
(Baby = 1)

411.   NumBaby   EXCLUDE: ANY STILLBORN

How many children have you given birth to, including any who live somewhere else and any who have died since birth?

1..20

412.   BirthInt   In the next set of questions, we want you to record some details about all the children you have ever given birth to. This includes children:
who live here;
children who live somewhere else, such as adult children; and
children who have died since birth.
Please enter details for each child, in the order in which they were born, starting with the one you gave birth to first.

For each child

413.   BirthDte   Please enter the Date of birth

PLEASE ENTER IN DATE OF BIRTH ORDER - ELDEST FIRST, YOUNGEST LAST.

AS A GUIDE, THE D.O.B. OF EACH HOUSEHOLD MEMBER IS LISTED BELOW

414.   BirthSex   Sex of child

Male..1
Female..2

415.   ChldLive   Is this child living with you?

Yes..1
No, lives elsewhere..2
No, deceased..3

Ask all women aged 16-49
(Sex = 2 & DVAge = 16-49)

416.   Pregnant   May I just check...

Are you pregnant now?

Yes..1
No/unsure..2

SHOWCARD 22

417.   MoreChld   Do you think that you will have any (more) children (after the one you are expecting)? Could you choose your answers from this card.

Yes..1
Probably yes..2
Probably not..3
No...4
Don't know..5

Ask if respondent answered don't know above
(MoreChld = DK)

418.   ProbMore   On the whole do you think...

You will probably have any/more children..1
Or you will probably not have any/more children.................................2

Ask if respondent is likely to have more children
(MoreChld = 1 or 2 or ProbMore = 1)

419.   TotChld   How many children do you think you will have born to you in total, including those you have had already who are still alive/ (and) the one you are expecting?

1..14

420.   NextAge   How old do you think you will be when you have your first/next baby (after the one you are expecting)?

1..97

FINANCIAL SITUATION

This section to be asked of household, not individuals
Ask HRP

421. Repay   The next section has questions on your Household's financial situation.

Do you or anyone in your household have to repay any credit card, hire purchase or other loans (that is, excluding mortgage repayments or other loans connected with the accommodation)?

THE QUESTIONS ON THE FINANCIAL SITUATION OF THE HOUSEHOLD MAY BE ANSWERED BY THE HRP OR SPOUSE OR RESPONSIBLE ADULT

Yes...1
No..2

Ask if anyone in the household has any loans to repay
(Repay = 1)

422. BurdRepy   To what extent is the repayment of such loans and the interest a financial burden or struggle for your household?

Would you say it is...

RUNNING PROMPT

a heavy burden/ struggle..1
a slight burden/ struggle...2
or not a burden/ struggle at all..3

Ask all households

SHOWCARD 23

423.   Afford   Looking at this card, can I just check whether your household could afford the following?

CODE ALL THAT APPLY

To pay for a week's annual holiday away from home...............................1
To eat meat, chicken or fish (or vegetarian equivalent) every second day....2
To pay an unexpected, but necessary, expense of £500.........................3
To keep your home adequately warm...4
Afford none of these (SPONTANEOUS ONLY)......................................5

424.   EndsMeet   A household may have different sources of income and more than one household member may contribute to it.

Thinking of your household's total monthly or weekly income, is your household able to make ends meet, that is pay your usual expenses.....

IF NOT MAKING ENDS MEET, CODE AS 'WITH GREAT DIFFICULTY' (CODE 1)

RUNNING PROMPT

with great difficulty...1
with difficulty...2
with some difficulty...3
fairly easily..4
easily...5
or very easily...6

425.   LowestIn   Thinking of the household's basic needs, what is the very minimum amount of money the household needs each month to pay its usual expenses?

Please answer in relation to the present circumstances of your household, and what you consider as usual expenses.

0.00..999999.99

426.   HowLong   For how long did this cover?

one week...1
two weeks...2
three weeks...3
four weeks...4
calendar month..5
two calendar months..7
eight times a year..8
nine times a year...9
ten times a year...10
three months/13 weeks...13
six months/26 weeks...26
one year/12 months/52 weeks..52
less than one week..90
one off/lump sum 95
none of these: EXPLAIN IN A NOTE <CTRL> + <M>.........................97

INCOME

Ask all adults (except proxy respondents)

SHOWCARD 24

427. Intro　　The next set of questions are about benefits.

Continue with benefits questions……………………………………………1

Ask if continuing with benefits questions
(Intro = 1)

SHOWCARD 24

428. Ben1Q　　Looking at this card, are you at present receiving any state benefits
in your own right: that is, where you are the named recipient?

CODE ALL THAT APPLY

Child Benefit………………………………………………………………………1
Guardian's Allowance……………………………………………………………2
Carer's Allowance………………………………………………………………3
Retirement pension (National Insurance), or Old Person's pension…………4
Widow's pension, Bereavement Allowance or Widowed Parents
(formerly Widowed Mother's) Allowance……………………………………5
War Disablement Pension or War Widow's/Widower's Pension
(and any related allowances)…………………………………………………6
Severe Disablement Allowance………………………………………………7
None of these……………………………………………………………………8

SHOWCARD 25

429. DisBen   And looking at this card, are you at present receiving any of the state benefits shown on this card - either in your own right, or on behalf of someone else in the household?

CODE ALL THAT APPLY

Care component of Disability Living Allowance......................................1
Mobility component of Disability Living Allowance...............................2
Attendance Allowance..3
None of these...4

Ask if receiving Attendance Allowance
(DisBen = 3)

430. Attall   Is this paid as part of your retirement pension or do you receive a separate payment?

Paid as part of pension..1
Separate payment...2

Ask all except proxy respondents

SHOWCARD 26

CODE ALL THAT APPLY

431. Ben2Q   Now looking at this card, are you at present receiving any of these benefits in your own right - that is, where you are the named recipient?

Job Seekers' Allowance (JSA)...1
Pension Credit..2
Income Support...3
Incapacity Benefit..4
Maternity Allowance...5
Industrial Injury Disablement Benefit..6
None of these...7

Ask all except proxy respondents

SHOWCARD 27

432　TxCred　　Now looking at this card, are you at present receiving any of these Tax Credits, in your own right: please include any lump sum payments received in the last six months?

Working Tax Credit (excluding any childcare tax credit)...........................1
Child Tax Credit (including any childcare tax credit)...............................2
None of these...3

SHOWCARD 28

433.　Inclus　　Did your last wage/salary include any of the items on this card?

CODE ALL THAT APPLY.

Statutory Sick Pay..1
Statutory Maternity Pay..2
Statutory Paternity Pay...3
Statutory Adoption Pay..4
Income Tax Refund..5
Mileage Allowance or fixed allowance for motoring...............................6
Motoring Expenses Refund..7
Tax credit...8
None of these..9

Ask all (except proxy respondents)

SHOWCARD 29

434.　Ben12m　　In the last 12 months, have you received any of the things shown on this card, in your own right?

A grant from the Social Fund for funeral expenses.................................1
A grant from Social Fund for maternity expenses/Sure Start
Maternity Grant...2
A Social Fund loan or Community Care grant.......................................3
None of these..4

Ask all aged 60 or over
(DVAge > 60)

435.   Winter   In the last 12 months have you received a winter fuel payment in your own right?

Yes...1

No..2

Ask all (except proxy respondents)

SHOWCARD 30

436.   Ben6m   In the last 6 months have you received any of the things on this card in your own right?

'Extended payment' of Housing Benefit/rent rebate,
or Council Tax Benefit (4 week payment only)......................................2
Widow's payment or Bereavement payment – lump sum.........................3
Child Maintenance Bonus..4
Lone Parent's Benefit Run-On..5
Any National Insurance or State Benefit not mentioned earlier.................6
Work-Search Premium...7
In-Work credit..8
Return to work payment..9
None of these...10

Code for each benefit mentioned
(Ben1Q, DisBen, Ben2Q, TxCred, Ben12m, Ben6m)

437.   BAmt   How much did you get last time?

IF COMBINED WITH ANOTHER BENEFIT AND UNABLE TO GIVE
SEPARATE AMOUNT, ENTER `Don't know` <CTRL> + <K>

0.00..997.00

If don't know or refusal at the amount of benefit received
(Ben1Amt = DK or Refusal)

438.   BAmtDK   INTERVIEWER: IS THIS `DON'T KNOW` BECAUSE IT'S PAID IN
COMBINATION WITH ANOTHER BENEFIT, AND YOU CANNOT
ESTABLISH A SEPARATE AMOUNT?

Yes (Please give full details in a Note)..1

No..2

Ask if amount of benefit received was greater than zero
(Ben1Amt > 0.00)

439.   Bpd   How long did this cover?

one week...1
two weeks..2
three weeks..3
four weeks..4
calendar month..5
two calendar months...7
eight times a year...8
nine times a year..9
ten times a year..10
three months/13 weeks...13
six months/26 weeks..26
one year/12 months/52 weeks..52
less than one week..90
one off lump sum..95
none of these: Explain in a note <Ctrl> + <M>..97

Ask if receiving Retirement pension or old person's pension
(Ben1Q = 4)

440.   BenUs   Is this the amount you usually get?

Yes...1
No..2
No such thing as a usual amount..3

Ask if not usual amount
(BenUs = 2)

441.   BUAmt   How much do you usually get?

IF COMBINED WITH ANOTHER BENEFIT AND UNABLE TO GIVE
SEPARATE AMOUNT, ENTER DON'T KNOW <CTRL+K>

0.00..997.00

442.   BUPd   How long does this cover?

one week..1
two weeks..2
three weeks...3
four weeks...4
calendar month...5
two calendar months..7
eight times a year...8
nine times a year..9
ten times a year...10
three months/13 weeks...13
six months/26 weeks...26
one year/12 months/52 weeks...52
less than one week...90
one off lump sum..95
none of these...97

Ask if receiving War Disablement Pension or War Widow's Pension
(Ben1Q = 6)

443.   WPentype   Do you receive...

RUNNING PROMPT

War Disablement Pension..1
or War Widow's Pension..2

Ask if receiving CARE component of Disability Living Allowance
(DisBen = 1)

444.   WhoReCar   Whom do you receive it for?

IF CURRENT HOUSEHOLD MEMBER, ENTER PERSON NUMBER
OTHERWISE ENTER 97

1..16, 97

Ask if receiving MOBILITY component of Disability Living Allowance
(DisBen = 2)

445.   WhoReMob   Whom do you receive it for?

IF CURRENT HOUSEHOLD MEMBER, ENTER PERSON NUMBER
OTHERWISE ENTER 97

1..16, 97

Ask if receiving Attendance Allowance
(DisBen = 3)

446.   WhoReAtt   Whom do you receive it for?

IF CURRENT HOUSEHOLD MEMBER, ENTER PERSON NUMBER
OTHERWISE ENTER 97

1..16, 97

Ask all adults

447.　SrcInc08　SHOWCARD 4

This card shows various possible sources of income. Can you please tell me which kinds of income you personally receive?

CODE ALL THAT APPLY

Earnings from employment...1
Earnings from self-employment...2
Pension from former employer..3
Personal Pension...4
State Pension..5
Child benefit...6
Income Support...7
Tax Credits...8
Other state benefits...9
Interest from savings..10
Interest from investments...11
Other kinds of regular allowance from outside the household.................12
Income from rent...13
Other sources..14
No source of income...15

Ask if has a source of income
(SrcInc08=1,2,3,4,5,6,7,8,9,10,11,12,13 or 14)

448.　GrossTel　Thinking of the sources you have mentioned, what is your total personal income before deductions for income tax, National Insurance etc, (that can be weekly, monthly or an annual amount)?

PROMPT ONLY IF NECESSARY. AN ESTIMATE IS ACCEPTABLE

0..99999997

449.　GrssTime　ASK OR RECORD

Is that a weekly, monthly or annual amount?

Weekly...1
Monthly..2

Annually..3

Ask if GrossTel =Refusal or Don't Know

450. TelBand   We put answers into income bands. Would you tell me which band represents your total personal income before all deductions. Is it...

RUNNING PROMPT

Less than £100 a week...1
£100 but less than £200 a week..2
£200 but less than £300 a week..3
£300 but less than £400 a week..4
£400 but less than £500 a week..5
£500 but less than £600 a week..6
£600 but less than £700 a week..7
£700 but less than £800 a week..8
£800 but less than £900 a week..9
£900 but less than £1000 a week...10
Over £1000 a week..11

Ask all (except proxy respondents)

451. OthSrc   SHOWCARD 31

Please tell me if you are receiving any of the following type of regular payments

CODE ALL THAT APPLY

Occupational pensions from former employer(s)....................1
Occupational pensions from a spouse's former employer(s)....................2
Private pensions or annuities..3
Regular redundancy payments from former employer(s)........................4
Government Training Schemes such as YT allowance............................5
None of these..6

Ask if receiving payments from occupational pensions from employer(s)
(OthSrc = 1)

452.   PFEmpNet   In total how much do you receive each month from the occupational pensions) from your former employer(s) AFTER tax is deducted? (i.e. NET)

DO NOT PROBE MONTH. ACCEPT CALENDAR MONTH OR 4 WEEKLY.

0.01..99999.97

453.   PFEmpGrs   In total how much do you receive each month from the occupational pension(s) from your former employer(s) BEFORE tax is deducted? (i.e. GROSS)?

DO NOT PROBE MONTH. ACCEPT CALENDAR MONTH OR 4 WEEKLY.

0.01..99999.97

Ask if receiving payments from occupational pensions from a spouse's former employer(s)
(OthSrc = 2)

454.   SpousNet   In total how much do you receive each month from the occupational penion(s) from your spouse's former employer(s) AFTER tax is deducted? (ie NET)

DO NOT PROBE MONTH. ACCEPT CALENDAR MONTH OR 4 WEEKLY.

0.01..99999.97

455.   SpousGrs   In total how much do you receive each month from the Occupational pension(s) from your spouse's former employer(s) BEFORE tax is deducted? (i.e. GROSS)?

DO NOT PROBE MONTH. ACCEPT CALENDAR MONTH OR 4 WEEKLY.

0.01..99999.97

Ask if receiving payments from private pension(s) or annuities
(OthSrc = 3)

456.   PrivPNet   In total how much do you receive each month from your private pension(s) or annuities tax is deducted? (ie NET)

DO NOT PROBE MONTH. ACCEPT CALENDAR MONTH OR 4 WEEKLY.

0.01..99999.97

457.   PrivPGrs   In total how much do you receive each month from your private pension(s) or annuities BEFORE tax is deducted? (i.e. GROSS)?

DO NOT PROBE MONTH. ACCEPT CALENDAR MONTH OR 4 WEEKLY.

0.01..99999.97

Ask if receiving regular redundancy payments from a former employer(s)
(OthSrc = 4)

458.   RedunNet   In total how much do you receive each month from regular redundancy payments from your former employer(s) AFTER tax is deducted? (i.e. NET)

DO NOT PROBE MONTH. ACCEPT CALENDAR MONTH OR 4 WEEKLY.

0.01..99999.97

459.   RedunGrs   In total how much do you receive each month from regular redundancy payments from your former employer(s) BEFORE tax is deducted? (i.e. GROSS)?

DO NOT PROBE MONTH. ACCEPT CALENDAR MONTH OR 4 WEEKLY.

0.01..99999.97

Ask if receiving payments from Government Training Schemes
(OthSrc = 5)

460.   TrainNet   In total how much do you receive each month from Government Training schemes, such as YT allowance, AFTER tax is deducted?
(ie NET)

DO NOT PROBE MONTH. ACCEPT CALENDAR MONTH OR 4 WEEKLY.

0.01..99999.97

461.   TrainGrs   In total how much do you receive each from Government Training Schemes, such as YT allowance, BEFORE tax is deducted?
(i.e. GROSS)?

DO NOT PROBE MONTH. ACCEPT CALENDAR MONTH OR 4 WEEKLY.

0.01..99999.97

Ask all (except proxy respondents)

462.   ReglrP   SHOWCARD 32

Taking your response from this card, please tell me if you are receiving any of the following type of regular payments

CODE ALL THAT APPLY

Educational grant..1
Regular payments from friends or relatives
outside the household..2
Maintenance, alimony or separation allowance....................................3
None of these...4

Ask if receiving an educational grant
(ReglrP = 1)

463.   EdGrnt   In total how much do you receive from your educational grant
EACH MONTH?

0.01..99999.97

Ask if receiving regular payments from friends or relatives outside household
(RegIrP = 2)

464. RegFr   In total how much do you receive from friends or relatives EACH MONTH?

                     0.01..99999.97

Ask if receiving maintenance, alimony or separation allowance
(RegIrP = 3)

465. RegMa   In total how much do you receive maintenance, alimony or separation allowances EACH MONTH?

                     0.01..99999.97

Ask all (except proxy respondents)

SHOWCARD 33

466. RegOPM   Taking your response from this card, please tell me if you are making any of the following type of regular payments

                     Regular payments to friends or relatives outside the household................2
                     Maintenance, alimony or separation allowance.....................................3
                     None of these...4

Ask if making regular payments to friends or relatives outside household
(RegOPM = 1)

467. RegFro   In total how much do you give to friends or relatives EACH MONTH?

                     0.01..99999.97

Ask if making payments of maintenance, alimony or separation allowance
(RegOPM = 2)

468. RegMaO   In total how much do you pay out in terms of maintenance, alimony or separation allowances EACH MONTH?

                     0.01..99999.97

Ask all (except proxy respondents)

469.   Rentpay   In the 12 months since (DATE), have you received any rent from property, for example, renting out a building, house, a flat, a room or land?

Yes..1
No...2

Ask if respondent is receiving rent
(Rentpay = 1)

470.   RentBF   How much did you receive in the 12 months since (DATE), BEFORE deducting income tax, but after deducting all allowable expenses?

ALLOWABLE EXPENSES INCLUDE INTEREST PAYMENTS, INSURANCE, REPAIRS AND MAINTENANCE, RATES AND SERVICES.

IF A PRECISE FIGURE IS NOT AVAILABLE, KEY D/K

0.01..99999.97

Ask if answered 'Don't know' to above question
(RentBF = Don't know)

SHOWCARD 34

471.   RentBApx   Perhaps you could give an approximate range?

REMIND: LAST 12 MONTHS... BEFORE TAX IS DEDUCTED... BUT AFTER DEDUCTING EXPENSES

Less than £1,000 per year...1
£1,001 to £3,000 per year...2
£3,001 to £5,000 per year...3
£5,001 to £10,000 per year...4
More than £10,000 per year..5

Ask if respondent is receiving rent
(Rentpay = 1)

472.   RentAFT   How much did you receive in the 12 months since (DATE), AFTER
deducting income tax, but after deducting all allowable expenses?

ALLOWABLE EXPENSES INCLUDE INTEREST PAYMENTS,
INSURANCE, REPAIRS AND MAINTENANCE, RATES AND SERVICES.

0.01..99999.97

Ask if answered 'Don't know' to above question
(RentAFT = Don't know)

SHOWCARD 34

473.   RentAApx   Perhaps you could give an approximate range?

REMIND: LAST 12 MONTHS... AFTER TAX IS DEDUCTED... AFTER
DEDUCTING EXPENSES

Less than £1,000 per year...1
£1,001 to £3,000 per year...2
£3,001 to £5,000 per year...3
£5,001 to £10,000 per year...4
More than £10,000 per year..5

**The next group of questions are only asked of those in paid work,
(including those temporarily away from job or on a government
scheme), but excluding unpaid family workers.**
(Wrking = 1   OR   JbAway = 1   OR   Stat = 1 or 3)
**The routing instructions above each question apply only to those who
meet the above criteria.**

Ask if an employee
(Stat = 1)

474. PyPeriod   The next questions are about earnings from your main job.

How long a period does your wage/salary usually cover?

one week..1
two weeks..2
three weeks..3
four weeks..4
calendar month...5
two calendar months..7
eight times a year...8
nine times a year..9
ten times a year..10
three months/13 weeks...13
six months/26 weeks...26
one year/12 months/52 weeks...52
less than one week...90
one off lump sum...95
None of these: Explain in a note <Ctrl> + <M>.....................97

Ask all, except those who are paid less than once a week, or in a one off sum, or answered 'none of these'
(PyPeriod <= 52)

475. TakeHome   How much is your usual take home pay per (period at PyPeriod)
after all deductions?

0.00..99999.97

Ask if paid less than once a week, or in a one off sum, or in none of these ways, or did not know how much money they usually took home
(PyPeriod = 90, 95 or 97 or TakeHome = DK)

SHOWCARD 35 or 36

476. TakHmEst   Please look at this card and estimate your usual take home pay per
(Period at PyPeriod) after all deductions?

0..32

Ask if an employee
(Stat = 1)

477.   GrossAm   How much are your usual gross earnings per (period at PyPeriod) before any deductions?

0.01..99999.97

Ask if respondent does not know how much their usual gross earnings are
(GrossAm = DK)

SHOWCARD 35 or 36

478.   GrossEst   Please look at this card and estimate your usual gross earnings per (Period at PyPeriod) before any deductions?

0..32

Ask if an employee
(Stat = 1)

479.   PaySlip   INTERVIEWER - CODE WHETHER PAYSLIP WAS CONSULTED

Pay slip consulted by respondent, but not by interviewer..........................1
Pay slip consulted by interviewer...2
Pay slip not consulted...3

Ask if answered PyPeriod
(1<PyPeriod>97)

480.   PayBonus   In your present job, have you ever received an occasional addition to pay in the last 12 months (that is since DATE 1 YEAR AGO) such as a Christmas bonus or a quarterly bonus?

EXCLUDE SHARES AND VOUCHERS.

Yes...1
No..2

Ask if respondent received a pay bonus
(PayBonus = 1)

481.   HowBonus   Was the bonus or commission paid...

RUNNING PROMPT

after tax was deducted (net)...1
or before tax was deducted (gross)..2
or some before and some after..3

If some or all tax was deducted, or they did not know if tax was deducted from pay bonus
(HowBonus = 1 or 3 or DK)

482.   NetBonus   What was the total amount you received in the last 12 months (that is since DATE 1 YEAR AGO) AFTER tax was deducted (i.e. net)?

0.01..99999.97

Ask if some or all tax was deducted from the pay bonus
(HowBonus = 2 or 3)

483.   GrsBonus   What was the total amount you received in the last 12 months (that is since DATE A YEAR AGO) before tax was deducted (i.e. gross)?

0.01..99999.97

Ask if an employee
(Stat = 1)

484.   PHlth   Some people these days have health insurance, like BUPA or AXA PPP healthcare, which pays the cost of private medical treatment.
Are you covered by any private medical insurance of this kind?

Yes..1
No...2

Ask if respondent has health insurance
(PHlth = 1)

485.   Policy   Is the insurance policy in your name, or are you included as a
Dependent on someone else's policy

Policy holder...1
Dependent...2

Ask if respondent is policy holder
(Policy=1)

486.   OthCov   Is anyone else covered by this policy?

Yes...1
No..2

Ask if anyone else is covered by the policy
(OthCov=1)

487.   PersCov   Enter number of additional persons also covered by this policy

1..16

Ask if respondent is policy holder
(Policy=1)

488.   SubsPay   Do you pay the whole subscription yourself (including the subscription for
your dependents), or does your employer pay all or part of it for you?

Employer pays it all, including any dependents......................................1
Employer pays for respondent only..2
Employer pays part and respondent pays part.......................................3
Respondent pays it all..4

Ask if self-employed
(Stat = 2)

489. BusAccts   You said earlier you were self-employed in your main job.

In this job/business are annual business accounts prepared for HM Revenue & Customs (formerly the Inland Revenue) for tax purposes?

INCLUDE IF PREPARED BY ACCOUNTANT

Yes..1
No...2
Not yet but will be..3

Ask if business accounts are prepared or will be
(BusAccts = 1,3)

490. Se1   The questions that follow are about just your own share of the business. What is the most recent period for which accounts have been prepared for HM Revenue and Customs (formerly the Inland Revenue)?

ENTER BEGINNING OF PERIOD
IF DAY OF MONTH NOT NONE, ENTER 15

ENTER DATE

491. Se2   ENTER END OF PERIOD (FOR WHICH ACCOUNTS HAVE BEEN PREPARED)
IF DAY OF MONTH NOT NONE, ENTER 15

ENTER DATE

492. SeWeeks   May I check, how many weeks does this cover?

IF COVERS FULL 12 MONTHS ENTER 52

1..104

493. Profit1   What was your share of the profit or loss figure shown on these accounts for this period?

0..9999997

494. Profit2   Did the answer in the previous question refer to profit or loss?

Profit/Earnings...1
Loss...2

495. ProfTax   Can I just check, is that figure before the reduction of income tax?

Yes (before tax)...1
No (after tax)..2

496. PrBefore   What was (your share of) the profit before tax and lump sum National Insurance deductions?

0..9999997

Ask if business accounts are not prepared
(BusAccts = 2)

497. GrsSEMJb   Now I'd like to ask you some questions about your income from your job/ business; that is, after paying for any materials, equipment or goods that you use(d) in your work.
On average, what was your WEEKLY or MONTHLY (or ANNUAL) income from this job/ business over the last 12 months - BEFORE deducting Income Tax and National Insurance contributions?

IF NOTHING OR MADE A LOSS, ENTER ZERO.
IF BUSINESS PARTNERSHIP, ENTER PERSON'S SHARE OF INCOME ONLY.
IF SELF-EMPLOYED LESS THAN 12 MONTHS, REFER JUST TO PERIOD SELF-EMPLOYED.

0.00..999999.97

Ask if respondent does not know gross income from job/ business
(GrsSEMJb = DK)

498. WorkAcc   Do you have separate bank or building society accounts for your work and your private finances?

Yes..1
No..2

Ask if respondent doesn't know gross income and has a separate account
(WorkAcc = 1)

SHOWCARD 37
(CARD SHOWS:

499. OwnSum

MONEY FROM THE WORK ACCOUNT
- USED FOR PAYMENTS TO YOURSELF AND ANY OTHER PERSONAL SPENDING
- USED TO PAY DOMESTIC BILLS (INCLUDING STANDING ORDERS)
- TRANSFERRED TO A PRIVATE ACCOUNT
- USED FOR ANY OTHER NON-BUSINESS USE)

Do you draw money from your work account for any non-business purposes, such as any of the things shown on this card?

(CODE 'YES' IF ANY APPLY)

Yes..1
No...2

Ask if respondent does draw money from business account for non-business purposes
(OwnSum = 1)

500. OwnAmt

Thinking of the last 12 months, on average how much did you take each month for these non-business purposes?

1..9997

501. OwnOther

Apart from drawings from the bank/building society, do/did you receive any other income from this job/business, for personal use?

Yes..1
No...2

Ask if respondent receives other income from job/business
(nOther = 1)

502. OwnOtAmt   On average, how much is that each month?

0..9997

Ask if a value is given above (including zero)
(*GrsSEMJb not equal to DK*)

503. GrossPer   How long does this cover?

one week...1
two weeks...2
three weeks..3
four weeks..4
calendar month...5
two calendar months...7
eight times a year...8
nine times a year..9
ten times a year..10
three months/13 weeks..13
six months/26 weeks...26
one year/12 months/52 weeks..52
less than one week..90
one off lump sum...95
none of these: EXPLAIN IN A NOTE <CTRL> + <M>............97

Ask if gross income is above zero
(*GrsSEMJb >= 1*)

504. NetSEMJb   On average, what is your WEEKLY or MONTHLY (or ANNUAL) income
from this job/ business over the last 12 months - AFTER deducting Income
Tax and National Insurance contributions?

0.00..999999.97

505.   NetPer   What period does this cover?

one week...1
two weeks...2
three weeks...3
four weeks...4
calendar month..5
two calendar months..7
eight times a year...8
nine times a year..9
ten times a year...10
three months/13 weeks...13
six months/26 weeks...26
one year/12 months/52 weeks..52
less than one week...90
one off lump sum..95
none of these: EXPLAIN IN A NOTE <CTRL> + <M>.........................97

Ask if gross income is zero
(GrsSEMJb = 0)

506.   LosSEMJb   On average, how much have you been LOSING WEEKLY or MONTHLY or ANNUALLY) from this job/ business over the last 12 months after deducting all business expenses?

0.00..999999.97

507. LossPer   What period does this cover?

one week..1
two weeks..2
three weeks..3
four weeks..4
calendar month...5
two calendar months...7
eight times a year...8
nine times a year..9
ten times a year..10
three months/13 weeks..13
six months/26 weeks...26
one year/12 months/52 weeks...52
less than one week..90
one off lump sum...95
none of these: EXPLAIN IN A NOTE <CTRL> + <M>...........................97

**Ask if respondent has a second or third job as an employee
(EmpSE2nd = 1 or EmpSE3rd = 1)**

508. PaySecJb   The next questions are about earnings from your second (and third) jobs.

509. SjNetAm   You said earlier you had another job(s), in which you were an employee.

In the last month, how much did you earn from your other job(s) as an
employee, AFTER DEDUCTIONS for tax and National Insurance (i.e. NET)?

0.01..99999.97

510. SjGrsAm   You said earlier you had another job(s), in which you were an employee.

In the last month, how much did you earn from your other job(s) as an
employee, BEFORE DEDUCTIONS for tax and National Insurance (i.e.
GROSS)?

0.01..99999.97

**Ask if respondent has a second or third job as self-employed
(EmpSE2nd = 2 or EmpSE3rd = 2)**

511.   SjPrfGrs   You said earlier you had another job(s), in which you were self-employed.

In the last 12 months (that is since DATE 1 YEAR AGO) how much have you earned from this work, BEFORE deducting income tax and National Insurance contributions, but...

–   after deducting all business expenses, and
–   before deducting money drawn for your own use?

IF MADE NO PROFIT ENTER 0.

0.00..99999.97

512.   SjPrfNet   In the last 12 months (that is since DATE 1 YEAR AGO) how much have you earned from this work, AFTER deducting income tax and National Insurance contributions, but...

–   after deducting all business expenses, and
–   before deducting money drawn for your own use?

IF MADE NO PROFIT ENTER 0.

0.00..99999.97

**Ask if respondent has a second or third job as self-employed and gross profit is zero
(Stat = 2 AND SjPrfGrs = 0)**

513.   SjLssGrs   In the last 12 months (that is since DATE 1 YEAR AGO) how much have you lost from this work, after deducting all business expenses?

IF MADE NO LOSS ENTER 0.

0.00..99999.97

Ask all
514.   OddJob   (Apart from your main job) do you earn any money from odd jobs or from work that you do from time to time?

PROMPT AS NECESSARY

INCLUDE BABYSITTING, MAIL ORDER AGENT, POOLS AGENT ETC.

Yes...1
No...2

Ask if respondent has odd/other jobs
(OddJob = 1)

515.   OddJEmp   In these job(s) do you work as an employee or are you self-employed?

Employee..1
self-employed...2

516.   OddJAmnt   In the last month (that is since DATE 1 MONTH AGO) how much have you earned from your odd/ occasional jobs?

0.00..99999.97

Ask all (except proxy respondents)
– NOTE: End of the section of questions that are only asked of those in paid work

517.   OthPay   Apart from anything you have already mentioned, have you received any payment from interest from savings, Bank or Building Society accounts, income from shares, bonds, unit trusts or gilt-edged stock or any unincorporated business in the last 12 months (that is since DATE 1 YEAR AGO)?

PROMPT AS NECESSARY
CODE ALL THAT APPLY - EXCLUDE BENEFITS NO LONGER RECEIVED.

Interest from savings, Bank or Building Society accounts..........................1
Income from shares, bonds, unit trusts or gilt-edged stock.......................2
Income from unincorporated business...3
Other..4
None of these..5

Ask if respondent is receiving income from some other source

(OthPay = 4)

518.   OthSourc   Please specify other source

ENTER TEXT OF AT MOST 100 CHARACTERS

Ask if respondent is receiving interest from savings
(OthPay = 1)

519.   Investpy   How much have you received in total from interest on savings, Bank or building Society accounts in the last 12 months?

0.01..99999.97

Ask if respondent is receiving income from an unincorporated business
(OthPay = 3)

520.   Unincpy   How much have you received in total from the unincorporated business in The last 12 months?

0.01..99999.97

Ask if respondent is receiving income from shares, bonds, unit trusts or gilt-edged stock
(OthPay = 2)

512.   Sharepy   How much have you received in total from shares, bonds, unit trusts or gilt-edged stock in the last 12 months?

0.01..99999.97

Ask if respondent is receiving income from another source
(OthPay = 4)

522.   OthRgPAm   (Apart from interest and income from shares)
How much have you received from other sources in the last 12 months?

0.01 .. 99999.97

Ask if proxy respondent

SHOWCARD 36

523.   NtIncEst   I would now like to ask you about the income of (NAME).
Please could you look at this card and estimate their total NET income (that is after deduction of tax, National Insurance and any expenses) (NAME) brings into the household in a year from all sources (benefits, employment, investments etc)?

0..32

Ask if household contains one or more children (under the age of 16)

524.   AskwIth   The next section is about child income. We only need to collect this information once for each child in the household. Who will answer the child income section for (child's name)?

ENTER PERSON NUMBER

1..16

525.   AskNowCH   DO YOU WANT TO ASK THIS SECTION FOR (CHILD'S NAME) NOW OR LATER?

IF YOU HAVE ALREADY ASKED THIS SECTION FOR (CHILD'S NAME), DO NOT CHANGE FROM CODE 1.

Yes, now/Already asked..1
Later..2

Ask if section is to be asked now
(AskNowCH =1)

526.   NCSOR   Has (CHILD'S NAME) received or earned an independent source of income the last 12 months?

Please ignore anything less than £30.00 per month, or money received from other household members.

Yes...1
No...2

Ask if child has received or earned an independent source of income (INCSOR = 1)

527.　ChInc　　How much was this income?

0.00..99999.00

528.　Chpypd　　What period did this cover?

one week	1
two weeks	2
three weeks	3
four weeks	4
calendar month	5
two calendar months	7
eight times a year	8
nine times a year	9
ten times a year	10
three months/13 weeks	13
six months/26 weeks	26
one year/12 months/52 weeks	52
less than one week	90
one off lump sum	95
none of these: EXPLAIN IN A NOTE <CTRL> + <M>	97

TRAILER MODULE
INDIVIDUAL MATERIAL DEPRIVATION

The following questions need to be answered by all adults aged 16+ years}

529. MobPhon   Do you have a mobile phone?

Yes 1
No because can't afford it..2
No for some other reason..3

530. Shoes   Do you have at least two pairs of properly fitting shoes?

INCLUDE ALL FOOTWEAR – BOOTS, SANDALS, TRAINERS etc
Yes..1
No because can't afford it..2
No for some other reason..3

531. Clothes   Do you replace worn-out clothes with new (not second-hand) ones?

INCLUDE HOMEMADE CLOTHES IF THEY ARE NEWLY MADE

Yes..1
No because can't afford it..2
No for some other reason..3

532. GetTog   Do you get together with friends or family from outside the household for a drink or meal at least once a month?

'A DRINK' CAN BE NON-ALCOHOLIC
GET TOGETHER' CAN BE AT HOME OR ELSEWHERE

Yes..1
No because can't afford it..2
No for some other reason..3

533.   Leisure   Do you regularly take part in a leisure activity that costs money such as sport, cinema, concerts etc?

THE ACTIVITY SHOULD OCCUR OUTSIDE THE HOME
SPECTATING COUNTS AS TAKING PART
Yes..1
No because can't afford it...2
No for some other reason...3

534.   Spenself   Do you spend some money on non-essential items for yourself each week?

Yes..1
No because can't afford it...2
No for some other reason...3

Ask if respondent needed a medical examination or treatment for a health problem but you did not receive it
(MedRec = 1)

535.   UnmetMed   How many times in the last 12 months have you needed a medical examination or treatment for a health problem, from a GP or specialist but not received it?

EXCLUDE DENTISTS AND OPHTHALMOLOGISTS

Not at all..1
1-2 times...2
3-5 times...3
6-9 times...4
10 times or more...5

TRAILER MODULE
INDIVIDUAL CHILD MATERIAL DEPRIVATION

The following questions are asked of the HRP about all the children in the household

536.   NewClot   Do ALL the children in your household have some new (not second-hand) clothes
INCLUDE HOMEMADE CLOTHES IF THEY ARE NEWLY MADE

Yes...1
No because can't afford it...2
No for some other reason...3

537.   ChShoes   Do ALL the children in your household have at least two pairs of properly fitting shoes?
INCLUDE ALL FOOTWEAR – BOOTS, SANDALS, TRAINERS etc

Yes...1
No because can't afford it...2
No for some other reason...3

538.   FruitVeg   Do ALL the children in your household eat fresh fruit or vegetables at least once a day?

Yes...1
No because can't afford it...2
No for some other reason...3

539.   ThreMeal   Do ALL the children in your household eat at least three meals a day?

Yes...1
No because can't afford it...2
No for some other reason...3

540.   MeatFish   Do they ALL eat one meal with meat, chicken or fish (or vegetarian equivalent) at least once a day?

Yes...1
No because can't afford it...2
No for some other reason...3

541.   HomeBook   Do they ALL have books at home suitable for their ages?

Yes...1
No because can't afford it...2
No for some other reason..3

542.   OutEquip   Do they ALL have outdoor leisure equipment suitable for their ages (bicycle, roller skates), etc?
VERY CHEAP OR SELF-MADE EQUIPMENT ARE TO BE INCLUDED

Yes...1
No because can't afford it...2
No for some other reason..3

543.   InGames   Do they ALL have indoor games suitable for their ages (building blocks, board games, computer games, etc

Yes...1
No because can't afford it...2
No for some other reason..3

544.   ChLeisur   Do they ALL have regular leisure activities that cost money (swimming, playing an instrument, youth organisations, sports etc.)?
THE ACTIVITY SHOULD OCCUR OUTSIDE THE HOME

Yes...1
No because can't afford it...2
No for some other reason..3

545.   Celbrate   Do they ALL have celebrations on special occasions (birthdays, religious events etc.)?

Yes...1
No because can't afford it...2
No for some other reason..3

546.   FrenRoun   Do they ALL invite friends round to play and eat from time to time?

     Yes...1
     No because can't afford it...2
     No for some other reason...3

547.   SchTrip   DO ALL the children who attend school participate in school trips and school events that cost money?

     Yes...1
     No because can't afford it...2
     No for some other reason...3
     Not applicable - no children who attend school....................................4

548.   WeekHol   Do they ALL go on holiday at least 1 week per year?

     Yes...1
     No because can't afford it...2
     No for some other reason...3

549.   Homewrk   Do ALL the children in your household who attend school have a suitable place at home to study or do homework?

     Yes...1
     No..2
     Not applicable...3

550.   PlayOut

     Do ALL the children in your household have an outdoor space in the neighbourhood where they can play safely?
     THIS CAN BE THE HOUSEHOLD'S GARDEN

     Yes...1
     No..2
     Not applicable...3

551.   UnMedCh   Was there any time in the last 12 months when at least one of the children in your household needed to consult a GP or specialist but did not?

EXCLUDE ALL DENTISTS AND OPHTHALOMOGISTS

Yes...1
No..2

Ask if a child needed to consult a GP or specialist but did not.
(UnMedCh = 1)

552.   ChMedRe   What was the main reason for not consulting a GP or specialist on this these occasions?

Could not afford to..1
Waiting list...2
Could not take the time because of work, care of other children or care of other persons...3
Too far to travel/no means of transport...4
Other reason..5

553.   UnDentCh   Was there any time in the last 12 months when at least one of the children in your household needed a dental examination or treatment but did not receive it?

Yes...1
No..2

Ask if a child needed a dental examination or treatment but did not receive it.
(UnDentCh = 1)

554.   ChDentRe   What was the main reason for not consulting a dentist on this (these) occasion(s)?

Could not afford to..1
Waiting list...2
Could not take the time because of work, care of other children or care of other persons...3
Too far to travel/no means of transport...4
Other reason..5

Summary of main topics included in GHS/GLF questionnaires: 1971 to 2009

Appendix F

Topic Area	Year included
ACCIDENTS THAT RESULTED IN SEEING A GP OR GOING TO HOSPITAL	1981, 1984 1987-89
ATTENDANCE AT ACTIVITIES ON SCHOOL PREMISES IN LAST 12 MONTHS	1984
BURGLARIES AND THEFTS FROM PRIVATE HOUSEHOLDS	1972-73, 1979-80, 1985-86, 1991, 1993, 1996
BUS TRAVEL	1982
CAR OWNERSHIP	1971-96, 1998, 2000-09
Driving licences and private motoring	1980
CAREER OPPORTUNITIES	1972
CARERS	1985, 1990, 1995, 2000
Carers aged 8-17	1996
CHILD CARE	
Pre-school children (aged under 5)	1971-79, 1986
Children aged 0-11	1991
Children under 14	1998
Children aged 0-12	2005-09
ETHNICITY AND COUNTRY OF BIRTH	
Colour, assessment of persons seen*	1971-92
Country of birth:	
of adults and their parents	1971-96, 1998, 2000-09
of children	1979-96, 1998, 2000-09
Year of entry to UK:	
Adults	1971-96, 1998, 2000-09
Children	1979-96, 1998, 2000-09
Ethnic origin	1983-96, 1998, 2000-09
National identity	2001-09
CONSUMER DURABLES	
Possession of various consumer durables	1972-76, 1978-96, 1998, 2000-09
Possession of a telephone	1972-76, 1979-96, 1998, 2000-09
Possession of a mobile telephone:	1992, 2000-09
Access to the Internet	2000-04
CONTRACEPTION AND STERILISATION	
Whether woman/partner has been sterilised for contraceptive reasons	1983-84, 1986-87, 1989, 1991,
Whether woman/partner has had other sterilising operation	1993, 1995, 1998, 2002
Details of any reversal of sterilisation operations	1983-84, 1986-87
Current use of contraception/reason for not using contraception	1983, 1986, 1989, 1991, 1993, 1995, 1998, 2002
Previous usual method of contraception	1989, 1991, 1993, 1995, 1998, 2002
Use of contraception	1989, 1991, 1993, 1995, 1998, 2002
Use of emergency contraception in previous 2 years	1993, 1995, 1998, 2002
Whether woman/partner would have difficulties in having (more) children	1983-84, 1986-87, 1989,

Reasons for difficulties in getting pregnant and whether consulted a doctor	**1991, 1993, 1995, 1998, 2002**
DRINKING	
Rating of drinking behaviour according to quantity-frequency (QF) index based on reported alcohol consumption in the 12 months before interview	**1978, 1980, 1982, 1984**
Rating of drinking behaviour according to average weekly alcohol consumption (AC) rating	**1986-98 (alternate yrs), 2000-02**
Alcohol consumption on the heaviest drinking day in the 7 days before interview	**1998, 2000-09**
Personal rating of own drinking behaviour	**1978-98 (alternate yrs), 2000-09**
Whether think drinking/smoking can damage health	**1978-90 (alternate yrs)**
Whether non-drinkers have always been non-drinkers or used to drink but stopped, and reasons	**1992-98 (alternate years), 2000-09**
Whether drink more or less than the recommended sensible amount	**1992-96 (alternate years)**
Whether drink more or less now than 5 years ago	**1998, 2000-09**
EDUCATION	
Current education	
Current education status	**1971-96, 1998, 2000-09**
Type of educational establishment currently attended:	
- by adults aged under 50	**1971-81, 1984-90**
- by adults aged under 70	**1991-96, 1998, 2000-09**
- by children aged 5-15	**1971-77**
Qualification/examination aimed at	**1971, 1974-76**
Expected date of completion of full-time education	**1971-76**
Whether intend to do any paid work while still in full-time education, and if so, when	**1971-76**
Whether currently attending any leisure or recreation classes	**1973-78, 1981, 1983, 1993-96**
Past education	
Age on leaving school	**1972-96, 1998**
Age on leaving last place of full-time education	**1971-96, 1998, 2000-09**
Type of educational establishment last attended full time	**1971-96, 1998**
Qualifications obtained	**1971-96, 1998, 2000-09**
Job training	**1971-84**
Students in institutional accommodation	**1981-87**
ELDERLY	**1979-80, 1985, 1987, 1991, 1994, 1996, 1998, 2001**
EMPLOYMENT	
Those currently working	
Main job - occupation and industry and employee/self-employed	**1971-96, 1998, 2000-09**
Subsidiary job - occupation and industry and	**1971-78, 1980-84**
- employee/self-employed	**1987-91**
Last job - occupation and industry and employee/self-employed	**1986**
Whether has a second job	**1992-96, 1998**
Whether present job was obtained through a government scheme	**1989-92**
Youth Opportunities Programme Schemes	**1982-84**
Youth Training Scheme	**1985-95**
Journey time to work	**1971-76, 1978**
Usual number of hours worked per week (excluding overtime)	**1971-96, 1998, 2005-09**
Hours of paid/unpaid overtime usually worked per week	**1973-83, 1998**
Usual number of hours worked per week (including paid/unpaid overtime)	**2000-09**

Usual number of days worked per week	**1973, 1979-84**
Number of days worked in reference week	**1977-78**
Length of time with present employer/present spell of self-employment	**1971-96, 1998, 2000-07**
Whether self-employed during the previous 12 months	**1986-91**
Number of changes of employer in 12 months before interview	**1971-76, 1979-91**
Number of new employee jobs started in 12 months before interview	**1977-78, 1983-91**
Source of hearing about job(S) started in 12 months before interview	**1971-77, 1980-84**
Whether paid by employer when sick	**1971-76, 1979-81**
Whether employer is in the public/private sector	**1983, 1985, 1987**
Trade Union and Staff Association membership	**1983**
Whether people work all or part of the time at home	**1993**
Whether does any unpaid work for members of the family	**1993-95**
Whether has ever been a company director	**1987**
Type of National Insurance contribution paid by:	
- married and widowed women	**1972-1980**
- married, widowed and separated women	**1981-1983**
Level of satisfaction with present job as a whole	**1971-83**
Level of satisfaction with specific aspects of present job	**1974-83**
Whether thinking of leaving present employer, and if so, why	**1971-76**
Whether signed on at an Unemployment Benefit Office in the reference week	**1984-90, 1994-96**
Absence from work in the reference week	**1971-72, 1974-84**
Sickness absence in the four weeks before interview	**1981-84**
Sickness absence in the 3 months before interview	**1992**
Whether registered as unemployed in the reference week	**1977-82**
Unemployment experience in 12 months before interview	**1975-77, 1983-84**
Economic activity status 12 months before interview	**1979-91, 2005-09**
Whether in employment prior to present job	**1986**
Whether on any government schemes	**1985-96**
Usual job of father	**1971-91**
Those currently unemployed	
Most recent job - occupation and industry and employee/self-employed	**1971-96, 1998, 2000-09**
Whether most recent job was obtained through a government scheme	**1989-92**
Whether has ever had a paid job	**1986-96, 1998, 2000-09**
Whether has ever worked for an employer as part of a government scheme	**1989-91**
Whether registered as unemployed in the reference week	**1971-83**
Methods of seeking work in the reference week	
Whether signed on at an Unemployment Benefit Office in the reference week	**1984-90, 1994-96**
Whether looking for full or part-time work	**1983**
Whether taking part in Youth Training Scheme or Youth Opportunities Programmes	**1984**
Whether last job was organised through Youth Opportunities Programme (16-19 yrs olds)	**1982**

For those who in the reference week were looking for work	**1991-96, 1998, 2000-09**
- would they have been able to start within 2 weeks if a job had been available	
For those who in the reference week were waiting to take up a new job already obtained	
- would they have started that job in the reference week if it had been available then	**1977-82**
- when was the new job obtained and when did they expect to start it	**1979**
Whether paid unemployment benefit (and supplementary allowances) for reference week	**1971-74**
When last worked and reasons for stopping work	**1971-73, 1974-79, 1986**
Reasons for leaving last job	**1981-82, 1986**
Whether last job was full/part time	**1986**
Length of current spell of unemployment	**1974-96, 1998**
Unemployment experience in 12 months before interview	**1975-77, 1983-84**
Economic activity status 12 months before interview	**1979-91**
Number of new employee jobs started in 12 months before interview	**1977, 1982-91**
Source of hearing about all jobs started in 12 months before interview	**1982-84**
Whether on any government schemes	**1985-96, 1998, 2000-09**
Whether does any unpaid work for members of the family and if so:	
number of hours a week and where	**1993-96, 1998, 2000-09**
for whom and type of work	**1993-96**
Whether has ever been a company director	**1987**
Type of National Insurance contribution paid in preceding two completed tax years by married/widowed/separated women aged 20-59, not working in week before interview	**1982-83**
Usual job of father	**1971-92**
The economically inactive	
Major activity in the reference week	
Last job - occupation and industry and employee/self-employed	**1971-96, 1998, 2000-09**
Usual job (of retired persons)	
- occupation and industry	**1973-76, 1979-88**
- employee/self-employed	
When finished last job	**1971-73, 1977-78, 1986**
Reasons for stopping work	**1971-73, 1978-82, 1986**
Whether registered as unemployed in the reference week	**1972-83**
Whether signed on at an Unemployment Benefit Office in the reference week	**1984-90, 1994-96**
Whether paid unemployment benefit (and supplementary allowance) for reference week	**1972-74**
Whether would like a regular paid job, whether looking for work, and if a job had been available would they have been able to start within 2 weeks	**1991-96, 1998, 2000-09**
Length of time currently out of employment	**1993-96, 1998, 2000-07**
Main reason for not looking for work	**1986-87**
Whether would like regular paid job	**1986-87**
Whether has ever had a paid job	**1986-96, 1998, 2000-09**
Whether has had a paid job in last 12 months	**1987-91**
Whether has ever worked for an employer as part of a government scheme	**1989-91**
Whether has had a paid job in previous 3 years	**1986**
Whether last job was full/part time	**1986**
Unemployment experience in 12 months before interview	**1975-77, 1983-84**
Economic activity status 12 months before interview	**1980-91**

Number of new employee jobs started in 12 months before interview	**1977, 1984-91**
Source of hearing about all jobs started in 12 months before interview	**1977**
Whether on any government schemes	**1985-96, 1998, 2000-09**
Whether does any unpaid work for members of the family and if so:	
number of hours a week and where	**1993-96, 1998, 2000-09**
for whom and type of work	**1993-96**
Whether has ever been a company director	**1987**
Type of National Insurance contribution paid in the preceding two completed tax years by Married/widowed/separated women aged 20-59, not working in week before interview	**1982**
Future work intentions	**1971-76**
Usual job of father	**1971-92**
FORESTS	
Whether ever visits forests or woodland areas, facilities visitors would like to see there	**1987**
HEALTH	
Acute sickness (restricted activity in a two-week reference period)*	**1971-76, 1979-96, 1998, 2000-09**
Chronic health problems	**1977-78**
Chronic sickness (longstanding illness or disability)	
Prevalence of longstanding illness or disability*	**1971-76, 1979-96, 1998, 2000-09**
Cause of the illness or disability*	**1971-75**
When the illness or disability started*	**1971**
Type of illness or disability*	**1988-89, 1994-96, 1998, 2000-09**
Prevalence of limiting longstanding illness or disability*	**1972-76, 1979-96, 1998, 2000-09**
When it started to limit activities and whether housebound or bedfast because of it*	**1972-76**
Dental health	**1983, 1985, 1987, 1989, 1991, 1993,**
	1995, 2003
General health in the 12 months before interview	**1977-96, 1998, 2000-07**
General health (0n a 5 point scale)	**2005-09**
Hearing	**1977-81, 1985, 1991-2, 1994-5, 1998, 2001-2,**
Medicine-taking in seven days before interview	**4th qtr 1972, 1973**
Short-term health problems	**1977-78**
Sight	**1977-82, 1985, 1987, 1994, 1990-94, 1998, 2001**
Tinnitus (sensation of noise in the ears or head)	**1981**

HEALTH SERVICES	
Day patient visits	**1971-96, 1998, 2000-09**
GP consultations	**1971-96, 1998, 2000-09**
Consultations in the two weeks before interview:	
number of consultations*	
NHS or private*	
type of doctor*	
site of consultation*	
cause of consultation*	**1971-75**
whether consulted because something was the matter, or for some other reason*	**1981**
whether consultation about reported longstanding illness or restricted activity*	**1983-84, 1986-87**
whether was given a prescription*	**1981-96, 1998, 2000-09**
whether was referred to hospital*	**1981-85, 1988-90**
whether was given National Insurance medical certificate	**1981-85**
whether saw a practice nurse and, if so, the number of times*	**2000-09**
Access to GPs	**1977**
Whether has used NHS Direct in the last year	**2004-09**
Health and personal social services	**1971-76, 1970-85, 1991, 1994, 1998, 2001**
Inpatient spells	
Spells in hospital as an inpatient in a three-month reference period:	**1971-1976**
Stays in hospital as an inpatient in a 12-month reference period:	
number of stays*	**1982-96, 1998, 2000-09**
number of nights on each stay*	**1992-96, 1998, 2000-09**
NHS or private patient	**1982-83, 1985-87,**
	1995-96, 1998, 2000-09
whether private patients were treated in an NHS/private hospital	**1998, 2000-09**
whether claimed for under private medical insurance	**1982-83, 1987**
Whether on waiting list for admission to hospital and length of time on list*	**1973-76**
Outpatient (OP) attendances	
Attendances at hospital OP departments in a three-month reference period:	
number of attendances*	**1971-96, 1998, 2000-09**
NHS or private	**1973-76, 1982-83, 1985-87,**
	1995-96, 1998, 2000-09
nature of complaint causing attendance*	**1974-76**
whether claimed for under private medical insurance	**1982-83, 1987, 1995**
number of casualty visits*	**1995-96, 1998, 2000-09**
Appointments with OP departments:	**1973-76**
HOUSEHOLD COMPOSITION	**1971-96, 1998, 2000-09**
Age*, sex*, marital status of household members	
Relationship to head of household*	
Family unit(s)	
Housewife	**1971-80**
HOUSING (see also MIGRATION)	
Accommodation: amenities	
Length of residence at present address*	
Age of building	**1971-96, 1998, 2000-04**
Type of accommodation	
Number of rooms and bedrooms	

Whether have separate kitchen	
Bath/WC: sole use, shared, none	**1971-90**
WC: inside or outside the accommodation	
Installation/replacement of bath or WC	**1971-76**
Cost of improvements made to the accommodation	
Floor level of main accommodation	**1973-96, 1998, 2000-04**
Whether there is a lift	**2001-04**
Central heating and fuel use	
Accommodation problems including damp, noise, pollution and crime	**2004-2009**
Debt and Indebtedness	**2009**
Housing costs	
Gross value	**1971-86**
Type of mortgage	**1972-77, 1979, 1981, 1984-86**
Current mortgage payments	**1972-77, 1979, 1981, 1984**
Purchase price of present home, amount of mortgage or loan and date mortgage started	**1985-86, 1992-93**
Current rent	**1972-77, 1979, 1981**
Amount of any rent rebate/allowance and/or rate rebate received	
Whether in receipt of housing benefit	**1985-95, 1998, 2000-09**
Whether rent paid by DSS or local authority	**1998, 2000-09**
Council Tax band for households containing person(s) aged 65 or over	**2001**
Tenure	
Whether present home is owned or rented	**1971-96, 1998, 2000-09**
Whether in co-ownership housing association scheme	**1981-95**
Change of tenure on divorce or remarriage	**1991-93**
Change of tenure on marriage or cohabitation	**1998**
Housing history of local authority tenants and owner occupiers who had become owners	**1985-86**
in the previous five years	
Whether ever rented from local authority, and if so, whether bought that accommodation	**1991-93**
Owner occupiers:	
- in whose name the property is owned	**1978-96, 1998, 2000-09**
- whether property is owned outright or being bought with a mortgage or loan	**1971-96, 1998, 2000-09**
- how outright owners originally acquired their home	**1978-80, 1982-83,1985-86**
- source of mortgage or loan	**1978-80, 1982-86,1992-93**
- whether currently using present home as security for a (second) mortgage or loan of	**1980-82, 1992-93**
any kind, and if so, details	
- whether owner occupiers with mortgage have taken out a remortgage on present home	**1985-87, 1992-93**
- whether recent owner occupiers had previously rented this accommodation	**1981-82, 1985-86**
- whether had rented present accommodation before deciding to buy	**1992-93**
- whether previous accommodation was owned and if so, details of the sale	**1992-93**
Renters:	
- in whose name the property is rented	**1985-96, 1998, 2000-05**
- from whom the accommodation is rented	**1971-96, 1998, 2000-09**
- whether landlord lives in the same building	**1971-72, 1975-76,**
	1979-96, 1998, 2000-04
- whether have considered buying present home and, if not, why not	**1980-89**
- tenure preference	**1985-88**
- whether previously owned/buying accommodation and reasons for leaving	**1995-96**

Local authority renters	**1990-91**
HOUSING SATISFACTION	**1978, 1988, 1990**
INCOME	
Income over 12 months before interview	**1971-78**
Current income	**1979-96, 1998, 2000-09**
INHERITANCE	**1995**
LEISURE / SOCIAL AND CULTURAL PARTICIPATION	
Arts and entertainments, museums, galleries, historic buildings	**1987, 2006**
Holidays away from home in four weeks before interview	**1973, 1977, 1980, 1983, 1986**
Leisure activities in the four weeks before interview	**1973, 1977, 1980, 1983,**
Social activities and hobbies in the four weeks before interview	**1973, 1977, 1980, 1983, 1986, 1987**
	1990, 1993, 1996, 2002
Involvement in groups, clubs and organisations, in last 12 months	**2006**
Whether did any voluntary arts/cultural work in the 4 weeks before interview	**2002**
Personal contact with family, relatives and friends in spare time	**2006**
Asking for help from neighbours	**2006**
Unpaid help given to others outside the home, in last 12 months	**2006**
LIBRARIES	**1987**
LONG-DISTANCE TRAVEL	**1971-72**
MARRIAGE, COHABITATION AND CHILDBIRTH	
Marital history	**1979-96, 1998, 2000-09**
Date of present marriage	**1971-78**
Expected family size	**1974-78**
Date of birth and sex of all liveborn children and whether they live with mother	**1979-96, 1998, 2000-09**
Date of birth of step, foster and adopted children living in the household, and how long they have lived there	**1979-87, 1989-96, 1998, 2000-09**
Whether women think they will have any (more) children, how many in all, and age at which they think will have their first/next baby	**1979-96, 1998, 2000-09**
Current cohabitation	**1979-96, 1998, 2000-09**
Cohabitation before current or most recent marriage	**1979, 1981-88**
Cohabitation before all marriages	**1989-96, 1998, 2000-09**
Number of cohabiting relationships that did not lead to marriage	**1998, 2000-09**
MIGRATION	
Past movement	
Length of residence at previous address*	**1971-77**
Details of previous accommodation	**1971-73, 1978-80**
Number of moves in last five years*	**1971-77, 1979-96, 1998, 2000-09**
Potential movement – people thinking of moving*	**1971-78, 1980-81, 1983**
Frustrated potential movement – people who had previously thought of moving*	**1974-76, 1980, 1983**
MOBILITY AIDS – difficult getting about without assistance	**1993, 1996, 2001**
PENSIONS	

Whether covered by employer's pension scheme	**1971-76, 1979, 1982-83, 1985,**
	1987-96, 1998, 2000-09
Whether the scheme is contributory, reasons for not belonging to the scheme	**1971-76, 1979, 1982-83, 1985, 1987**
Whether ever belonged to present employer's pension scheme	**1985, 1987**
Whether in receipt of a pension from a previous employer	**1983, 1985, 1987**
Whether ever belonged to a previous employer's pension scheme	
Length of time in last employer's pension scheme and in last job	**1985**
Whether retained any pension rights from any previous employer	**1971-76, 1979, 1982-83,**
	1985, 1987
Whether pays Additional Voluntary Contributions into employer's pension scheme	**1987**
Whether has a stakeholder pension	**2001-09**
Whether has a group personal pension	**2003-09**
Whether currently belongs to a personal pension scheme and whether employer contributes	**1991-96, 1998, 2000-07**
Whether has ever contributed towards a personal pension	**1987-96, 1998, 2000-09**
Date the personal pension was taken out	
Whether belonged to an employer's pension scheme during the 6 months prior to taking out a personal pension	**1989-90**
Whether makes any other income tax deductible pension contributions	**1993-96, 1998, 2000-09**
- whether free standing additional voluntary contributions	**2000-09**
PRIVATE MEDICAL INSURANCE	**1982-83, 1986-87, 1995**
SHARE OWNERSHIP	**1987-88, 1992-96, 1998**
SMOKING	
Cigarette smoking	
Prevalence of cigarette smoking	**1972-76, 1978-98 (alternate years),**
	2000-09
Current cigarette smokers:	
number of cigarettes smoked per day	**1972-76, 1978-98 (alternate years),**
type of cigarette smoked mainly	**2000-09**
usual brand of cigarette smoked	**1984-98 (alternate years), 2000-09**
age started smoking cigarettes regularly	**1988-99 (alternate years), 2000-09**
whether would find it difficult to not smoke for a day	
whether would like to give up smoking altogether	**1992-98 (alternate years),**
when is the first cigarette of the day smoked	**2000-09**
whether or not intends to give up smoking in the future	**2003-09**
Regular cigarette smokers:	
age started smoking cigarettes regularly	**1972-73**
Occasional cigarette smokers:	
whether ever smoked cigarettes regularly	
age started smoking cigarettes regularly	**1972-73**
how long ago stopped smoking cigarettes regularly	
Current non-smokers:	

whether ever smoked cigarettes regularly	**1972-76, 1978-98 (alternate years),**
	2000-09
age started smoking cigarettes regularly	
number smoked per day when smoking regularly	**1972-73, 1980-98 (alternate years),**
how long ago stopped smoking cigarettes regularly	**2000-09**
Cigar smoking	**1972-76, 1978-98 (alternate years),**
	2000-09
Pipe smoking	**1972, 1978, 1986-98 (alternate years),**
	2000-09
SOCIAL CAPITAL	
Opinion of local services, amenities, organisations, safety in the area, local problems	**2000, 2004**
SOCIAL MOBILITY	**2005**
Opinion of living standards across the generations	
- mother and father's main job, year of birth and qualifications	
- household financial problems	
SPORT	**1987, 1990, 1993, 1996, 2002**
VOLUNTARY WORK	**1981, 1987, 1992, 2002**
* including children	

Smoking and drinking among adults, 2009

A report on the 2009 General Lifestyle Survey

Authors: **Simon Robinson**
            Helen Harris
Editor: **Steven Dunstan**

Office for National Statistics

A National Statistics publication

National Statistics are produced to high professional standards set out in the Code of Practice for Official Statistics. They are produced free from political influence.

About us

The Office for National Statistics

The Office for National Statistics (ONS) is the executive office of the UK Statistics Authority, a non-ministerial department which reports directly to Parliament. ONS is the UK government's single largest statistical producer. It compiles information about the UK's society and economy, and provides the evidence-base for policy and decision-making, the allocation of resources, and public accountability. The Director-General of ONS reports directly to the National Statistician who is the Authority's Chief Executive and the Head of the Government Statistical Service.

The Government Statistical Service

The Government Statistical Service (GSS) is a network of professional statisticians and their staff operating both within the Office for National Statistics and across more than 30 other government departments and agencies.

Contacts

This publication

For information about the content of this publication, contact the General Lifestyle Survey
Tel: 01633 455678
Email: socialsurveys@ons.gsi.gov.uk

Principal Research Officer: Steven Dunstan

Other customer enquiries

ONS Customer Contact Centre
Tel: 0845 601 3034
International: +44 (0)845 601 3034
Minicom: 01633 815044
Email: info@statistics.gsi.gov.uk
Fax: 01633 652747
Post: Room 1.101, Government Buildings,
Cardiff Road, Newport, South Wales NP10 8XG
www.ons.gov.uk

Media enquiries

Tel: 0845 604 1858
Email: press.office@ons.gsi.gov.uk

Copyright and reproduction

This publication is available for download at:
www.ons.gov.uk

Contents

List of Contributors

Authors: Simon Robinson

                                  Helen Harris

General Lifestyle Survey team: Paul Horton

                                  Teresa McCloy

                                  Mike Tom

                                  Jayne White

Reviewers: NHS Information Centre for Health and Social Care

                                  ONS Centre for Health Analysis and Life Events

                                  Mike Prestwood

Acknowledgements

A large scale survey is a collaborative effort and the authors wish to thank the interviewers and other ONS staff who contributed to the study. The authors would also like to thank the sponsors for both their contribution and ongoing commitment to the survey. Also, the help of respondents who gave up their time to be interviewed is gratefully appreciated, without their co-operation the survey would not be possible.

Introduction

In 2008 the Office for National Statistics (ONS) launched the Integrated Household Survey (IHS). In the IHS questionnaires are comprised of two sections: a suite of core IHS questions followed by individual survey modules. In 2009 the modules of the IHS were:

- General LiFestyle Survey (GLF)
- Living Cost and Food Survey (LCF)
- Opinions Survey (OPN)
- English Housing Survey (EHS)
- Labour Force Survey (LFS)
- Annual Population Survey (APS)
- Life Opportunities Survey (LOS)

Questions on smoking and drinking behaviour formed part of the General Household Survey (GHS) until 2008 when, to mark its entry into the IHS, it was renamed the General LiFestyle Survey (GLF). This report provides information about smoking and drinking based on data collected by the GLF in 2009. It also includes tables showing data on the trends and changes in smoking and drinking measured by the GLF in 2008 and by the GHS over several decades.

An overview of the General Lifestyle Survey

The GLF is a multi-purpose continuous survey carried out by the Office for National Statistics (ONS). It collects information on a range of topics from people living in private households in Great Britain. The survey started as the GHS in 1971 and has been carried out continuously since then, except for breaks to review it in 1997/1998 and to redevelop it in 1999/2000.

The survey presents a picture of households, families and people living in Great Britain. This information is used by government departments and other organisations, such as educational establishments, businesses and charities, to contribute to policy decisions and for planning and monitoring purposes.

The interview consists of questions relating to the household, answered by the household reference person[1] or spouse, and an individual questionnaire, asked of all resident adults aged 16 and over. Demographic and health information is also collected about children in the household. The GLF collects data on a wide range of core topics which are included on the survey every year. These are:

- demographic information about households, families and people
- housing tenure and household accommodation
- access to and ownership of consumer durables, including vehicles
- employment

- education
- health and use of health services
- smoking
- drinking
- family information, including marriage, cohabitation and fertility
- income

The 2009 GLF was sponsored by ONS; the NHS Information Centre for Health and Social Care; Department for Work and Pensions; HM Revenue & Customs; and Scottish Government.

The GHS was conducted on a financial year basis between 1994 and 2005, with fieldwork spread evenly across the year from April to March. However, in 2005 the survey period reverted to a calendar year and the whole of the annual sample was dealt with in the nine months April to December 2005. From 2006 the GHS ran from January to December.

Another change in 2005 was that, in line with European requirements, the GHS adopted a longitudinal sample design, in which respondents remain in the sample for four years (waves) with around a quarter of the sample being replaced each year. Approximately 70 per cent of the 2009 sample was also interviewed in 2008. More details are given in Appendix B.

The response rate for the 2009 survey was 73 per cent, giving an achieved sample size of 8,206 households and 15,325 adults aged 16 and over. The smoking and drinking questions were answered in person by 13,488 of these adults (interviews obtained by proxy from another member of the household do not include all questions on smoking and drinking).

Other GLF results for 2009

Results for other GLF topics will be combined with those from other sources in Social Trends and other reports to be published in 2011. Tables from all GLF topic areas are published on the ONS website: www.statistics.gov.uk/StatBase/Product.asp?vlnk=5756. Technical information about the GLF in the form of appendices is also available, including:

- a glossary of definitions and terms used throughout the report and notes on how these have changed over time (Appendix A)
- information about the sample design and response (Appendix B)
- sampling errors (Appendix C)
- weighting (Appendix D)
- the household and individual questionnaires used in 2009, excluding self-completion forms and prompt cards (Appendix E)
- a list of the main topics covered by the survey since 1971 (Appendix F)

Smoking

As smoking is the leading cause of preventable illness and premature death in Great Britain, reducing its prevalence is a key element in improving public health. The GLF and GHS have been monitoring smoking prevalence for over 35 years.

Respondents to the GHS aged 16 and over were asked questions about smoking behaviour in alternate years from 1974 to 1998. Following the review of the GHS carried out in 1997, the smoking questions became part of the continuous survey and have been included every year from 2000 onwards. Note however, that in order to keep the tables in this report to a manageable size they only show data from each fourth year from 1974 to 1998.

This report updates information about trends in cigarette smoking presented in earlier GLF and GHS reports and on the ONS website. It also discusses variations according to personal characteristics such as sex, age, socio-economic classification and economic activity status, and comments briefly on the prevalence of cigarette smoking in different parts of Great Britain. Smoking prevalence in relation to ethnicity is not included in this report; the 2005 report[2] covered this topic in some detail, based on five years' combined data, to give large enough samples for analysis in minority ethnic groups. Other topics covered in 2009 include cigarette consumption, type of cigarette smoked, how old respondents were when they started smoking, and dependence on cigarettes.

Government policy and targets for the reduction of smoking

In December 1998 *Smoking Kills – a White Paper on tobacco*[3] was released, which included targets for reducing the prevalence of cigarette smoking among adults in England to 24 per cent by 2010. In 2004 the Department of Health agreed a Public Service Agreement (PSA) which revised the target downwards: to reduce the prevalence of cigarette smoking among adults in England to 21 per cent or less by 2010[4]. In 2010 the white paper *Healthy Lives, Healthy People*[5] set out the government's long term policy for improving public health that includes the announcement that a new *Tobacco Control Plan* will be published in 2011.

Since smoking is estimated to be the cause of about a third of all cancers, reducing smoking is also one of three key commitments at the heart of the *NHS Cancer Plan*, which was published in 2000[6]. In particular, the *Cancer Plan* focused on the need to reduce the comparatively high rates of smoking among those in manual socio-economic groups, which result in much higher death rates from cancer among unskilled workers than among professionals. The more recent PSA targets mentioned in the previous paragraph also included reducing prevalence among routine and manual groups to 26 per cent or less by 2010.

Legislation came into force in February 2003 banning cigarette advertising on billboards and in the press and magazines in the UK, and further restrictions on advertising at the point of sale were introduced in December 2004. A ban on smoking in enclosed public places came into force in Scotland during the spring of 2006 with similar bans in England and Wales being introduced in

2007. On 1 October 2007 it became illegal in Great Britain to sell tobacco products to anyone under the age of 18. In England, from 1 October 2011, it will become illegal to sell tobacco products from vending machines.

The reliability of smoking estimates

As noted in earlier GHS reports, it is likely that the survey underestimates cigarette consumption and, perhaps to a lesser extent, prevalence (the proportion of people who smoke). For example, evidence suggests (Kozlowski, 1986[7]) that when respondents are asked how many cigarettes they smoke each day, there is a tendency to round the figure down to the nearest multiple of 10. Underestimates of consumption are likely to occur in all age groups. Under-reporting of prevalence, however, is most likely to occur among young people. To protect their privacy, particularly when they are being interviewed in their parents' home, young people aged 16 and 17 complete the smoking and drinking sections of the questionnaire themselves, so that neither the questions nor their responses are heard by anyone else who may be present.[8]

The prevalence of cigarette smoking

Trends in the prevalence of cigarette smoking

In 2009, 21 per cent of the adult population of Great Britain were cigarette smokers. The overall prevalence of smoking has been at this level since 2007.

The prevalence of cigarette smoking fell substantially in the 1970s and the early 1980s, from 45 per cent in 1974 to 35 per cent in 1982. The rate of decline then slowed, with prevalence falling by only about one percentage point every two years until 1994, after which it levelled out at about 27 per cent before resuming a slow decline in the 2000s.

Smoking prevalence was higher among men than women from 1974 until 2008 but in 2008 the difference between men and women was not statistically significant. In 2009, smoking prevalence was slightly higher among men (22 per cent) than among women (20 per cent).

Figure 1.1   Prevalence of cigarette smoking: by sex*
Great Britain

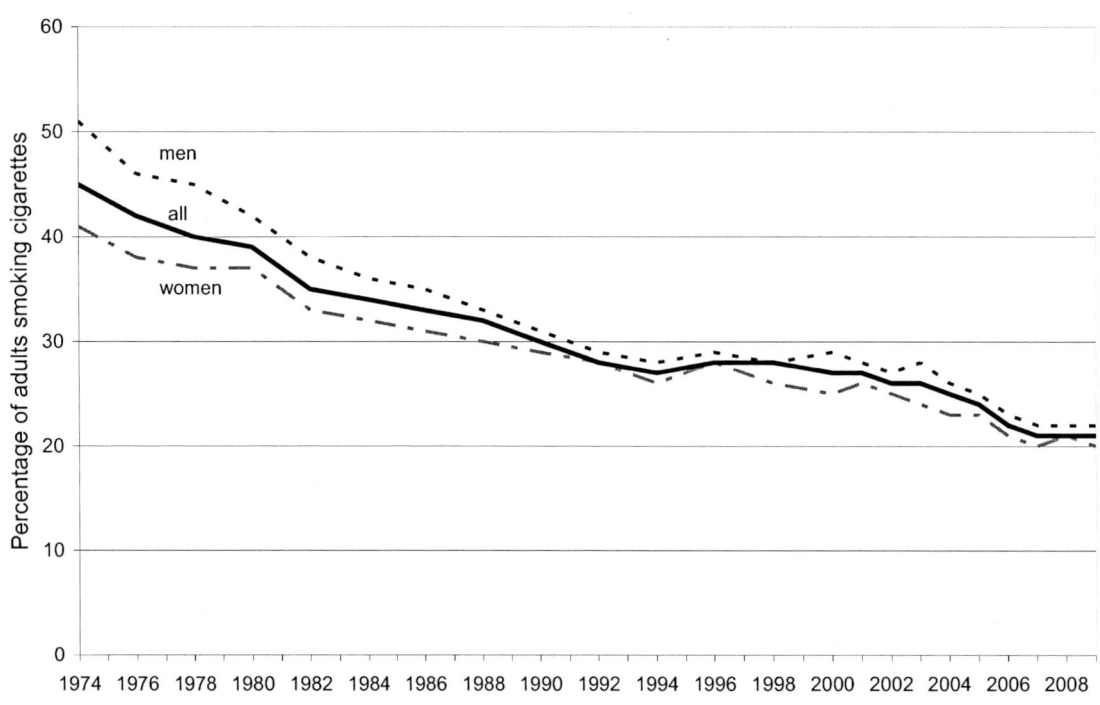

* weighted data are shown from 1998 onwards

Source: General Lifestyle Survey, Office for National Statistics

The difference in smoking prevalence between men and women has decreased considerably since the 1970s. In 1974, for example, 51 per cent of men smoked cigarettes, compared with 41 per cent of women. This 10-point difference has narrowed to just 2 points in 2009.

Overall, the proportion of respondents saying that they had never smoked did not change significantly between 2008 and 2009. There was, however, a significant increase in males aged 20 to 24 reporting that they have never smoked, rising from 61 per cent in 2008 to 71 per cent in 2009. This finding should be treated with caution as it is based on a small number of respondents. The proportion of women who reported being ex-smokers did not change but the proportion of men who reported being ex-smokers decreased from 30 per cent to 28 per cent.

Over the last 30 years there have been falls in the prevalence of smoking in all age groups. Since the survey began, the GHS has shown considerable fluctuation in smoking prevalence among those aged 16 to 19, particularly if young men and young women are considered separately. However, this is mainly because of the relatively small sample size in this age group and occurred within a pattern of overall decline in smoking prevalence in this age group from 31 per cent in 1998 to 24 per cent in 2009. Since the early 1990s the prevalence of cigarette smoking has been higher among those aged 20 to 34 than among those in other age groups. In 2009, this group has the same prevalence as the 35 to 49 group: 26 per cent of the 20 to 24, 25 per cent of the 25 to 34, and 25 per cent of the 35 to 49 age group were smokers. Smoking prevalence continued to be lowest among adults aged 60 and over at 14 per cent.

Figure 1.1, Tables 1.1-1.3

Cigarette smoking and marital status

The prevalence of cigarette smoking varies considerably according to marital status. The groups with the highest proportion of smokers were cohabiting adults (33 per cent) and single adults (27 per cent). Smoking prevalence was much lower among married people (15 per cent) than among those in any of the three other marital status categories (single; cohabiting; and widowed, divorced or separated). This is not explained by the association between age and marital status (for example, married people and those who are widowed, divorced or separated are older, on average, than single people). Table 1.5 shows that in every age group, married people were less likely to be smokers than other respondents. For example, among those aged 25 to 34, 32 per cent of those who were single and 33 per cent of those who were cohabiting were smokers, compared with only 15 per cent of those who were married.

Tables 1.4-1.5

Cigarette smoking and socio-economic classification

The National Statistics Socio-Economic Classification (NS-SEC), which was introduced in 2001, does not allow categories to be collapsed into broad non-manual and manual groupings. So, since the *Cancer Plan* targets for England relate particularly to those in the manual socio-economic groups, the old socio-economic groupings have been recreated for this report in Table 1.6. As a result of the new occupation coding, the classifications are not exactly the same, and comparisons with previous years should be made with caution.

The GHS has consistently shown striking differences in the prevalence of cigarette smoking in relation to socio-economic group, with smoking being considerably more prevalent among those in manual groups than among those in non-manual groups. In the 1970s, 1980s and 1990s, the prevalence of cigarette smoking fell more sharply among those in non-manual than in manual groups, so that differences between the groups became proportionately greater (table not shown).

In the period between 1998 and 2009 smoking continued to fall more quickly in the non-manual group than in the manual group. In the non-manual group smoking fell by a quarter over this period while in the manual group it fell by a fifth. In England in 2009, 26 per cent of those in manual groups were cigarette smokers, compared with 33 per cent in 1998. In the non-manual group 16 per cent were smokers in 2009 compared with 22 per cent in 1998.

Figure 1.2   **Prevalence of cigarette smoking by socio-economic group***

England

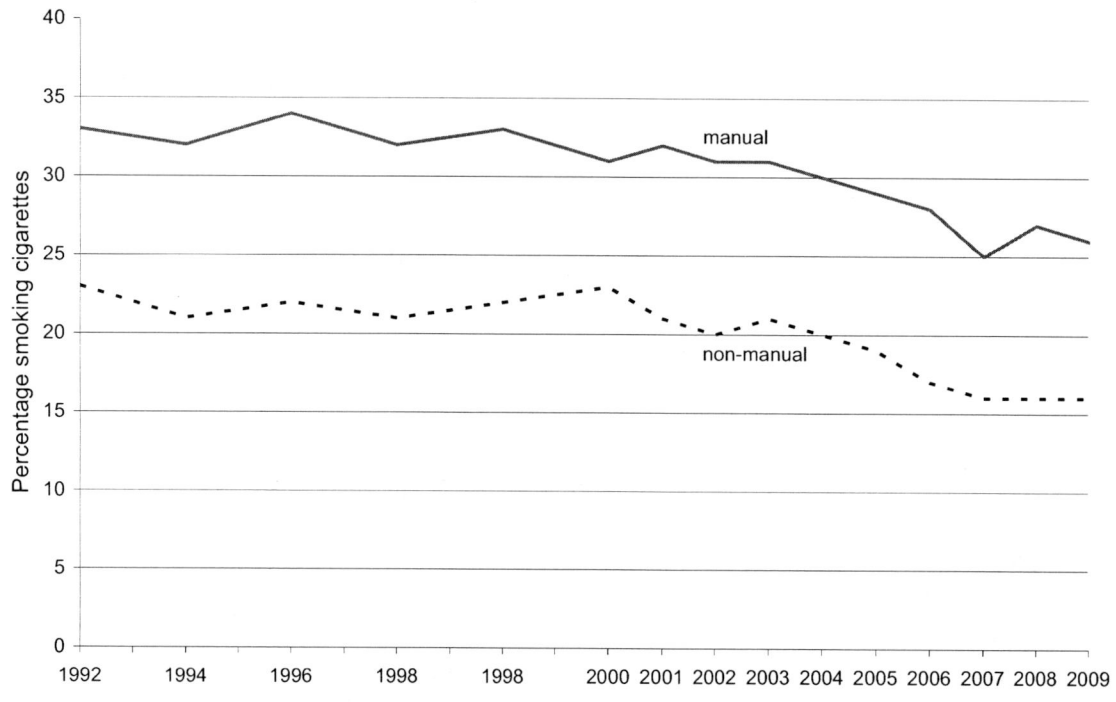

* weighted data are shown from 1998 onwards

Source: General Lifestyle Survey, Office for National Statistics

However, caution is advisable when making comparisons over this period: the re-created socio-economic groups may have been affected by the change from head of household to household reference person as the basis for assessing socio-economic group, and by revisions to the way in which occupation is coded.

Table 1.7 shows similar trends in England since 2001 using the new socio-economic classification[9] (NS-SEC) of the household reference person. The previously mentioned Public Service Agreement (PSA) target was to reduce the prevalence of smoking among those in households classified as routine or manual to 26 per cent or lower by 2010. Over the period 2001 to 2009, the prevalence of cigarette smoking fell by five percentage points among those in routine and manual households (from 33 per cent to 28 per cent), and by eight percentage points among those in intermediate households (from 27 per cent to 19 per cent). Smoking prevalence fell by four percentage points among those in managerial and professional households (from 19 per cent in 2001 to 15 per cent in 2009). In England, smoking is nearly twice as common in routine and manual households as it is in managerial and professional households (28 per cent compared to 15 per cent).

The prevalence of cigarette smoking in Great Britain in 2009 in relation to the eight- and three-category versions of NS-SEC is shown in Table 1.8. As was the case with the socio-economic groupings used previously, there were striking differences between the various classes. Smoking prevalence was lowest among those in higher professional households (10 per cent) and highest, at 32 per cent, among those whose household reference person was in a routine occupation. Between 2008 and 2009 the percentage of women smokers in the intermediate classification decreased from 22 per cent to 16 per cent, leading to a fall in smoking prevalence from 21 per cent to 17 per cent among all adults in that group. In Great Britain, smoking is nearly twice as common in routine and manual households as it is in managerial and professional households (29 per cent compared to 15 per cent).

Figure 1.2, Tables 1.6-1.8

Cigarette smoking and economic activity

Those who were economically active were more likely to smoke than those who were not, but this is largely explained by the lower prevalence of smoking among those aged 60 and over, who form the majority of economically inactive people.

Smoking prevalence was highest among economically inactive people aged 16 to 59: 30 per cent of this group were smokers, compared with 22 per cent of economically active people and only 13 per cent of economically inactive people aged 60 and over. Prevalence was particularly high among economically inactive people aged 16 to 59 whose last job was a routine or manual one, 50 per cent of them were cigarette smokers. This figure shows a significant increase from 2008, when the smoking prevalence of the same group was 42 per cent.

It should be noted that these figures refer to the socio-economic classification of the current or last job of the individual whereas the figures in the previous section refer to the socio-economic classification of the current or last job of the household reference person.

Table 1.9

Variation in cigarette smoking between countries and regions

The data presented so far have been mainly for Great Britain, but the PSA targets and those included in the *NHS Cancer Plan* related to England only. Table 1.10 shows that in 2009, overall prevalence in England was 21 per cent, the same as in Great Britain as a whole.

In every previous year except 2004, smoking prevalence has been higher in Scotland than in England, although the difference has not always been large enough to be statistically significant. In 2009, 25 per cent of adults in Scotland were smokers, a significantly higher proportion than in England. In Wales, 23 per cent of adults were smokers. This figure is not significantly different to the ones for England or Scotland due to sample size.

The region of England with the highest prevalence was the North West, where 23 per cent of people were cigarette smokers. The prevalence of cigarette smoking was lowest, at 18 per cent, in the South West.

Care should be taken in interpreting the results for regional variation in any one year because sample sizes in some regions are small, making them subject to relatively high levels of sampling error.

Tables 1.10-1.12

Cigarette consumption

The overall decline in smoking prevalence in Great Britain since the mid 1970s has been due to a fall in the proportions of both light to moderate smokers (defined as fewer than 20 cigarettes per day) and heavy smokers (20 cigarettes or more per day). The proportion of adults smoking on average 20 or more cigarettes a day fell, between 1974 and 2009, from 26 per cent to 7 per cent among men and from 13 per cent to 5 per cent among women. Over the same period the proportion smoking fewer than 20 per day fell from 25 per cent to 15 per cent for men and from 28 per cent to 15 per cent for women.

In all age groups, respondents were much more likely to be light to moderate than heavy smokers, the difference was most pronounced among those aged under 35. For example, 21 per cent of both men and women aged 25 to 34 were light to moderate smokers in 2009, and only 6 per cent and 3 per cent respectively were heavy smokers.

The overall reported number of cigarettes smoked per male and female smoker has changed little since the early 1980s. As in previous years, male smokers smoked slightly more cigarettes a day on average than female smokers: in 2009, men smoked on average 14 cigarettes a day, compared with 13 for women. Among both men and women smokers, cigarette consumption varied by age. The highest average was 16 cigarettes a day among men in the 50 to 59 age group although the difference between this group and the 35 to 49 and 60 and over age groups was not statistically significant.

GHS reports have consistently shown cigarette consumption levels to be higher among men and women smokers in manual socio-economic groups than among those in non-manual groups. A similar pattern is evident in relation to NS-SEC. In 2009, smokers in households where the household reference person was in a routine or manual occupation smoked an average of 14 cigarettes a day, compared with 12 a day for those in managerial or professional households.

Tables 1.13-1.16

Cigarette type

Filter cigarettes continue to be the most widely smoked type of cigarette, especially among women, but there has been a marked increase since the early 1990s in the proportion of smokers who smoke mainly hand-rolled tobacco. In 1990, 18 per cent of men smokers and 2 per cent of women smokers said they smoked mainly hand-rolled cigarettes, but by 2009 this had risen to 37 per cent and 21 per cent respectively. It should be noted that this increase in the proportion of smokers smoking mainly hand-rolled tobacco coincides with a fall in the prevalence of cigarette smoking from 30 per cent in 1990 to 21 per cent in 2009, so that the proportion of all adults who smoke hand-rolled tobacco has not increased so sharply: it rose from about 3 per cent to about 6 per cent (no table shown).

Figure 1.3, Tables 1.17-1.18

Figure 1.3   Type of cigarette smoked: by sex:
Great Britain

(a) Men

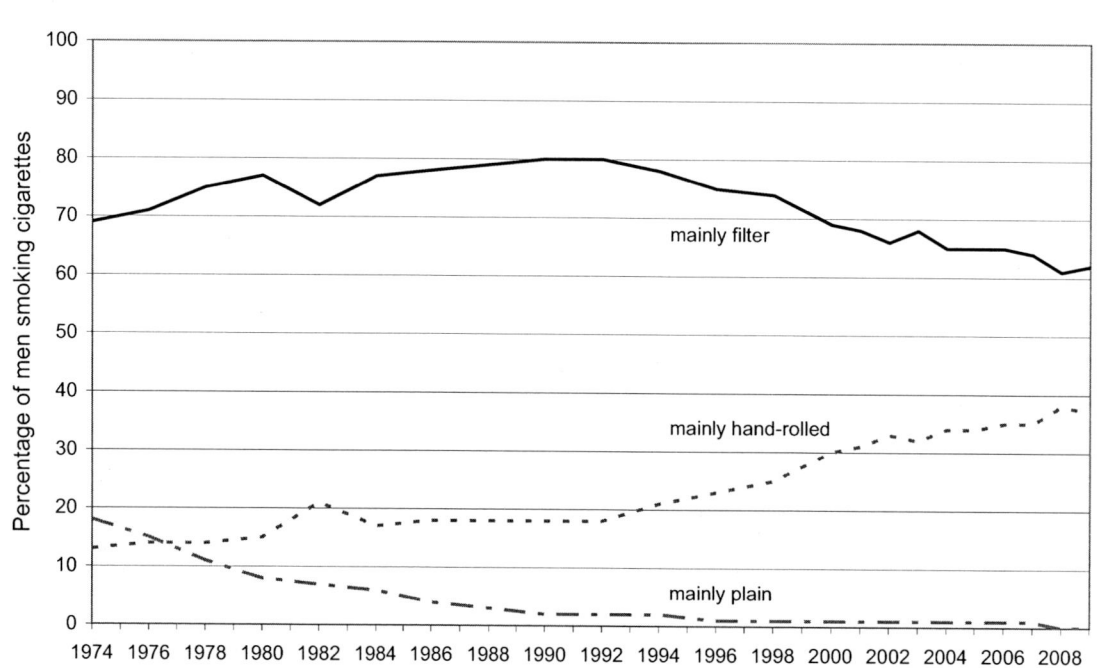

(b) Women

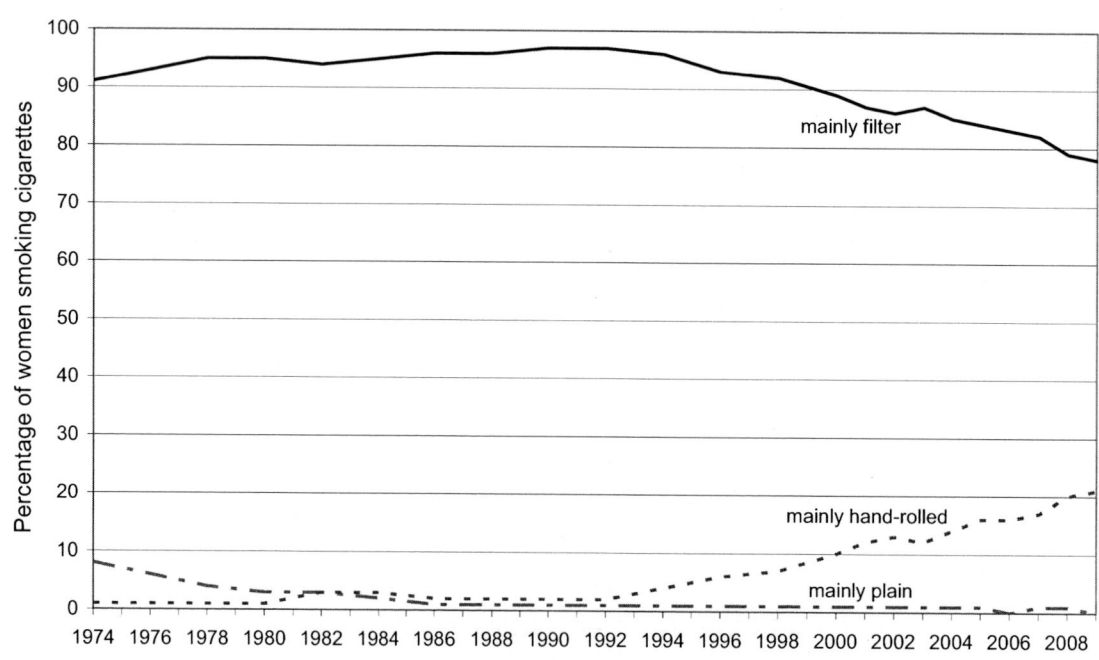

Source: General Lifestyle Survey, Office for National Statistics

Tar yield

In 1986, 40 per cent of those who smoked manufactured cigarettes smoked brands yielding 15 mg or more of tar per cigarette. In the following decade, the proportion smoking this type of cigarette fell to zero. Initially, this was partly due to smokers switching to lower tar brands, but the main factor has been the requirement for manufacturers to reduce substantially the tar yields of existing brands. Following legislation in 1992, they were required to reduce the tar yield to no more than 12 mg per cigarette by the beginning of 1998. A European Union directive which came into force at the end of 2002 further reduced the maximum tar yield to 10 mg per cigarette from January 2004.

The effect of the recent changes in legislation can be seen in Table 1.20, in that there have been no brands with a yield of 12 mg or more since 2003, even though these were the main brand of more than a third of smokers in previous years. There was a corresponding increase in the next highest category: the proportion of smokers smoking brands with a yield of 10 to 11mg increased from 13 per cent in 1998 to 71 per cent in 2003 staying at about the same level until 2007 when it dropped to 62 per cent[10]. In 2009 the proportion of smokers smoking brands with a yield of 10 to 11mg was 59 per cent.

There was a difference in tar yield of cigarettes smoked according to the socio-economic class of the smoker's household reference person. Those in managerial and professional households were more likely than other smokers to smoke lower tar cigarettes: 36 per cent of smokers in managerial and professional households smoked cigarettes with a tar yield less than 8 mg, compared with only 18 per cent of smokers in routine and manual households.

Tables 1.19-1.22

Cigar and pipe smoking

A decline in the prevalence of pipe and cigar smoking among men has been evident since the survey began, with most of the reduction occurring in the 1970s and 1980s.

In 2009 only 2 per cent of men smoked at least one cigar a month, compared with 34 per cent in 1974. Only a small number of women smoked cigars in 1974, and since 1978 the percentages have been scarcely measurable on the GHS.

Less than half of 1 per cent of men in 2009 said they smoked a pipe (rounded to zero in the tables), and they were almost all aged 50 and over. Cigar smoking is slightly more common among men aged 30 and over than it is among men aged under 30.

Figure 1.4, Tables 1.23-1.24

Figure 1.4   **Type of tobacco product smoked by men**

Great Britain

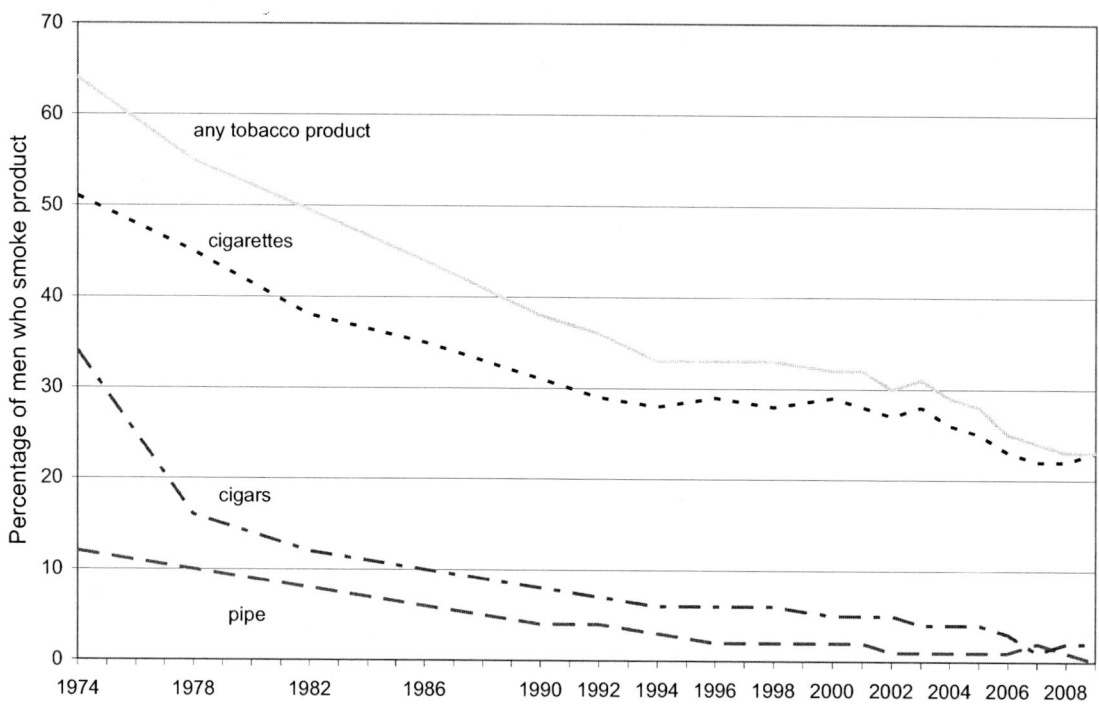

Source: General Lifestyle Survey, Office for National Statistics

Age started smoking

The White Paper *Smoking Kills* noted that people who start smoking at an early age are more likely than other smokers to smoke for a long period of time and more likely to die from a smoking-related disease.

About two-thirds of respondents who were either current smokers or who had smoked regularly at some time in their lives had started smoking before they were 18. Almost two-fifths had started smoking regularly before the age of 16 even though it has been illegal to sell cigarettes to people aged under 16 since 1908 and has recently become illegal to sell cigarettes to people under 18 years of age[11]. Men were more likely than women to have started smoking before they were 16 (42 per cent of men who had ever smoked regularly, compared with 37 per cent of women in 2009).

Since the early 1990s there has been an increase in the proportion of women taking up smoking before the age of 16. In 1992, 28 per cent of women who had ever smoked started before they were 16. In 2009 the corresponding figure was 37 per cent. There has been little change since 1992 in the proportion of men who had ever smoked who had started smoking regularly before the age of 16.

As the GHS has shown in previous years, there was an association between age started smoking regularly and socio-economic classification based on the current or last job of the household reference person. In managerial and professional households, 33 per cent of smokers had started smoking before they were 16, compared with 47 per cent of those in routine and manual households.

Current heavy smokers were more likely than light or ex-smokers to have started smoking at an early age. Of those smoking 20 or more cigarettes a day, 52 per cent started smoking regularly before they were 16, compared with 39 per cent of those currently smoking fewer than 10 cigarettes a day.

Tables 1.25-1.27

Dependence on cigarette smoking

Since 1992 the GHS/GLF has asked three questions relevant to the likelihood of a smoker giving up. First, whether they would like to stop smoking, and then two indicators of dependence: whether they think they would find it easy or difficult not to smoke for a whole day and how soon after waking they smoke their first cigarette. There has been little change since 1992 in any of the three measures.

In 2009, 63 per cent of smokers said they would like to stop smoking altogether and 57 per cent of smokers felt that it would be either very or fairly difficult to go without smoking for a whole day. Not surprisingly, heavier smokers were more likely to say they would find it difficult – 81 per cent of those smoking 20 or more cigarettes a day did so, compared with only 28 per cent of those smoking fewer than 10 cigarettes a day.

In 2009, 15 per cent of smokers had their first cigarette within five minutes of waking up. Heavy smokers were more likely than light smokers to smoke immediately on waking: 32 per cent of those smoking 20 or more cigarettes did so, compared with only 3 per cent of those smoking fewer than 10 a day.

Smokers in routine and manual households were more likely than those in managerial and professional households to say they would find it difficult to go without smoking for a whole day (61 per cent compared with 50 per cent). However, once amount smoked was taken into account (smokers in the routine and manual group smoke more on average than smokers in other social classes) the pattern of association was less clear.

Overall, smokers in managerial and professional households were less likely than those in routine and manual households to have had their first cigarette within five minutes of waking than those in routine and manual households (11 per cent compared with 18 per cent).

Tables 1.28-1.33

Notes and references

1   The term 'household reference person' is defined in appendix A of the GLF overview report. Available at: www.statistics.gov.uk/StatBase/Product.asp?vlnk=5756

2   Goddard E, General Household Survey 2005, Smoking and drinking among adults, 2005, ONS 2006.

3   Smoking kills – a White Paper on tobacco. The Stationery Office (London 1998)

4   Available at www.hm-treasury.gov.uk/spend_sr04_psaindex.htm

5   Healthy lives, healthy people: our strategy for public health in England, Department of Health, 2010: available at http://www.dh.gov.uk/prod_consum_dh/groups/dh_digitalassets/@dh/@en/@ps/documents/digitalasset/dh_122347.pdf

6   The NHS Cancer Plan, Department of Health, 2000: available at www.dh.gov.uk/assetRoot/04/01/45/13/04014513.pdf

7   Kozlowski L T, Pack size, reported smoking rates and public health, American Journal of Public Health, 76 (11) pp1337–8 November 1986

8   See Chapter 4, General Household Survey 1992, HMSO 1994. This includes a discussion of the differences found when smoking prevalence reported by young adults on the GHS was compared with prevalence among secondary school children

9   Further information on National Statistics Socio-Economic Classification is available at: www.ons.gov.uk/about-statistics/classifications/current/ns-sec/index.html

10   An error was found in the automated procedure for coding the brand of cigarette smoked which was introduced when the GHS moved to computerised interviewing in April 1994. The net effect of this was that from 1994 to 2000, some brands were wrongly assigned to a low tar category. The coding procedure was revised for the 2001 survey. Corrected data for 1998 and 2000 are given in Tables 1.19 and 1.20

11   The legal minimum age was raised to 18 on 1 October 2007.

Smoking tables

Figures for unweighted sample sizes are rounded independently. The sum of component items does not, therefore, necessarily add to the totals shown.

The following conventions have been used within tables:
- Category not available.
* Information is suppressed as a measure of disclosure control.

Table 1.1 Prevalence of cigarette smoking by sex and age: 1974 to 2009

Persons aged 16 and over   Great Britain

Age	Unweighted							Weighted												Weighted base 2009 (000s) =100%[3]	Unweighted sample[3] 2009
	1974	1978	1982	1986	1990	1994	1998	1998	2000	2001	2002	2003	2004	2005[1]	2006[2]	2007[2]	2008[2]	2009[2]		
								Percentage smoking cigarettes													
Men																				
16-19	42	35	31	30	28	28	30	30	30	25	22	27	23	23	20	22	18	24	1,083	280
20-24	52	45	41	41	38	40	42	41	35	40	37	38	36	34	33	32	29	24	1,232	280
25-34	56	48	40	37	36	34	37	38	39	38	36	38	35	34	33	29	30	27	2,867	690
35-49	55	48	40	37	34	31	32	33	31	31	29	32	31	29	26	25	24	26	5,578	1,530
50-59	53	48	42	35	28	27	27	28	27	26	27	26	26	25	23	22	23	22	3,088	1,030
60 and over	44	38	33	29	24	18	16	16	16	16	17	16	15	14	13	13	13	15	5,753	2,340
All aged 16 and over	51	45	38	35	31	28	28	30	29	28	27	28	26	25	23	22	22	22	19,602	6,160
Women																				
16-19	38	33	30	30	32	27	31	32	28	31	29	25	25	26	20	20	26	24	1,092	290
20-24	44	43	40	38	39	38	39	39	35	35	38	34	29	30	29	30	31	28	1,444	330
25-34	46	42	37	35	34	30	33	33	32	31	33	31	28	29	26	23	25	24	3,148	890
35-49	49	43	38	34	33	28	28	29	27	28	27	28	28	26	25	23	23	23	6,411	1,940
50-59	48	42	40	35	29	26	27	27	28	25	24	23	22	23	22	21	20	20	3,422	1,180
60 and over	26	24	23	22	20	17	16	16	15	17	14	14	14	13	12	12	12	13	6,747	2,660
All aged 16 and over	41	37	33	31	29	26	26	26	25	26	25	24	23	23	21	20	21	20	22,263	7,290
Total																				
16-19	40	34	30	30	30	27	31	31	29	28	25	26	24	24	20	21	22	24	2,175	560
20-24	48	44	40	39	38	39	40	40	35	37	38	36	32	32	31	31	30	26	2,676	620
25-34	51	45	38	36	35	32	35	35	35	34	34	34	31	31	30	26	27	25	6,015	1,580
35-49	52	45	39	36	34	30	30	31	29	29	28	30	29	27	25	24	24	25	11,988	3,470
50-59	51	45	41	35	29	27	27	28	27	26	26	25	24	24	22	21	22	21	6,510	2,220
60 and over	34	30	27	25	21	17	16	16	16	17	15	15	14	14	12	12	13	14	12,500	5,000
All aged 16 and over	45	40	35	33	30	27	27	28	27	27	26	26	25	24	22	21	21	21	41,865	13,450

1 2005 data includes last quarter of 2004/05 data due to survey change from financial year to calendar year.
2 Results from 2006 include longitudinal data (see Appendix B).
3 Trend tables show unweighted and weighted figures for 1998 to give an indication of the effect of the weighting. Bases for earlier years can be found in GLF/GHS reports for each year.

Source: General Lifestyle Survey, Office for National Statistics

Table 1.2 Ex-regular cigarette smokers by sex and age: 1974 to 2009

Persons aged 16 and over   Great Britain

Age	Unweighted							Weighted											Weighted base 2009 (000s) =100%[3]	Unweighted sample[3] 2009
	1974	1978	1982	1986	1990	1994	1998	1998	2000	2001	2002	2003	2004	2005[1]	2006[2]	2007[2]	2008[2]	2009[2]		
	Percentage of ex-regular cigarette smokers																			
Men																				
16-19	3	4	4	5	4	5	5	5	3	4	3	5	4	3	4	1	3	3	1,083	280
20-24	9	9	9	11	8	7	8	9	7	9	7	7	8	7	11	9	11	6	1,232	280
25-34	18	18	20	20	16	16	13	13	12	15	13	13	15	14	16	17	17	17	2,867	690
35-49	21	26	32	33	32	27	22	21	20	20	20	20	20	19	20	21	25	24	5,578	1,530
50-59	30	35	38	38	42	40	41	40	36	36	35	32	34	34	31	33	31	31	3,088	1,030
60 and over	37	43	47	52	52	55	54	54	52	47	51	50	50	51	49	49	50	48	5,753	2,340
All aged 16 and over	23	27	30	32	32	31	31	29	27	27	28	27	28	27	27	28	30	28	19,602	6,160
Women																				
16-19	4	5	6	7	6	6	7	8	6	6	5	6	4	4	4	2	3	6	1,092	290
20-24	9	8	9	9	8	10	8	8	11	12	10	10	8	9	11	11	10	10	1,444	330
25-34	12	14	15	16	14	14	14	14	13	16	16	16	14	15	17	16	18	18	3,148	890
35-49	10	13	15	20	20	21	19	19	19	19	17	16	18	18	18	19	19	21	6,411	1,940
50-59	13	18	19	18	20	22	25	25	24	24	26	27	27	25	25	25	23	23	3,422	1,180
60 and over	11	16	20	23	27	29	29	29	29	29	30	29	28	29	30	29	31	31	6,747	2,660
All aged 16 and over	11	14	16	18	19	21	21	20	20	21	21	21	20	21	21	21	22	22	22,263	7,290

1 2005 data includes last quarter of 2004/5 data due to survey change from financial year to calendar year.
2 Results from 2006 include longitudinal data (see Appendix B).
3 Trend tables show unweighted and weighted figures for 1998 to give an indication of the effect of the weighting. Bases for earlier years can be found in GLF/GHS reports for each year.

Source: General Lifestyle Survey, Office for National Statistics

Table 1.3 Percentage who have never smoked cigarettes regularly by sex and age: 1974 to 2009

Persons aged 16 and over   Great Britain

Age	Unweighted							Weighted											Weighted base 2009 (000s) =100%[3]	Unweighted sample[3] 2009
	1974	1978	1982	1986	1990	1994	1998	1998	2000	2001	2002	2003	2004	2005[1]	2006[2]	2007[2]	2008[2]	2009[2]		
	Percentage who have never smoked regularly																			
Men																				
16-19	56	61	65	65	68	67	64	65	67	71	75	68	72	74	77	77	80	74	1,083	280
20-24	38	46	50	47	54	53	49	50	58	51	55	54	55	59	56	59	61	71	1,232	280
25-34	26	33	39	43	48	50	50	49	49	47	51	49	50	53	51	54	54	56	2,867	690
35-49	24	26	28	30	34	42	46	45	49	49	51	48	50	52	54	53	50	50	5,578	1,530
50-59	16	17	20	26	31	33	32	32	37	38	38	41	40	41	46	45	46	48	3,088	1,030
60 and over	18	18	20	19	24	27	30	30	32	36	32	34	35	35	38	38	37	38	5,753	2,340
All aged 16 and over	25	29	32	34	37	40	41	42	44	45	46	45	46	47	50	50	49	50	19,602	6,160
Women																				
16-19	58	62	64	62	62	67	62	61	66	63	66	69	70	70	76	78	71	70	1,092	290
20-24	47	49	51	54	53	52	53	53	54	53	52	55	62	61	61	60	59	62	1,444	330
25-34	42	44	48	48	52	55	53	53	54	53	51	53	58	56	57	61	57	58	3,148	890
35-49	41	44	47	46	48	51	52	52	54	53	55	55	54	56	58	58	57	56	6,411	1,940
50-59	38	39	41	47	51	52	48	48	48	51	50	50	51	51	53	55	56	57	3,422	1,180
60 and over	63	60	57	55	54	54	55	56	56	54	55	57	58	58	58	58	57	56	6,747	2,660
All aged 16 and over	49	49	51	51	52	54	53	53	54	53	54	55	57	57	58	59	58	57	22,263	7,290

1 2005 data includes last quarter of 2004/5 data due to survey change from financial year to calendar year.
2 Results from 2006 include longitudinal data (see Appendix B).
3 Trend tables show unweighted and weighted figures for 1998 to give an indication of the effect of the weighting. Bases for earlier years can be found in GLF/GHS reports for each year.

Source: General Lifestyle Survey, Office for National Statistics

Table 1.4 Cigarette-smoking status by sex and marital status

Persons aged 16 and over   *Great Britain: 2009*[1]

Marital status	Current cigarette smokers			Current non-smokers of cigarettes		Weighted base (000s)= 100%	Unweighted sample
	Light to moderate (under 20 per day)	Heavy (20 or more per day)	Total	Ex-regular cigarette smokers	Never or only occasionally smoked cigarettes		
		Percentages					
Men							
Single	20	6	27	13	61	*4,766*	*1,180*
Married/cohabiting	13	6	19	33	48	*12,652*	*4,280*
Married couple	11	5	16	36	49	*10,577*	*3,670*
Cohabiting couple	25	9	35	20	45	*2,075*	*610*
Widowed/divorced/separated	16	12	29	36	35	*2,185*	*700*
All aged 16 and over	15	7	22	28	50	*19,602*	*6,160*
Women							
Single	22	7	28	12	59	*4,199*	*1,190*
Married/cohabiting	13	4	17	23	60	*13,443*	*4,540*
Married couple	11	4	14	23	63	*11,181*	*3,860*
Cohabiting couple	26	5	31	24	45	*2,262*	*680*
Widowed/divorced/separated	15	6	22	30	48	*4,621*	*1,560*
All aged 16 and over	15	5	20	22	57	*22,263*	*7,290*
Total							
Single	21	7	27	13	60	*8,965*	*2,370*
Married/cohabiting	13	5	18	28	54	*26,095*	*8,820*
Married couple	11	4	15	29	56	*21,758*	*7,530*
Cohabiting couple	26	7	33	22	45	*4,337*	*1,290*
Widowed/divorced/separated	16	8	24	32	44	*6,805*	*2,260*
All aged 16 and over	15	6	21	25	54	*41,865*	*13,450*

1   Results for 2009 include longitudinal data (see Appendix B).

Source: General Lifestyle Survey, Office for National Statistics

Table 1.5 Cigarette-smoking status by age and marital status

Persons aged 16 and over   *Great Britain: 2009[1]*

Marital status	Age					
	16-24	25-34	35-49	50-59	60 and over	Total
	Percentage smoking cigarettes					
Single	23	32	35	27	20	27
Married/cohabiting	32	22	20	18	12	18
Married couple	20	15	17	17	11	15
Cohabiting couple	38	33	35	30	17	33
Widowed/divorced/separated	*	52	39	31	17	24
All aged 16 and over	25	25	25	21	14	21
Weighted base (000s)= 100%						
Single	4,052	1,752	1,890	510	761	8,965
Married/cohabiting	792	4,142	8,719	4,999	7,444	26,095
Married couple	291	2,551	7,143	4,620	7,154	21,758
Cohabiting couple	500	1,591	1,576	379	290	4,337
Widowed/divorced/separated	8	121	1,380	1,001	4,296	6,805
All aged 16 and over	4,852	6,015	11,988	6,510	12,500	41,865
Unweighted sample						
Single	1,000	450	490	160	270	2,370
Married/cohabiting	180	1,090	2,570	1,730	3,240	8,820
Married couple	50	670	2,100	1,590	3,110	7,530
Cohabiting couple	130	420	470	140	130	1,290
Widowed/divorced/separated	0	40	410	320	1,490	2,260
All aged 16 and over	1,180	1,580	3,470	2,220	5,000	13,450

1 Results for 2009 include longitudinal data (see Appendix B).

* Information is suppressed for low cell counts as a measure of disclosure control.

Shaded figures indicate the estimates are unreliable and any analysis using these figures may be invalid. Any use of these shaded figures must be accompanied by this disclaimer.

Source: General Lifestyle Survey, Office for National Statistics

Table 1.6 Prevalence of cigarette smoking by sex and whether household reference person is in a non-manual socio-economic group: England 1992 to 2009

Persons aged 16 and over																England
Socio-economic group of household reference person[3]	Unweighted				Weighted											Weighted base 2009 (000s) =100%[5]	Unweighted sample[5] 2009
	1992	1994	1996	1998	1998	2000	2001	2002	2003	2004	2005[4]	2006[2]	2007[2]	2008[2]	2009[2]		
Percentage smoking cigarettes																	
Men																	
Non-manual	22	21	21	21	22	24	22	21	22	22	19	18	18	16	17	8,908	2,770
Manual	35	34	35	34	35	34	34	32	33	31	31	29	27	28	27	6,852	2,160
Total[6]	29	28	28	28	29	29	28	27	27	26	25	23	22	21	22	16,765	5,220
Women																	
Non-manual	23	21	22	21	22	22	20	20	20	19	18	16	16	16	15	10,491	3,420
Manual	30	30	33	31	31	29	31	30	29	28	28	27	24	26	25	7,288	2,360
Total[6]	27	25	27	26	26	25	25	25	24	23	22	21	19	20	20	18,991	6,160
All persons																	
Non-manual	23	21	22	21	22	23	21	20	21	20	19	17	16	16	16	19,400	6,190
Manual	33	32	34	32	33	31	32	31	31	30	29	28	25	27	26	14,140	4,520
Total[6]	28	26	28	27	28	27	27	26	25	25	24	22	21	21	21	35,756	11,370

1   Figures for 1992 to 1996 are taken from Department of Health bulletin Statistics on smoking: England, 1978 onwards. Figures for 2001 to 2006 are based on the NS-SEC classification recoded to produce SEG and should therefore be treated with caution.

2   Results from 2006 include longitudinal data (see Appendix B).

3   Head of household in years before 2000.

4   2005 data includes last quarter of 2004/5 data due to survey change from financial year to calendar year.

5   Trend tables show unweighted and weighted figures for 1998 to give an indication of the effect of the weighting. Bases for earlier years can be found in GLF/GHS reports for each year.

6   Respondents whose head of household/household reference person was a full time student, in the Armed forces, had an inadequately described occupation, had never worked or were long-term unemployed are not shown as separate categories but are included in the total

Source: General Lifestyle Survey, Office for National Statistics

Table 1.7 Prevalence of cigarette smoking by sex and socio-economic classification of the household reference person: England, 2001 to 2009

Persons aged 16 and over   *England*

Socio-economic classification of household reference person	Weighted									Weighted base 2009 (000s) = 100%[4]	Unweighted sample[4] 2009
	2001	2002	2003	2004	2005[2]	2006[1]	2007[1]	2008[1]	2009[1]		
	Percentage smoking cigarettes										
Men											
Managerial and professional	21	20	20	20	18	17	16	15	15	7,298	2,270
Intermediate	29	27	28	26	24	22	21	21	20	2,761	860
Routine and manual	34	32	34	32	32	32	28	31	29	5,725	1,810
Total[3]	28	27	27	26	25	23	22	21	22	16,777	5,220
Women											
Managerial and professional	17	17	17	17	16	14	14	14	14	7,689	2,490
Intermediate	26	25	24	22	22	20	18	21	18	3,455	1,120
Routine and manual	31	31	30	30	29	28	24	27	27	6,719	2,180
Total[3]	25	25	24	23	22	21	19	20	20	19,019	6,160
All persons											
Managerial and professional	19	19	18	19	17	15	15	14	15	14,987	4,760
Intermediate	27	26	26	24	23	21	20	21	19	6,216	1,980
Routine and manual	33	31	32	31	31	29	26	29	28	12,444	3,980
Total[3]	27	26	25	25	24	22	21	21	21	35,796	11,380

1 Results from 2006 include longitudinal data (see Appendix B).

2 2005 data includes last quarter of 2004/5 data due to survey change from financial year to calendar year.

3 Respondents whose household reference person was a full time student, had an inadequately described occupation, had never worked or was long-term unemployed these are not shown as separate categories but are included in the total.

4 Trend tables show unweighted and weighted figures for 1998 to give an indication of the effect of the weighting. Bases for earlier years can be found in GLF/GHS reports for each year.

Source: General Lifestyle Survey, Office for National Statistics

Table 1.8　Prevalence of cigarette smoking by sex and socio-economic classification based on the current or last job of the household reference person

Persons aged 16 and over　　　　　　　　　　　　　　　　　　　*Great Britain: 2009[1]*

Socio-economic classification of household reference person[2]	Men		Women		Total	
	Percentage smoking cigarettes					
Managerial and professional						
Large employers and higher managerial	12		13		13	
Higher professional	11	15	10	14	10	15
Lower managerial and professional	18		16		17	
Intermediate						
Intermediate	19	21	16	19	17	20
Small employers and own account	23		21		22	
Routine and manual						
Lower supervisory and technical	25		27		26	
Semi-routine	31	30	26	27	28	29
Routine	34		30		32	
Total[2]	22		20		21	
Weighted bases (000s) =100%						
Large employers and higher managerial	1,282		1,326		2,607	
Higher professional	2,092		1,789		3,881	
Lower managerial and professional	4,976		5,668		10,642	
Intermediate	1,292		2,176		3,468	
Small employers and own account	1,893		1,859		3,753	
Lower supervisory and technical	2,472		2,303		4,775	
Semi-routine	2,247		3,218		5,464	
Routine	2,134		2,388		4,521	
Total[2]	19,563		22,150		41,713	
Unweighted sample						
Large employers and higher managerial	420		440		860	
Higher professional	630		590		1,220	
Lower managerial and professional	1,570		1,870		3,450	
Intermediate	400		710		1,100	
Small employers and own account	600		610		1,210	
Lower supervisory and technical	800		760		1,550	
Semi-routine	690		1,040		1,730	
Routine	690		790		1,480	
Total[2]	6,140		7,250		13,400	

1　Results for 2009 include longitudinal data (see Appendix B).

2　Respondents whose household reference person was a full time student, had an inadequately described occupation, had never worked or was long-term unemployed are not shown as separate categories but are included in the total.

Source: General Lifestyle Survey, Office for National Statistics

Table 1.9 Prevalence of cigarette smoking by sex and socio-economic classification based on own current or last job, whether economically active or inactive, and, for economically inactive persons, age

Persons aged 16 and over
Great Britain: 2009[1]

Socio-economic classification	Men					Women					All persons				
	Active	Inactive 16-59	Inactive 60 and over	Total inactive	Total	Active	Inactive 16-59	Inactive 60 and over	Total inactive	Total	Active	Inactive 16-59	Inactive 60 and over	Total inactive	Total
							Percentage smoking cigarettes								
Managerial and professional	16	25	8	10	15	15	14	10	11	14	16	17	9	11	15
Intermediate	21	42	14	18	21	19	21	11	13	19	20	26	12	15	20
Routine and manual	31	59	19	29	30	30	45	17	26	27	31	50	18	27	29
Total[2]	23	35	13	20	22	21	28	13	19	20	22	30	13	19	21
Weighted bases (000s) =100%															
Managerial and professional	5,493	241	1,557	1,799	7,292	4,979	638	1,299	1,936	6,915	10,472	879	2,856	3,735	14,207
Intermediate	2,201	126	669	795	2,996	2,927	470	1,449	1,919	4,846	5,128	596	2,118	2,714	7,842
Routine and manual	4,439	617	1,905	2,522	6,966	4,016	1,203	2,561	3,765	7,784	8,455	1,821	4,466	6,287	14,750
Total[2]	13,419	1,822	4,352	6,174	19,602	12,974	3,523	5,763	9,287	22,263	26,393	5,346	10,115	15,461	41,865
Unweighted sample															
Managerial and professional	1,610	70	660	720	2,340	1,530	200	520	720	2,250	3,150	270	1,180	1,440	4,590
Intermediate	660	40	270	310	970	900	140	580	720	1,620	1,560	180	850	1,030	2,590
Routine and manual	1,280	170	780	950	2,230	1,230	400	990	1,380	2,620	2,510	570	1,760	2,330	4,850
Total[2]	3,870	500	1,790	2,280	6,160	3,960	1,070	2,260	3,330	7,290	7,830	1,560	4,050	5,610	13,450

1 Results for 2009 include longitudinal data (see Appendix B).

2 Full time students, those who had never worked or were long-term unemployed, and those whose occupation was inadequately described are not shown as separate categories but are included in the total.

Shaded figures indicate the estimates are unreliable and any analysis using these figures may be invalid. Any use of these shaded figures must be accompanied by this disclaimer.

Source: General Lifestyle Survey, Office for National Statistics

Table 1.10 Prevalence of cigarette smoking by sex and country: 1978 to 2009

Persons aged 16 and over   *Great Britain*

Country	Unweighted						Weighted											Weighted base 2009 (000s) =100%³	Unweighted sample³ 2009
	1978	1982	1986	1990	1994	1998	1998	2000	2001	2002	2003	2004	2005¹	2006²	2007²	2008²	2009²		
							Percentage smoking cigarettes												
Men																			
England	44	37	34	31	28	28	29	29	28	27	27	26	25	23	22	21	22	16,816	5,230
Wales	44	36	33	30	28	28	29	25	27	27	29	24	24	19	21	20	21	1,035	370
Scotland	48	45	37	33	31	33	35	30	32	29	35	29	28	25	24	23	25	1,751	550
Great Britain	45	38	35	31	28	28	30	29	28	27	28	26	25	23	22	22	22	19,602	6,160
Women																			
England	36	32	31	28	25	26	26	25	25	25	24	23	22	21	19	20	20	19,121	6,190
Wales	37	34	30	31	27	26	27	24	26	27	26	22	21	20	20	21	24	1,162	430
Scotland	42	39	35	35	29	29	29	30	30	28	28	22	25	25	24	24	24	1,980	670
Great Britain	37	33	31	29	26	26	26	25	26	25	24	23	23	21	20	21	20	22,263	7,290
All persons																			
England	40	35	32	29	26	27	28	27	27	26	25	25	24	22	21	21	21	35,937	11,430
Wales	40	35	31	31	27	27	28	25	27	27	27	23	22	20	21	21	23	2,198	800
Scotland	45	42	36	34	30	30	31	30	31	28	31	25	27	25	24	24	25	3,731	1,220
Great Britain	40	35	33	30	27	27	28	27	27	26	26	25	24	22	21	21	21	41,865	13,450

1 2005 data includes last quarter of 2004/5 data due to survey change from financial year to calendar year.
2 Results from 2006 include longitudinal data (see Appendix B).
3 Trend tables show unweighted and weighted figures for 1998 to give an indication of the effect of the weighting. Bases for earlier years can be found in GLF/GHS reports for each year.

Source: General Lifestyle Survey, Office for National Statistics

Table 1.11 Prevalence of cigarette smoking by sex, country, and region of England: 1998 to 2009

Persons aged 16 and over													*Great Britain*
Government Office Region	Weighted											*Weighted base 2009 (000s) =100%[3]*	*Unweighted sample[3] 2009*
	1998	2000	2001	2002	2003	2004	2005[1]	2006[2]	2007[2]	2008[2]	2009[2]		
Men				Percentage smoking cigarettes									
England													
North East	28	27	33	24	30	28	28	25	21	17	20	*702*	*250*
North West	29	29	28	28	30	27	26	26	25	25	24	*2,584*	*750*
Yorkshire and the Humber	30	29	30	27	25	30	27	24	21	24	23	*1,732*	*600*
East Midlands	27	27	28	24	31	27	25	21	22	20	19	*1,589*	*550*
West Midlands	32	27	27	25	26	26	23	25	25	21	22	*1,754*	*530*
East of England	26	27	27	25	28	26	25	22	20	20	20	*1,980*	*660*
London	34	31	29	29	28	26	25	24	22	21	26	*2,199*	*520*
South East	28	28	26	27	25	25	24	21	21	21	21	*2,803*	*840*
South West	26	30	27	27	26	25	26	22	21	21	19	*1,472*	*540*
All England	29	29	28	27	27	26	25	23	22	21	22	*16,816*	*5,230*
Wales	29	25	27	27	29	24	24	19	21	20	21	*1,035*	*370*
Scotland	35	30	32	29	35	29	28	25	24	23	25	*1,751*	*550*
Great Britain	30	29	28	27	28	26	25	23	22	22	22	*19,602*	*6,160*
Women													
England													
North East	30	28	26	29	27	30	30	25	22	23	23	*925*	*330*
North West	32	30	29	28	30	28	23	23	22	22	22	*2,677*	*840*
Yorkshire and the Humber	28	26	28	27	24	26	23	23	23	25	22	*1,931*	*700*
East Midlands	26	24	27	24	24	28	25	19	17	19	18	*1,724*	*620*
West Midlands	26	24	22	21	24	21	21	19	21	19	21	*2,058*	*630*
East of England	24	23	25	25	22	23	21	17	16	18	18	*2,160*	*740*
London	27	24	26	21	20	19	20	19	17	18	19	*2,622*	*640*
South East	21	23	23	25	22	20	21	19	17	18	18	*3,196*	*990*
South West	25	24	22	24	22	21	25	23	20	22	17	*1,828*	*700*
All England	26	25	25	25	24	23	22	21	19	20	20	*19,121*	*6,190*
Wales	27	24	26	27	26	22	21	20	20	21	24	*1,162*	*430*
Scotland	29	30	30	28	28	22	25	25	24	24	24	*1,980*	*670*
Great Britain	26	25	26	25	24	23	23	21	20	21	20	*22,263*	*7,290*
All persons													
England													
North East	29	27	29	27	28	29	29	25	22	21	22	*1,627*	*580*
North West	31	30	29	28	30	28	24	25	23	23	23	*5,261*	*1,580*
Yorkshire and the Humber	29	28	29	27	25	28	25	23	22	25	22	*3,664*	*1,300*
East Midlands	27	25	28	24	27	27	25	20	19	20	19	*3,313*	*1,170*
West Midlands	29	26	24	23	25	23	22	22	23	20	22	*3,812*	*1,160*
East of England	25	25	26	25	25	24	23	19	18	19	19	*4,139*	*1,400*
London	31	27	27	24	24	22	22	21	19	19	22	*4,822*	*1,160*
South East	24	25	24	26	24	22	22	20	19	20	19	*5,999*	*1,830*
South West	25	27	24	25	24	23	25	23	21	21	18	*3,300*	*1,240*
All England	28	27	27	26	25	25	24	22	21	21	21	*35,937*	*11,430*
Wales	28	25	27	27	27	23	22	20	21	21	23	*2,198*	*800*
Scotland	31	30	31	28	31	25	27	25	24	24	25	*3,731*	*1,220*
Great Britain	28	27	27	26	26	25	24	22	21	21	21	*41,865*	*13,450*

1   2005 data includes last quarter of 2004/5 data due to survey change from financial year to calendar year.
2   Results from 2006 include longitudinal data (see Appendix B).
3   Trend tables show unweighted and weighted figures for 1998 to give an indication of the effect of the weighting. Bases for earlier years can be found in GHS reports for each year.

Source: General Lifestyle Survey, Office for National Statistics

Table 1.12 Cigarette-smoking status by sex, country and region of England: 2009

Persons aged 16 and over   *Great Britain: 2009[1]*

Government Office Region	Current cigarette smokers				Current non-smokers of cigarettes			*Weighted base (000s) =100%*	*Unweighted sample*
	Heavy (20 or more per day)	Moderate (10-19 per day)	Light (fewer than 10 per day)	All current smokers	Ex-regular cigarette smokers	Never or only occasionally smoked cigarettes			
				Percentages					
Men									
England									
North East	10	8	2	20	29	51	*702*	*250*
North West	8	8	7	24	30	46	*2,584*	*750*
Yorkshire and the Humber	7	9	6	23	27	50	*1,732*	*600*
East Midlands	6	8	5	19	28	53	*1,589*	*550*
West Midlands	7	8	6	22	29	49	*1,754*	*530*
East of England	5	8	7	20	31	50	*1,980*	*660*
London	6	8	12	26	24	50	*2,199*	*520*
South East	6	8	6	21	31	49	*2,803*	*840*
South West	6	7	6	19	33	48	*1,472*	*540*
All England	7	8	7	22	29	49	*16,816*	*5,230*
Wales	7	10	4	21	25	54	*1,035*	*370*
Scotland	8	10	6	25	24	51	*1,751*	*550*
Great Britain	7	8	7	22	28	50	*19,602*	*6,160*
Women									
England									
North East	10	9	4	23	23	54	*925*	*330*
North West	6	9	7	22	23	55	*2,677*	*840*
Yorkshire and the Humber	5	11	6	22	21	57	*1,931*	*700*
East Midlands	4	9	5	18	21	61	*1,724*	*620*
West Midlands	5	9	7	21	24	55	*2,058*	*630*
East of England	3	7	8	18	24	58	*2,160*	*740*
London	5	8	6	19	22	59	*2,622*	*640*
South East	4	8	6	18	23	58	*3,196*	*990*
South West	3	7	6	17	27	57	*1,828*	*700*
All England	5	8	6	20	23	57	*19,121*	*6,190*
Wales	7	11	6	24	21	55	*1,162*	*430*
Scotland	7	12	5	24	17	59	*1,980*	*670*
Great Britain	5	9	6	20	22	57	*22,263*	*7,290*
Total									
England									
North East	10	8	3	22	26	53	*1,627*	*580*
North West	7	9	7	23	27	50	*5,261*	*1,580*
Yorkshire and the Humber	6	10	6	22	24	53	*3,664*	*1,300*
East Midlands	5	9	5	19	24	57	*3,313*	*1,170*
West Midlands	6	9	7	22	26	52	*3,812*	*1,160*
East of England	4	7	7	19	27	54	*4,139*	*1,400*
London	6	8	8	22	23	55	*4,822*	*1,160*
South East	5	8	6	19	27	54	*5,999*	*1,830*
South West	4	7	6	18	29	53	*3,300*	*1,240*
All England	6	8	7	21	26	53	*35,937*	*11,430*
Wales	7	11	5	23	23	54	*2,198*	*800*
Scotland	7	11	6	25	20	55	*3,731*	*1,220*
Great Britain	6	9	6	21	25	54	*41,865*	*13,450*

1 Results for 2009 include longitudinal data (see Appendix B).

Source: General Lifestyle Survey, Office for National Statistics

Table 1.13 Cigarette-smoking status by sex: 1974 to 2009

Persons aged 16 and over *Great Britain*

	Unweighted							Weighted										
	1974	1978	1982	1986	1990	1994	1998	1998	2000	2001	2002	2003	2004	2005[1]	2006[2]	2007[2]	2008[2]	2009[2]
								Percentages										
Men																		
Current cigarette smokers																		
Light to moderate (under 20 per day)	25	22	20	20	17	17	18	19	18	19	17	18	18	17	15	16	15	15
Heavy (20 or more per day)	26	23	18	15	14	12	10	11	10	10	10	10	9	8	8	7	7	7
Total current cigarette smokers	51	45	38	35	31	28	28	30	29	28	27	28	26	25	23	22	22	22
Ex-regular cigarette smokers	23	27	30	32	32	31	31	29	27	27	28	27	28	27	27	28	30	28
Never or only occasionally	25	29	32	34	37	40	41	42	44	45	46	45	46	47	50	50	49	50
Weighted base (000s) =100%[3]								*19,229*	*20,350*	*19,913*	*19,561*	*19,187*	*19,561*	*19,496*	*19,918*	*19,994*	*19,498*	*19,602*
Unweighted sample[3]	*9850*	*10480*	*9200*	*8870*	*8110*	*7640*	*6580*		*6590*	*7060*	*6840*	*8100*	*6870*	*10040*	*7680*	*7240*	*6700*	*6160*
Women																		
Current cigarette smokers																		
Light to moderate (under 20 per day)	28	23	22	21	20	18	19	19	19	19	18	18	17	17	16	15	15	15
Heavy (20 or more per day)	13	13	11	10	9	8	7	7	6	7	7	7	6	6	5	5	5	5
Total current cigarette smokers	41	37	33	31	29	26	26	26	25	26	25	24	23	23	21	20	21	20
Ex-regular cigarette smokers	11	14	16	18	19	21	21	20	20	21	21	21	20	21	21	21	22	22
Never or only occasionally	49	49	51	51	52	54	53	53	54	53	54	55	57	57	58	59	58	57
Weighted base (000s) =100%[3]								*21,654*	*22,044*	*21,987*	*22,236*	*21,842*	*22,396*	*22,315*	*22,721*	*22,594*	*22,435*	*22,263*
Unweighted sample[3]	*11,480*	*12,160*	*10,640*	*10,300*	*9,440*	*9,110*	*7,830*		*7,500*	*8,300*	*7,950*	*9,330*	*8,030*	*11,630*	*9,000*	*8,380*	*7,930*	*7,290*

1 2005 data includes last quarter of 2004/5 data due to survey change from financial year to calendar year.
2 Results from 2006 include longitudinal data (see Appendix B).
3 Trend tables show unweighted and weighted figures for 1998 to give an indication of the effect of the weighting. For the weighted data (1998 and 2000 to 2006) the weighted base (000s) is the base for percentages. Unweighted data (up to 1998) are based on the unweighted sample.

Source: General Lifestyle Survey, Office for National Statistics

Table 1.14 Cigarette-smoking status by sex and age

Persons aged 16 and over   *Great Britain: 2009[1]*

Age	Current cigarette smokers			Current non-smokers of cigarettes		Weighted base (000s) =100%	Unweighted sample
	Light to moderate (under 20 per day)	Heavy (20 or more per day)	All current smokers	Ex-regular cigarette smokers	Never or only occasionally smoked cigarettes		
			Percentages				
Men							
16-19	23	*	24	3	74	1,083	280
20-24	20	3	24	6	71	1,232	280
25-34	21	6	27	17	56	2,867	690
35-49	17	10	26	24	50	5,578	1,530
50-59	13	8	22	31	48	3,088	1,030
60 and over	9	5	15	48	38	5,753	2,340
All aged 16 and over	15	7	22	28	50	19,602	6,160
Women							
16-19	19	5	24	6	70	1,092	290
20-24	23	5	28	10	62	1,444	330
25-34	21	3	24	18	58	3,148	890
35-49	16	7	23	21	56	6,411	1,940
50-59	15	6	20	23	57	3,422	1,180
60 and over	9	4	13	31	56	6,747	2,660
All aged 16 and over	15	5	20	22	57	22,263	7,290
Total							
16-19	21	3	24	4	72	2,175	560
20-24	22	4	26	8	66	2,676	620
25-34	21	4	25	17	57	6,015	1,580
35-49	17	8	25	22	53	11,988	3,470
50-59	14	7	21	27	52	6,510	2,220
60 and over	9	5	14	39	47	12,500	5,000
All aged 16 and over	15	6	21	25	54	41,865	13,450

1   Results for 2009 include longitudinal data (see Appendix B).

Source: General Lifestyle Survey, Office for National Statistics

Table 1.15   Average daily cigarette consumption per smoker by sex and age: 1974 to 2009

Current cigarette smokers aged 16 and over   *Great Britain*

Age	Unweighted							Weighted											Weighted base 2009 (000s)= 100%[3]	Unweighted sample[3] 2009
	1974	1978	1982	1986	1990	1994	1998	1998	2000	2001	2002	2003	2004	2005[1]	2006[2]	2007[2]	2008[2]	2009[2]		
							Mean number of cigarettes per day													
Men																				
16-19	16	14	12	12	13	10	10	10	12	11	11	13	11	13	10	10	10	8	255	60
20-24	19	17	16	15	16	13	14	13	12	12	12	12	11	11	12	12	11	11	290	70
25-34	19	19	17	16	16	15	13	13	13	13	13	13	12	12	13	12	12	12	775	200
35-49	20	20	20	19	19	18	17	18	17	17	17	16	16	15	16	16	15	15	1,468	380
50-59	18	20	18	17	17	20	18	18	17	18	18	18	18	17	16	16	16	16	666	210
60 and over	14	15	16	15	15	14	16	16	15	15	16	15	14	15	18	15	15	15	834	320
All aged 16 and over	18	18	17	16	17	16	16	15	15	15	15	15	15	14	15	14	14	14	4,287	1,240
Women																				
16-19	12	13	11	11	11	10	10	10	10	12	12	10	11	10	9	9	11	12	258	70
20-24	14	14	14	12	13	13	12	11	10	11	10	11	11	11	11	10	11	10	401	100
25-34	15	16	16	14	15	14	12	12	12	12	12	12	11	12	11	10	10	10	749	230
35-49	15	16	15	16	15	15	15	15	14	15	15	14	14	14	14	14	14	14	1,485	450
50-59	13	14	14	14	15	15	15	15	15	15	15	15	15	15	15	14	14	14	698	230
60 and over	10	11	11	12	12	13	12	12	12	12	13	13	13	13	13	13	13	14	900	340
All aged 16 and over	13	14	14	14	14	14	13	13	13	13	13	13	13	13	13	13	13	13	4,491	1,400

1   2005 data includes last quarter of 2004/5 data due to survey change from financial year to calendar year.
2   Results from 2006 include longitudinal data (see Appendix B).
3   Trend tables show unweighted and weighted figures for 1998 to give an indication of the effect of the weighting. Bases for earlier years can be found in GLF/GHS reports for each year.

Source: General Lifestyle Survey, Office for National Statistics

Table 1.16 Average daily cigarette consumption per smoker by sex, and socio-economic classification based on the current or last job of the household reference person

Current cigarette smokers aged 16 and over			*Great Britain: 2009[1]*
Socio-economic classification of household reference person[2]	Men	Women	Total
	Mean number of cigarettes a day		
Managerial and professional			
Large employers and higher managerial	12	9	10
Higher professional	11 12	10 11	10 12
Lower managerial and professional	12	12	12
Intermediate			
Intermediate	12 14	13 13	13 14
Small employers and own account	15	14	15
Routine and manual			
Lower supervisory and technical	15	13	14
Semi-routine	15 16	13 13	14 14
Routine	18	13	15
Total[2]	14	13	13
Weighted bases (000s) =100%			
Large employers and higher managerial	151	177	328
Higher professional	235	170	405
Lower managerial and professional	876	890	1,766
Intermediate	241	353	594
Small employers and own account	429	398	827
Lower supervisory and technical	619	606	1,225
Semi-routine	691	845	1,536
Routine	719	709	1,428
Total[2]	4,280	4,457	8,737
Unweighted sample			
Large employers and higher managerial	50	50	100
Higher professional	60	50	110
Lower managerial and professional	250	270	530
Intermediate	70	100	170
Small employers and own account	130	120	240
Lower supervisory and technical	180	190	370
Semi-routine	200	270	470
Routine	220	230	450
Total[2]	1,240	1,390	2,630

1 Results for 2009 include longitudinal data (see Appendix B).

2 Respondents whose household reference person was a full time student, had an inadequately described occupation, had never worked or was long-term unemployed are not shown as separate categories but are included in the total.

Source: General Lifestyle Survey, Office for National Statistics

Table 1.17 Type of cigarette smoked by sex: 1974 to 2009

Current cigarette smokers aged 16 and over   Great Britain

Type of cigarette smoked	Unweighted							Weighted										
	1974	1978	1982	1986	1990	1994	1998	1998	2000	2001	2002	2003	2004	2005[1]	2006[2]	2007[2]	2008[2]	2009[2]
Men								Percentages										
Mainly filter	69	75	72	78	80	78	74	74	69	68	66	68	65	65	65	64	61	62
Mainly plain	18	11	7	4	2	2	1	1	1	1	1	1	1	1	1	1	0	0
Mainly hand-rolled	13	14	21	18	18	21	25	25	30	31	33	32	34	34	35	35	38	37
Weighted base (000s) =100%[3]								5,687	5,802	5,643	5,246	5,367	5,158	4,927	4,618	4,428	4,186	4,292
Unweighted sample[3]	4,990	4,650	3,470	3,070	2,510	2,150	1,860		1,800	1,900	1,760	2,170	1,750	2,400	1,660	1,470	1,320	1,240
	%	%	%	%	%	%	%	%	%	%	%	%	%	%	%	%	%	
Women																		
Mainly filter	91	95	94	96	97	96	92	92	89	87	86	87	85	84	83	82	79	78
Mainly plain	8	4	3	1	1	1	1	1	1	1	1	1	1	1	0	1	1	0
Mainly hand-rolled	1	1	3	2	2	4	7	8	10	12	13	12	14	16	16	17	20	21
Weighted base (000s) =100%[3]								5,735	5,619	5,635	5,560	5,287	5,156	5,060	4,743	4,449	4,624	4,506
Unweighted sample[3]	4,600	4,420	3,520	3,190	2,750	2,340	2,040		1,900	2,100	1,960	2,230	1,830	2,580	1,820	1,600	1,540	1,410

1 2005 data includes last quarter of 2004/5 data due to survey change from financial year to calendar year.
2 Results from 2006 include longitudinal data (see Appendix B).
3 Trend tables show unweighted and weighted figures for 1998 to give an indication of the effect of the weighting. For the weighted data (1998 and 2000 to 2006) the weighted base (000s) is the base for percentages. Unweighted data (up to 1998) are based on the unweighted sample.

Source: General Lifestyle Survey, Office for National Statistics

Table 1.18 Type of cigarette smoked by sex and age

Current cigarette smokers aged 16 and over   Great Britain: 2009[1]

Type of cigarette smoked	Age					
	16-24	25-34	35-49	50-59	60 and over	All aged 16 and over
	Percentages					
Men						
Mainly filter	73	67	58	66	55	62
Mainly plain	*	*	*	0	*	0
Mainly hand-rolled	26	33	42	34	45	37
Weighted base (000s) =100%	547	777	1,474	666	829	4,292
Unweighted sample	140	200	380	210	320	1,240
Women						
Mainly filter	82	70	75	84	84	78
Mainly plain	1	*	0	0	0	0
Mainly hand-rolled	16	29	24	16	16	21
Weighted base (000s) =100%	659	751	1,487	700	909	4,506
Unweighted sample	170	230	450	230	340	1,410
Total						
Mainly filter	78	68	67	75	70	71
Mainly plain	1	1	0	0	*	0
Mainly hand-rolled	21	31	33	25	30	29
Weighted base (000s) =100%	1,206	1,528	2,961	1,366	1,738	8,798
Unweighted sample	300	430	830	440	660	2,650

1 Results for 2009 include longitudinal data (see Appendix B).
* Information is suppressed for low cell counts as a measure of disclosure control.

Source: General Lifestyle Survey, Office for National Statistics

Table 1.19 Grouped tar yield per cigarette: 1986 to 2009

Current smokers of manufactured cigarettes   *Great Britain*

Tar yield	Unweighted					Weighted										
	1986	1988	1990	1992	1998	1998	2000	2001	2002	2003	2004	2005[1]	2006[2]	2007[2]	2008[2]	2009[2]
							Percentages									
less than 10mg	19	21	24	25	28	28	27	26	27	26	26	24	25	38	37	38
10mg to 14mg	32	58	54	68	70	69	71	71	71	71	71	73	72	62	63	59
15mg or more	40	17	19	4	0	0	0	0	0	0	0	0	0	-	-	-
No regular brand/dk tar	10	4	4	3	2	2	2	2	2	3	3	3	3	-	-	3
Weighted base (000s) =100%[3]						*9,568*	*9,104*	*8,850*	*8,317*	*8,306*	*7,812*	*7,510*	*6,987*	*6,539*	*6,187*	*6,217*
Unweighted sample[3]	*5,620*	*5,360*	*4,740*	*4,660*	*3,290*		*2,960*	*3,170*	*2,870*	*3,420*	*2,720*	*3,760*	*2,610*	*2,260*	*2,020*	*1,870*

1 2005 data includes last quarter of 2004/5 data due to survey change from financial year to calendar year.
2 Results from 2006 include longitudinal data (see Appendix B).
3 Trend tables show unweighted and weighted figures for 1998 to give an indication of the effect of the weighting. For the weighted data (1998 and 2000 to 2006) the weighted base (000s) is the base for percentages. Unweighted data (up to 1998) are based on the unweighted sample.
- No data available.

Source: General Lifestyle Survey, Office for National Statistics

Table 1.20 Tar yield per cigarette: 1998 to 2009

Current smokers of manufactured cigarettes   *Great Britain*

Tar yield	Weighted										
	1998	2000	2001	2002	2003	2004	2005[1]	2006[2]	2007[2]	2008[2]	2009[2]
					Percentages						
Less than 4mg	5	5	3	2	2	1	1	1	3	3	2
4 to 7mg	17	22	17	17	17	19	17	17	22	20	23
8 to 9mg	11	9	7	8	7	6	6	7	12	14	13
10 to 11mg	13	27	35	34	71	71	73	72	62	63	59
12 to 14mg	51	34	36	37	0	0	0	0	-	-	-
No regular brand/dk tar yield	2	2	2	2	3	3	3	3	-	-	3
Weighted base (000s) =100%	*9,568*	*9,104*	*8,850*	*8,317*	*8,306*	*7,812*	*7,510*	*6,989*	*6,539*	*5,796*	*6,217*
Unweighted sample	*3,290*	*2,960*	*3,170*	*2,870*	*3,420*	*2,720*	*3,760*	*2,610*	*2,260*	*2,020*	*1,870*

1 2005 data includes last quarter of 2004/5 data due to survey change from financial year to calendar year.
2 Results from 2006 include longitudinal data (see Appendix B).
- No data available.

Source: General Lifestyle Survey, Office for National Statistics

Table 1.21 Tar yields by sex and age of smoker

Current smokers of manufactured cigarettes aged 16 and over					Great Britain: 2009[1]	
Tar yield					Weighted base (000s) =100%	Unweighted sample
Less than 4mg	4 to 7mg	8 to 9mg	10 to 11mg	No regular brand/dk tar yield		
Percentages						
Men						
16-19	*	16	11	66	*	191	40
20-24	0	10	15	72	*	209	50
25-34	*	26	9	59	5	519	130
35-49	2	26	9	59	4	853	220
50-59	*	19	12	65	2	439	130
60 and over	*	21	8	65	6	454	180
Total	1	22	10	62	4	2,665	750
Women						
16-19	0	19	13	62	6	200	60
20-24	*	27	15	53	4	351	80
25-34	2	28	14	54	3	526	170
35-49	2	22	14	59	4	1,127	340
50-59	2	24	14	59	*	586	190
60 and over	5	26	16	51	2	763	290
Total	2	24	14	56	3	3,552	1,110
Total						
16-19	*	18	12	64	5	390	100
20-24	*	21	15	60	3	560	130
25-34	1	27	12	56	4	1,045	300
35-49	2	24	12	59	4	1,980	560
50-59	2	22	13	62	*	1,025	320
60 and over	4	24	13	56	3	1,217	460
Total	2	23	13	59	3	6,217	1,870

1 Results for 2009 include longitudinal data (see Appendix B).
Shaded figures indicate the estimates are unreliable and any analysis using these figures may be invalid. Any use of these shaded figures must be accompanied by this disclaimer.
* Information is suppressed for low cell counts as a measure of disclosure control.

Source: General Lifestyle Survey, Office for National Statistics

Table 1.22 Tar yields by sex and socio-economic classification based on the current or last job of the household reference person

Current smokers of manufactured cigarettes aged 16 and over   *Great Britain: 2009[1]*

Socio-economic class of household reference person[2]	Tar yields					Weighted base (000s) =100%	Unweighted sample
	Less than 4mg	4 to 7mg	8 to 9mg	10 to 11mg	No regular brand/dk tar yield		
Percentages							
Men							
Managerial and professional	4	32	9	53	2	*893*	*260*
Intermediate	0	26	9	61	4	*427*	*120*
Routine and manual	*	14	10	70	5	*1,179*	*340*
Total[2]	1	22	10	62	4	*2,665*	*750*
Women							
Managerial and professional	3	32	15	48	3	*1,066*	*330*
Intermediate	2	26	17	51	4	*632*	*190*
Routine and manual	2	19	13	64	2	*1,590*	*510*
Total[2]	2	24	14	56	3	*3,552*	*1,110*
All persons							
Managerial and professional	4	32	12	50	2	*1,960*	*590*
Intermediate	1	26	14	55	4	*1,059*	*310*
Routine and manual	1	17	12	67	4	*2,769*	*840*
Total[2]	2	23	13	59	3	*6,217*	*1,870*

1 Results for 2009 include longitudinal data (see Appendix B).

2 Respondents whose household reference person was a full time student, had an inadequately described occupation, had never worked or was long-term unemployed are not shown as separate categories but are included in the total.

Source: General Lifestyle Survey, Office for National Statistics

Table 1.23 Prevalence of smoking by sex and type of product smoked: 1974 to 2009

Persons aged 16 and over   *Great Britain*

	Unweighted							Weighted										
	1974	1978	1982[1]	1986	1990	1994	1998	1998	2000	2001	2002	2003	2004	2005[2]	2006[3]	2007[3]	2008[3]	2009[3]
								Percentage smoking										
Men																		
Cigarettes[4]	51	45	38	35	31	28	28	30	29	28	27	28	26	25	23	22	22	22
Pipe	12	10	..	6	4	3	2	2	2	2	1	1	1	1	1	1	1	0
Cigars[5]	34	16	12	10	8	6	6	6	5	5	5	4	4	4	3	2	2	2
All smokers[6]	64	55	45	44	38	33	33	34	32	32	30	31	29	28	25	24	23	23
Weighted base (000s) = 100%[7]								*19,225*	*20,350*	*19,972*	*19,561*	*19,187*	*19,561*	*19,498*	*19,920*	*19,996*	*19,518*	*19,607*
Unweighted sample[7]	*9,860*	*10,440*	*9,170*	*8,880*	*8,120*	*7,660*	*6,580*		*6,590*	*7,070*	*6,840*	*8,100*	*6,870*	*10,040*	*7,680*	*7,240*	*6,700*	*6,160*
Women																		
Cigarettes[4]	41	37	33	31	29	26	26	26	25	26	25	24	23	23	21	20	20	20
Cigars[5]	3	1	0	1	0	0	0	0	0	0	0	0	0	0	0	0	0	0
All smokers[6]	41	37	34	31	29	26	26	27	26	26	25	24	23	23	21	20	21	20
Weighted base (000s) = 100%[7]								*21,653*	*22,044*	*22,032*	*22,236*	*21,842*	*22,393*	*22,315*	*22,723*	*22,594*	*22,458*	*22,266*
Unweighted sample[7]	*11,420*	*12,080*	*10,560*	*10,310*	*9,460*	*9,140*	*7,830*		*7,500*	*8,320*	*7,950*	*9,330*	*8,030*	*11,630*	*9,010*	*8,380*	*7,940*	*7,290*

1 In 1982 and 1984 men were not asked about pipe smoking, and therefore the figures for all smokers exclude those who smoked only a pipe.
2 2005 data includes last quarter of 2004/5 data due to survey change from financial year to calendar year.
3 Results from 2006 include longitudinal data (see Appendix B).
4 Figures for cigarettes include all smokers of manufactured and hand-rolled cigarettes.
5 For 1974 the figures include occasional cigar smokers, that is, those who smoked less than one cigar a month.
6 The percentages for cigarettes, pipes and cigars add to more than the percentage for all smokers because some people smoked more than one type of product.
7 Trend tables show unweighted and weighted figures for 1998 to give an indication of the effect of the weighting. For the weighted data (1998 and 2000 to 2009) the weighted base (000s) is the base for percentages. Unweighted data (up to 1998) are based on the unweighted sample.

Source: General Lifestyle Survey, Office for National Statistics

Table 1.24 Prevalence of smoking among men by age and type of product smoked

Men aged 16 and over   *Great Britain: 2009[1]*

Age	Cigarettes[2]	Pipe[3]	Cigars[3]	All smokers[4]	*Weighted base (000s) =100%*	*Unweighted sample*
	Percentage smoking					
16-19	24	0	*	24	*1,083*	*280*
20-24	24	0	1	24	*1,232*	*280*
25-29	25	*	1	25	*1,383*	*310*
30-34	30	*	3	32	*1,489*	*380*
35-49	26	*	2	27	*5,578*	*1,530*
50-59	22	1	2	23	*3,088*	*1,030*
60 and over	15	1	2	17	*5,753*	*2,340*
All aged 16 and over	22	0	2	23	*19,607*	*6,160*

1 Results for 2009 include longitudinal data (see Appendix B).
2 Figures for cigarettes include all smokers of both manufactured and hand-rolled cigarettes.
3 Young people aged 16-17 were not asked about cigar or pipe-smoking.
4 The percentages for cigarettes, pipes and cigars add to more than the percentage for all smokers because some people smoked more than one type of product.

Source: General Lifestyle Survey, Office for National Statistics

Table 1.25 Age started smoking regularly by sex: 1992 to 2009

Persons aged 16 and over who had ever smoked regularly   *Great Britain*

Age started smoking regularly	Unweighted				Weighted											
	1992	1994	1996	1998	1998	2000	2001	2002	2003	2004	2005[1]	2006[2]	2007[2]	2008[2]	2009[2]
						Percentages									
Men															
Under 16	40	41	41	43	42	43	42	42	42	42	41	41	41	40	42
16-17	27	27	27	26	26	27	26	28	26	26	26	26	26	27	26
18-19	17	16	17	17	17	15	16	16	16	16	17	17	18	18	16
20-24	12	11	11	10	11	11	11	11	11	10	11	12	11	11	12
25 and over	4	4	3	4	4	5	4	4	4	5	5	4	4	4	5
Weighted base (000s) =100%					*11,146*	*11,016*	*10,608*	*10,469*	*10,431*	*10,506*	*10,194*	*9,931*	*9,919*	*9,028*	*8,415*
Unweighted sample	*5,140*	*4,520*	*4,300*	*3,850*		*3,620*	*3,880*	*3,700*	*4,410*	*3,700*	*5,280*	*3,900*	*3,680*	*3,090*	*2,720*
Women															
Under 16	28	30	32	31	32	33	35	33	35	35	36	36	36	37	37
16-17	28	28	28	29	28	27	27	28	26	18	27	28	27	27	28
18-19	19	19	17	18	17	19	17	18	19	18	17	17	18	18	17
20-24	15	13	13	14	14	12	12	13	13	12	12	12	13	12	11
25 and over	10	9	9	8	8	8	9	7	7	7	7	6	6	7	7
Weighted base (000s) =100%					*10,101*	*9,663*	*10,222*	*10,067*	*9,738*	*9,591*	*9,589*	*9,404*	*9,183*	*8,426*	*8,058*
Unweighted sample	*4640*	*4180*	*3990*	*3640*		*3300*	*3820*	*3590*	*4140*	*3450*	*4990*	*3700*	*3450*	*2280*	*2,600*
All persons															
Under 16	34	36	37	37	37	38	39	38	38	39	39	39	39	38	39
16-17	27	28	28	27	27	27	26	28	26	27	27	27	27	27	27
18-19	18	18	17	18	17	17	17	17	17	17	17	17	18	18	17
20-24	14	12	12	12	12	11	12	12	12	11	11	12	12	11	11
25 and over	7	7	6	6	6	6	6	5	6	6	6	5	5	5	6
Weighted base (000s) =100%					*21,247*	*20,679*	*20,830*	*20,537*	*20,169*	*20,097*	*19,783*	*19,337*	*19,103*	*17,454*	*16,473*
Unweighted sample	*9,780*	*8,700*	*8,290*	*7,500*		*6,960*	*7,700*	*7,280*	*8,550*	*7,150*	*10,260*	*7,640*	*7,130*	*5,970*	*5,320*

1 2005 data includes last quarter of 2004/5 data due to survey change from financial year to calendar year.
2 Results from 2006 include longitudinal data (see Appendix B).

Source: General Lifestyle Survey, Office for National Statistics

Table 1.26 Age started smoking regularly by sex and socio-economic classification based on the current or last job of the household reference person

Persons aged 16 and over who had ever smoked regularly   *Great Britain 2009[1]*

Age started smoking regularly	Socio-economic classification of household reference person[2]			
	Managerial & professional	Intermediate	Routine & manual	Total
	Percentages			
Men				
Under 16	35	38	50	42
16-17	25	28	25	26
18-19	22	15	11	16
20-24	12	14	11	12
25 and over	6	5	4	5
Weighted base (000s) =100%	*3,246*	*1,342*	*3,333*	*8,415*
Unweighted sample	*1,060*	*440*	*1,080*	*2,720*
Women				
Under 16	31	32	44	37
16-17	28	27	28	28
18-19	22	20	12	17
20-24	14	13	8	11
25 and over	6	8	8	7
Weighted base (000s) =100%	*2,934*	*1,410*	*3,243*	*8,058*
Unweighted sample	*950*	*460*	*1,040*	*2,600*
All persons				
Under 16	33	35	47	39
16-17	26	27	26	27
18-19	22	18	11	17
20-24	13	13	9	11
25 and over	6	7	6	6
Weighted base (000s) =100%	*6,180*	*2,752*	*6,577*	*16,473*
Unweighted sample	*2,000*	*900*	*2,120*	*5,320*

1 Results for 2009 include longitudinal data (see Appendix B).

2 Respondents whose household reference person was a full time student, had an inadequately described occupation, had never worked or was long-term unemployed are not shown as separate categories but are included in the total.

Source: General Lifestyle Survey, Office for National Statistics

Table 1.27 Age started smoking regularly by sex, whether current smoker and if so, cigarettes smoked a day

Persons aged 16 and over who had ever smoked regularly   *Great Britain: 2009[1]*

Age started smoking regularly	Current smoker				Ex-regular smoker	All who have ever smoked regularly
	20 or more a day	10-19 a day	0-9 a day	All current smokers[2]		
				Percentages		
Men						
Under 16	53	49	34	46	39	42
16-17	24	24	23	24	26	26
18-19	10	12	21	14	18	16
20-24	8	9	15	10	12	12
25 and over	4	6	6	5	4	5
Weighted base (000s) =100%	*887*	*1,103*	*847*	*2,845*	*5,570*	*8,415*
Unweighted sample	*250*	*300*	*210*	*760*	*1,950*	*2,720*
Women						
Under 16	50	46	42	46	31	37
16-17	28	26	23	26	29	28
18-19	8	13	18	13	20	17
20-24	11	9	11	10	12	11
25 and over	3	6	5	5	8	7
Weighted base (000s) =100%	*790*	*1,351*	*913*	*3,060*	*4998*	*8,058*
Unweighted sample	*230*	*380*	*260*	*880*	*1,720*	*2,600*
All persons						
Under 16	52	47	39	46	35	39
16-17	26	25	23	25	28	27
18-19	9	12	20	14	19	17
20-24	9	9	13	10	12	11
25 and over	4	6	5	5	6	6
Weighted base (000s) =100%	*1677*	*2454*	*1,760*	*5,904*	*10,568*	*16,473*
Unweighted sample	*480*	*680*	*470*	*1,640*	*3,680*	*5,320*

1 Results for 2009 include longitudinal data (see Appendix B).
2 Includes a few smokers who did not say how many cigarettes a day they smoked.

Source: General Lifestyle Survey, Office for National Statistics

Table 1.28 Proportion of smokers who would like to give up smoking altogether, by sex and number of cigarettes smoked per day: 1992 to 2009

Current cigarette smokers aged 16 and over   Great Britain

Number of cigarettes smoked a day	Unweighted				Weighted											Weighted base 2009 (000s) =100%[3]	Unweighted sample[3] 2009
	1992	1994	1996	1998	1998	2000	2001	2002	2003	2004	2005[1]	2006[2]	2007[2]	2008[2]	2009[2]		

Percentage who would like to stop altogether

Men
20 or more	68	70	66	69	69	74	70	68	64	67	66	67	62	62	59	1,324	410
10-19	70	72	69	73	73	76	71	71	67	68	68	68	66	65	65	1,651	480
0-9	58	61	62	62	62	64	62	62	61	64	68	65	69	59	60	1,307	340
All smokers[4]	66	69	66	69	69	72	68	68	64	67	68	67	66	62	62	4,298	1,250
Women																	
20 or more	70	69	69	68	68	73	66	67	64	70	67	67	61	64	63	1,107	340
10-19	72	71	70	75	75	76	67	71	71	70	70	72	68	66	66	1,985	620
0-9	58	62	59	65	65	63	60	67	66	67	67	69	66	69	63	1,399	440
All smokers[4]	68	68	67	70	70	71	65	69	67	69	68	70	66	67	64	4,506	1,410
Total																	
20 or more	69	70	68	69	69	74	68	68	64	68	67	67	62	63	61	2,430	750
10-19	71	71	70	74	74	76	69	71	69	69	69	70	67	66	66	3,636	1,100
0-9	58	61	60	64	64	63	61	65	64	66	68	67	67	64	61	2,706	780
All smokers[4]	67	68	67	69	69	72	66	68	66	68	68	68	66	65	63	8,804	2,650

1 2005 data includes last quarter of 2004/5 data due to survey change from financial year to calendar year
2 Results from 2006 include longitudinal data (see Appendix B).
3 Trend tables show unweighted and weighted figures for 1998 to give an indication of the effect of the weighting. Bases for earlier years can be found in GLF/GHS reports for each year.
4 Includes a few smokers who did not say how many cigarettes a day they smoked.

Source: General Lifestyle Survey, Office for National Statistics

Table 1.29 Proportion of smokers who would find it difficult to go without smoking for a day, by sex and number of cigarettes smoked per day: 1992 to 2009

Current cigarette smokers aged 16 and over   Great Britain

Number of cigarettes smoked a day	Unweighted				Weighted											Weighted base 2009 (000s) =100%[3]	Unweighted sample[3] 2009
	1992	1994	1996	1998	1998	2000	2001	2002	2003	2004	2005[1]	2006[2]	2007[2]	2008[2]	2009[2]		

Percentage who would find it difficult not to smoke for a day

Men
20 or more	76	78	78	78	78	78	74	77	78	77	77	80	81	79	78	1,316	410
10-19	54	57	54	54	54	56	55	57	53	57	60	64	63	61	58	1,644	480
0-9	20	17	20	25	23	14	21	23	19	16	23	24	26	23	28	1,307	340
All smokers[4]	55	56	56	56	56	53	52	56	53	52	55	59	58	55	55	4,283	1,240
Women																	
20 or more	86	86	87	87	86	88	87	86	83	82	84	84	90	86	86	1,107	340
10-19	68	68	66	66	65	67	65	66	64	67	65	70	65	67	68	1,981	620
0-9	23	20	24	24	25	22	24	21	22	21	27	27	26	28	28	1,399	440
All smokers[4]	61	60	61	59	59	58	58	59	56	57	58	60	59	59	60	4,502	1,400
Total																	
20 or more	80	82	83	82	82	82	80	81	80	79	80	82	85	82	81	2,422	750
10-19	61	63	60	61	60	62	61	62	58	62	63	67	64	64	63	3,625	1,100
0-9	21	19	23	24	24	18	22	22	21	19	25	26	26	25	28	2,706	780
All smokers[4]	58	59	58	58	57	56	55	57	55	55	56	59	58	57	57	8,785	2,650

1 2005 data includes last quarter of 2004/5 data due to survey change from financial year to calendar year.
2 Results from 2006 include longitudinal data (see Appendix B).
3 Trend tables show unweighted and weighted figures for 1998 to give an indication of the effect of the weighting. Bases for earlier years can be found in GLF/GHS reports for each year.
4 Includes a few smokers who did not say how many cigarettes a day they smoked.

Source: General Lifestyle Survey, Office for National Statistics

Table 1.30 Proportion of smokers who have their first cigarette within five minutes of waking, by sex and number of cigarettes smoked per day: 1992 to 2009

Current cigarette smokers aged 16 and over *Great Britain*

Number of cigarettes smoked a day	Unweighted				Weighted											Weighted base 2009 (000s) =100%[3]	Unweighted sample[3] 2009
	1992	1994	1996	1998	1998	2000	2001	2002	2003	2004	2005[1]	2006[2]	2007[2]	2008[2]	2009[2]		
Percentage smoking within 5 minutes of waking																	
Men																	
20 or more	29	31	29	31	32	30	30	31	31	34	34	35	36	35	29	1,324	410
10-19	10	13	9	11	11	13	11	11	11	13	15	13	13	14	12	1,647	480
0-9	2	2	3	2	2	2	3	3	4	1	2	2	3	2	4	1,293	340
All smokers[4]	16	18	16	16	17	16	15	16	16	17	17	18	17	17	15	4,279	1,240
Women																	
20 or more	29	34	32	31	31	32	35	31	31	33	31	37	34	36	35	1,107	340
10-19	10	9	11	12	12	12	12	12	12	15	11	12	16	11	15	1,983	620
0-9	1	0	1	1	1	2	2	2	3	2	2	2	3	4	2	1,394	440
All smokers[4]	14	14	15	14	14	14	15	14	14	16	14	15	16	15	16	4,498	1,400
Total																	
20 or more	29	33	30	31	31	31	32	31	31	34	33	36	35	36	32	2,430	750
10-19	10	11	10	12	12	13	11	11	11	14	13	12	14	13	13	3,630	1,100
0-9	2	1	2	2	2	2	2	3	3	1	2	2	3	3	3	2,686	770
All smokers[4]	15	16	15	15	15	15	15	15	15	17	16	16	17	16	15	8,777	2,640

1 2005 data includes last quarter of 2004/5 data due to survey change from financial year to calendar year.
2 Results from 2006 include longitudinal data (see Appendix B).
3 Trend tables show unweighted and weighted figures for 1998 to give an indication of the effect of the weighting. Bases for earlier years can be found in GLF/GHS reports for each year.
4 Includes a few smokers who did not say how many cigarettes a day they smoked.

Source: General Lifestyle Survey, Office for National Statistics

Table 1.31 Proportion of smokers who would like to give up smoking, by sex, socio-economic classification of household reference person, and number of cigarettes smoked a day

Current cigarette smokers aged 16 and over   *Great Britain: 2009[1]*

Number of cigarettes smoked a day	Socio-economic classification [2]			Total
	Managerial & professional	Intermediate	Routine & manual	
	Percentage who would like to stop altogether			
Men				
20 or more	61	55	60	59
10-19	75	64	61	65
0-9	62	50	64	60
All smokers[3]	67	57	61	62
Women				
20 or more	54	65	67	63
10-19	66	70	66	66
0-9	65	66	58	63
All smokers[3]	63	67	64	64
Total				
20 or more	57	60	63	61
10-19	70	67	64	66
0-9	64	59	61	61
All smokers[3]	65	62	63	63
Weighted base (000s)=100%				
Men				
20 or more	*272*	*219*	*731*	*1,324*
10-19	*506*	*258*	*764*	*1,651*
0-9	*480*	*192*	*532*	*1,307*
All smokers[3]	*1,263*	*670*	*2,035*	*4,298*
Women				
20 or more	*243*	*225*	*536*	*1,107*
10-19	*497*	*310*	*1030*	*1,985*
0-9	*497*	*216*	*594*	*1,399*
All smokers[3]	*1,243*	*751*	*2,169*	*4,506*
Total				
20 or more	*514*	*445*	*1,267*	*2,430*
10-19	*1,003*	*568*	*1,795*	*3,636*
0-9	*977*	*408*	*1127*	*2,706*
All smokers[3]	*2,506*	*1,421*	*4,204*	*8,804*
Unweighted sample				
Men				
20 or more	*90*	*70*	*220*	*410*
10-19	*140*	*70*	*230*	*480*
0-9	*130*	*50*	*150*	*340*
All smokers[3]	*360*	*200*	*610*	*1,250*
Women				
20 or more	*80*	*60*	*170*	*340*
10-19	*150*	*90*	*330*	*620*
0-9	*150*	*70*	*190*	*440*
All smokers[3]	*380*	*220*	*690*	*1,410*
Total				
20 or more	*160*	*140*	*390*	*750*
10-19	*290*	*170*	*560*	*1,100*
0-9	*280*	*120*	*330*	*780*
All smokers[3]	*740*	*420*	*1,300*	*2,650*

1 Results for 2009 include longitudinal data (see Appendix B).
2 Respondents whose household reference person was a full time student, had an inadequately described occupation, had never worked or was long-term unemployed are not shown as separate categories but are included in the total.
3 Includes a few smokers who did not say how many cigarettes a day they smoked.
Shaded figures indicate the estimates are unreliable and any analysis using these figures may be invalid. Any use of these shaded figures must be accompanied by this disclaimer.

Source: General Lifestyle Survey, Office for National Statistics

Table 1.32 Proportion of smokers who would find it difficult to go without smoking for a day, by   sex, socio-economic classification of household reference person, and number of cigarettes smoked a day

Current cigarette smokers aged 16 and over   *Great Britain: 2009[1]*

Number of cigarettes smoked a day	Socio-economic classification[2]			Total
	Managerial & professional	Intermediate	Routine & manual	
	Percentage who would find it difficult to stop for a day			
Men				
20 or more	74	78	78	78
10-19	50	63	60	58
0-9	30	29	29	28
All smokers[3]	47	58	58	55
Women				
20 or more	81	83	89	86
10-19	68	68	70	68
0-9	24	30	31	28
All smokers[3]	53	61	64	60
Total				
20 or more	77	80	83	81
10-19	58	66	66	63
0-9	27	30	30	28
All smokers[3]	50	60	61	57
Weighted base (000s)=100%				
Men				
20 or more	*272*	*216*	*726*	*1,316*
10-19	*506*	*258*	*758*	*1,644*
0-9	*483*	*192*	*530*	*1,307*
All smokers[3]	*1,266*	*667*	*2,021*	*4,283*
Women				
20 or more	*243*	*225*	*536*	*1,107*
10-19	*495*	*310*	*1,028*	*1,981*
0-9	*497*	*216*	*594*	*1,399*
All smokers[3]	*1,241*	*751*	*2,167*	*4,502*
Total				
20 or more	*514*	*441*	*1,262*	*2,422*
10-19	*1,001*	*568*	*1,786*	*3,625*
0-9	*980*	*408*	*1,124*	*2,706*
All smokers[3]	*2,507*	*1,417*	*4,188*	*8,785*
Unweighted sample				
Men				
20 or more	*90*	*70*	*220*	*410*
10-19	*140*	*70*	*230*	*480*
0-9	*130*	*50*	*150*	*340*
All smokers[3]	*360*	*200*	*600*	*1,240*
Women				
20 or more	*80*	*60*	*170*	*340*
10-19	*150*	*90*	*330*	*620*
0-9	*150*	*70*	*190*	*440*
All smokers[3]	*380*	*220*	*690*	*1,400*
Total				
20 or more	*160*	*130*	*390*	*750*
10-19	*290*	*170*	*560*	*1,100*
0-9	*280*	*120*	*330*	*780*
All smokers[3]	*740*	*420*	*1,290*	*2,650*

1 Results for 2009 include longitudinal data (see Appendix B).

2 Respondents whose household reference person was a full time student, had an inadequately described occupation, had never worked or was long-term unemployed are not shown as separate categories but are included in the total.

3 Includes a few smokers who did not say how many cigarettes a day they smoked.

Shaded figures indicate the estimates are unreliable and any analysis using these figures may be invalid. Any use of these shaded figures must be accompanied by this disclaimer.

Source: General Lifestyle Survey, Office for National Statistics

Table 1.33 Proportion of smokers who have their first cigarette within five minutes of waking, by sex, socio-economic classification of household reference person, and number of cigarettes smoked a day

Current cigarette smokers aged 16 and over   *Great Britain: 2009[1]*

Number of cigarettes smoked a day	Socio-economic classification[2]			Total
	Managerial & professional	Intermediate	Routine & manual	
	Percentage who smoke within 5 minutes of waking			
Men				
20 or more	31	19	30	29
10-19	9	11	12	12
0-9	4	0	6	4
All smokers[3]	12	11	17	15
Women				
20 or more	22	41	36	35
10-19	12	11	18	15
0-9	*	*	4	2
All smokers[3]	9	18	19	16
Total				
20 or more	27	30	33	32
10-19	10	11	15	13
0-9	2	*	5	3
All smokers[3]	11	14	18	15
Weighted base (000s)=100%				
Men				
20 or more	*272*	*219*	*731*	*1,324*
10-19	*506*	*258*	*760*	*1,647*
0-9	*475*	*190*	*527*	*1,293*
All smokers[3]	*1,259*	*667*	*2,026*	*4,279*
Women				
20 or more	*243*	*225*	*536*	*1,107*
10-19	*495*	*310*	*1,030*	*1,983*
0-9	*497*	*210*	*594*	*1,394*
All smokers[3]	*1,241*	*746*	*2,169*	*4,498*
Total				
20 or more	*514*	*445*	*1,267*	*2,430*
10-19	*1000*	*568*	*1,791*	*3,630*
0-9	*972*	*400*	*1,121*	*2,686*
All smokers[3]	*2,499*	*1,413*	*4,195*	*8,777*
Unweighted sample				
Men				
20 or more	*90*	*70*	*220*	*410*
10-19	*140*	*70*	*230*	*480*
0-9	*130*	*50*	*140*	*340*
All smokers[3]	*360*	*200*	*600*	*1,240*
Women				
20 or more	*80*	*60*	*170*	*340*
10-19	*150*	*90*	*330*	*620*
0-9	*150*	*70*	*190*	*440*
All smokers[3]	*380*	*220*	*690*	*1,400*
Total				
20 or more	*160*	*140*	*390*	*750*
10-19	*290*	*170*	*560*	*1,100*
0-9	*280*	*110*	*330*	*770*
All smokers[3]	*740*	*410*	*1,290*	*2,640*

1 Results for 2009 include longitudinal data (see Appendix B).

2 Respondents whose household reference person was a full time student, had an inadequately described occupation, had never worked or was long-term unemployed are not shown as separate categories but are included in the total.

3 Includes a few smokers who did not say how many cigarettes a day they smoked.

Shaded figures indicate the estimates are unreliable and any analysis using these figures may be invalid. Any use of these shaded figures must be accompanied by this disclaimer.

* Information is suppressed for low cell counts as a measure of disclosure control.

Source: General Lifestyle Survey, Office for National Statistics

Drinking

The Department of Health estimates that the harmful use of alcohol costs the NHS around £2.7bn a year and 7 per cent of all hospital admissions are alcohol related. Drinking can lead to over 40 medical conditions, including cancer, stroke, hypertension, liver disease and heart disease. The General LiFestyle Survey (GLF) and its predecessor the General Household Survey (GHS) have, between them, been measuring drinking behaviour for over 30 years.

Questions about drinking alcohol were included in the General Household Survey (GHS) every two years from 1978 to 1998. Following the review of the GHS, the questions about drinking in the last seven days form part of the continuous survey, and have been included every year from 2000 onwards. Questions designed to measure average weekly alcohol consumption were included from 2000 to 2002 and in 2005 and 2006. The General LiFestyle Survey (GLF) has included both sets of questions in both 2008 and 2009. Before 1988 questions about drinking were asked only of those aged 18 and over, but since then respondents aged 16 and 17 have answered the questions using a self-completion questionnaire.

This report presents information on the frequency of drinking alcohol, the amounts consumed in the week before the interview took place and average weekly consumption. It also presents data on the association between consumption of alcohol and characteristics of individuals such as sex, age, socio-economic classification, and region of residence.

Measuring alcohol consumption

Obtaining reliable information about drinking behaviour is difficult, and social surveys consistently record lower levels of consumption than would be expected from data on alcohol sales. This is partly because people may consciously or unconsciously underestimate how much alcohol they consume. Drinking at home is particularly likely to be underestimated because the quantities consumed are not measured and are likely to be larger than those dispensed in licensed premises.

There are different methods for obtaining survey information on drinking behaviour. One approach is to ask people to recall all episodes of drinking during a set period[1]. However, this is time-consuming and is not suitable for the GLF, where drinking is only one of a number of subjects covered.

In 2009 two measures of alcohol consumption were used:

- average weekly alcohol consumption;
- maximum amount drunk on any one day in the previous seven days

Average weekly alcohol consumption

Questions to establish average weekly alcohol consumption were included on the GHS in their current form periodically since 1986. The measure was developed in response to earlier medical guidelines suggesting maximum recommended weekly amounts of alcohol of 21 units for men and 14 units for women. These guidelines have now been replaced by daily alcohol limits but the average weekly figures continue to provide a consistent measure of alcohol consumption through which trends can be monitored. Respondents are asked how often over the last year they have drunk normal strength beer; strong beer (6 per cent or greater ABV[2]); wine; spirits; fortified wines and; alcopops, and how much they have usually drunk on any one day. This information is combined to give an estimate of the respondent's weekly alcohol consumption (averaged over a year) in units of alcohol.

The method used for calculating usual weekly alcohol consumption is to multiply the number of units of each type drunk on a usual drinking day by the frequency with which it was drunk using the factors shown below, and then to total across all drinks.

Drinking frequency	Multiplying factor
Almost every day	7.0
5 or 6 days a week	5.5
3 or 4 days a week	3.5
Once or twice a week	1.5
Once or twice a month	0.375 (1.5 ÷ 4)
Once every couple of months	0.115 (6 ÷ 52)
Once or twice a year	0.029 (1.5 ÷ 52)

Maximum daily amount drunk last week

These questions were included in the GHS from 1998 onwards, following the publication in 1995 of an inter-departmental review of the effects of drinking[3]. This concluded that it was more appropriate to set benchmarks for daily than for weekly consumption of alcohol, partly because of concern about the health and social risks associated with single episodes of intoxication. The levels of the limits were set after consideration of evidence of associations between alcohol consumption and increased risk of haemorrhagic stroke, hypertension and some types of cancer.

The report stated that low levels of alcohol consumption are associated with reduced risk of cardiovascular heart disease in men aged over 40 and postmenopausal women: 'In terms of all cause mortality and morbidity the benefit can be largely gained by drinking as little as 1 unit a day on a regular basis. Consumption above 2 units a day does not confer any major additional health benefit'.

The report also provided evidence, however, that 'men who drink more than 3 to 4 units a day run an increasingly significant risk of illness and death from a number of conditions, including haemorrhagic stroke, some cancers, accidents and hypertension'.

The report concluded that regular consumption of between three and four units[4] a day for men and two to three units a day for women does not carry a significant health risk, but that consistently drinking above these levels is not advisable because of the progressive health risk it carries. The government's advice on sensible drinking is now based on these daily limits.

The sensible drinking limits for women are set slightly lower than those for men because:

'The tissue in a woman's body contains a lower proportion of water than a man's and this means that, in a man and a woman of the same weight, a given amount of alcohol will produce a higher tissue concentration in the woman. In addition the average woman weighs 58kg, considerably less than the average man (70 kg), and has correspondingly less tissue to absorb the alcohol. Taking these two factors together means the same amount of alcohol will produce a significantly higher tissue concentration in the average woman. In addition, women may metabolise alcohol at a slower rate than men, so the alcohol may remain in their tissues longer'.

People responding to the GLF are asked on how many days they drank alcohol during the previous week. They are then asked how much of each of six different types of drink (normal strength beer; strong beer; wine; spirits; fortified wines; and alcopops) they drank on their heaviest drinking day during the previous week. These amounts are converted to units of alcohol and added to give an estimate of the number of units the respondent consumed on that day.

Recent changes in methodology

The conversion of volumes of alcoholic drinks to units of alcohol is based on assumptions about the size of a given measure (for example, a glass of wine) and the alcohol content of the type of drink, that is, the percentage of alcohol by volume (ABV). In recent years there have been changes to both of these factors and these have been reflected in revisions to the conversion method which was first used on the 2006 data.

The survey does not ask about the specific ABV of every alcoholic drink consumed but assumes an average for each type of drink. The revised method changed the number of units assumed to be in drinks in the 'normal strength beer, lager and cider' and 'strong beer, lager and cider' categories but the main impact was on drinks in the 'wine' category.

The revised method has had a large impact on the estimates of units of alcohol consumed from wine because it changed both the assumed ABV of wine (from 9 to 12 per cent) and the size of a glass of wine. Wine is sold on licensed premises and consumed at home in a variety of glass sizes. Until 2006 a glass of wine was assumed to be 125 ml. In 2006 and 2007 an average size of 170 ml was assumed. The changes in both glass size and ABV of wine resulted in the number of units assumed to be in a glass of wine doubling from 1 to 2 units. The changes in conversion factors are discussed in detail in a paper in the National Statistics Methodology series[5].

In addition to the revised method, a question about wine glass size has been included in the survey since 2008. Respondents are now asked whether they have consumed small (125 ml), standard (175 ml) or large (250 ml) glasses of wine. The data from this question are used when calculating the number of units of alcohol consumed by the respondent. It is now assumed that a small glass contains 1.5 units, a standard glass contains 2 units and a large glass contains 3 units.

The main impact of the 2006 change in methodology can be seen in the 2006 data for which figures using both the original and revised methods were produced[6]. There are also two sets of figures based on the 2008 data to show the effect of introducing the new glass size question. In tables showing time series there are, therefore, three sections showing the original method up to 2006, then the revised method from 2006 to 2008 and finally the updated method from 2008 which uses the data about wine glass size.

The addition of the wine glass size question has had little effect on the estimates of average weekly alcohol consumption but has slightly reduced the proportion of women exceeding 3 units on their heaviest drinking day in the week before interview. There are two reasons for this. Firstly, when glass size was analysed by sex and age, for most groups the average size was close to the average assumed under the previous method but for women aged 45 to 64 average size was lower and for men and women aged 65 and over it was much lower. Secondly, approximately 60 per cent of the units of alcohol consumed by women come from wine whereas only around 25 per cent of men's units do so. This means that any change to the calculation of units of alcohol coming from wine has a much greater effect on the total units for women than on the total for men.

Trends in alcohol consumption

Due to the change in methodology, this section contains discussion of both the trend up to 2006 and the trend since 2006. Figures 2.1 and 2.2 show the trends to 2006 only.

Trends in average weekly alcohol consumption

During the 1990s the GHS showed a slight increase in overall weekly alcohol consumption among men and a much more marked one among women. Following an increase between 1998 and 2000, there has been a decline since 2002 in the proportion of men drinking more than, on average, 21 units a week and in the proportion of women drinking more than 14 units (Figure 2.1). At first sight, the fall appears most marked between 2002 and 2005, but this is largely due to the longer time interval between surveys. The proportion of men drinking more than 21 units a week on average fell from 29 per cent in 2000 to 23 per cent in 2006. There was also a fall in the proportion of women drinking more than 14 units a week (from 17 per cent in 2000 to 12 per cent in 2006).

Figure 2.1   **Percentage of men drinking more than 21 units a week, and women drinking more than 14 units a week: original method**

Great Britain

Percentages

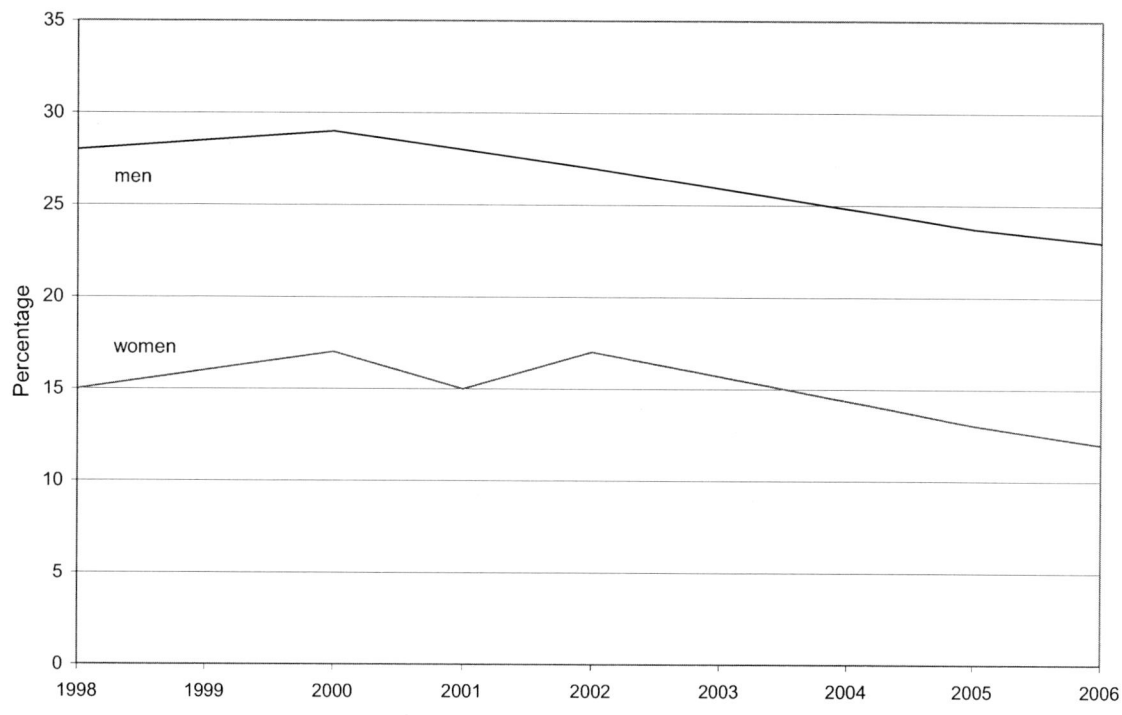

Source: General Household Survey, Office for National Statistics

The fall in consumption between 2000 and 2006 occurred among men and women in all age groups, but was most evident among those aged 16 to 24. Among young men in this age group the proportion drinking more than 21 units a week fell from 41 per cent in 2000 to 26 per cent in 2006 and among young women the proportion drinking more than 14 units a week fell from 33 per cent to 19 per cent over the same period.

This trend seems to be continuing under the new methodology; between 2006 and 2009 the proportion of men drinking more than 21 units a week fell from 31 per cent to 26 per cent and the proportion of women drinking more than 14 units a week fell from 20 per cent to 18 per cent. These falls were driven by falls in the younger age groups. Among men, the percentage drinking more than 21 units a week fell in the 16 to 24 (from 30 to 21 per cent) and 25 to 44 age groups (from 33 to 26 per cent). Among women, the percentage drinking more than 14 units a week fell in the 25 to 44 age group from 23 to 19 per cent.

On the average weekly measure, heavy drinking is defined as consuming more than 50 units a week for men and consuming more than 35 units a week for women. In the 16 to 24 age group there were significant falls, between 2000 and 2006, in the proportion of men and women drinking heavily (from 14 per cent to 7 per cent for men and from 9 per cent to 5 per cent for women). Under the new methodology, between 2006 and 2009, the proportion of men who drink more than

50 units a week fell from 8 per cent to 7 per cent and the proportion of women who drink more than 35 units a week fell from 5 per cent to 4 per cent.

The average number of units of alcohol consumed in a week rose steadily in the 1990s and reached a peak of around 17 units for men and 7.5 units for women in the period 2000 to 2002. These levels fell to 14.8 units for men and 6.2 units for women in 2006. The figures produced using the updated methodology suggests that the average number of units consumed may be continuing to fall from 2006 onwards but there is no statistically significant change between 2008 and 2009.

Figure 2.2   **Average weekly alcohol units: by sex. Original method**

Great Britain

Number of units

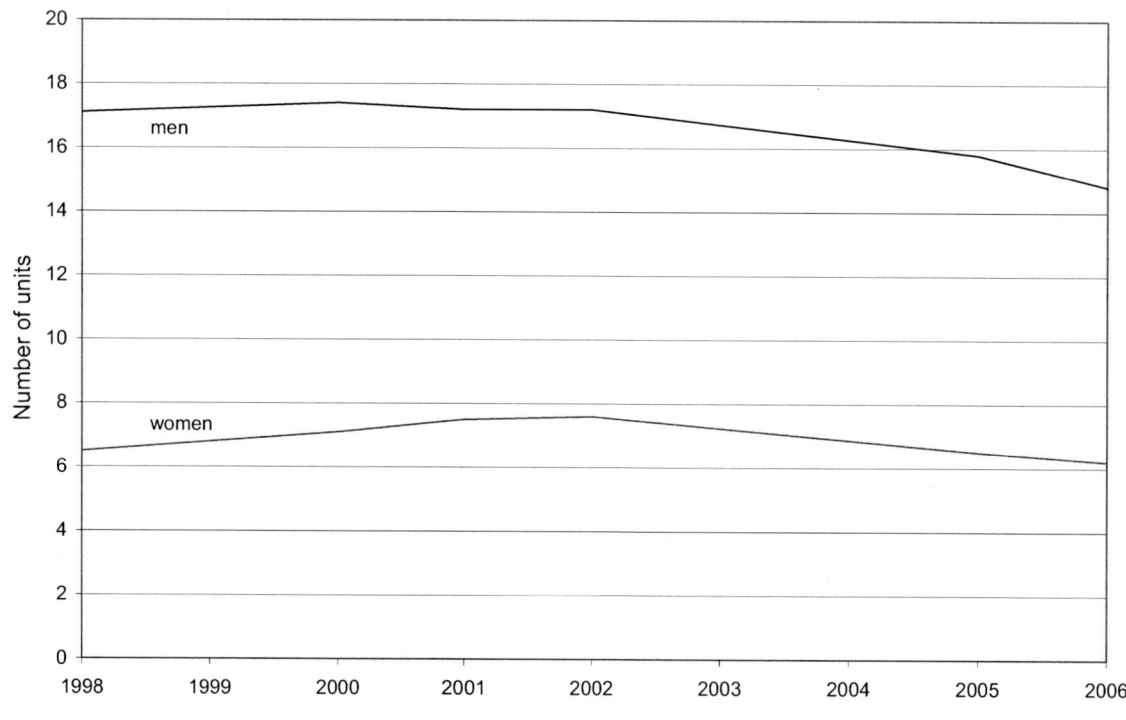

Source: General Household Survey, Office for National Statistics

The British Beer and Pub Association (BBPA) makes annual estimates of per capita alcohol consumption using data provided by HM Revenue and Customs[7]. These show a steady increase in consumption from 1998 to 2004, followed by a decline of about 5 per cent to 2006, and then a further decline of about 7 per cent from 2006 to 2009. The decline measured by the GHS is much greater, at about 15 per cent between 2002 and 2006. Both sources show that there has been a fall in consumption in recent years, but two factors are likely to account for the different sizes of the falls:

1.   There may be an increased tendency among respondents to under-report consumption. Recent extensive publicity about the dangers of drinking, in particular binge drinking, may

have led some people to moderate their behaviour, but might equally have made people less inclined to admit to how much they have been drinking

2.   The introduction of updated methods of estimating units occurs as a step change, whereas the actual changes which the updated method takes into account happened over a number of years. It is therefore likely that progressive underestimation of wine consumption has occurred as glass sizes and alcoholic strength have increased

Tables 2.1-2.2

Trends in abstinence

The falls in average consumption in recent years (shown in figure 2.2) are partly due to rises in the proportion of people who abstain from alcohol altogether. The table below shows the trend in abstinence since 1998.

Figure 2.3   **Percentage of adults who report never drinking alcohol**

Great Britain

Percentages

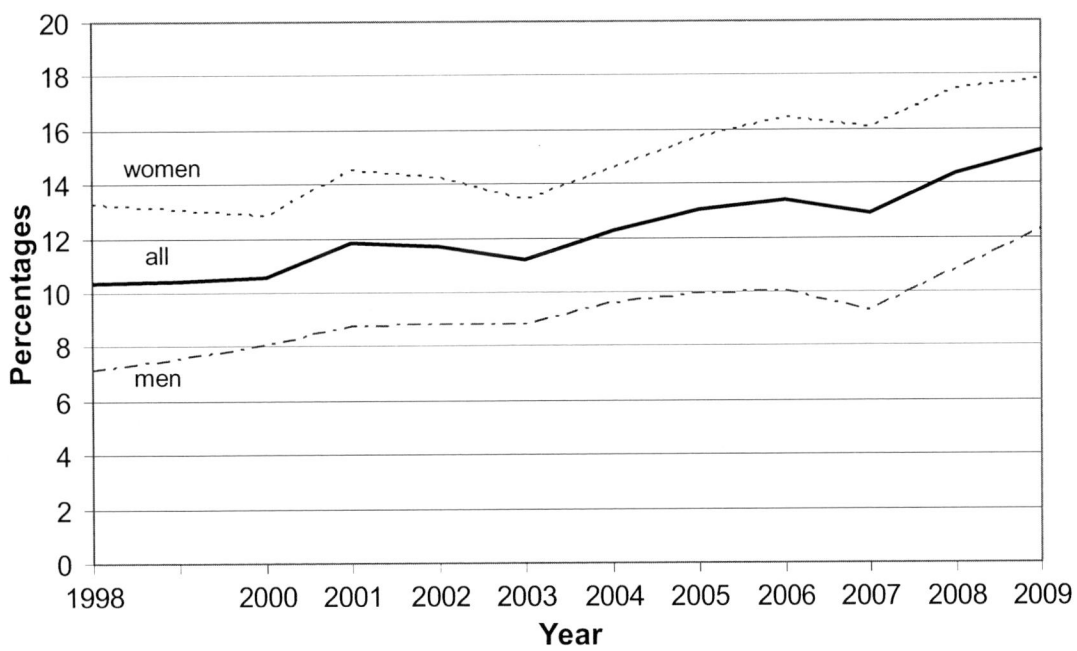

Source: General Lifestyle Survey, Office for National Statistics

The proportion of people who abstain from alcohol altogether increased from 10 per cent in 1998 to 15 per cent in 2009. The biggest falls in the average weekly consumption figures were from 12.1 to 10.2 units between 2002 and 2006 using the original method of converting volumes to units and from 13.5 to 11.9 units between 2006 and 2009 using the revised method. Excluding non-drinkers from the analyses causes the average consumption figures to rise but the falls between the years remain. The figures for 2002 to 2006 fall from 13.7 to 11.8 units and the figures for 2006 to 2009 fall from 15.6 to 14.0 units. This shows that the falls in alcohol consumption as measured by the GHS/GLF are largely due to people who drink alcohol drinking less.

Trends in last week's drinking

There has been a fall in the proportions of men and women who say that they had an alcoholic drink in the previous week compared with five years ago. Table 2.3 shows that following a period of little change between 1998 and 2003, the figures fell from 75 per cent of men and 60 per cent of women in 2003 to 72 per cent and 57 per cent in 2005; the figures were then fairly stable until 2007. The proportion of men and women reporting drinking alcohol in the last seven days fell from 72 per cent of men and 57 per cent of women in 2007 to 68 per cent of men and 54 per cent of women in 2009.

The proportions of men exceeding four units and women exceeding three units on their heaviest drinking day were fairly stable between 1998 and 2004 but have since decreased. The figures produced using the original method of converting to units show falls for both men and women between 2004 and 2006. The figures produced using the revised method show a continuing downward trend. The proportion of men exceeding 4 units on their heaviest drinking day was 41 per cent in 2007 and 37 per cent in 2009. The proportions for women exceeding 3 units were 34 per cent in 2007 and 29 per cent in 2009.

The figures for heavy drinking follow a similar pattern for men. There was little change between 1998 and 2004 in the proportion of men drinking heavily (more than 8 units) on at least one day in the previous week. Since 2004 this proportion has decreased from 22 per cent to 18 per cent in 2006. Using the revised methodology this trend seems to be continuing with the proportion falling from 23 per cent in 2006 to 20 per cent in 2009. There appears to be a similar downward trend in the proportion of women drinking heavily (more than 6 units) on at least one day in the previous week, falling from 10 per cent in 2002 to 8 per cent in 2006. Using the revised method of converting volumes to units of alcohol the proportion of women drinking heavily was 15 per cent in 2006 and 13 per cent in 2009.

The most pronounced changes have occurred for men in the 16 to 24 age group where the proportion drinking more than 4 units on their heaviest drinking day fell from 50 per cent in 2000 to 39 per cent in 2006 and the proportion drinking more than 8 units decreased from 37 per cent to 27 per cent over the same period. Since the introduction of the revised methodology in 2006 however, there has been little significant change. The falls between 2008 and 2009, from 42 per cent to 36 per cent exceeding 4 units and from 30 to 24 per cent drinking heavily, should be treated with caution due to the small sample size for this age group.

There have also been marked falls for women in this age group with the proportion drinking more than 3 units on their heaviest drinking day falling from 42 per cent in 2000 to 34 per cent in 2006 and the proportion drinking more than 6 units falling from 27 per cent to 20 per cent. It is too soon to tell whether this trend will continue under the revised methodology. So far there are no significant changes in this age group in the proportion exceeding 3 units or in the proportion exceeding 6 units between 2006 and 2009.

Tables 2.3- 2.4

Average weekly alcohol consumption in 2009

Weekly alcohol consumption and sex and age

In 2009 average levels of alcohol consumption were similar in all age groups from 16 to 64 at around 12 or 13 units a week but were about a third lower among those aged 65 and over at 8.2 units a week. The average consumption for men was twice that of women (16.3 units compared with 8.0 units). The difference between men and women was particularly large in the 65 and over age group. In this group average consumption for women was 4.6 units per week but for men was nearly three times that at 12.7 units.

Table 2.5

Weekly alcohol consumption and household socio-economic class

A review of information on inequalities in health, undertaken by the Department of Health[8], noted that both mortality and morbidity show a clear association with socio-economic position, with death rates much higher among unskilled men than among those in professional households (overall, up to 22,000 premature deaths a year are thought to be attributable to alcohol misuse[9]). Over many years, the GHS showed little difference in usual weekly alcohol consumption between those in non-manual and manual households. Where differences existed, it was those in the non-manual categories who tended to have the higher weekly consumption. When the revised method of converting volumes of alcohol to units was introduced in 2006 these differences were amplified. This is due, at least in part, to the relatively low prevalence of wine consumption in routine and manual households compared with the other groups.

The socio-economic classification of a household is based upon the current or last job of the household reference person. The classification takes into account the occupation and details of employment status (whether an employer, self-employed or employee; whether a supervisor, manager etc). The 40 operational categories and sub-categories are usually collapsed into 8 or 3 classes for analysis[10]. Using the three-category classification, average weekly consumption in 2009 was highest, at 13.5 units, in the managerial and professional group, and lowest, at 10.7 units, among those in routine and manual worker households. This difference is found for both men and women but is particularly pronounced for women where the managerial and professional group average 9.7 units and the routine and manual group average 6.6 units a week.

Table 2.6

Weekly alcohol consumption, income and economic activity

A clear association between household income and alcohol consumption can be seen in table 2.7. As household income rises from £400 per week, so does average weekly alcohol consumption. The group with the highest income has the highest average consumption. Among those living in households with a gross income of more than £1,000 a week, men drank on average 18.7 units as week, and women 10.8 units. In households with an income of £200 or less the levels were 16.1 units and 5.7 units respectively.

In the 16 to 64 age group people who are economically inactive tend to drink less than those who are working. Among people aged between 16 and 64 and in full-time employment those earning £600.01 or more a week showed higher average weekly consumption that those earning £600 or less.

Tables 2.7-2.9

Variation in average weekly alcohol consumption between countries and regions

There were no significant differences in average weekly alcohol consumption between countries in Great Britain. In the English regions average weekly consumption was highest in the North East (14.4 units) and lowest in London (9.3 units). Average weekly consumption in London was significantly lower than in all other regions apart from the West Midlands where it was similarly low. In the West Midlands average consumption was lower than in the North West, North East, South East and Yorkshire and the Humber.

Table 2.10

Abstinence in 2009

In 2009, 85 per cent of adults consumed alcohol and 15 per cent of adults abstained from drinking alcohol. Abstinence was more common among women (18 per cent) than among men (12 per cent). Levels of abstinence were highest, at 26 per cent, among women aged 65 and over and were next highest among men and women aged from 16 to 24 at 17 per cent. The levels of abstinence among men aged 65 and over (14 per cent) were similar to those among women aged 25 to 44 (14 per cent) and women aged 45 to 64 (15 per cent). Only 10 per cent of men aged 25 to 64 were non-drinkers.

Of those who reported never drinking alcohol, 57 per cent said they had always been a non-drinker and 43 per cent said they had given up drinking. Of those who had always been non-drinkers, 48 per cent said the main reason was that they didn't like it and 28 per cent said it was for religious reasons. Of those who had given up drinking, 51 per cent had done so for health reasons and 22 per cent gave up because they didn't like it.

Drinking in the week before interview in 2009

Frequency of drinking during the last week

Patterns of drinking behaviour in 2009 were broadly similar to those described in earlier GHS and GLF reports. Men were more likely than women to have had an alcoholic drink in the week before interview: 68 per cent of men and 54 per cent of women had had a drink on at least one day during the previous week. Men also drank on more days of the week than women: 18 per cent of men and 10 per cent of women had drunk on at least five of the preceding seven days. Men were much more likely than women to have drunk alcohol every day during the previous week (10 per cent compared with 6 per cent).

The proportions drinking during the last week also varied between age groups. Those in the youngest and oldest age groups (16 to 24 and 65 and over) were less likely than those in the middle age range to report drinking alcohol during the previous week. The proportion who had drunk alcohol in the previous week was particularly low among women aged 65 and over; 43 per cent of whom had done so, compared with 66 per cent of men in that age group and 59 per cent of women aged 45 to 64.

The age group with the highest proportion of people who didn't drink in the last week was the 65 and over group (47 per cent). This was also the group with the highest proportion of people who drank every day (14 per cent). The proportion of people who drink every day rises as age group rises. For example, 2 per cent of men and 1 per cent of women aged 16 to 24 had drunk every day during the previous week, compared with 19 per cent of men and 10 per cent of women aged 65 and over.

Table 2.11

Maximum daily amount drunk last week

Two measures of daily consumption are shown. The first is the proportion of men exceeding four units and women exceeding three units on their heaviest drinking day. This measure is based on the government recommendations that men should not regularly drink more than three to four units and women more than two to three units of alcohol a day but is not the same as the recommendations since there is no measure of how regular this drinking is. In the following sections this measure will be referred to as drinking more than '4/3 units'. The second measure is intended to indicate heavy drinking that would be likely to lead to intoxication and is set at more than eight units on one day for men and more than six units for women and is referred to as drinking more than '8/6 units'.

The proportion of people who exceeded 4/3 units on at least one day during the previous week was higher for men (37 per cent) than it was for women (29 per cent). The proportion drinking heavily was also greater for men (20 per cent) than for women (13 per cent).

It was noted earlier that older people tend to drink more frequently than younger people. However, among both men and women, those aged 65 and over were significantly less likely than respondents in other age groups to have exceeded 4/3 units on at least one day. For example, 20 per cent of men over 65 exceeded four units on at least one day during the previous week. The corresponding figures for the younger three age-bands were 36 per cent, 44 per cent and 41 per cent (16 to 24, 25 to 44 and 45 to 64 respectively). Among women, 11 per cent of those aged 65 and over exceeded three units on at least one day. The corresponding figures for the younger three age-bands were 37 per cent, 36 per cent and 32 per cent (16 to 24, 25 to 44 and 45 to 64 respectively).

Similar patterns were evident for heavy drinking: 24 per cent of men aged 16 to 24, 27 per cent of men aged 25 to 44, 21 per cent of men aged 45 to 64, but only 5 per cent of those aged 65 and over, had drunk more than eight units on at least one day during the previous week. Among women the figures for the corresponding age groups were 24 per cent, 19 per cent and 11 per cent compared with only 2 per cent of women in the oldest age group.

Table 2.12b shows the above analysis with those people who did not consume alcohol in the week before interview excluded. When looking only at those people who drank alcohol in the last week, over half (54 per cent) consumed more than 4/3 units and over a quarter (27 per cent) consumed more than 8/6 units on at least one day. The proportion exceeding 4/3 units varied with age group. In the 16 to 24 group, 69 per cent of those who consumed alcohol in the last week consumed more than 4/3 units on their heaviest drinking day. This is higher than the 62 per cent who exceeded 4/3 units in the 25 to 44 group, which in turn is higher than the 56 per cent who did so in the 45 to 64 age group. The proportion of drinkers exceeding 4/3 units was lowest, at 29 per cent, in the 65 and over group.

Among those who consumed alcohol in the week before interview, the differences between age groups in heavy drinking were even more marked. In the 16 to 24 age group 46 per cent of those who consumed alcohol in the last week consumed more than 8/6 units on their heaviest drinking day. The corresponding figures for the other age groups were 35 per cent, 25 per cent and 6 per cent (25 to 44, 45 to 64 and 65 and over respectively).

Overall, men and women who consumed alcohol in the week before interview were just a likely as each other to consume more than 4/3 units on their heaviest drinking day but men were more likely than women to consume more than 8/6 units on that day (30 per cent compared with 24 per cent). Differences between men and women varied with age group. In the 16 to 24 age group, there were no significant differences between men and women in the proportion drinking more than 4/3 units or in the proportion drinking heavily on their heaviest drinking day. In the 25 to 44 and 45 to 64 age groups, there was no significant difference between men and women in the proportion exceeding 4/3 units but a higher proportion of men than of women reported heavy drinking (39 per cent compared with 32 per cent in the 25 to 44 group and 30 per cent compared with 19 per cent in the 45 to 64 group). In the 65 and over group a higher proportion of men than of women consumed more than 4/3 units (31 per cent and 26 per cent) and a higher proportion of men than of women reported heavy drinking (8 per cent and 4 per cent).

Tables 2.12-2.12b

Drinking last week and socio-economic characteristics

Households where the household reference person was classified as managerial and professional had the highest proportions of both men and women who had an alcoholic drink in the last seven days (77 per cent and 65 per cent), while men and women in routine and manual households had the lowest (59 per cent and 44 per cent). There was a similar pattern in the proportions drinking on five or more days in the previous week. For example, 18 per cent of people in managerial and professional households had an alcoholic drink on five or more days in the previous week. In households where the reference person was in an occupation in the 'routine and manual' classification, this proportion was much lower, at 10 per cent.

Variations in amounts drunk were also marked, particularly for women. Women in large employer/higher managerial households were twice as likely than those in the routine group to have drunk more than three units on any one day (44 per cent compared with 20 per cent), and were also twice as likely to have drunk heavily on at least one day in the previous week (18 per cent compared with 9 per cent). A similar but less pronounced pattern was seen for men. In large employer/higher managerial households 49 per cent of men exceeded four units on their heaviest drinking day in the week before interview. In the routine group this falls to 35 per cent. Men in large employer/higher managerial households were also more likely to have drunk heavily on at least one day in the previous week than those in the routine group (25 per cent compared with 19 per cent).

Overall the proportion of people exceeding 4/3 units was greater in managerial and professional households (38 per cent) than in routine and manual households (28 per cent); the proportion drinking heavily was also greater in managerial and professional households (19 per cent) than in routine and manual households (15 per cent).

Tables 2.13-2.14

Drinking last week and household income

As the level of gross weekly household income rises, the proportion of people who drank alcohol in the previous week also rises. In households with a gross weekly income of over £1,000, 74 per cent drank in the previous week and 17 per cent drank on five or more days compared with 46 per cent and 11 per cent in households with a gross weekly income of £200 or less.

The proportions of people exceeding 4/3 units and of people drinking heavily rose with increasing gross weekly household income. In households with a gross weekly income of £200 or less, for example, 30 per cent of men drank more than 4 units and 14 per cent drank more than 8 units on at least one day in the previous week. In households with an income of over £1,000 the figures were 46 per cent and 26 per cent respectively. The difference for women was even more marked. In households with income of £200 or less per week, 17 per cent of women exceeded 3 units and 8 per cent exceeded 6 units on their heaviest drinking day. These proportions rise to 43 and 19 per cent respectively in households with income in excess of £1,000 per week.

Tables 2.15-2.16

Drinking last week, economic activity and earnings from employment

Variations in alcohol consumption by economic status reflect differences in both the income and age profiles of the groups. Among men aged 16 to 64, those in employment were most likely to have drunk alcohol during the previous week – 74 per cent had done so compared with 58 per cent of the unemployed and 52 per cent of those who were economically inactive. Working men were more likely than unemployed and economically inactive men to have drunk more than 4 units on one day – 44 per cent, compared with 37 per cent and 31 per cent respectively. Working men were also more likely than economically inactive men to have drunk more than 8 units on one day – 26 per cent compared with 17 per cent. As noted above, lower levels of drinking among economically inactive men are probably due in part to the large proportion of this group who are aged 60 to 64.

Among women aged 16 to 64, 64 per cent of those who were working; 44 per cent of those who were unemployed; and 45 per cent of those who were economically inactive had drunk alcohol in the previous week. Working women were more likely than the economically inactive to have drunk more than 3 units on one day - 38 per cent, compared with 25 per cent. Working women were also more likely than the economically inactive to have drunk more than 6 units on one day - 18 per cent, compared with 11 per cent.

Among those aged 16 to 64 and working full time, drinking behaviour showed a similar pattern of association with earnings from employment as it did with household income. The prevalence of alcohol consumption was highest among those earning the most. In the £800.01 or more group 83 per cent of adults had consumed alcohol in the week before interview – higher than any other group. The figures for drinking on five or more days in the week are less straight forward. Prevalence of this was higher for those earning over £600.01 per week than it was for those earning between £200.01 and £600 per week. For those earning £200 or less however, the figures were more similar to the over £600.01 group. The sample size in this very low income group is small and the figures are therefore subject to quite high levels of sampling error.

High earners were similarly more likely to exceed 4/3 units than low earners. For example, 52 per cent of adults earning over £800 per week exceeded 4/3 units compared with 38 per cent of those earning £200 or less per week. The relationship between earnings and heavy drinking is similar. The proportion of people who drank heavily on at least one day in the week before interview is similar in the middle and high income groups at between 25 and 28 per cent but is lower in the low income groups at 19 per cent.

Tables 2.17-2.20

Variation in drinking last week between countries and regions

Care should be taken in interpreting the results for geographical variation in any one year because sample sizes in some regions are small, making them subject to relatively high levels of sampling error.

In 2009 a higher proportion of men (69 per cent) and women (55 percent) in England consumed alcohol in the week before interview than did so in Scotland (58 per cent and 48 per cent respectively). Men in England and men in Wales were more likely than men in Scotland to have had an alcoholic drink on at least five days in that week (19 per cent and 17 per cent compared with 12 per cent). There were, however, no significant differences between the countries of Great Britain in the proportions of men and women consuming more than 4/3 units on their heaviest drinking day or in the proportions reporting heavy drinking (more than 8/6 units) on that day. It should be noted, however, that the countries of Great Britain also conduct their own health surveys that include questions on drinking and that results between surveys can differ.[11]

Of the English regions, London had the lowest prevalence of drinking in the week before interview (57 per cent of men, 46 per cent of women, 51 per cent of adults). The West Midlands had the next lowest prevalence with the other regions being broadly similar to each other. The highest proportions of adults exceeding 4/3 units on their heaviest drinking day were found in the North East, North West and in Yorkshire and the Humber (40, 39 and 41 per cent of adults). The lowest proportions doing so were in London, the West Midlands and the South West (26, 27 and 28 per cent of adults). The North East, North West and Yorkshire and the Humber also showed the highest levels of heavy drinking (21, 21 and 22 per cent of adults) while the West Midlands showed the lowest at 11 per cent.

Tables 2.21-2.22

Notes and references

1   Goddard E. Obtaining information about drinking through surveys of the general population. National Statistics Methodology Series NSM 24 (ONS 2001)

2   ABV is the percentage of Alcohol by Volume.

3   Sensible drinking: the report of an inter-departmental group. (Department of Health 1995).

4   A unit of alcohol is defined as 10ml of pure ethanol. This is equivalent to a standard measure of spirits (25ml at 40% ABV) or half a pint of standard strength beer (284ml at 3.6% ABV)

5   Goddard E Estimating alcohol consumption from survey data: updated method of converting volumes to units National Statistics Methodology Series NSM 37 (ONS 2007), www.statistics.gov.uk/statbase/product.asp?vlnk=15067

6   Goddard E Smoking and drinking among adults, 2006. (ONS 2008), www.statistics.gov.uk/statbase/product.asp?vlnk=5756

7   BBPA Statistical Handbook 2010: a compilation of drinks industry statistics. (British Beer & Pub Association, Brewing Publications Ltd, 2010).

8   Inequalities in Health, (The Stationery Office 1998) also available at www.archive.official-documents.co.uk/document/doh/ih/contents.htm

9   Safe. Sensible. Social. The next steps in the National Alcohol Strategy. (Department of Health 2007). www.dh.gov.uk/en/Publicationsandstatistics/publications/PublicationsPolicyandGuidance/DH_075218

10   Further information on the National Statistics Socio-economic Classification is available at: http://www.ons.gov.uk/about-statistics/classifications/current/ns-sec/index.html

11   A discussion of the differences between countries based on health surveys is available at: http://www.scotland.gov.uk/Publications/2010/08/31093025/0

Alcohol consumption tables

Table 2.1   Average weekly alcohol consumption (units), by sex and age: 1992-2009

Persons aged 16 and over   Great Britain

Age	Unweighted				Weighted						2006[3]	2008[3]	2008[4] Updated method	2009[4]	Weighted base 2009 (000's) =100%	Unweighted sample[5] 2009
	1992	1994	1996	1998	1998	2000	2001	2002	2005[1]	2006[2]						
Men																
16-24	19.1	17.4	20.3	23.6	25.5	25.9	24.8	21.5	18.2	16.4	18.6	16.3	16.3	14.8	2,281	550
25-44	18.2	17.5	17.6	16.5	17.1	17.7	18.4	18.7	16.2	15.6	19.7	16.6	16.8	16.4	6,649	1,680
45-64	15.6	15.5	15.6	17.3	17.4	16.8	16.1	17.5	17.7	16.0	20.8	18.7	18.7	18.7	6,558	2,190
65 and over	9.7	10.0	11.0	10.7	10.6	11.0	10.8	10.7	10.4	10.4	13.5	13.6	13.2	12.7	4,017	1,710
Total	15.9	15.4	16.0	16.4	17.1	17.4	17.2	17.2	15.8	14.8	18.7	16.7	16.6	16.3	19,505	6,130
Women																
16-24	7.3	7.7	9.5	10.6	11.0	12.6	14.1	14.1	10.9	9.0	10.8	10.0	10.3	10.3	2,540	620
25-44	6.3	6.2	7.2	7.1	7.1	8.1	8.3	8.4	7.1	6.8	10.1	9.5	9.6	8.7	7,479	2,180
45-64	5.3	5.3	5.9	6.4	6.4	6.2	6.8	6.7	6.3	6.2	9.8	9.1	9.0	8.9	7,218	2,540
65 and over	2.7	3.2	3.5	3.3	3.2	3.5	3.6	3.8	3.5	3.5	5.1	4.9	4.7	4.6	5,005	1,940
Total	5.4	5.4	6.3	6.4	6.5	7.1	7.5	7.6	6.5	6.2	9.0	8.4	8.4	8.0	22,242	7,280
All persons																
16-24	12.9	12.3	14.7	16.6	18.0	19.3	19.4	17.6	14.3	12.5	14.6	13.0	13.1	12.5	4,821	1,180
25-44	11.8	11.4	11.9	11.4	12.0	12.9	13.3	13.3	11.3	11.0	14.6	12.8	12.9	12.3	14,127	3,860
45-64	10.2	10.2	10.5	11.6	11.7	11.4	11.3	11.9	11.7	10.9	15.0	13.7	13.6	13.6	13,777	4,730
65 and over	5.6	6.0	6.8	6.5	6.3	6.7	6.6	6.8	6.5	6.5	8.7	8.8	8.5	8.2	9,022	3,650
Total	10.2	10.0	10.7	11.0	11.5	12.0	12.1	12.1	10.8	10.2	13.5	12.3	12.2	11.9	41,747	13,410

1   2005 data includes last quarter of 2004/5 data due to survey change from financial year to calendar year.
2   Results from 2006 include longitudinal data (see Appendix B).
3   Figures produced using the updated methodology for converting volumes of alcohol to units assuming an average wine glass size
4   Figures produced using the updated methodology including data on wine glass size
5   Figures for unweighted sample have been rounded independently. The sum of component items does not therefore necessarily add to the totals shown.

Source: General Lifestyle Survey, Office for National Statistics

Table 2.2   Weekly alcohol consumption: percentage exceeding specified amounts by sex and age: 1992-2009

Persons aged 16 and over   Great Britain

Age	Unweighted data				Weighted data						2006[3]	2008[3]	2008[4] Updated method	2009[4]	Weighted base 2009 (000's) =100%	Unweighted sample[5] 2009
	1992	1994	1996	1998	1998	2000	2001	2002	2005[1]	2006[2]						
Men																
Percentage of men who drank more than 21 units																
16-24	32	29	35	36	38	41	40	37	27	26	30	25	25	21	2,281	550
25-44	31	30	30	27	28	30	30	29	26	24	33	27	27	26	6,649	1,680
45-64	25	27	26	30	30	28	26	28	25	24	34	31	31	31	6,558	2,190
65 and over	15	17	18	16	16	17	15	15	14	14	21	22	22	20	4,017	1,710
Total	26	27	27	27	28	29	28	27	24	23	31	27	27	26	19,505	6,130
Percentage of men who drank more than 50 units																
16-24	9	9	10	13	14	14	15	12	9	7	9	7	7	6	2,281	550
25-44	8	7	6	6	6	7	7	8	5	5	9	6	6	7	6,649	1,680
45-64	6	6	5	6	7	6	5	6	6	6	10	8	8	8	6,558	2,190
65 and over	2	3	3	3	3	3	2	3	3	2	5	6	5	5	4,017	1,710
Total	6	6	6	6	7	7	7	7	6	5	8	7	7	7	19,505	6,130
Women																
Percentage of women who drank more than 14 units																
16-24	17	19	22	25	25	33	32	33	24	19	24	22	22	23	2,540	620
25-44	14	15	16	16	16	19	17	19	14	14	23	21	21	19	7,479	2,180
45-64	11	12	13	16	15	14	14	14	13	12	21	21	21	20	7,218	2,540
65 and over	5	7	7	6	6	7	6	7	5	5	10	10	9	10	5,005	1,940
Total	11	13	14	15	15	17	15	17	13	12	20	19	19	18	22,242	7,280
Percentage of women who drank more than 35 units																
16-24	4	4	5	6	7	9	10	10	6	5	7	6	7	6	2,540	620
25-44	2	2	2	2	2	3	3	3	2	2	6	5	5	4	7,479	2,180
45-64	1	2	2	2	2	2	2	2	2	2	6	5	5	4	7,218	2,540
65 and over	0	1	1	1	1	1	1	1	1	1	2	2	1	1	5,005	1,940
Total	2	2	2	2	2	3	3	3	2	2	5	4	4	4	22,242	7,280

1   2005 data includes last quarter of 2004/5 data due to survey change from financial year to calendar year.

2   Results from 2006 include longitudinal data (see Appendix B).

3   Figures produced using the updated methodology for converting volumes of alcohol to units assuming an average wine glass size

4   Figures produced using the updated methodology including data on wine glass size

5   Figures for unweighted sample have been rounded independently. The sum of component items does not therefore necessarily add to the totals shown.

Source: General Lifestyle Survey, Office for National Statistics

Table 2.3   Drinking last week, by sex and age: 1998 to 2009

Persons aged 16 and over   *Great Britain*

Drinking last week	1998	2000	2001	2002	2003	2004	2005[1]	2006[2]	2007[2]	2008[2]	2009[2]	Weighted base 2009 (000s)=100%	Unweighted sample 2009[3]
					Percentages								
Men													
Drank last week													
16-24	70	70	70	69	70	66	64	60	64	63	55	2,341	570
25-44	79	78	78	77	77	76	74	73	74	72	70	6,660	1,680
45-64	77	77	76	76	78	76	77	76	76	74	72	6,579	2,190
65 and over	65	67	68	67	69	68	66	67	67	66	66	4,022	1,710
Total	75	75	75	74	75	73	72	71	72	70	68	19,603	6,160
Drank on 5 or more days last week													
16-24	13	11	14	11	14	8	10	8	9	6	7	2,341	570
25-44	21	19	19	19	20	20	18	17	18	14	13	6,660	1,680
45-64	29	26	25	26	26	28	28	26	27	24	23	6,579	2,190
65 and over	25	28	27	28	29	28	26	27	29	27	27	4,022	1,710
Total	23	22	22	22	23	23	22	21	22	19	18	19,603	6,160
Women													
Drank last week													
16-24	62	64	59	61	61	60	56	53	54	52	51	2,552	630
25-44	65	67	66	65	65	62	62	60	61	59	59	7,483	2,180
45-64	61	61	61	63	64	62	61	61	61	60	59	7,232	2,540
65 and over	45	43	45	46	45	45	43	44	45	43	43	5,003	1,940
Total	59	60	59	59	60	58	57	56	57	55	54	22,271	7,290
Drank on 5 or more days last week													
16-24	8	7	8	7	4	5	5	3	4	2	2	2,552	630
25-44	12	11	11	11	10	9	11	9	11	9	7	7,483	2,180
45-64	15	15	17	17	17	18	17	15	15	15	14	7,232	2,540
65 and over	14	14	15	15	16	16	14	15	15	15	14	5,003	1,940
Total	13	13	13	13	13	13	13	11	12	11	10	22,271	7,290

1 2005 data includes last quarter of 2004/5 data due to survey change from financial year to calendar year.

2 Results from 2006 include longitudinal data (see Appendix B).

3 Figures for unweighted sample have been rounded independently. The sum of component items does not therefore necessarily add to the totals shown.
   Bases for earlier years can be found in GLF/GHS reports for each year.

Source: General Lifestyle Survey, Office for National Statistics

Table 2.4 Maximum drunk on any one day last week by sex and age: 1998 to 2009

Persons aged 16 and over — *Great Britain*

Maximum daily amount	1998	2000	2001	2002	2003	2004	2005[1]	2006[2]	2006[3]	2007	2008	2008[4] updated method	2009	Weighted base 2009 (000s)=100%	Unweighted sample 2009[5]
					Percentages										
Men															
Drank more than 4 units on at least one day															
16-24	52	50	50	49	51	47	42	39	42	44	42	42	36	2,342	570
25-44	48	45	49	46	47	48	42	42	48	48	41	42	44	6,664	1,690
45-64	37	38	37	38	41	37	35	33	42	44	40	41	41	6,578	2,190
65 and over	16	16	18	16	19	20	16	14	21	23	21	21	20	4,022	1,710
Total	39	39	40	38	40	39	35	33	40	41	37	37	37	19,606	6,160
Drank more than 8 units on at least one day															
16-24	39	37	37	35	37	32	30	27	30	32	30	30	24	2,342	570
25-44	29	27	30	28	30	31	25	25	31	31	26	27	27	6,664	1,690
45-64	17	17	17	18	20	18	16	15	21	24	21	21	21	6,578	2,190
65 and over	4	5	5	5	6	7	4	4	7	8	7	7	5	4,022	1,710
Total	22	21	22	21	23	22	19	18	23	24	21	21	20	19,606	6,160
Women															
Drank more than 3 units on at least one day															
16-24	42	42	40	42	40	39	36	34	39	40	37	36	37	2,548	630
25-44	28	31	31	31	30	28	26	27	40	43	38	37	36	7,481	2,180
45-64	17	19	19	19	20	20	18	17	35	36	35	32	32	7,229	2,540
65 and over	4	4	5	5	4	5	4	4	14	14	13	10	11	5,005	1,940
Total	21	23	23	23	23	22	20	20	33	34	32	29	29	22,263	7,290
Drank more than 6 units on at least one day															
16-24	24	27	27	28	26	24	22	20	25	24	23	24	24	2,548	630
25-44	11	13	14	13	13	13	11	12	21	22	20	20	19	7,481	2,180
45-64	5	5	5	5	5	6	4	4	12	13	13	13	11	7,229	2,540
65 and over	1	1	1	1	1	1	1	0	2	3	2	2	2	5,005	1,940
Total	8	10	10	10	9	9	8	8	15	15	14	14	13	22,263	7,290

1 2005 data includes last quarter of 2004/5 data due to survey change from financial year to calendar year.

2 Results from 2006 include longitudinal data (see Appendix B).

3 Figures produced using the updated methodology for converting volumes of alcohol to units assuming an average wine glass size

4 Figures produced from 2008 are using the updated methodology including data on wine glass size

5 Figures for unweighted sample have been rounded independently. The sum of component items does not therefore necessarily add to the totals shown. Bases for earlier years can be found in GLF/GHS reports for each year.

Source: General Lifestyle Survey, Office for National Statistics

Table 2.5   Average weekly alcohol consumption (units), by sex and age

Persons aged 16 and over   *Great Britain: 2009[1]*

Age	Average weekly alcohol consumption			Weighted base (000's) =100%			Unweighted sample[2]		
	Men	Women	Total	Men	Women	Total	Men	Women	Total
16-24	14.8	10.3	12.5	2,281	2,540	4,821	550	620	1,180
25-44	16.4	8.7	12.3	6,649	7,479	14,127	1,680	2,180	3,860
45-64	18.7	8.9	13.6	6,558	7,218	13,777	2,190	2,540	4,730
65 and over	12.7	4.6	8.2	4,017	5,005	9,022	1,710	1,940	3,650
Total	16.3	8.0	11.9	19,505	22,242	41,747	6,130	7,280	13,410

1 Results for 2009 include longitudinal data (see Appendix B).

2 Figures for unweighted sample have been rounded independently. The sum of component items does not therefore necessarily add to the totals shown.

Source: General Lifestyle Survey, Office for National Statistics

Table 2.6   Average weekly alcohol consumption (units), by sex and socio-economic class based on the current or last job of the household reference person

Persons aged 16 and over   *Great Britain: 2009[1]*

Socio-economic classification of household reference person	Men		Women		Total	
Managerial and professional						
Large employer and higher managerial	19.9 ⎤		11.7 ⎤		15.7 ⎤	
Higher professional	17.3 ⎬ 17.5		9.8 ⎬ 9.7		13.8 ⎬ 13.5	
Lower managerial and professional	17.0 ⎦		9.2 ⎦		12.8 ⎦	
Intermediate						
Intermediate	15.0 ⎤ 15.8		6.8 ⎤ 7.8		9.8 ⎤ 11.4	
Small employers/own account workers	16.3 ⎦		9.1 ⎦		12.7 ⎦	
Routine and manual						
Lower supervisory and technical	15.4 ⎤		7.1 ⎤		11.4 ⎤	
Semi-routine	14.9 ⎬ 15.4		6.7 ⎬ 6.6		10.1 ⎬ 10.7	
Routine	15.9 ⎦		6.1 ⎦		10.7 ⎦	
Total[4]	16.3		8.0		11.9	
Weighted bases (000's) =100%						
Large employer and higher managerial	1,276		1,332		2,608	
Higher professional	2,084		1,787		3,871	
Lower managerial and professional	4,927		5,664		10,591	
Intermediate	1,289		2,177		3,466	
Small employers/own account workers	1,890		1,849		3,740	
Lower supervisory and technical	2,462		2,296		4,758	
Semi-routine	2,235		3,211		5,447	
Routine	2,130		2,382		4,512	
Total[4]	19,505		22,242		41,747	
Unweighted sample						
Large employer and higher managerial	420		440		860	
Higher professional	630		590		1,220	
Lower managerial and professional	1,560		1,870		3,440	
Intermediate	400		710		1,100	
Small employers/own account workers	600		600		1,210	
Lower supervisory and technical	790		750		1,550	
Semi-routine	690		1,040		1,720	
Routine	690		790		1,480	
Total[4]	6,130		7,280		13,410	

1   Results for 2009 include longitudinal data (see Appendix B).
2   Full-time students, members of the Armed Forces, the long-term unemployed and those who have never worked
    are not shown as separate categories but are included in the totals.

Source: General Lifestyle Survey, Office for National Statistics

Table 2.7 Average weekly alcohol consumption (units), by sex and usual gross weekly household income (£)

Persons aged 16 and over   *Great Britain: 2009[1]*

Usual gross weekly household income (£)	Average weekly alcohol consumption			Weighted base (000's) =100%			Unweighted sample[2]		
	Men	Women	Total	Men	Women	Total	Men	Women	Total
Up to 200.00	16.1	5.7	9.9	2,674	3,970	6,644	830	1,340	2,170
200.01 - 400.00	12.8	6.7	9.4	3,289	4,194	7,483	1,180	1,500	2,680
400.01 - 600.00	14.7	7.5	10.8	2,854	3,257	6,111	960	1,120	2,080
600.01 - 800.00	16.7	8.9	12.8	2,819	2,787	5,606	840	880	1,720
800.01 - 1000.00	18.3	9.0	13.6	2,084	2,067	4,151	620	630	1,250
1000.01 or more	18.7	10.8	14.8	4,489	4,455	8,944	1,300	1,310	2,610
Total	16.3	8.0	11.9	18,208	20,731	38,939	5,720	6,790	12,510

1 Results for 2009 include longitudinal data (see Appendix B).

2 Figures for unweighted sample have been rounded independently. The sum of component items does not therefore necessarily add to the totals shown.

Source: General Lifestyle Survey, Office for National Statistics

Table 2.8 Average weekly alcohol consumption (units), by sex and economic activity status

Persons aged 16-64   *Great Britain: 2009[1]*

Economic activity status	Average weekly alcohol consumption			Weighted base (000's) =100%			Unweighted sample[2]		
	Men	Women	Total[3]	Men	Women	Total[3]	Men	Women	Total[3]
Working	17.3	9.7	13.5	11,531	11,763	23,294	3,300	3,580	6,880
Unemployed	16.6	11.0	14.4	1,359	868	2,227	360	250	600
Economically inactive	16.8	7.0	10.5	2,590	4,603	7,192	770	1,520	2,280
Total[3]	17.2	9.0	12.9	15,480	17,234	32,713	4,420	5,340	9,760

1 Results for 2009 include longitudinal data (see Appendix B).

2 Figures for unweighted sample have been rounded independently. The sum of component items does not therefore necessarily add to the totals shown.

3 Full-time students, members of the Armed Forces, the long-term unemployed and those who have never worked are not shown as separate categories but are included in the totals.

Source: General Lifestyle Survey, Office for National Statistics

Table 2.9   Average weekly alcohol consumption (units), by sex and usual gross weekly earnings (£)

Persons aged 16-64 in full-time employment   *Great Britain: 2009[1]*

Usual gross weekly earnings (£)	Average weekly alcohol consumption			Weighted base (000's) =100%			Unweighted sample[2]		
	Men	Women	Total	Men	Women	Total	Men	Women	Total
Up to 200.00	16.7	10.3	13.9	605	484	1,090	180	150	330
200.01 - 300.00	16.3	8.2	12.1	1,194	1,288	2,482	330	380	710
300.01 - 400.00	19.7	8.9	14.5	1,511	1,411	2,922	440	410	850
400.01 - 600.00	15.6	10.2	13.7	2,855	1,545	4,400	790	450	1,240
600.01 - 800.00	19.3	11.7	16.9	1,485	684	2,169	420	210	630
800.01 or more	20.8	13.0	18.7	1,760	643	2,402	530	190	710
Total	18.0	9.9	14.8	9,410	6,054	15,464	2,680	1,790	4,470

1 Results for 2009 include longitudinal data (see Appendix B).

2 Figures for unweighted sample have been rounded independently. The sum of component items does not therefore necessarily add to the totals shown.

Source: General Lifestyle Survey, Office for National Statistics

Table 2.10   Average weekly alcohol consumption (units), by sex, country, and region of England

Persons aged 16 and over   *Great Britain: 2009[1]*

Government Office Region	Average weekly alcohol consumption			Weighted base (000's) =100%			Unweighted sample[2]		
	Men	Women	Total	Men	Women	Total	Men	Women	Total
North East	21.0	9.4	14.4	700	918	1,617	250	330	580
North West	17.3	9.0	13.1	2,565	2,676	5,242	740	840	1,580
Yorkshire and the Humber	17.7	9.8	13.6	1,735	1,922	3,657	590	700	1,290
East Midlands	16.3	7.8	11.9	1,587	1,719	3,306	550	620	1,170
West Midlands	14.0	6.9	10.2	1,748	2,062	3,810	530	630	1,160
East of England	15.8	7.8	11.6	1,962	2,161	4,123	650	740	1,390
London	13.4	6.0	9.3	2,184	2,622	4,806	520	640	1,160
South East	17.1	8.4	12.5	2,773	3,190	5,964	830	990	1,820
South West	17.6	7.9	12.2	1,469	1,826	3,294	540	700	1,240
England	16.4	8.0	11.9	16,722	19,098	35,820	5,210	6,190	11,390
Wales	16.7	8.6	12.4	1,029	1,164	2,193	370	430	800
Scotland	15.0	7.8	11.2	1,754	1,980	3,734	550	670	1,220
Great Britain	16.3	8.0	11.9	19,505	22,242	41,747	6,130	7,280	13,410

1 Results for 2009 include longitudinal data (see Appendix B).

2 Figures for unweighted sample have been rounded independently. The sum of component items does not therefore necessarily add to the totals shown.

Source: General Lifestyle Survey, Office for National Statistics

Table 2.11   Whether drank last week and number of drinking days by sex and age

Persons aged 16 and over   *Great Britain: 2009[1]*

Drinking days last week	Age									
	16-24		25-44		45-64		65 and over		Total	
				Percentages						
Men										
0	45		30		28		34		32	
1	24		21		15		16		19	
2	14		18		15		11		15	
3	7		11		12		7		10	
4	3		7		8		4		6	
5	3		5		5		5		5	
6	2	7	3	13	5	23	3	27	4	18
7	2		5		12		19		10	
% who drank last week	55		70		72		66		68	
Weighted base (000's) =100%	*2,341*		*6,660*		*6,579*		*4,022*		*19,603*	
Unweighted sample[2]	*570*		*1,680*		*2,190*		*1,710*		*6,160*	
Women										
0	49		41		41		57		46	
1	24		23		17		16		20	
2	15		14		14		6		12	
3	7		9		9		4		8	
4	2		5		6		3		5	
5	0		3		4		2		3	
6	1	2	2	7	3	14	1	14	2	10
7	1		3		7		10		6	
% who drank last week	51		59		59		43		54	
Weighted base (000's) =100%	*2,552*		*7,483*		*7,232*		*5,003*		*22,271*	
Unweighted sample[2]	*630*		*2,180*		*2,540*		*1,940*		*7,290*	
All persons										
0	47		36		35		47		39	
1	24		22		16		16		19	
2	14		16		14		8		14	
3	7		10		10		6		9	
4	3		6		7		4		5	
5	2		4		4		3		4	
6	1	4	2	10	4	18	2	20	3	14
7	1		4		10		14		8	
% who drank last week	53		64		65		53		61	
Weighted base (000's) =100%	*4,894*		*14,144*		*13,811*		*9,025*		*41,874*	
Unweighted sample[2]	*1,190*		*3,870*		*4,740*		*3,650*		*13,450*	

1 Results for 2009 include longitudinal data (see Appendix B).

2 Figures for unweighted sample have been rounded independently. The sum of component items does not therefore necessarily add to the totals shown.

Source: General Lifestyle Survey, Office for National Statistics

Table 2.12   Maximum drunk on any one day last week, by sex and age

Persons aged 16 and over   *Great Britain: 2009[1]*

Maximum daily amount	Age				
	16-24	25-44	45-64	65 and over	Total

				Percentages		
Men						
Drank nothing last week	45	30	28	34	32	
Up to 4 units	19	27	31	45	31	
More than 4, up to 8 units	11	36	17	44	20	41	15	20	17	37
More than 8 units	24		27		21		5		20	
Women						
Drank nothing last week	50	41	41	57	46	
Up to 3 units	13	23	27	32	25	
More than 3, up to 6 units	13	37	17	36	20	32	9	11	16	29
More than 6 units	24		19		11		2		13	
All persons						
Drank nothing last week	48	36	35	47	39	
Up to 4/3 units	16	25	29	38	28	
More than 4/3, up to 8/6 units	12	36	17	40	20	36	12	15	16	33
More than 8/6 units	24		23		16		3		16	
Weighted base (000's) = 100%						
Men	*2,342*	*6,664*	*6,578*	*4,022*	*19,606*
Women	*2,548*	*7,481*	*7,229*	*5,005*	*22,263*
All persons	*4,890*	*14,145*	*13,807*	*9,028*	*41,869*
Unweighted sample					
Men	*570*	*1,690*	*2,190*	*1,710*	*6,160*
Women	*630*	*2,180*	*2,540*	*1,940*	*7,290*
All persons	*1,190*	*3,870*	*4,740*	*3,650*	*13,450*

1   Results for 2009 include longitudinal data (see Appendix B).

2   Figures for unweighted sample have been rounded independently. The sum of component items does not therefore necessarily add to the totals shown.

Source: General Lifestyle Survey, Office for National Statistics

Table 2.12b   Maximum drunk on any one day by those who consumed alcohol last week, by sex and age

Persons aged 16 and over who drank alcohol last week   *Great Britain: 2009[1]*

Maximum daily amount	Age					
	16-24	25-44	45-64	65 and over	Total	
			Percentages			
Men						
Up to 4 units	35	38	42	69	45	
More than 4, up to 8 units	21	24	28	23	25	
More than 8 units	45	39	30	8	30	
	65	62	58	31	55	
Women						
Up to 3 units	27	39	46	74	46	
More than 3, up to 6 units	25	30	34	22	29	
More than 6 units	48	32	19	4	24	
	73	61	54	26	54	
All persons						
Up to 4/3 units	31	38	44	71	46	
More than 4/3, up to 8/6 units	23	26	31	22	27	
More than 8/6 units	46	35	25	6	27	
	69	62	56	29	54	
Weighted base (000's) = 100%						
Men	1,279	4,684	4,735	2,643	13,342	
Women	1,280	4,388	4,276	2,135	12,079	
All persons	2,559	9,073	9,011	4,779	25,422	
Unweighted sample[2]						
Men	300	1,210	1,630	1,150	4,280	
Women	310	1,280	1,530	850	3,970	
All persons	610	2,490	3,160	2,000	8,250	

1 Results for 2009 include longitudinal data (see Appendix B).

2 Figures for unweighted sample have been rounded independently. The sum of component items does not therefore necessarily add to the totals shown.

Source: General Lifestyle Survey, Office for National Statistics

Table 2.13 Drinking last week, by sex, and socio – economic classification based on the current or last job of the household reference person

Persons aged 16 and over   *Great Britain: 2009[1]*

Socio-economic classification of household reference person	Men	Women	All persons
	Percentage who drank last week		
Managerial and professional			
Large employer and higher managerial	87	73	80
Higher professional	77 77	69 65	74 71
Lower managerial and professional	75	62	68
Intermediate			
Intermediate	69	52	58
Small employers/own account workers	66 67	57 55	62 60
Routine and manual			
Lower supervisory and technical	62	49	56
Semi-routine	56 59	45 44	50 51
Routine	60	37	48
Total[2]	68	54	61
	Percentage who drank on 5 or more days last week		
Managerial and professional			
Large employer and higher managerial	29	15	22
Higher professional	24 23	16 14	20 18
Lower managerial and professional	20	13	16
Intermediate			
Intermediate	17	9	12
Small employers/own account workers	21 19	12 10	16 14
Routine and manual			
Lower supervisory and technical	17	8	13
Semi-routine	11 14	6 7	8 10
Routine	13	7	10
Total[2]	18	10	14
Weighted bases (000's) =100%			
Large employer and higher managerial	1,280	1,332	2,612
Higher professional	2,087	1,787	3,874
Lower managerial and professional	4,981	5,678	10,659
Intermediate	1,289	2,181	3,471
Small employers/own account workers	1,898	1,854	3,752
Lower supervisory and technical	2,467	2,301	4,768
Semi-routine	2,243	3,209	5,452
Routine	2,137	2,381	4,518
Total[2]	18,953	21,431	40,384
Unweighted sample			
Large employer and higher managerial	420	440	860
Higher professional	630	590	1,220
Lower managerial and professional	1,580	1,880	3,450
Intermediate	400	710	1,100
Small employers/own account workers	600	610	1,210
Lower supervisory and technical	790	750	1,550
Semi-routine	690	1,040	1,730
Routine	690	790	1,480
Total[2]	5,970	7,040	13,010

1 Results for 2009 include longitudinal data (see Appendix B).

2 Full-time students, members of the Armed Forces, the long term unemployed and those who have never worked are not shown as separate categories but are included in the totals.

Source: General Lifestyle Survey, Office for National Statistics

Table 2.14 Maximum number of units drunk on any one day last week, by sex and socio-economic classification based on the current or last job of the household reference person

Persons aged 16 and over   *Great Britain: 2009[1]*

Socio-economic classification of household reference person	Men	Women	All persons
	Percentage who drank more than 4/3 units on at least one day last week[3]		
Managerial and professional			
Large employer and higher managerial	49	44	46
Higher professional	40 / 41	39 / 35	39 / 38
Lower managerial and professional	39	32	35
Intermediate			
Intermediate	35	24	28
Small employers/own account workers	37 / 36	32 / 28	35 / 32
Routine and manual			
Lower supervisory and technical	35	28	32
Semi-routine	32 / 34	22 / 23	26 / 28
Routine	35	20	27
Total[2]	37	29	33
	Percentage who drank more than 8/6 units on at least one day last week[3]		
Managerial and professional			
Large employer and higher managerial	25	18	21
Higher professional	23 / 23	18 / 15	21 / 19
Lower managerial and professional	22	14	18
Intermediate			
Intermediate	21	12	15
Small employers/own account workers	19 / 20	12 / 12	16 / 15
Routine and manual			
Lower supervisory and technical	18	13	16
Semi-routine	19 / 19	11 / 11	14 / 15
Routine	19	9	14
Total[2]	20	13	16
Weighted bases (000's) =100%			
Large employer and higher managerial	*1,280*	*1,332*	*2,612*
Higher professional	*2,085*	*1,787*	*3,872*
Lower managerial and professional	*4,985*	*5,675*	*10,660*
Intermediate	*1,289*	*2,177*	*3,466*
Small employers/own account workers	*1,903*	*1,857*	*3,760*
Lower supervisory and technical	*2,469*	*2,301*	*4,770*
Semi-routine	*2,241*	*3,203*	*5,444*
Routine	*2,132*	*2,385*	*4,517*
Total[2]	*18,956*	*21,423*	*40,379*
Unweighted sample			
Large employer and higher managerial	*420*	*440*	*860*
Higher professional	*630*	*590*	*1,220*
Lower managerial and professional	*1,580*	*1,880*	*3,450*
Intermediate	*400*	*710*	*1,100*
Small employers/own account workers	*610*	*610*	*1,210*
Lower supervisory and technical	*800*	*750*	*1,550*
Semi-routine	*690*	*1,040*	*1,720*
Routine	*690*	*790*	*1,480*
Total[2]	*5,970*	*7,040*	*13,010*

1 Results for 2009 include longitudinal data (see Appendix B).
2 Full-time students, members of the Armed Forces, the long term unemployed and those who have never worked are not shown as separate categories but are included in the totals.
3 The first of each pair of figures shown relates to men, and the second, to women.

Source: General Lifestyle Survey, Office for National Statistics

Table 2.15   Drinking last week, by sex and usual gross weekly household income

Persons aged 16 and over   *Great Britain: 2009[1]*

Drinking last week	Usual gross weekly household income (£)						
	Up to 200.00	200.01 - 400.00	400.01 - 600.00	600.01 - 800.00	800.01 - 1000.00	1000.01 or more	Total[2]
				Percentages			
Drank last week							
Men	55	61	68	68	75	78	68
Women	39	45	52	58	64	70	54
All persons	46	52	59	63	70	74	61
Drank on 5 or more days							
Men	16	18	17	18	17	20	18
Women	7	9	9	11	9	14	10
All persons	11	13	13	14	13	17	14
Weighted base (000's) =100%							
Men	*2,686*	*3,289*	*2,867*	*2,848*	*2,086*	*4,523*	*18,300*
Women	*3,977*	*4,194*	*3,254*	*2,797*	*2,077*	*4,465*	*20,765*
All persons	*6,663*	*7,483*	*6,121*	*5,646*	*4,164*	*8,988*	*39,064*
Unweighted sample[3]							
Men	*830*	*1,180*	*960*	*850*	*620*	*1,310*	*5,750*
Women	*1,340*	*1,500*	*1,120*	*880*	*630*	*1,320*	*6,800*
All persons	*2,180*	*2,680*	*2,080*	*1,730*	*1,250*	*2,630*	*12,550*

1   Results for 2009 include longitudinal data (see Appendix B).

2   The total includes those for whom household income was not available

3   Figures for unweighted sample have been rounded independently. The sum of component items does not therefore necessarily add to the totals shown.

Source: General Lifestyle Survey, Office for National Statistics

Table 2.16   Maximum drunk on any one day last week by sex and usual gross weekly household income

Persons aged 16 and over   *Great Britain: 2009[1]*

Drinking last week	Usual gross weekly household income (£)						
	Up to 200.00	200.01 - 400.00	400.01 - 600.00	600.01 - 800.00	800.01 - 1000.00	1000.01 or more	Total[2]
				Percentages			
Drank more than 4/3 units on at least one day last week[3]							
Men	30	28	36	39	43	46	37
Women	17	22	26	31	35	43	29
All persons	22	24	31	35	39	45	33
Drank more than 8/6 units on at least one day last week[3]							
Men	14	13	21	22	26	26	20
Women	8	8	13	16	16	19	13
All persons	10	10	17	19	21	23	16
Weighted base (000's) =100%							
Men	*2,689*	*3,289*	*2,863*	*2,853*	*2,086*	*4,523*	*18,303*
Women	*3,971*	*4,190*	*3,257*	*2,797*	*2,077*	*4,462*	*20,754*
All persons	*6,659*	*7,479*	*6,119*	*5,650*	*4,164*	*8,985*	*39,057*
Unweighted sample							
Men	*840*	*1,180*	*960*	*850*	*620*	*1,310*	*5,750*
Women	*1,340*	*1,500*	*1,120*	*880*	*630*	*1,310*	*6,800*
All persons	*2,180*	*2,680*	*2,080*	*1,740*	*1,250*	*2,630*	*12,550*

1 Results for 2009 include longitudinal data (see Appendix B).
2 The total includes those for whom household income was not available
3 The first of each pair of figures shown relates to men, and the second, to women.

Source: General Lifestyle Survey, Office for National Statistics

Table 2.17   Drinking last week, by sex and economic activity status

Persons aged 16-64   *Great Britain: 2009[1]*

Drinking last week	Economic activity status			
	Working	Unemployed	Economically inactive	Total
			Percentages	
Drank last week				
Men	74	58	52	69
Women	64	44	45	58
All persons	69	53	48	63
Drank on 5 or more days last week				
Men	17	12	15	16
Women	10	7	8	9
All persons	13	10	10	13
Weighted base (000's) =100%				
Men	*11,585*	*1,382*	*2,601*	*15,571*
Women	*11,760*	*882*	*4,620*	*17,265*
All persons	*23,345*	*2,264*	*7,221*	*32,837*
Unweighted sample[2]				
Men	*3,310*	*360*	*770*	*4,440*
Women	*3,580*	*250*	*1,520*	*5,350*
All persons	*6,890*	*610*	*2,300*	*9,800*

1 Results for 2009 include longitudinal data (see Appendix B).

2 Figures for unweighted sample have been rounded independently.
   The sum of component items does not therefore necessarily add to the totals shown.

Source: General Lifestyle Survey, Office for National Statistics

Table 2.18   Maximum drunk on any one day last week, by sex and economic activity status

Persons aged 16-64   *Great Britain: 2009[1]*

Drinking last week	Economic activity status			
	Working	Unemployed	Economically inactive	Total
		Percentages		
Drank more than 4/3 units on at least one day[2]				
Men	44	37	31	41
Women	38	29	25	34
All persons	41	34	27	38
Drank more than 8/6 units on at least one day[2]				
Men	26	24	17	24
Women	18	17	11	16
All persons	22	22	13	20
Weighted base (000's) =100%				
Men	*11,584*	*1,385*	*2,604*	*15,575*
Women	*11,758*	*877*	*4,616*	*17,255*
All persons	*23,342*	*2,262*	*7,219*	*32,830*
Unweighted sample[3]				
Men	*3,310*	*360*	*770*	*4,450*
Women	*3,580*	*250*	*1,520*	*5,350*
All persons	*6,890*	*610*	*2,290*	*9,790*

1 Results for 2009 include longitudinal data (see Appendix B).

2 The first of each pair of figures shown relates to men, and the second, to women.

3 Figures for unweighted sample have been rounded independently.
  The sum of component items does not therefore necessarily add to the totals shown.

Source: General Lifestyle Survey, Office for National Statistics

Table 2.19   Drinking last week, by sex and usual gross weekly earnings

Persons aged 16-64 in full-time employment   *Great Britain: 2009[1]*

Drinking last week	Usual gross weekly earnings[2] (£)						
	Up to 200.00	200.01 -300.00	300.01 -400.00	400.01 -600.00	600.01 -800.00	800.01 or more	Total
				Percentages			
Drank last week							
Men	70	64	76	72	79	85	75
Women	55	56	64	68	71	77	65
All persons	64	60	70	71	77	83	71
Drank on 5 or more days							
Men	26	12	17	13	22	21	17
Women	11	7	8	9	15	18	10
All persons	20	9	12	12	20	21	15
Weighted base (000's) =100%							
Men	*607*	*1,217*	*1,516*	*2,857*	*1,486*	*1,760*	*9,443*
Women	*479*	*1,288*	*1,411*	*1,545*	*686*	*643*	*6,051*
All persons	*1,086*	*2,505*	*2,926*	*4,402*	*2,172*	*2,402*	*15,494*
Unweighted sample[3]							
Men	*180*	*330*	*440*	*790*	*420*	*530*	*2,690*
Women	*150*	*380*	*410*	*450*	*210*	*190*	*1,790*
All persons	*330*	*720*	*850*	*1,240*	*630*	*710*	*4,480*

1 Results for 2009 include longitudinal data (see Appendix B).

2 Usual gross weekly earnings for the respondent

3 Figures for unweighted sample have been rounded independently.
   The sum of component items does not therefore necessarily add to the totals shown.

Source: General Lifestyle Survey, Office for National Statistics

Table 2.20 Maximum drunk on any one day last week, by sex and usual gross weekly earnings

Persons aged 16-64 in full-time employment   *Great Britain: 2009[1]*

Drinking last week	Usual gross weekly earnings[2] (£)						
	Up to 200.00	200.01 -300.00	300.01 -400.00	400.01 -600.00	600.01 -800.00	800.01 or more	Total
	Percentages						
Drank more than 4/3 units on at least one day[3]							
Men	42	41	48	44	46	52	46
Women	32	33	38	44	44	54	41
All persons	38	37	43	44	45	52	44
Drank more than 8/6 units on at least one day[3]							
Men	21	21	29	28	29	29	27
Women	17	17	20	22	20	27	20
All persons	19	19	25	26	26	28	24
Weighted base (000's) =100%							
Men	*612*	*1,208*	*1,516*	*2,857*	*1,489*	*1,760*	*9,442*
Women	*481*	*1,288*	*1,411*	*1,545*	*686*	*643*	*6,053*
All persons	*1,093*	*2,496*	*2,926*	*4,402*	*2,175*	*2,402*	*15,495*
Unweighted sample[4]							
Men	*180*	*330*	*440*	*790*	*420*	*530*	*2,690*
Women	*150*	*380*	*410*	*450*	*210*	*190*	*1,790*
All persons	*330*	*710*	*850*	*1,240*	*630*	*710*	*4,480*

1 Results for 2009 include longitudinal data (see Appendix B).
2 Usual gross weekly earnings for the respondent
3 The first of each pair of figures shown relates to men, and the second, to women
4 Figures for unweighted sample have been rounded independently.
  The sum of component items does not therefore necessarily add to the totals shown.

Source: General Lifestyle Survey, Office for National Statistics

Table 2.21   Drinking last week, by sex, country, and region of England

Persons aged 16 and over   *Great Britain: 2009[1]*

Government Office Region	Drinking last week		Weighted base (000's) =100%	Unweighted sample[2]
	Drank last week	Drank on 5 or more days last week		
Men		Percentages		
North East	75	19	702	250
North West	71	16	2,582	750
Yorkshire and the Humber	70	17	1,738	600
East Midlands	70	21	1,591	550
West Midlands	66	21	1,757	530
East of England	71	20	1,975	660
London	57	17	2,189	520
South East	73	21	2,803	840
South West	75	22	1,472	540
England	69	19	16,808	5,230
Wales	66	17	1,035	370
Scotland	58	12	1,759	560
Great Britain	68	18	19,603	6,160
Women				
North East	57	10	925	330
North West	56	9	2,679	840
Yorkshire and the Humber	60	11	1,927	700
East Midlands	56	10	1,724	620
West Midlands	52	12	2,066	630
East of England	57	13	2,161	740
London	46	8	2,628	650
South East	59	12	3,190	990
South West	54	11	1,826	700
England	55	11	19,127	6,190
Wales	52	7	1,164	430
Scotland	48	8	1,980	670
Great Britain	54	10	22,271	7,290
All persons				
North East	65	14	1,627	580
North West	63	12	5,262	1,580
Yorkshire and the Humber	65	14	3,665	1,300
East Midlands	63	15	3,315	1,170
West Midlands	58	16	3,822	1,170
East of England	64	16	4,136	1,400
London	51	12	4,817	1,160
South East	65	16	5,993	1,830
South West	64	16	3,298	1,240
England	62	15	35,935	11,420
Wales	58	12	2,199	800
Scotland	53	10	3,739	1,230
Great Britain	61	14	41,874	13,450

1 Results for 2009 include longitudinal data (see Appendix B).
2 Figures for unweighted sample have been rounded independently.
  The sum of component items does not therefore necessarily add to the totals shown.

Source: General Lifestyle Survey, Office for National Statistics

Table 2.22   Maximum drunk on any one day last week, by sex, country, and region of England

Persons aged 16 and over   *Great Britain: 2009[1]*

Government Office Region	Drank more than 4/3 units on at least one day[2]	Drank more than 8/6 units on at least one day[2]	Weighted base (000's) =100%	Unweighted sample[3]
Men				
North East	45	27	702	250
North West	43	25	2,585	750
Yorkshire and the Humber	45	27	1,738	600
East Midlands	37	19	1,591	550
West Midlands	32	16	1,757	530
East of England	34	20	1,980	660
London	31	16	2,191	520
South East	39	20	2,803	840
South West	34	17	1,472	540
England	37	20	16,818	5,240
Wales	38	20	1,029	370
Scotland	34	20	1,759	560
Great Britain	37	20	19,606	6,160
Women				
North East	36	17	925	330
North West	34	17	2,678	840
Yorkshire and the Humber	37	18	1,925	700
East Midlands	31	13	1,724	620
West Midlands	23	8	2,066	630
East of England	28	10	2,167	740
London	22	11	2,620	640
South East	31	13	3,190	990
South West	24	9	1,824	700
England	29	13	19,119	6,190
Wales	32	15	1,164	430
Scotland	26	14	1,980	670
Great Britain	29	13	22,263	7,290
All persons				
North East	40	21	1,627	580
North West	39	21	5,263	1,580
Yorkshire and the Humber	41	22	3,663	1,300
East Midlands	34	16	3,315	1,170
West Midlands	27	11	3,822	1,170
East of England	31	15	4,147	1,400
London	26	13	4,811	1,160
South East	34	17	5,993	1,830
South West	28	13	3,296	1,240
England	33	16	35,937	11,430
Wales	35	17	2,193	800
Scotland	30	17	3,739	1,230
Great Britain	33	16	41,869	13,450

1 Results for 2009 include longitudinal data (see Appendix B).

2 The first of each pair of figures shown relates to men, and the second, to women.

3 Figures for unweighted sample have been rounded independently.
   The sum of component items does not therefore necessarily add to the totals shown.

Source: General Lifestyle Survey, Office for National Statistics

Table 3.1 Trends in household size: 1971 to 2009

(a) Households and (b) Persons

Great Britain

Number of persons in household (all ages)	Unweighted								Weighted										
	1971	1975	1981	1985	1991	1995	1996	1998	1998	2000	2001	2002	2003	2004	2005[1]	2006[2]	2007[2]	2008[2]	2009[2]
(a) Households	%	%	%	%	%	%	%	%	%	%	%	%	%	%	%	%	%	%	%
								Percentage of households of each size											
1	17	20	22	24	26	28	27	29	31	32	31	31	30	31	31	30	30	30	31
2	31	32	31	33	34	35	34	36	34	34	34	35	36	35	35	34	33	34	33
3	19	18	17	17	17	16	16	15	16	15	16	16	15	15	15	16	16	16	15
4	18	17	18	17	16	15	15	14	14	13	13	13	13	13	13	14	14	14	14
5	8	8	7	6	6	5	5	5	4	5	4	4	5	4	4	4	5	5	5
6 or more	6	5	4	2	2	2	2	2	2	2	2	2	2	2	2	2	2	2	2
Weighted base (000's) =100%[3]	*11,990*	*12,100*	*12,010*	*9,990*	*9,960*	*9,760*	*9,160*	*8,640*	*24,450*	*24,845*	*24,592*	*24,529*	*24,423*	*24,688*	*24,829*	*24,815*	*24,724*	*24,838*	*25,190*
Unweighted sample[3,4]										*8,220*	*8,990*	*8,620*	*10,280*	*8,700*	*12,800*	*9,730*	*9,090*	*8,730*	*8,200*
Average (mean) household size	2.91	2.78	2.70	2.56	2.48	2.40	2.43	2.36	2.32	2.30	2.33	2.31	2.32	2.30	2.30	2.34	2.35	2.37	2.35
(b) Persons	%	%	%	%	%	%	%	%	%	%	%	%	%	%	%	%	%	%	%
								Percentage of persons in households of each size											
1	6	7	8	10	11	12	11	12	13	14	13	13	13	14	14	13	13	13	13
2	22	23	23	26	27	29	28	30	30	30	29	30	31	30	31	29	28	29	28
3	20	19	19	20	20	20	20	19	20	20	20	20	20	19	19	20	21	20	19
4	25	25	27	27	25	24	25	24	23	22	23	22	22	23	22	23	24	23	24
5	15	14	14	12	11	10	10	10	9	9	9	9	9	9	9	10	10	10	10
6 or more	13	11	9	6	5	5	6	5	4	5	5	5	5	5	5	5	5	5	5
Weighted base (000's) =100%[3]	*34,850*	*33,580*	*32,410*	*25,560*	*24,660*	*23,390*	*22,270*	*20,400*	*56,751*	*57,106*	*57,260*	*56,570*	*56,721*	*56,873*	*56,985*	*58,041*	*58,081*	*58,829*	*59,192*
Unweighted sample[3,4]										*19,270*	*21,180*	*20,150*	*24,490*	*20,420*	*30,070*	*22,920*	*21,470*	*20,500*	*18,990*

1 2005 data includes last quarter of 2004/5 data due to survey change from financial year to calendar year.

2 Results from 2006 onwards include longitudinal data (see Appendix B).

3 Trend tables show unweighted and weighted figures for 1998 to give an indication of the effect of the weighting. For the weighted data (1998 and 2000 to 2009) the weighted base (000's) is the base for percentages. Unweighted data (up to 1998) are based on the unweighted sample.

4 All unweighted bases are rounded to the nearest 10

Source: General Lifestyle Survey, Office for National Statistics

Table 3.2   Trends in household type: 1971 to 2009

(a) Households and (b) Persons

Great Britain

Household type	Unweighted 1971	1975	1981	1985	1991	1995	1996	1998	Weighted 1998	2000	2001	2002	2003	2004	2005[1]	2006[2]	2007[2]	2008[2]	2009[2]
(a) Households	%	%	%	%	%	%	%	%	%	%	%	%	%	%	%	%	%	%	%
Percentage of households of each type																			
1 adult aged 16-59	5	6	7	8	10	12	11	13	15	16	15	16	15	16	16	15	14	13	13
2 adults aged 16-59	14	14	13	15	16	17	15	16	16	17	17	16	16	16	16	16	15	15	15
Youngest person aged 0-4	18	15	13	13	14	13	13	13	12	11	11	11	11	11	11	11	11	12	10
Youngest person aged 5-15	21	22	22	18	16	16	17	16	16	15	16	16	16	16	16	16	15	15	15
3 or more adults	13	11	13	12	12	10	11	9	10	10	11	10	11	10	10	11	12	12	12
2 adults, 1 or both aged 60 or over	17	17	17	17	16	16	16	17	15	15	15	15	16	16	16	16	16	16	16
1 adult aged 60 or over	12	15	15	16	16	15	16	16	15	16	15	15	15	15	15	16	16	17	18
Weighted base (000's) =100%³	11,930	12,090	12,010	9,990	9,960	9,760	9,160	8,640	24,450	24,845	24,592	24,529	24,423	24,688	24,829	24,815	24,724	24,838	25,190
Unweighted sample³,⁴										8,220	8,990	8,620	10,280	8,700	12,800	9,730	9,090	8,730	8,200
(b) Persons	%	%	%	%	%	%	%	%	%	%	%	%	%	%	%	%	%	%	%
Percentage of persons in each type of household																			
1 adult aged 16-59	2	2	3	3	4	5	5	5	7	7	7	7	6	7	7	6	6	6	6
2 adults aged 16-59	10	10	10	12	13	14	13	14	14	14	14	14	14	14	14	14	13	13	14
Youngest person aged 0-4	27	23	21	21	22	20	21	21	19	19	18	18	18	17	17	18	18	19	18
Youngest person aged 5-15	31	34	33	28	25	26	27	25	26	25	25	26	25	25	25	25	25	25	24
3 or more adults	15	13	16	17	16	15	15	13	15	15	16	15	16	16	15	17	17	17	18
2 adults, 1 or both aged 60 or over	11	12	12	13	13	14	13	14	13	13	13	13	14	14	14	13	13	14	14
1 adult aged 60 or over	4	5	6	6	7	6	7	7	7	7	7	6	7	7	7	7	7	7	7
Weighted base (000's) =100%³	34,720	33,560	32,410	25,560	24,660	23,390	22,270	20,400	56,751	57,106	57,260	56,570	56,721	56,873	56,985	58,041	58,081	58,829	59,192
Unweighted sample³,⁴										19,270	21,180	20,150	24,490	20,420	30,070	22,920	21,470	20,500	18,990

1 2005 data includes last quarter of 2004/5 data due to survey change from financial year to calendar year.

2 Results from 2006 onwards include longitudinal data (see Appendix B).

3 Trend tables show unweighted and weighted figures for 1998 to give an indication of the effect of the weighting. For the weighted data (1998 and 2000 to 2009) the weighted base (000's) is the base for percentages. Unweighted data (up to 1998) are based on the unweighted sample.

4 All unweighted bases are rounded to the nearest 10

Source: General Lifestyle Survey, Office for National Statistics

Table 3.3 Percentage living alone, by age: 1973 to 2009

All persons aged 16 and over   Great Britain

Percentage who lived alone

	Unweighted								Weighted[1]										
	1973	1983	1987	1991	1993	1995	1996	1998	1998	2000	2001	2002	2003	2004	2005[2]	2006[3]	2007[3]	2008[3]	2009[3]
16-24	2	2	3	3	4	5	4	4	4	5	5	5	4	4	5	3	3	2	2
25-44	2	4	6	7	8	9	8	10	12	12	12	12	12	12	12	11	11	10	10
45-64	8	9	10	11	11	12	11	14	15	16	15	15	14	16	16	15	15	15	16
65-74	26	28	28	29	28	27	31	27	28	29	27	27	27	26	26	26	25	25	27
75 and over	40	47	50	50	50	51	47	48	48	50	49	48	48	47	48	50	51	51	50
All aged 16 and over	9	11	12	14	14	15	14	16	17	17	16	17	16	17	17	16	16	15	16
Unweighted sample [4,5]																			
16-24	3,810	3,500	3,560	2,820	2,570	2,320	2,230	1,890		1,870	2,060	2,020	2,430	2,070	2,990	2,160	2,020	1,870	1,790
25-44	8,170	7,020	7,420	7,120	6,880	6,760	6,490	5,860		5,390	6,120	5,580	6,840	5,710	8,230	6,060	5,450	5,070	4,520
45-64	7,950	5,950	5,800	5,490	5,360	5,620	5,110	4,890		4,800	5,150	5,170	5,950	5,200	7,650	6,070	5,790	5,690	5,210
65-74	2,850	2,490	2,390	2,200	2,300	2,130	1,940	1,860		1,670	1,880	1,770	2,270	1,790	2,750	2,190	2,200	2,200	2,180
75 and over	1,430	1,490	1,600	1,600	1,580	1,450	1,490	1,370		1,340	1,470	1,440	1,680	1,400	2,130	1,730	1,670	1,580	1,630
All aged 16 and over	24,210	20,450	20,760	19,230	18,690	18,270	17,260	15,870		15,080	16,690	15,970	19,180	16,180	23,750	18,210	17,120	16,410	15,330

1 Weighted bases are shown in Table 3.21.

2 2005 data includes last quarter of 2004/5 data due to survey change from financial year to calendar year.

3 Results from 2006 onwards include longitudinal data (see Appendix B).

4 Trend tables show unweighted and weighted figures for 1998 to give an indication of the effect of the weighting. For the weighted data (1998 and 2000 to 2009) the weighted base (000's) is the base for percentages. Unweighted data (up to 1998) are based on the unweighted sample.

5 All unweighted bases are rounded to the nearest 10

Source: General Lifestyle Survey, Office for National Statistics

Table 3.4   Percentage of men and women living alone by age

All persons aged 16 and over   *Great Britain: 2009[1]*

	Percentage living alone		
	Men	Women	Total
16-24	2	2	2
25-44	13	7	10
45-64	17	15	16
65-74	22	32	27
75 and over	36	60	50
All aged 16 and over	15	17	16
All persons[2]	12	14	13
Weighted bases (000's) =100%			
16-24	*3,625*	*3,496*	*7,121*
25-44	*8,182*	*8,217*	*16,399*
45-64	*7,427*	*7,705*	*15,132*
65-74	*2,417*	*2,664*	*5,081*
75 and over	*1,774*	*2,558*	*4,332*
All aged 16 and over	*23,425*	*24,640*	*48,064*
All persons[2]	*29,233*	*29,958*	*59,192*
Unweighted sample[3]			
16-24	*900*	*890*	*1,790*
25-44	*2,110*	*2,410*	*4,520*
45-64	*2,500*	*2,710*	*5,210*
65-74	*1,080*	*1,100*	*2,180*
75 and over	*700*	*930*	*1,630*
All aged 16 and over	*7,290*	*8,030*	*15,330*
All persons[3]	*9,200*	*9,790*	*18,990*

1   Results for 2009 include longitudinal data (see Appendix B)

2   Including children.

3   All unweighted bases are rounded to the nearest 10

Source: General Lifestyle Survey, Office for National Statistics

Table 3.5 Type of household: 1979 to 2009

(a) Households and (b) Persons

Household type	Unweighted						Weighted									Great Britain	
	1979	1985	1991	1995	1996	1998	1998	2000	2001	2002	2003	2004	2005[1]	2006[2]	2007[2]	2008[2]	2009[2]
(a) Households	%	%	%	%	%	%	%	%	%	%	%	%	%	%	%	%	%
							Percentage of households of each type										
1 person only	23	24	26	28	27	29	31	32	31	31	30	31	31	31	31	30	31
2 or more unrelated adults	3	4	3	2	3	2	3	3	3	2	3	3	3	2	2	2	2
Married/cohabiting couple																	
with dependent children	31	28	25	24	25	23	22	21	22	21	21	21	21	22	22	22	22
with non-dependent children only	7	8	8	6	6	6	6	6	6	6	6	6	6	6	7	7	7
no children	27	27	28	29	28	30	28	28	29	28	29	29	29	28	27	28	27
Married couple																	
with dependent children	..	..	..	..	23	20	19	18	18	18	18	18	17	18	18	18	18
with non-dependent children	..	..	..	..	6	5	6	6	6	6	6	6	5	6	7	7	7
no children	..	..	..	..	25	26	24	24	23	23	23	23	23	23	22	23	22
Cohabiting couple																	
with dependent children	..	..	..	..	3	3	3	3	3	3	4	3	3	4	4	4	4
with non-dependent children	..	..	..	..	0	0	0	0	0	0	0	0	0	0	0	0	1
no children	..	..	..	..	4	4	5	5	5	5	5	5	5	5	5	5	5
Lone parent																	
with dependent children	4	4	6	7	7	7	7	7	7	8	7	7	7	7	6	6	6
with non-dependent children only	4	4	4	3	3	3	3	2	2	2	3	3	3	3	3	3	3
Two or more families	1	1	1	1	1	1	1	1	1	1	1	1	1	1	1	1	1
Weighted base (000's) =100%[3,4,5]	11,450	9,990	9,960	9,740	9,140	8,620	24,389	24,787	24,493	24,449	24,326	24,613	24,751	24,727	24,621	24,730	25,058
Unweighted sample[3,4,5]							8,200	8,200	8,960	8,590	10,250	8,680	12,760	9,710	9,050	8,730	8,200
(b) Persons	%	%	%	%	%	%	%	%	%	%	%	%	%	%	%	%	%
							Percentage of persons in each type of household										
1 person only	9	10	11	12	11	12	13	14	13	13	13	14	14	13	13	13	13
2 or more unrelated adults	2	3	2	2	3	2	3	3	3	3	3	4	3	3	2	3	2
Married/cohabiting couple																	
with dependent children	49	45	41	40	42	39	38	36	37	36	37	36	36	37	38	37	37
with non-dependent children only	9	11	11	9	9	8	9	9	9	9	9	9	8	9	10	10	10
no children	20	21	23	25	24	26	25	25	25	25	25	25	26	24	24	24	23
Married couple																	
with dependent children	..	..	..	..	37	34	33	32	32	32	31	31	30	31	31	31	31
with non-dependent children	..	..	..	..	9	8	8	9	9	8	8	8	8	9	10	10	10
no children	..	..	..	..	21	22	21	21	20	21	21	21	21	20	19	19	19
Cohabiting couple																	
with dependent children	..	..	..	..	4	5	5	5	5	5	6	5	5	5	6	7	6
with non-dependent children	..	..	..	..	0	0	0	0	0	0	1	1	0	0	1	1	1
no children	..	..	..	..	3	4	4	4	5	4	5	5	5	5	4	5	4
Lone parent																	
with dependent children	5	5	7	8	8	9	8	9	8	9	9	8	9	9	8	7	8
with non-dependent children only	3	4	3	3	3	3	3	2	2	2	3	3	3	3	3	3	3
Two or more families	2	1	2	1	1	2	2	2	2	2	2	2	2	2	2	2	2
Weighted base (000's) =100%[3,4,5]	30,550	25,450	24,660	23,330	22,190	20,350	56,605	56,955	56,921	56,245	56,319	56,565	56,663	57,684	57,668	58,442	58,747
Unweighted sample[3,4,5]							20,350	19,220	21,070	20,050	24,350	20,320	29,910	22,820	21,320	20,500	18,990

1 2005 data includes last quarter of 2004/5 data due to survey change from financial year to calendar year.
2 Results from 2006 onwards include longitudinal data (see Appendix B).
3 Trend tables show unweighted and weighted figures for 1998 to give an indication of the effect of the weighting. For the weighted data (1998 and 2000 to 2009) the weighted base (000's) is the base for percentages. Unweighted data (up to 1998) are based on the unweighted sample.
4 Total includes a very small number of same sex cohabitees.
5 All unweighted bases are rounded to the nearest 10
.. Data are not available (not collected in these years).

Source: General Lifestyle Survey, Office for National Statistics

Table 3.6 Family type, and marital status of lone parents: 1971 to 2009

Families with dependent children[1]   *Great Britain*

Family type	Unweighted								Weighted										
	1971	1975	1981	1985	1991	1995	1996	1998	1998	2000	2001	2002	2003	2004	2005[2]	2006[3]	2007[3]	2008[3]	2009[3]
	%	%	%	%	%	%	%	%	%	%	%	%	%	%	%	%	%	%	%
Married/cohabiting couple[4]	92	90	87	86	81	78	79	75	76	74	75	73	74	75	74	75	77	77	77
Lone mother	7	9	11	12	18	20	20	22	21	23	22	24	23	23	24	22	21	20	20
single	1	1	2	3	6	8	7	9	8	11	10	12	11	11	11	10	10	11	10
widowed	2	2	2	1	1	1	1	1	1	1	1	0	0	1	1	1	0	0	1
divorced	2	3	4	5	6	7	6	8	7	7	7	7	7	7	8	7	6	5	6
separated	2	2	2	3	4	5	5	5	5	5	4	5	5	4	4	4	4	4	3
Lone father	1	1	2	2	1	2	2	2	3	3	3	2	3	2	2	3	3	3	3
All lone parents	8	10	13	14	19	22	21	25	24	26	25	27	26	25	26	25	23	23	23
Weighted base (000's) =100%[5]	4,860	4,780	4,450	3,350	3,140	3,020	2,980	2,660	7,182	7,105	7,146	7,206	7,071	7,000	7,025	7,271	7,277	7,273	7,261
Unweighted sample[5,6]								2,660	2,460	2,700	2,580	3,170	2,570	3,830	2,890	2,690	2,530	2,260

1 Dependent children are persons aged under 16, or aged 16-18 and in full-time education, in the family unit, and living in the household.
2 2005 data includes last quarter of 2004/5 data due to survey change from financial year to calendar year.
3 Results from 2006 onwards include longitudinal data (see Appendix B).
4 Including married women whose husbands were not defined as resident in the household.
5 Trend tables show unweighted and weighted figures for 1998 to give an indication of the effect of the weighting. For the weighted data (1998 and 2000 to 2009) the weighted base (000's) is the base for percentages. Unweighted data (up to 1998) are based on the unweighted sample.
6 All unweighted bases are rounded to the nearest 10

Source: General Lifestyle Survey, Office for National Statistics

Table 3.7 Families with dependent children: 1972 to 2009

Dependent children [1]

Great Britain

Percentage of all dependent children in each family type

	Unweighted								Weighted										
	1972	1975	1981	1985	1991	1995	1996	1998	1998	2000	2001	2002	2003	2004	2005[2]	2006[3]	2007[3]	2008[3]	2009[3]
	%	%	%	%	%	%	%	%	%	%	%	%	%	%	%	%	%	%	%
Married/cohabiting couple with																			
1 dependent child	16	17	18	19	17	16	17	15	17	17	17	18	18	18	18	19	19	20	20
2 or more dependent children	76	74	70	69	66	64	63	62	61	58	60	57	58	60	57	57	58	59	59
Lone mother with																			
1 dependent child	2	3	3	4	5	5	5	6	6	7	6	8	7	7	8	7	7	7	6
2 or more dependent children	5	6	7	7	12	14	13	15	13	15	15	15	14	14	15	15	13	12	13
Lone father with																			
1 dependent child	0	0	1	1	0	1	0	1	1	1	1	1	1	1	1	1	1	1	1
2 or more dependent children	1	1	1	1	1	1	1	1	1	2	1	1	2	1	1	1	1	1	1
Weighted base (000's) =100% [4]	9,470	9,290	8,220	5,970	5,800	5,560	5,430	4,900	12,799	12,641	12,606	12,451	12,368	12,190	12,189	12,549	12,382	12,314	12,350
Unweighted sample [4,5]									4,900	4,500	4,850	4,560	5,740	4,580	6,830	5,170	4,770	4,450	3,980

1 Dependent children are persons aged under 16, or aged 16-18 and in full-time education, in the family unit, and living in the household.

2 2005 data includes last quarter of 2004/5 data due to survey change from financial year to calendar year.

3 Results from 2006 onwards include longitudinal data (see Appendix B).

4 Trend tables show unweighted and weighted figures for 1998 to give an indication of the effect of the weighting. For the weighted data (1998 and 2000 to 2009) the weighted base (000's) is the base for percentages. Unweighted data (up to 1998) are based on the unweighted sample.

5 All unweighted bases are rounded to the nearest 10

Source: General Lifestyle Survey, Office for National Statistics

Table 3.8 Average (mean) number of dependent children by family type: 1971 to 2009

Families with dependent children[1]   *Great Britain*

Family type	Average (mean) number of children																		
	Unweighted								Weighted[2]										
	1971	1975	1981	1985	1991	1995	1996	1998	1998	2000	2001	2002	2003	2004	2005[3]	2006[4]	2007[4]	2008[4]	2009[4]
Married/cohabiting couple[5]	2.0	2.0	1.9	1.8	1.9	1.9	1.9	1.9	1.8	1.8	1.8	1.8	1.8	1.8	1.8	1.8	1.7	1.7	1.7
Married couple	..	..	..	..	1.9	..	1.9	1.9	1.8	1.8	1.9	1.8	1.8	1.8	1.8	1.8	1.8	1.7	1.7
Cohabiting couple	..	..	..	..	..	..	1.7	1.7	1.7	1.7	1.6	1.6	1.7	1.6	1.6	1.6	1.6	1.6	1.7
Lone parent	1.8	1.7	1.6	1.6	1.7	1.7	1.7	1.7	1.6	1.7	1.7	1.6	1.6	1.6	1.6	1.7	1.6	1.6	1.6
Total: all families with dependent children	2.0	1.9	1.8	1.8	1.8	1.8	1.8	1.8	1.8	1.8	1.8	1.7	1.8	1.8	1.7	1.7	1.7	1.7	1.7
Unweighted sample [6,7]																			
Married/cohabiting couple	*4,480*	*4,300*	*3,890*	*2,890*	*2,540*	*2,360*	*2,330*	*2,000*		*1,800*	*2,000*	*1,890*	*2,370*	*1,950*	*2,880*	*2,170*	*2,060*	*1,940*	*1,710*
Married couple	*..*	*..*	*..*	*..*	*..*	*..*	*2,090*	*1,750*		*1,560*	*1,720*	*1,640*	*1,970*	*1,650*	*2,420*	*1,830*	*1,690*	*1,590*	*1,400*
Cohabiting couple	*..*	*..*	*..*	*..*	*..*	*..*	*240*	*250*		*250*	*280*	*250*	*400*	*300*	*460*	*340*	*370*	*350*	*310*
Lone parent	*380*	*480*	*560*	*460*	*600*	*660*	*640*	*650*		*660*	*680*	*680*	*780*	*610*	*930*	*710*	*610*	*580*	*550*
Total	*4,860*	*4,780*	*4,450*	*3,350*	*3,140*	*3,020*	*2,960*	*2,660*		*2,460*	*2,690*	*2,570*	*3,150*	*2,550*	*3,810*	*2,870*	*2,670*	*2,520*	*2,250*

1 Dependent children are persons aged under 16, or aged 16-18 and in full-time education, in the family unit, and living in the household.
2 Weighted bases are shown in Table 3.21.
3 2005 data includes last quarter of 2004/5 data due to survey change from financial year to calendar year.
4 Results from 2006 onwards include longitudinal data (see Appendix B).
5 Including married women whose husbands were not defined as resident in the household.
6 Trend tables show unweighted and weighted figures for 1998 to give an indication of the effect of the weighting. For the weighted data (1998 and 2000 to 2009) the weighted base (000's) is the base for percentages. Unweighted data (up to 1998) are based on the unweighted sample.
7 All unweighted bases are rounded to the nearest 10
.. Data are not available (not collected in these years).

Source: General Lifestyle Survey, Office for National Statistics

Table 3.9   Age of youngest dependent child by family type

Families with dependent children[1]   *Great Britain: 2008[2] and 2009[2] combined*

Family type		Age of youngest dependent child					
		0-4	5-9	10-15	16 and over	*Unweighted sample[3]*	Total
							%
Married/cohabiting							
couple[4]	%	42	23	27	8	*5,710*	77
Lone mother	%	33	25	32	9	*1,550*	20
Lone father	%	15	19	44	22	*190*	3
All lone parents	%	31	25	34	11	*1,740*	23
Total	%	40	24	28	8	*7,450*	100

1   Dependent children are persons aged under 16, or aged 16-18 and in full-time education, in the family unit, and living in the household.

2   Results for 2008 & 2009 include longitudinal data (see Appendix B).

3   Including married women whose husbands were not defined as resident in the household.

4   All unweighted bases are rounded to the nearest 10

Source: General Lifestyle Survey, Office for National Statistics

Table 3.10   Stepfamilies with dependent children by family type

Stepfamilies with dependent children[1]

(Family unit head aged 16-59)   *Great Britain: 2009[2]*

Type of stepfamily	
	%
Couple with child(ren) from the woman's previous marriage/ cohabitation	86
Couple with child(ren) from the man's previous marriage/ cohabitation	8
Couple with child(ren) from both partners' previous marriage/ cohabitation	7
Weighted base (000's) = 100%	*527*
Unweighted sample[3]	*210*

1   Dependent children are persons under 16, or aged 16-18 and in full-time education, in the family unit, and living in the household.

2   Results for 2009 include longitudinal data (see Appendix B).

3   All unweighted bases are rounded to the nearest 10

Source: General Lifestyle Survey, Office for National Statistics

Table 3.11 Usual gross weekly household income of families with dependent children by family type

Families with dependent children[1]   *Great Britain: 2009[2]*

Family type		Usual gross weekly household income[3]							Weighted base (000's) = 100%[4]	Unweighted sample[5]
		£0.00-£100.00	£100.01 -£200.00	£200.01-£300.00	£300.01-£400.00	£400.01-£500.00	£500.01-£700.00	£700.01 and over		
Married couple	%	3	3	5	5	6	17	62	4,307	1,300
Cohabiting couple	%	2	6	7	7	12	28	38	923	300
Lone mother[6]	%	5	25	21	16	12	11	9	1,401	480
Single	%	7	35	24	12	9	7	7	734	240
Divorced	%	3	14	20	19	16	17	12	410	140
Separated	%	6	18	14	25	14	16	6	208	70
Lone father	%	12	24	13	10	9	18	13	199	60
All lone parents	%	6	25	20	16	12	12	9	1,600	530
All families with dependent children	%	4	8	9	8	8	17	47	6,830	2,130

1   Dependent children are persons aged under 16, or aged 16-18 and in full-time education, in the family unit, and living in the household.

2   Results for 2009 include longitudinal data (see Appendix B).

3   From 2007, income includes council tax benefit/rebate

4   Bases exclude cases where income is not known.

5   All unweighted bases are rounded to the nearest 10

6   Includes around twenty widowed lone mothers.

Note: Shaded figures indicate the estimates are unreliable and any analysis using these figures may be invalid. Any use of these shaded figures must be accompanied by this disclaimer.

Source: General Lifestyle Survey, Office for National Statistics

Table 3.12 The distribution of the population by sex and age: 1971 to 2009

All persons
Great Britain

Age	Unweighted								Weighted										
	1971	1975	1981	1985	1991	1995	1996	1998	1998	2000	2001	2002	2003	2004	2005¹	2006²	2007²	2008²	2009²
	%	%	%	%	%	%	%	%	%	%	%	%	%	%	%	%	%	%	%
Males																			
0- 4	9	8	7	7	8	7	7	8	6	6	6	6	6	6	6	6	6	6	6
5-15³	19	18	18	16	15	16	16	16	15	15	15	15	15	15	14	14	14	14	13
16-44³	39	40	41	42	41	39	39	38	42	42	42	41	40	40	40	41	41	41	40
45-64	24	23	22	22	22	24	23	24	23	24	24	25	25	25	25	25	25	25	25
65-74	7	8	8	9	8	8	8	9	8	8	8	8	8	8	8	8	8	8	8
75 and over	3	3	4	4	5	5	6	5	5	5	5	6	6	6	6	6	6	6	6
Weighted base (000's) =100%⁴	*16,910*	*16,240*	*15,740*	*12,550*	*11,910*	*11,380*	*10,780*	*9,830*	*27,921*	*28,134*	*28,212*	*27,524*	*27,732*	*27,802*	*27,732*	*28,382*	*28,478*	*29,059*	*29,233*
Unweighted sample⁴										*9,320*	*10,170*	*9,710*	*11,920*	*9,910*	*14,580*	*11,060*	*10,400*	*9,950*	*9,200*
	%	%	%	%	%	%	%	%	%	%	%	%	%	%	%	%	%	%	%
Females																			
0- 4	8	6	6	6	7	6	7	7	6	6	6	5	5	5	5	6	6	6	6
5-15³	16	17	16	15	14	14	15	14	14	14	14	14	13	13	13	13	12	12	12
16-44³	37	38	39	41	39	39	39	38	40	40	40	40	40	40	39	40	39	40	39
45-64	24	24	22	21	22	24	23	24	23	24	24	24	24	25	25	25	25	26	26
65-74	9	10	10	10	10	9	9	9	9	8	9	9	9	9	9	9	9	9	9
75 and over	5	6	7	8	8	8	7	8	8	8	8	8	8	8	8	8	8	8	9
Weighted base (000's) =100%⁴	*17,870*	*17,330*	*16,680*	*13,520*	*12,740*	*12,010*	*11,490*	*10,560*	*28,828*	*28,973*	*29,048*	*29,047*	*28,989*	*29,072*	*29,253*	*29,659*	*29,603*	*29,770*	*29,958*
Unweighted sample⁴										*9,940*	*11,010*	*10,440*	*12,570*	*10,510*	*15,490*	*11,860*	*11,080*	*10,560*	*9,790*
	%	%	%	%	%	%	%	%	%	%	%	%	%	%	%	%	%	%	%
Total																			
0- 4	8	7	6	6	7	7	7	7	6	6	6	6	6	6	6	6	6	6	6
5-15³	17	17	17	15	15	15	15	15	14	14	14	14	14	14	14	13	13	13	13
16-44³	38	39	40	42	40	39	39	38	41	41	41	40	40	40	40	40	40	40	40
45-64	24	23	22	21	22	24	23	24	23	24	24	24	25	25	25	25	25	25	26
65-74	8	9	9	9	9	9	9	9	8	8	8	8	9	9	9	8	8	8	9
75 and over	4	4	5	6	7	6	7	7	7	7	7	7	7	7	7	7	7	7	7
Weighted base (000's) =100%⁴ ⁵	*34,780*	*33,570*	*32,410*	*26,070*	*24,660*	*23,390*	*22,270*	*20,400*	*56,749*	*57,106*	*57,260*	*56,571*	*56,721*	*56,873*	*56,985*	*58,041*	*58,081*	*58,829*	*59,192*
Unweighted sample⁴ ⁵										*19,270*	*21,180*	*20,150*	*24,490*	*20,420*	*30,070*	*22,920*	*21,470*	*20,500*	*18,990*

1 2005 data includes last quarter of 2004/5 data due to survey change from financial year to calendar year.

2 Results from 2006 onwards include longitudinal data (see Appendix B).

3 These age-groups were 5-14 and 15-44 in 1971 and 1975

4 Trend tables show unweighted and weighted figures for 1998 to give an indication of the effect of the weighting. For the weighted data (1998 and 2000 to 2009) the weighted base (000's) is the base for percentages. Unweighted data (up to 1998) are based on the unweighted sample.

5 All unweighted bases are rounded to the nearest 10

Source: General Lifestyle Survey, Office for National Statistics

Table 3.13   Percentage of males and females by age

All persons   *Great Britain: 2009[1]*

Age		Males	Females	Weighted base (000's) =100%	Unweighted sample[2]
0-4	%	52	48	3,634	1,130
5-15	%	52	48	7,493	2,530
16-19	%	53	47	3,532	940
20-24	%	49	51	3,589	860
25-29	%	49	51	3,649	940
30-34	%	51	49	3,514	970
35-39	%	51	49	4,546	1,300
40-44	%	49	51	4,691	1,310
45-49	%	48	52	4,279	1,330
50-54	%	48	52	3,799	1,230
55-59	%	49	51	3,353	1,210
60-64	%	51	49	3,702	1,440
65-69	%	48	52	2,729	1,180
70-74	%	47	53	2,352	1,000
75 and over	%	41	59	4,332	1,630
Total	%	49	51	59,192	18,990

1   Results for 2009 include longitudinal data (see Appendix B).
2   All unweighted bases are rounded to the nearest 10

Source: General Lifestyle Survey, Office for National Statistics

Table 3.14   Socio-economic classification based on own current or last job by sex and age

All persons aged 16 and over   *Great Britain: 2009[1]*

Socio-economic classification[2]	Age group						
	16-24	25-34	35-44	45-54	55-64	65 and over	All
	%	%	%	%	%	%	%
Men							
Higher managerial and professional	3	18	21	19	18	15	17
Lower managerial and professional	10	24	27	24	23	21	22
Intermediate	8	7	5	5	6	4	6
Small employers and own account	3	8	12	12	15	12	11
Lower supervisory and technical	12	14	12	14	12	18	14
Semi-routine	22	14	10	10	10	11	12
Routine	14	12	11	12	14	16	13
Never worked and long-term unemployed	29	4	3	3	3	3	6
Weighted base (000's)=100%	*2,257*	*3,271*	*4,422*	*3,746*	*3,424*	*4,110*	*21,230*
Unweighted sample[3]	*560*	*810*	*1,170*	*1,170*	*1,240*	*1,740*	*6,690*
Women							
Higher managerial and professional	2	12	13	8	6	2	7
Lower managerial and professional	12	30	32	31	26	19	26
Intermediate	20	19	15	18	18	22	19
Small employers and own account	1	4	5	4	7	5	5
Lower supervisory and technical	4	4	4	7	6	6	5
Semi-routine	24	18	19	20	23	23	21
Routine	12	9	7	8	11	16	11
Never worked and long-term unemployed	25	5	5	3	3	7	7
Weighted base (000's)=100%	*2,274*	*3,286*	*4,415*	*4,001*	*3,453*	*5,120*	*22,548*
Unweighted sample[3]	*570*	*940*	*1,320*	*1,290*	*1,340*	*1,980*	*7,440*
Total							
Higher managerial and professional	3	15	17	13	12	8	12
Lower managerial and professional	11	27	29	27	24	20	24
Intermediate	14	13	10	12	12	14	12
Small employers and own account	2	6	9	8	11	8	8
Lower supervisory and technical	8	9	8	10	9	11	9
Semi-routine	23	16	14	15	16	17	17
Routine	13	10	9	10	13	16	12
Never worked and long-term unemployed	27	4	4	3	3	6	6
Weighted base (000's)=100%	*4,531*	*6,557*	*8,837*	*7,747*	*6,877*	*9,230*	*43,779*
Unweighted sample[3]	*1,130*	*1,750*	*2,490*	*2,460*	*2,580*	*3,720*	*14,130*

1   Results for 2009 include longitudinal data (see Appendix B).

2   Full-time students and persons in inadequately described occupations are excluded.

3   All unweighted bases are rounded to the nearest 10

Source: General Lifestyle Survey, Office for National Statistics

Table 3.15

Table 3.15   Ethnic groups: 2001 to 2009

All persons   Great Britain

Ethnic group	2001	2002	2003	2004	2005[1]	2006[2]	2007[2]	2008[2]	2009[2]
	%	%	%	%	%	%	%	%	%
White British	89	88	87	87	86	87	87	87	86
Other White	3	3	3	4	3	4	3	3	4
(White total)	92	91	91	90	90	91	90	91	90
Mixed background	1	1	1	1	1	1	1	1	1
Indian	2	2	2	2	2	2	2	2	2
Pakistani	2	1	2	1	1	2	1	1	1
Bangladeshi	2	0	1	1	1	1	0	1	1
Other Asian background	0	1	1	1	1	1	1	1	1
(Asian total)	4	4	4	4	5	6	4	4	4
Chinese	0	0	0	1	0	1	0	0	0
Black Caribbean	1	1	1	1	1	1	1	1	1
Black African	1	1	1	1	2	1	2	1	2
(Black total)	2[3]	2[3]	3[3]	3[3]	3[3]	2[3]	3[3]	3[3]	3[3]
Other ethnic group	1	1	1	1	1	0	1	1	1
Weighted base (000's) = 100%	57,034	56,302	56,581	56,722	56,847	57,886	57,937	57,681	58,344
Unweighted sample [4]	21,100	20,050	24,430	20,370	30,010	22,870	21,430	20,500	18,990

1 2005 data includes last quarter of 2004/5 data due to survey change from financial year to calendar year.
2 Results from 2006 onwards include longitudinal data (see Appendix B).
3 Including other Black groups not shown separately.
4 All unweighted bases are rounded to the nearest 10

Source: General Lifestyle Survey, Office for National Statistics

Table 3.16   Age by ethnic group

All persons   Great Britain: 2007[1], 2008[1] and 2009[1] combined

Age	White British	Other White	Mixed back-ground	Indian	Pakistani	Bangladeshi	Other Asian background	Chinese	Black Caribbean	Black African	Other Black background	Other ethnic group	All
	%	%	%	%	%	%	%	%	%	%	%	%	%
0-15	18	13	49	20	33	37	27	15	21	34	41	22	19
16-24	11	11	18	9	18	17	11	12	15	16	15	14	12
25-44	27	41	24	45	28	32	42	37	30	35	27	38	28
45-64	27	23	6	19	17	13	17	28	24	13	11	22	26
65 and over	17	12	2	7	5	2	4	8	11	3	7	4	16
Unweighted sample [2,3]	53,760	2,020	600	850	550	220	460	160	490	690	60	480	60,340

1 Results from 2007 onwards include longitudinal data (see Appendix B).
2 Weighted bases not shown for combined data sets.
3 All unweighted bases are rounded to the nearest 10
Note: Shaded figures indicate the estimates are unreliable and any analysis using these figures may be invalid. Any use of these shaded figures must be accompanied by this disclaimer.

Source: General Lifestyle Survey, Office for National Statistics

Table 3.17 Sex by ethnic group

All persons   Great Britain: 2007[1], 2008[1] and 2009[1] combined

Ethnic group		Male	Female	Unweighted sample [2,3]
White British	%	49	51	53,760
Other White	%	48	52	2,020
Mixed background	%	46	54	600
Indian	%	52	48	850
Pakistani	%	50	50	550
Bangladeshi	%	52	48	220
Other Asian background	%	48	52	460
Chinese	%	48	52	160
Black Caribbean	%	49	51	490
Black African	%	48	52	690
Other Black background	%	54	46	60
Other ethnic group	%	53	47	480

1   Results from 2007 onwards include longitudinal data (see Appendix B).
2   Weighted bases not shown for combined data sets.
3   All unweighted bases are rounded to the nearest 10
Note: Shaded figures indicate the estimates are unreliable and any analysis using these figures may be invalid. Any use of these shaded figures must be accompanied by this disclaimer.

Source: General Lifestyle Survey, Office for National Statistics

Table 3.18 Ethnic group by Government Office Region

All persons   *Great Britain: 2007[1], 2008[1] and 2009[1] combined*

Government Office Region	Ethnic group												
	White British	Other White	Mixed back-ground	Indian	Pakistani	Bangladeshi	Other Asian background	Chinese	Black Caribbean	Black African	Other Black background	Other ethnic group	Total
	%	%	%	%	%	%	%	%	%	%	%	%	%
England													
North East	4	1	0	0	0	0	1	2	*	*	0	2	4
North West	13	6	6	4	14	1	2	8	4	2	*	7	12
Yorkshire and the													
Humber	9	3	7	6	14	5	3	11	3	2	*	9	9
East Midlands	7	8	7	16	1	4	3	*	6	6	*	8	7
West Midlands	9	5	11	10	19	4	6	10	24	3	13	8	9
East of England	10	11	8	3	14	0	5	16	3	6	*	5	10
London	8	29	38	42	17	78	64	32	56	72	59	41	13
South East	15	13	11	13	17	3	8	14	3	8	7	11	14
South West	9	5	6	1	*	0	3	*	0	0	*	2	8
Wales	6	3	2	0	0	2	1	3	0	0	0	2	5
Scotland	9	16	2	4	3	*	4	4	*	1	7	6	9
Unweighted sample[2,3]	*53,760*	*2,020*	*600*	*850*	*550*	*220*	*460*	*160*	*490*	*690*	*60*	*480*	*60,340*

1 Results from 2007 onwards include longitudinal data (see Appendix B).

2 Weighted bases not shown for combined data sets.

3 All unweighted bases are rounded to the nearest 10

* Information is suppressed for low cell counts as a measure of disclosure control.

Note: Shaded figures indicate the estimates are unreliable and any analysis using these figures may be invalid. Any use of these shaded figures must be accompanied by this disclaimer

Source: General Lifestyle Survey, Office for National Statistics

Table 3.19

Average household size by ethnic group of household reference person

Households   *Great Britain: 2007[1], 2008[1] and 2009[1] combined*

Ethnic group	Average (mean) household size	Unweighted sample[2,3]
White British	2.30	23,630
Other White	2.37	860
Mixed background	2.39	120
Indian	2.96	300
Pakistani	4.11	140
Bangladeshi	4.96	50
Other Asian background	3.03	130
Chinese	2.84	60
Black Caribbean	2.46	220
Black African	3.15	220
Other black background	2.29	20
Other ethnic group	2.69	170
Total	2.35	25,900

1 Results from 2007 onwards include longitudinal data (see Appendix B).

2 Weighted bases not shown for combined data sets.

3 All unweighted bases are rounded to the nearest 10

Source: General Lifestyle Survey, Office for National Statistics

Table 3.20   Percentage born in the UK by age and ethnic group

All persons   *Great Britain: 2007[1], 2008[1] and 2009[1] combined*

Ethnic group	Percentage born in the United Kingdom			Unweighted sample[2,3]		
	Age			Age		
	Under 25	25 and over	Total	Under 25	25 and over	Total
White British	99	97	97	15,050	38,670	53,730
Other White	53	30	35	460	1,550	2,010
Mixed background	94	68	85	420	190	610
Indian	79	33	46	250	590	850
Pakistani	84	21	53	280	260	540
Bangladeshi	89	18	56	120	100	220
Other Asian Background	57	5	26	180	260	440
Chinese	64	14	28	40	120	160
Black Caribbean	95	51	67	180	310	490
Black African	52	13	33	330	350	680
Other Black background	94	39	69	30	30	60
Other ethnic group	50	19	30	170	300	470
Total	94	89	91	17,520	42,730	60,250

1   Results from 2007 onwards include longitudinal data (see Appendix B).

2   Weighted base not shown for combined data sets.

3   All unweighted bases are rounded to the nearest 10

Note: Shaded figures indicate the estimates are unreliable and any analysis using these figures may be invalid. Any use of these shaded figures must be accompanied by this disclaimer.

Source: General Lifestyle Survey, Office for National Statistics

Table 3.21   Weighted bases for Tables 3.3 and 3.8

(a) Persons aged 16 and over   *Great Britain*

	1998	2000	2001	2002	2003	2004	2005[1]	2006[2]	2007[2]	2008[2]	2009[2]	Table Reference
16-24	6,139	6,191	6,192	6,286	6,381	6,470	6,511	6,856	6,749	7,082	7,121	3.3
25-44	17,117	17,130	17,275	16,404	16,304	16,225	16,177	16,541	16,455	16,475	16,399	3.3
45-64	13,226	13,519	13,540	13,757	13,927	14,102	14,244	14,503	14,729	14,933	15,132	3.3
65-74	4,767	4,719	4,729	4,792	4,822	4,849	4,863	4,847	4,867	4,974	5,081	3.3
75 and over	3,836	3,888	3,898	3,993	4,014	4,044	4,067	4,162	4,210	4,257	4,332	3.3
All aged 16 and over	45,085	45,447	45,632	45,232	45,448	45,689	45,861	46,909	47,011	47,720	48,064	3.3

(b) Families with dependent children[3]   *Great Britain*

	1998	2000	2001	2002	2003	2004	2005	2006	2007	2008	2009	Table Reference
Married/cohabiting couple[4]	5,465	5,232	5,366	5,244	5,207	5,237	5,174	5,422	5,542	5,576	5,574	3.8
Married couple	4,765	4,496	4,580	4,515	4,330	4,431	4,348	4,560	4,523	4,562	4,598	3.8
Cohabiting couple	700	736	785	729	877	806	827	862	1,019	1,014	976	3.8
Lone parent	1,717	1,861	1,739	1,922	1,821	1,715	1,806	1,798	1,679	1,666	1,641	3.8
Total	7,182	7,093	7,105	7,166	7,028	6,952	6,980	7,219	7,221	7,242	7,215	3.8

1 2005 data includes last quarter of 2004/5 data due to survey change from financial year to calendar year.

2 Results from 2006 onwards include longitudinal data (see Appendix B).

3 Dependent children are persons aged under 16, or aged 16-18 and in full-time education, in the family unit, and living in the household.

4 Including married women whose husbands were not defined as resident in the household.

Source: General Lifestyle Survey, Office for National Statistics

Table 4.1 Housing tenure: 1971 to 2009

Households

Tenure	Unweighted								Weighted										
	1971	1975	1981	1985	1991	1995	1996	1998	1998	2000	2001	2002	2003	2004	2005[1]	2006[2]	2007[2]	2008[2]	2009[2]
	%	%	%	%	%	%	%	%	%	%	%	%	%	%	%	%	%	%	%
Owner occupied, owned outright	22	22	23	24	25	25	26	28	26	27	27	29	29	30	30	30	31	32	32
Owner occupied, with mortgage	27	28	31	37	42	42	41	41	42	41	41	40	40	39	38	40	40	39	37
Rented from council[3]	31	33	34	28	24	18	19	16	17	16	15	14	13	13	12	12	11	10	10
Rented from housing association[4]	1	1	2	2	3	4	5	5	5	6	6	7	7	7	7	8	8	9	8
Rented with job or business	5	3	2	2	1	2	**	**	**	**	**	**	**	**	**	**	**	**	**
Rented privately, unfurnished[5]	12	10	6	5	4	5	7	7	7	7	7	8	8	8	8	8	7	8	11
Rented privately, furnished	3	3	2	2	2	3	3	2	3	3	3	3	3	3	3	3	2	2	2
Weighted base (000's) =100%[6]									24,436	24,838	24,592	24,508	24,418	24,677	24,826	24,815	24,718	24,835	25,180
Unweighted sample[6,7]	11,940	11,970	11,940	9,930	9,920	9,720	9,160	8,630		8,220	8,990	8,610	10,280	8,700	12,800	9,730	9,090	8,730	8,200

1 2005 data includes last quarter of 2004/5 data due to survey change from financial year to calendar year.
2 Results from 2006 onwards include longitudinal data (see Appendix B).
3 Council includes local authorities.
4 Since 1996 housing associations are more correctly described as Registered Social Landlords (RSLs).
5 Unfurnished includes the answer 'partly furnished'.
6 Trend tables show unweighted and weighted figures for 1998 to give an indication of the effect of the weighting. For the weighted data (1998 and 2000 to 2009) the weighted base (000's) is the base for percentages. Unweighted data (up to 1998) are based on the unweighted sample.
7 All unweighted bases are rounded to the nearest 10.
** From 1996 onwards, accommodation that is provided as part of the employment contract of a member of the household, has been allocated to "rented privately". Squatters are also included in this category.

Source: General Lifestyle Survey, Office for National Statistics

Table 4.2 Type of accommodation: 1971 to 2009

Households

Great Britain

Type of accommodation[1]	Unweighted data								Weighted data											
	1971	1975	1981	1985	1991	1995	1996	1998	1998	2000	2001	2002	2003	2004	2005[2]	2006[3]	2007[3]	2008[3]	2009[3]
	%	%	%	%	%	%	%	%	%	%	%	%	%	%	%	%	%	%	%
Detached house	16	15	16	19	19	22	21	23	21	21	21	22	22	22	22	23	23	24	23
Semi-detached house	33	34	32	31	32	31	32	33	32	31	31	32	32	31	31	30	31	31	31
Terraced house	30	28	31	29	29	28	27	26	26	28	28	27	27	27	28	28	28	27	27
Purpose-built flat or maisonette	13	14	15	15	14	15	15	15	17	16	16	16	15	16	16	15	15	14	15
Converted flat or maisonette/rooms	6	8	5	5	4	4	5	4	4	4	4	4	4	4	4	3	3	3	4
With business premises/other	2	1	1	1	1	1	0	0	0	0	0	0	0	0	0	0	0	0	0
Weighted base (000's) =100%[4]	11,850	12,040	11,980	9,890	9,920	9,730	9,130	8,620	24,398	24,806	24,520	24,421	24,378	24,644	24,780	24,780	24,668	24,778	25,137
Unweighted sample[4,5]										8,210	8,960	8,580	10,260	8,680	12,780	9,710	9,070	8,700	8,180

1 Tables for type of accommodation exclude households living in caravans.
2 2005 data includes last quarter of 2004/5 data due to survey change from financial year to calendar year.
3 Results from 2006 onwards include longitudinal data (see Appendix B).
4 Trend tables show unweighted and weighted figures for 1998 to give an indication of the effect of the weighting. For the weighted data (1998 and 2000 to 2009) the weighted base (000's) is the base for percentages. Unweighted data (up to 1998) are based on the unweighted sample.
5 All unweighted bases are rounded to the nearest 10.

Source: General Lifestyle Survey, Office for National Statistics

Households

Table 4.3 Type of accommodation occupied by households renting from a council compared with other households: 1981 to 2009

Great Britain

Type of accommodation[1]	Unweighted						Weighted										
	1981	1987	1991	1995	1996	1998	1998	2000	2001	2002	2003	2004	2005[2]	2006[3]	2007[3]	2008[3]	2009[3]
	%	%	%	%	%	%	%	%	%	%	%	%	%	%	%	%	%
Renting from council																	
Detached house	1	1	1	0	1	1	1	1	1	0	1	1	1	1	1	1	1
Semi-detached house	30	28	28	28	28	29	27	27	26	27	27	26	26	24	24	24	23
Terraced house	34	35	34	33	31	28	27	31	29	30	30	27	28	28	30	31	32
Purpose-built flat or maisonette	33	34	35	38	38	40	43	40	42	40	41	43	42	45	43	42	42
Converted flat or maisonette	2	2	3	1	2	2	2	2	2	2	2	3	2	1	2	2	2
Weighted base (000's) =100%[1]							*4,021*	*3,870*	*3,695*	*3,404*	*3,075*	*3,312*	*3,044*	*2,862*	*2,702*	*2,449*	*2,501*
Unweighted sample[1]	*4,010*	*2,600*	*2,340*	*1,770*	*1,750*	*1,410*		*1,240*	*1,330*	*1,140*	*1,230*	*1,100*	*1,480*	*1,030*	*910*	*800*	*770*
	%	%	%	%	%	%	%	%	%	%	%	%	%	%	%	%	%
Other households																	
Detached house	24	25	25	25	25	27	26	24	25	25	25	25	25	26	26	27	26
Semi-detached house	33	33	33	32	33	33	32	32	32	32	33	32	31	31	32	32	31
Terraced house	29	28	28	27	27	26	26	27	27	26	27	27	28	28	28	26	27
Purpose-built flat or maisonette	6	7	8	10	9	10	11	11	11	12	11	12	12	11	11	11	12
Converted flat or maisonette	7	5	5	4	5	4	5	5	4	4	4	4	4	4	3	3	4
Weighted base (000's) =100%[1]							*20,328*	*20,896*	*20,808*	*20,980*	*21,282*	*21,304*	*21,717*	*21,894*	*21,948*	*22,307*	*22,615*
Unweighted sample[1]	*7,900*	*7,510*	*7,580*	*7,950*	*7,380*	*7,190*		*6,950*	*7,630*	*7,430*	*9,020*	*7,570*	*11,290*	*8,680*	*8,150*	*7,900*	*7,410*
	%	%	%	%	%	%	%	%	%	%	%	%	%	%	%	%	%
All households																	
Detached house	16	18	19	22	21	23	22	21	21	22	22	22	22	23	23	24	23
Semi-detached house	32	32	32	31	32	33	32	31	31	32	32	31	31	30	31	31	31
Terraced house	31	30	29	28	27	26	26	28	28	27	27	27	28	28	28	27	27
Purpose-built flat or maisonette	15	14	14	15	15	15	17	16	16	16	15	16	16	15	15	14	15
Converted flat or maisonette	5	5	4	4	5	4	4	4	4	4	4	4	4	3	3	3	4
Weighted base (000's) =100%[4]							*24,349*	*24,766*	*24,503*	*24,384*	*24,357*	*24,616*	*24,761*	*24,755*	*24,650*	*24,755*	*25,116*
Unweighted sample[4,5]	*11,910*	*10,110*	*9,920*	*9,720*	*9,130*	*8,600*		*8,190*	*8,960*	*8,570*	*10,250*	*8,670*	*12,770*	*9,700*	*9,060*	*8,700*	*8,180*

1 Tables for type of accommodation exclude households living in caravans.
2 2005 data includes last quarter of 2004/5 data due to survey change from financial year to calendar year.
3 Results from 2006 onwards include longitudinal data (see Appendix B).
4 Trend tables show unweighted and weighted figures for 1998 to give an indication of the effect of the weighting. For the weighted data (1998 and 2000 to 2009) the weighted base (000's) is the base for percentages. Unweighted data (up to 1998) are based on the unweighted sample.
5 All unweighted bases are rounded to the nearest 10.

Source: General Lifestyle Survey, Office for National Statistics

Table 4.4 (a) Type of accommodation by tenure
(b) Tenure by type of accommodation

Households   *Great Britain: 2009[1]*

Tenure		Type of accommodation[2]							Weighted base (000's) =100%	Unweighted sample[7]
		Detached house	Semi-detached house	Terraced house	All houses	Purpose-built flat or maisonette	Converted flat or maisonette/ rooms	All flats/ rooms		
(a)										
Owner occupied, owned outright	%	37	34	21	92	6	2	8	*7,967*	*3,060*
Owner occupied, with mortgage	%	27	34	29	91	7	2	9	*9,370*	*2,810*
All owners	%	32	34	25	91	7	2	9	*17,337*	*5,870*
Rented from council[3]	%	1	23	32	56	42	2	44	*2,501*	*770*
Rented from housing association[4]	%	1	24	30	55	41	5	45	*2,048*	*630*
Social sector tenants	%	1	23	31	55	42	3	45	*4,550*	*1,400*
Rented privately, unfurnished[5]	%	10	23	34	67	21	13	33	*2,722*	*780*
Rented privately, furnished	%	5	17	23	44	32	24	56	*508*	*130*
Private renters[6]	%	9	22	32	63	22	15	37	*3,230*	*910*
Total	%	23	31	27	81	15	4	19	*25,116*	*8,180*
(b)									Total	
		%	%	%	%	%	%	%	%	
Owner occupied, owned outright		50	35	25	36	13	14	13	32	
Owner occupied, with mortgage		44	42	40	42	18	21	19	37	
All owners		94	77	64	78	31	35	32	69	
Rented from council[3]		0	8	12	7	28	5	24	10	
Rented from housing association[4]		0	6	9	5	22	10	20	8	
Social sector tenants		1	14	20	12	50	16	43	18	
Rented privately, unfurnished[5]		5	8	13	9	15	36	19	11	
Rented privately, furnished		0	1	2	1	4	13	6	2	
Private renters[6]		5	9	15	10	19	50	25	13	
Weighted base (000's) =100%		*5,856*	*7,698*	*6,834*	*20,388*	*3,777*	*951*	*4,728*	*25,116*	
Unweighted sample[7]		*2,100*	*2,620*	*2,180*	*6,900*	*1,050*	*230*	*1,280*	*8,180*	

1 Results for 2009 include longitudinal data (see Appendix B).
2 Tables for type of accommodation exclude households living in caravans.
3 Council includes local authorities.
4 Since 1996, housing associations are more correctly described as Registered Social Landlords (RSLs).
5 Unfurnished includes the answer 'partly furnished'.
6 Tenants whose accommodation goes with the job of someone in the household have been allocated to 'rented privately'. Squatters are also included.
7 All unweighted bases are rounded to the nearest 10.

Source: General Lifestyle Survey, Office for National Statistics

Table 4.5   **(a) Household type by tenure**
                         (b) Tenure by household type

Households   *Great Britain: 2009[1]*

Tenure		Household type							Weighted base (000's) =100%	Unweighted sample[6]
		1 adult aged 16-59	2 adults aged 16-59	Small family	Large family	Large adult household	2 adults, 1 or both aged 60 or over	1 adult aged 60 or over		
(a)										
Owner occupied, owned outright	%	7	7	3	1	13	37	32	8,011	3,080
Owner occupied, with mortgage	%	14	24	27	5	23	5	2	9,370	2,810
All owners	%	11	16	16	3	18	20	16	17,381	5,890
Rented from council[2]	%	18	8	18	7	11	10	28	2,501	770
Rented from housing association[3]	%	20	8	20	6	9	10	27	2,057	630
Social sector tenants	%	19	8	18	7	10	10	28	4,558	1,400
Rented privately, unfurnished[4]	%	18	22	24	7	11	6	12	2,726	780
Rented privately, furnished	%	29	29	14	3	15	2	8	515	130
Private renters[5]	%	20	23	22	6	12	5	12	3,240	910
Total	%	13	15	17	4	16	16	18	25,180	8,200
(b)									Total	
		%	%	%	%	%	%	%	%	
Owner occupied, owned outright		16	15	6	5	25	73	58	32	
Owner occupied, with mortgage		40	57	58	47	53	12	5	37	
All owners		56	72	64	52	78	84	63	69	
Rented from council[2]		13	5	10	16	7	6	16	10	
Rented from housing association[3]		12	4	9	12	5	5	13	8	
Social sector tenants		25	9	20	28	12	11	28	18	
Rented privately, unfurnished[4]		15	15	15	18	8	4	8	11	
Rented privately, furnished		4	4	2	1	2	0	1	2	
Private renters[5]		19	19	17	20	10	4	9	13	
Weighted base (000's) =100%		3,361	3,899	4,315	1,055	3,986	4,133	4,430	25,180	
Unweighted sample[6]		870	1,150	1,390	360	1,090	1,800	1,540	8,200	

1 Results for 2009 include longitudinal data (see Appendix B).

2 Council includes local authorities.

3 Since 1996, housing associations are more correctly described as Registered Social Landlords (RSLs).

4 Unfurnished includes the answer 'partly furnished'.

5 Tenants whose accommodation goes with the job of someone in the household have been allocated to 'rented privately'. Squatters are also included in the privately rented category.

6 All unweighted bases are rounded to the nearest 10.

Source: General Lifestyle Survey, Office for National Statistics

Table 4.6 Housing profile by family type: lone-parent families compared with other families

Families with dependent children[1] *Great Britain: 2008[2] and 2009[2] combined*

	Lone-parent families	Other families
	%	%
Tenure[3]		
Owner occupied, owned outright	5	8
Owner occupied, with mortgage	29	68
Rented from council	22	7
Rented from housing association	22	6
Rented privately unfurnished	17	8
Rented privately furnished	2	1
Central heating	%	%
Yes	97	98
No	3	2
Type of accommodation	%	%
Detached house	8	28
Semi-detached house	33	35
Terraced house	40	29
Purpose-built flat or maisonette	17	7
Converted flat or maisonette/rooms	2	1
Bedroom standard[4]	%	%
2 or more below standard	1	0
1 below standard	9	5
Equals standard	54	32
1 above standard	30	42
2 or more above standard	5	21
Persons per room	%	%
Under 0.5	22	9
0.5-0.99	72	75
1.0-1.49	6	15
1.5 or above	*	1
Unweighted sample[5,6]	*1,060*	*3,620*

1 Dependent children are persons aged under 16, or aged 16-18 and in full-time education, and living in the household.

2 Results for 2008 & 2009 include longitudinal data.

3 Percentage does not total 100% due to remaining percentage is unknown tenure

4 For the bedroom standard definition (see Appendix A)

5 Weighted base not shown for combined data sets.

6 All unweighted bases are rounded to the nearest 10.

* Information is suppressed for low cell counts as a measure of disclosure control.

Source: General Lifestyle Survey, Office for National Statistics

Table 4.7 Type of accommodation by household type

Households　　*Great Britain: 2009[1]*

Household type		Type of accommodation[2]							Weighted base ('000's) =100%	Unweighted sample[3]
		Detached house	Semi-detached house	Terraced house	All houses	Purpose-built flat or maisonette	Converted flat or maisonette/ rooms	All flats/ rooms		
One adult aged 16-59	%	11	21	27	59	30	11	41	3,356	870
Two adults aged 16-59	%	20	25	31	76	17	7	24	3,897	1,150
Small family	%	21	36	32	88	10	2	12	4,321	1,400
Large family	%	19	34	36	88	10	2	12	1,055	360
Large adult household	%	30	37	27	94	6	1	6	3,986	1,090
Two adults, one or both aged 60 or over	%	37	34	21	92	7	1	8	4,118	1,790
One adult aged 60 or over	%	20	29	24	73	24	3	27	4,394	1,530
Total	%	23	31	27	81	15	4	19	25,127	8,180

1 Results for 2009 include longitudinal data (see Appendix B).
2 Tables for type of accommodation exclude households living in caravans.
3 All unweighted bases are rounded to the nearest 10.

Source: General Lifestyle Survey, Office for National Statistics

---

Table 4.8 Usual gross weekly income by tenure[6]

Households　　*Great Britain: 2009[1]*

Usual gross weekly income (£)	Tenure									Total
	Owners			Social sector tenants			Private renters			
	Owned outright	With mortgage	All owners	Council[2]	Housing association[3]	Social sector tenants	Unfurnished private[4]	Furnished private	Private renters[5]	
Income of household reference person										
Mean	424	643	543	207	198	203	396	370	361	457
Lower quartile	146	353	204	103	102	103	170	84	137	159
Median	250	531	411	166	167	166	308	277	276	325
Upper quartile	458	769	666	272	262	268	475	523	449	565
Income of household reference person and partner										
Mean	535	890	728	259	242	251	508	455	458	604
Lower quartile	175	487	278	120	115	120	197	140	164	196
Median	326	746	551	195	193	195	384	299	319	419
Upper quartile	594	1,099	915	339	322	333	653	549	598	771
Total household income										
Mean	570	951	778	291	268	280	545	516	503	649
Lower quartile	184	532	299	126	124	125	215	160	191	214
Median	357	804	612	212	209	210	415	339	369	465
Upper quartile	662	1,163	989	388	359	372	682	650	653	835
Weighted base ('000's) =100%	*8,011*	*9,370*	*17,381*	*2,501*	*2,057*	*4,558*	*2,079*	*506*	*3,229*	*25,179*
Unweighted sample[7]	*3,080*	*2,810*	*5,890*	*770*	*630*	*1,400*	*600*	*130*	*910*	*8,200*

1 Results for 2009 include longitudinal data (see Appendix B).
2 Council includes local authorities.
3 Since 1996, housing associations are more correctly described as Registered Social Landlords (RSLs).
4 Unfurnished includes the answer 'partly furnished'.
5 Tenants whose accommodation goes with the job of someone in the household have been allocated to 'rented privately'. Squatters are also included in the privately rented category.
6 From 2007, income includes council tax benefit/rebate.
7 All unweighted bases are rounded to the nearest 10.

Source: General Lifestyle Survey, Office for National Statistics

Table 4.9   (a) Age of household reference person by tenure
            (b) Tenure by age of household reference person

Household reference persons
Great Britain: 2009[1]

Tenure		Age of household reference person[2]								Weighted base (000's) =100%	Unweighted sample[7]
		Under 25	25-29	30-44	45-59	60-64	65-69	70-79	80 and over		
(a)											
Owner occupied, owned outright	%	*	0	5	22	16	14	26	17	8,011	3,080
Owner occupied, with mortgage	%	1	7	46	37	5	2	1	0	9,370	2,810
All owners	%	1	4	27	30	10	7	13	8	17,381	5,890
Rented from council[3]	%	3	7	27	23	7	9	13	11	2,501	770
Rented from housing association[4]	%	6	5	27	24	9	5	13	11	2,057	630
Social sector tenants	%	4	6	27	24	8	7	13	11	4,558	1,400
Rented privately, unfurnished[5]	%	10	15	38	18	6	3	6	5	2,726	780
Rented privately, furnished	%	18	23	34	13	5	1	3	3	515	130
Private renters[6]	%	12	16	38	17	6	3	5	4	3,240	910
Total	%	3	6	29	27	9	7	12	8	25,180	8,200
(b)										Total	
		%	%	%	%	%	%	%	%	%	
Owner occupied, owned outright		*	1	5	25	56	67	70	67	32	
Owner occupied, with mortgage		19	44	60	51	20	9	4	1	37	
All owners		20	45	66	76	76	76	74	68	69	
Rented from council[3]		11	12	9	9	8	13	11	13	10	
Rented from housing association[4]		16	7	8	7	8	6	9	11	8	
Social sector tenants		27	19	17	16	16	19	20	25	18	
Rented privately, unfurnished[5]		40	28	14	7	7	5	5	6	11	
Rented privately, furnished		13	8	2	1	1	0	1	1	2	
Private renters[6]		53	36	17	8	8	5	6	7	13	
Weighted base (000's) =100%		700	1,433	7,206	6,876	2,323	1,698	2,964	1,979	25,180	
Unweighted sample[7]		180	360	1,980	2,230	860	710	1,180	700	8,200	

1 Results for 2009 include longitudinal data (see Appendix B).

2 Boxed figures indicate median age-groups.

3 Council includes local authorities.

4 Since 1996, housing associations are more correctly described as Registered Social Landlords (RSLs).

5 Unfurnished includes the answer 'partly furnished'.

6 Tenants whose accommodation goes with the job of someone in the household have been allocated to 'rented privately'. Squatters are also included in the privately rented category.

7 All unweighted bases are rounded to the nearest 10.

* Information is suppressed for low cell counts as a measure of disclosure control.

Source: General Lifestyle Survey, Office for National Statistics

Table 4.10 Tenure by sex and marital status of household reference person

Household reference persons

Great Britain: 2009[1]

Tenure	Males						Females						Total
	Married	Cohabiting	Single	Widowed	Divorced/ separated	All males	Married	Cohabiting	Single	Widowed	Divorced/ separated	All females	
	%	%	%	%	%	%	%	%	%	%	%	%	%
Owner occupied, owned outright	37	8	20	62	23	32	28	9	16	65	22	31	32
Owner occupied, with mortgage	47	57	32	3	31	42	49	46	27	5	31	30	37
All owners	84	66	52	65	54	74	76	55	43	70	53	61	69
Rented from council[2]	4	8	11	15	18	7	9	11	20	13	18	14	10
Rented from housing association[3]	4	5	14	10	14	6	6	11	14	11	14	11	8
Social sector tenants	8	13	26	25	31	14	15	22	34	23	31	25	18
Rented privately, unfurnished[4]	7	19	15	9	12	10	8	21	19	6	14	12	11
Rented privately, furnished	1	3	7	1	3	2	1	2	3	0	2	2	2
Private renters[5]	8	21	22	10	15	12	9	23	23	7	15	14	13
Weighted base (000's) =100%	*9,567*	*1,474*	*2,089*	*836*	*1,286*	*15,294*	*2,438*	*849*	*2,070*	*2,314*	*2,199*	*9,886*	*25,180*
Unweighted sample[6]	*3,340*	*440*	*510*	*290*	*380*	*4,980*	*800*	*250*	*640*	*780*	*740*	*3,220*	*8,200*

1 Results for 2009 include longitudinal data (see Appendix B).

2 Council includes local authorities.

3 Since 1996, housing associations are more correctly described as Registered Social Landlords (RSLs).

4 Unfurnished includes the answer 'partly furnished'.

5 Tenants whose accommodation goes with the job of someone in the household have been allocated to 'rented privately'. Squatters are also included in the privately rented category.

6 All unweighted bases are rounded to the nearest 10.

Source: General Lifestyle Survey, Office for National Statistics

Table 4.11 Housing tenure by ethnic group of household reference person

Households

Great Britain: 2007[1], 2008[1], 2009[1] combined

Tenure	Ethnic group												Total
	White British	Other White background	Mixed background	Indian	Pakistani	Bangladeshi	Chinese	Other Asian background	Black Caribbean	Black African	Other Black background	Other ethnic group	
	%	%	%	%	%	%	%	%	%	%	%	%	%
Owner occupied, owned outright	34	20	10	25	29	0	20	8	16	2	*	8	32
Owner occupied, with mortgage	40	29	30	51	40	27	41	41	25	28	16	40	39
Rented from council	9	11	23	1	14	51	12	13	35	27	27	15	10
Rented from housing association	8	9	21	5	7	13	6	9	17	15	24	14	8
Rented privately unfurnished	7	21	10	9	5	7	7	12	3	19	19	13	8
Rented privately furnished	1	9	5	7	5	*	14	17	2	9	*	5	2
Unweighted sample[2,3]	*23,620*	*860*	*120*	*300*	*130*	*50*	*60*	*130*	*220*	*220*	*20*	*170*	*25,890*

1 Results from 2007 onwards include longitudinal data (see Appendix B).
2 Weighted bases not shown for combined data sets.
3 All unweighted bases are rounded to the nearest 10.
Note: Shaded figures indicate the estimates are unreliable and any analysis using these figures may be invalid. Any use of these shaded figures must be accompanied by this disclaimer.
* Information is suppressed for low cell counts as a measure of disclosure control.

Source: General Lifestyle Survey, Office for National Statistics

403

Table 4.12 (a) **Socio-economic classification and economic activity status of household reference person by tenure**
(b) **Tenure by socio-economic classification and economic activity status of household reference person**

Household reference persons

Great Britain: 2009[1]

(a)

Socio-economic classification and economic activity status of household reference person[2]	Tenure									
	Owners			Social sector tenants			Private renters			Total
	Owned outright	With mortgage	All owners	Council[3]	Housing association[4]	Social sector tenants	Unfurnished private[5]	Furnished private	Private Renters[6]	
	%	%	%	%	%	%	%	%	%	%
Economically active HRP:										
Large employers and higher managerial	3	9	6	0	*	*	3	6	3	5
Higher professional	5	13	9	1	1	1	7	12	7	7
Lower managerial and professional	10	32	22	6	4	5	19	19	19	18
Intermediate	4	8	6	3	3	3	6	11	6	6
Small employers and own account	5	8	7	4	2	3	7	4	7	6
Lower supervisory and technical	4	10	7	5	5	5	7	4	7	7
Semi-routine	4	7	6	11	11	11	11	8	11	7
Routine	3	6	5	8	10	9	7	8	7	6
Never worked and long-term unemployed	0	0	0	4	4	4	3	*	3	1
Economically inactive HRP	63	6	32	58	59	58	30	27	30	37
Weighted base (000's) =100%	*7,910*	*9,109*	*17,018*	*2,452*	*2,022*	*4,474*	*2,630*	*447*	*3,077*	*24,570*
Unweighted sample[7]	*3,040*	*2,730*	*5,780*	*750*	*620*	*1,380*	*750*	*110*	*860*	*8,010*

(b)

	Owned outright	With mortgage	All owners	Council[3]	Housing association[4]	Social sector tenants	Unfurnished private[5]	Furnished private	Private Renters[6]	Weighted base (000's)[7]	Unweighted sample[7]
Economically active HRP:											
Large employers and higher managerial %	18	72	90	0	*	*	7	2	9	*1,143*	*360*
Higher professional %	20	66	86	1	1	2	9	3	12	*1,841*	*540*
Lower managerial and professional %	17	65	82	3	2	5	11	2	13	*4,510*	*1,370*
Intermediate %	22	52	74	6	5	11	11	3	15	*1,352*	*410*
Small employers and own account %	28	49	77	6	3	9	13	1	14	*1,531*	*470*
Lower supervisory and technical %	17	55	73	8	6	14	12	1	13	*1,640*	*500*
Semi-routine %	18	36	54	15	12	28	16	2	18	*1,806*	*560*
Routine %	18	38	56	14	14	28	13	3	15	*1,400*	*430*
Never worked and long-term unemployed %	5	13	19	29	26	55	25	*	26	*313*	*80*
Economically inactive HRP %	55	6	61	16	13	29	9	1	10	*9,033*	*3,310*
Total %	32	37	69	10	8	18	11	2	13	*24,570*	*8,010*

1 Results for 2009. include longitudinal data (see Appendix B).
2 Full-time students are classified as economically inactive.
3 Council includes local authorities.
4 Since 1996, housing associations are more correctly described as Registered Social Landlords (RSLs).
5 Unfurnished includes the answer 'partly furnished'.
6 Tenants whose accommodation goes with the job of someone in the household have been allocated to 'rented privately'. Squatters are also included in the privately rented category.
7 All unweighted bases are rounded to the nearest 10.

Note: Shaded figures indicate the estimates are unreliable and any analysis using these figures may be invalid. Any use of these shaded figures must be accompanied by this disclaimer.
* Information is suppressed for low cell counts as a measure of disclosure control.

Source: General Lifestyle Survey, Office for National Statistics

Table 4.13 (a) **Length of residence of household reference person by tenure**
(b) **Tenure by length of residence of household reference person**

Household reference persons *Great Britain: 2009[1]*

(a)

Length of residence[2] (years)	Owners			Social sector tenants			Private renters			Total
	Owned outright	With mortgage	All owners	Council[3]	Housing association[4]	Social sector tenants	Unfurnished private[5]	Furnished private	Private renters[6]	
	%	%	%	%	%	%	%	%	%	%
Less than 12 months	0	2	1	2	5	4	14	27	16	3
12 months but less than 2 years	1	4	2	4	6	5	19	28	20	5
2 years but less than 3 years	3	8	6	6	8	7	15	12	14	7
3 years but less than 5 years	4	18	12	14	13	13	19	12	18	13
5 years but less than 10 years	13	30	22	23	26	24	16	8	15	22
10 years or more	78	38	57	51	42	47	18	13	17	50
Weighted base (000's) =100%	*8,011*	*9,370*	*17,381*	*2,501*	*2,057*	*4,558*	*2,726*	*515*	*3,240*	*25,180*
Unweighted sample[7]	*3,080*	*2,810*	*5,890*	*770*	*630*	*1,400*	*780*	*130*	*910*	*8,200*

(b)

Length of residence[2] (years)	Owned outright	With mortgage	All owners	Council[3]	Housing association[4]	Social sector tenants	Unfurnished private[5]	Furnished private	Private renters[6]	Weighted base (000's) =100%	Unweighted sample[7]
Less than 12 months	% 5	16	21	6	13	19	44	16	60	*861*	*260*
12 months but less than 2 years	% 6	27	33	7	10	17	39	11	50	*1,299*	*410*
2 years but less than 3 years	% 13	43	57	9	9	18	22	3	25	*1,829*	*550*
3 years but less than 5 years	% 11	53	64	11	8	19	16	2	18	*3,207*	*930*
5 years but less than 10 years	% 19	51	71	11	10	20	8	1	9	*5,475*	*1,670*
10 years or more	% 50	29	79	10	7	17	4	1	4	*12,509*	*4,380*
Total	% 32	37	69	10	8	18	11	2	13	*25,180*	*8,200*

1 Results for 2009 include longitudinal data (see Appendix B).
2 Boxed figures indicate median length of residence.
3 Council includes local authorities.
4 Since 1996, housing associations are more correctly described as Registered Social Landlords (RSLs).
5 Unfurnished includes the answer 'partly furnished'.
6 Tenants whose accommodation goes with the job of someone in the household have been allocated to 'rented privately'. Squatters are also included in the privately rented category.
7 All unweighted bases are rounded to the nearest 10.

Note: Derivation changed in 2005 to reflect the year the accommodation was purchased/commencement of rental agreement.

Source: General Lifestyle Survey, Office for National Statistics

Table 4.14 Persons per room: 1971 to 2009

Households   Great Britain

Persons per room	Unweighted								Weighted										
	1971	1975	1981	1985	1991	1995	1996	1998	1998	2000	2001	2002	2003	2004	2005	2006[1]	2007[1]	2008[1]	2009[1]
	%	%	%	%	%	%	%	%	%	%	%	%	%	%	%	%	%	%	%
Under 0.5	37	39	42	45	50	52	51	55	55	57	57	57	58	58	58	58	58	57	57
0.5 to 0.65	25	25	25	26	24	25	24	23	23	22	22	23	22	22	23	23	22	23	22
0.66 to 0.99	24	23	23	21	19	18	19	18	18	16	16	16	16	16	15	15	15	15	16
1	9	8	7	6	5	5	5	4	4	4	4	3	3	3	3	3	3	3	4
Over 1 to 1.5	4	3	2	1	1	1	1	1	1	1	1	1	1	1	1	1	1	1	1
Over 1.5	1	0	0	0	0	0	0	0	0	0	0	0	0	0	0	0	0	0	0
Weighted base (000's) =100%[2,3]	*11,990*	*12,100*	*12,000*	*9,980*	*9,650*	*9,750*	*9,150*	*8,640*	*24,450*	*24,845*	*24,592*	*24,529*	*24,423*	*24,688*	*24,829*	*24,813*	*24,724*	*24,838*	*25,190*
Unweighted sample[2,3]										*8,220*	*8,990*	*8,620*	*10,280*	*8,700*	*12,800*	*9,730*	*9,090*	*8,730*	*8,200*
Mean persons per room	..	0.57	0.56	0.52	0.50	0.48	0.49	0.47	0.46	0.45	0.46	0.45	0.45	0.45	0.45	0.45	0.45	0.45	0.45

1 Results from 2006 onwards include longitudinal data (see Appendix B).

2 Trend tables show unweighted and weighted figures for 1998 to give an indication of the effect of the weighting. For the weighted data (1998 and 2000 to 2009) the weighted base (000's) is the base for percentages. Unweighted data (up to 1998) are based on the unweighted sample.

3 All unweighted bases are rounded to the nearest 10.

Note: 2005 data includes last quarter of 2004/5 data due to survey change from financial year to calendar year.

.. No data available

Source: General Lifestyle Survey, Office for National Statistics

Table 4.15 Persons per room and mean household size by tenure

Households

Persons per room	Tenure[2]									
	Owners			Social sector tenants			Private renters			Total
	Owned outright	With mortgage	All owners	Council[3]	Housing association[4]	Social sector tenants	Unfurnished private[5]	Furnished private	Private renters[6]	
	%	%	%	%	%	%	%	%	%	%
Under 0.5	81	45	62	53	53	53	41	43	41	57
0.5 to 0.65	13	29	22	18	21	19	30	22	28	22
0.66 to 0.99	5	23	14	17	17	17	21	19	21	16
1	0	3	2	7	8	7	6	13	8	4
Over 1	0	1	0	4	2	3	2	*	2	1
Weighted base (000's) =100%	8,011	9,370	17,381	2,501	2,057	4,558	2,726	515	3,240	25,180
Unweighted sample[7]	3,080	2,810	5,890	770	630	1,400	780	130	910	8,200
Mean persons per room	0.33	0.50	0.42	0.51	0.50	0.50	0.52	0.54	0.53	0.45
Mean household size	1.87	2.84	2.39	2.20	2.11	2.16	2.42	2.23	2.39	2.35

1 Results for 2009 include longitudinal data (see Appendix B).
2 Boxed figures indicate median density of occupation.
3 Council includes local authorities.
4 Since 1996, housing associations are more correctly described as Registered Social Landlords (RSLs).
5 Unfurnished includes the answer 'partly furnished'.
6 Tenants whose accommodation goes with the job of someone in the household have been allocated to 'rented privately'. Squatters are also included in the privately rented category.
7 All unweighted bases are rounded to the nearest 10.
* Information is suppressed for low cell counts as a measure of disclosure control.

Source: General Lifestyle Survey, Office for National Statistics

Table 4.16 Closeness of fit relative to the bedroom standard by tenure

Households *Great Britain: 2009[1]*

Difference from bedroom standard[2] (bedrooms)	Tenure									
	Owners			Social sector tenants			Private renters			Total
	Owned outright	With mortgage	All owners	Council[3]	Housing association[4]	Social sector tenants	Unfurnished private[5]	Furnished private	Private renters[6]	
	%	%	%	%	%	%	%	%	%	%
1 or more below standard	0	2	1	7	6	6	4	6	5	3
Equals standard	8	20	14	52	57	54	45	42	45	25
1 above standard	32	40	37	31	26	29	35	26	33	35
2 or more above standard	60	38	48	11	11	11	16	26	17	37
Weighted base (000's) =100%	*8,011*	*9,370*	*17,381*	*2,501*	*2,057*	*4,558*	*2,726*	*515*	*3,240*	*25,180*
Unweighted sample[7]	*3,080*	*2,810*	*5,890*	*770*	*630*	*1,400*	*780*	*130*	*910*	*8,200*

1 Results for 2009 include longitudinal data (see Appendix B).
2 For the bedroom standard definition (see Appendix A)
3 Council includes local authorities.
4 Since 1996, housing associations are more correctly described as Registered Social Landlords (RSLs).
5 Unfurnished includes the answer 'partly furnished'.
6 Tenants whose accommodation goes with the job of someone in the household have been allocated to 'rented privately'. Squatters are also included in the privately rented category.
7 All unweighted bases are rounded to the nearest 10.

Source: General Lifestyle Survey, Office for National Statistics

Table 4.17 Cars or vans: 1972 to 2009

Households   Great Britain

Cars or vans	Unweighted								Weighted										
	1972	1975	1981	1985	1991	1995	1996	1998	1998	2000	2001	2002	2003	2004	2005¹	2006²	2007²	2008²	2009²
	%	%	%	%	%	%	%	%	%	%	%	%	%	%	%	%	%	%	%
Households with:																			
no car or van	48	44	41	38	32	29	30	28	28	27	28	27	26	27	25	23	23	22	23
one car or van	43	45	44	45	44	45	46	44	45	45	44	45	45	45	45	44	44	44	45
two cars or vans	8	10	12	14	19	22	21	23	22	22	23	22	24	24	25	26	27	27	25
three or more cars or vans	1	1	2	3	4	4	4	6	6	6	5	5	5	5	6	7	6	7	7
Weighted base (000's) =100%³	11,620	11,930	11,990	9,960	9,910	9,760	9,160	8,640	24,450	24,845	24,592	24,529	24,423	24,688	24,829	24,815	24,724	24,838	25,190
Unweighted sample³,⁴										8,220	8,990	8,620	10,280	8,700	12,800	9,730	9,090	8,730	8,200

1 2005 data includes last quarter of 2004/5 data due to survey change from financial year to calendar year.

2 Results from 2006 onwards include longitudinal data (see Appendix B).

3 Trend tables show unweighted and weighted figures for 1998 to give an indication of the effect of the weighting. For the weighted data (1998 and 2000 to 2009) the weighted base (000's) is the base for percentages. Unweighted data (up to 1998) are based on the unweighted sample.

4 All unweighted bases are rounded to the nearest 10.

Source: General Lifestyle Survey, Office for National Statistics

Table 4.18 Availability of a car or van by socio-economic classification of household reference person

Households | Great Britain: 2009[1]

Socio-economic classification of household reference person[2]		Number of cars or vans available to household			Weighted base (000's) =100%	Unweighted sample[3]
		None	1	2 or more		
Economically active HRP						
Large employers and higher managerial	%	4	31	65	1,143	360
Higher professional	%	5	45	49	1,841	540
Lower managerial and professional	%	9	43	48	4,510	1,370
Intermediate	%	15	51	34	1,352	410
Small employers and own account	%	3	38	59	1,531	470
Lower supervisory and technical	%	9	45	45	1,640	500
Semi-routine	%	26	49	26	1,809	560
Routine	%	21	49	30	1,400	430
Never worked and long-term unemployed	%	65	25	10	3127	80
Economically inactive HRP	%	41	48	11	9,040	3,310
Total	%	23	45	32	24,580	8,020

1 Results for 2009 include longitudinal data (see Appendix B).

2 Full-time students are classed as economically inactive.

3 All unweighted bases are rounded to the nearest 10.

Note: Shaded figures indicate the estimates are unreliable and any analysis using these figures may be invalid. Any use of these shaded figures must be accompanied by this disclaimer.

Source: General Lifestyle Survey, Office for National Statistics

Table 4.19 Consumer durables, central heating and cars: 1972 to 2009

Households   Great Britain

	1972	1975	1981	1985	1991	1993	1995	1996	1998	Weighted 1998	2000	2001	2002	2003	2004	2005[1]	2006[2]	2007[2]	2008[2]	2009[2]
Percentage of households with:																				
Colour television	93	96	74	86	95	95	97	97	98	97	98	98	99	..	..	99	99	99	99	99
Home computer	..	..	..	13	21	24	25	27	34	34	45	50	54	58	60	63	69	71	74	76
Washing machine	66	71	78	81	87	88	90	90	92	91	93	92	93	94	95	95	95	96	96	96
Telephone	42	54	75	81	88	90	93	94	96	96	98	98	99	99	99	99	99	99	100	100
fixed telephone[3]	..	..	..	..	..	..	..	..	..	..	93	93	92	92	92	92	92	92	92	91
mobile telephone[3]	..	..	..	..	..	..	..	..	..	..	58	70	75	76	79	80	83	81	82	84
Central heating	37	43	59	69	82	83	86	88	90	90	92	92	93	93	94	95	95	96	96	97
Car or van																				
one	52	56	59	62	67	68	71	70	72	72	73	72	73	74	73	75	77	77	78	77
more than one	9	11	14	17	23	23	26	24	28	27	28	28	28	29	29	30	33	34	34	32
Weighted base (000's)																				
= 100%[4]	11,660	11,930	11,720	9,990	9,960	9,850	9,760	9,160	8,640	24,450	24,575	24,592	24,529	24,423	24,688	24,829	24,815	24,724	24,838	25,190
Unweighted sample[4,5]											8,210	8,990	8,620	10,280	8,700	12,800	9,730	9,090	8,730	8,200

1 2005 data includes last quarter of 2004/5 data due to survey change from financial year to calendar year.

2 Results from 2006 onwards include longitudinal data (see Appendix B).

3 Percentages for fixed and mobile telephones sum to greater than 100 because many households owned both.

4 Trend tables show unweighted and weighted figures for 1998 to give an indication of the effect of the weighting. For the weighted data (1998 and 2000 to 2009) the weighted base (000's) is the base for percentages. Unweighted data (up to 1998) are based on the unweighted sample.

5 All unweighted bases are rounded to the nearest 10.

** Data not available - either not available until 2000 or consumer durable item not on GHS list that year.

Source: General Lifestyle Survey, Office for National Statistics

Table 4.20 Consumer durables, central heating and cars by socio-economic classification of household reference person

Household reference persons | *Great Britain: 2009[1]*

Consumer durables	Socio-economic classification of household reference person[2]								Economically inactive	Total
	Economically active									
	Large employers and higher managerial	Higher professional	Lower managerial and professional	Intermediate	Small employers and own account	Lower supervisory and technical	Semi-routine	Routine		
Percentage of households with:										
Television	99	99	99	98	98	99	99	99	99	99
Home computer	98	96	95	90	92	89	83	78	51	76
Washing machine	100	100	99	98	99	99	98	98	92	96
Telephone (fixed or mobile)	100	100	100	100	100	100	100	100	99	100
fixed telephone[3]	98	96	95	90	94	88	82	82	91	91
mobile telephone[3]	90	90	91	90	91	92	92	92	73	84
Central heating	99	98	98	97	96	97	97	97	96	97
Car or van - more than one	65	49	48	34	59	45	26	30	11	32
Weighted base (000's) = 100%[4]	*1,143*	*1,841*	*4,510*	*1,352*	*1,531*	*1,640*	*1,809*	*1,400*	*9,035*	*24,575*
Unweighted sample[4]	*360*	*540*	*1,370*	*410*	*470*	*500*	*560*	*430*	*3,310*	*8,020*

1 Results for 2009 include longitudinal data (see Appendix B).
2 Where the household reference person had never worked or was long-term unemployed these are not shown as a separate category, but are included in the total. Full-time students are classified as economically inactive.
3 Percentages for fixed and mobile telephones sum to greater than 100 because many households owned both.
4 All unweighted bases are rounded to the nearest 10.

Source: General Lifestyle Survey, Office for National Statistics

412

Table 4.21 Consumer durables, central heating and cars by usual gross weekly household income[1]

Households

Consumer durables	Usual gross weekly household income (£)							Total
	0.00-100	100.01-200	200.01-300	300.01-400	400.01-500	500.01-700	700.01 or more	
Percentage of households with:								
Television	96	98	99	98	99	99	100	99
Home computer	49	43	61	72	81	90	96	76
Washing machine	87	91	95	97	98	99	100	96
Telephone	99	99	100	99	100	100	100	100
fixed telephone[3]	79	85	87	87	90	93	96	90
mobile telephone[3]	72	69	81	85	87	91	92	84
Central heating	97	95	96	96	96	97	99	97
Car or van - more than one	11	5	11	14	21	35	60	31
Weighted base (000's) =100%[4]	1,901	3,617	2,687	2,253	1,978	3,276	7,782	23,493
Unweighted sample[4]	580	1,220	950	800	670	1,040	2,390	7,640

1 From 2007, income includes council tax benefit/rebate.

2 Results for 2009 include longitudinal data (see Appendix B).

3 Percentages for fixed and mobile telephones sum to greater than 100 because many households owned both.

4 All unweighted bases are rounded to the nearest 10.

Source: General Lifestyle Survey, Office for National Statistics

Table 4.22   Consumer durables, central heating and cars by household type

Households   *Great Britain: 2009[1]*

Consumer durables	Household type							
	1 adult aged 16-59	2 adults aged 16-59	Small family	Large family	Large adult household	2 adults, 1 or both aged 60 or over	1 adult aged 60 or over	Total
Percentage of households with:								
Television	96	98	99	100	99	100	99	99
Home computer	74	92	94	94	95	68	34	76
Washing machine	94	99	99	99	100	99	87	96
Telephone (fixed or mobile)	99	100	100	100	100	100	99	100
fixed telephone[2]	76	89	88	90	95	98	94	91
mobile telephone[2]	88	92	92	93	90	83	62	84
Central heating	96	97	99	99	98	97	95	97
Car or van - more than one	6	45	42	46	63	30	2	32
Weighted base (000's) =100%	*3,363*	*3,899*	*4,321*	*1,055*	*3,986*	*4,133*	*4,433*	*25,190*
Unweighted sample[3]	*870*	*1,150*	*1,400*	*360*	*1,090*	*1,800*	*1,540*	*8,200*

1 Results for 2009 include longitudinal data (see Appendix B).

2 Percentages for fixed and mobile telephones sum to greater than 100 because many households owned both.

3 All unweighted bases are rounded to the nearest 10.

Source: General Lifestyle Survey, Office for National Statistics

Table 4.23

Consumer durables, central heating and cars: lone-parent families compared with other families

Families with dependent children[1]   *Great Britain: 2008[2] and 2009[2] combined*

Consumer durables	Lone-parent families	Other families
Percentage of households with:		
Television	100	99
Home computer	85	96
Washing machine	98	99
Telephone (fixed or mobile)	99	100
fixed telephone[3]	78	94
mobile telephone[3]	93	91
Central heating	97	98
Car or van - one or more	61	94
Unweighted sample[4,5]	*1,060*	*3,620*

1 Dependent children are persons aged under 16, or aged 16-18 and in full time education, and living in the household.

2 Results for 2008 & 2009 include longitudinal data (see Appendix B).

3 Percentages for fixed and mobile telephones sum to greater than 100 because many households owned both.

4 Weighted base not shown for combined data sets.

5 All unweighted bases are rounded to the nearest 10.

Source: General Lifestyle Survey, Office for National Statistics

Table 5.1   Sex by marital status

All persons aged 16 and over   *Great Britain: 2009[1]*

Marital status[2]	Men		Women	
Married	52		49	
Civil Partnership[3]	0		0	
Cohabiting	10		10	
Single	28		22	
Widowed	4		10	
Divorced	4	6	8	9
Separated	2		2	
Weighted base (000's) =100%	*23,425*		*24,640*	
Unweighted sample[4,5]	*7,290*		*8,030*	

1 Results for 2009 include longitudinal data (see Appendix B).

2 Marital status as recorded at the beginning of the interview.

3 Since December 2005 same sex couples have been able to obtain legal recognition of their partnership by registering as Civil Partners.

4 Total includes a very small number of same sex cohabitees.

5 All unweighted bases are rounded to the nearest 10.

Source: General Lifestyle Survey, Office for National Statistics

Table 5.2   (a)   **Age by sex and marital status**
            (b)   **Marital status by sex and age**

Persons aged 16 and over   *Great Britain: 2009[1]*

Age	Marital status[2]						Total[4]
	Married[3]	Cohabiting	Single	Widowed	Divorced	Separated	
(a)	%	%	%	%	%	%	%
Men							
16-24	1	8	51	0	0	*	15
25-34	10	37	21	0	2	11	15
35-44	23	31	13	0	18	24	20
45-54	22	14	8	3	25	17	17
55-64	21	8	4	14	32	23	15
65-74	14	2	3	24	17	13	10
75 and over	9	1	1	58	5	10	8
Weighted base (000's) =100%	*12,168*	*2,381*	*6,548*	*869*	*1,024*	*366*	*23,425*
Unweighted sample[5]	*4,180*	*710*	*1,660*	*310*	*310*	*110*	*7,290*
	%	%	%	%	%	%	%
Women							
16-24	2	14	54	0	*	*	14
25-34	13	37	18	0	2	9	15
35-44	22	29	13	2	17	35	19
45-54	23	10	6	2	31	30	17
55-64	19	7	3	11	27	16	14
65-74	13	2	3	24	16	7	11
75 and over	6	0	2	62	7	2	10
Weighted base (000's) =100%	*12,094*	*2,381*	*5,342*	*2,469*	*1,875*	*416*	*24,640*
Unweighted sample[5]	*4,170*	*710*	*1,520*	*830*	*630*	*150*	*8,030*
	%	%	%	%	%	%	%
Total							
16-24	2	11	52	0	*	2	15
25-34	12	37	20	0	2	10	15
35-44	23	30	13	1	17	30	19
45-54	23	12	7	2	29	24	17
55-64	20	7	4	12	29	20	15
65-74	14	2	3	24	16	10	11
75 and over	7	1	2	61	6	6	9
Weighted base (000's) =100%	*24,262*	*4,763*	*11,890*	*3,338*	*2,899*	*782*	*48,064*
Unweighted sample[5]	*8,350*	*1,420*	*3,180*	*1,140*	*960*	*260*	*15,330*

Table 5.2

(b) Age		Marital status[2]						Weighted base (000's) =100%	Unweighted sample[5]
		Married[3]	Cohabiting	Single	Widowed	Divorced	Separated		
Men									
16-24	%	3	5	91	0	0	*	3,625	900
25-34	%	36	25	38	0	1	1	3,587	890
35-44	%	60	16	18	0	4	2	4,595	1,220
45-54	%	70	8	13	1	7	2	3,909	1,220
55-64	%	71	5	8	4	9	2	3,518	1,280
65-74	%	73	2	7	9	7	2	2,417	1,080
75 and over	%	60	1	5	29	3	2	1,774	700
Total	%	52	10	28	4	4	2	23,425	7,290
Women									
16-24	%	8	10	82	0	0	*	3,496	890
25-34	%	46	24	28	0	1	1	3,576	1,020
35-44	%	59	15	15	1	7	3	4,641	1,390
45-54	%	68	6	8	1	14	3	4,169	1,330
55-64	%	67	5	5	8	14	2	3,536	1,380
65-74	%	58	2	5	22	11	1	2,664	1,100
75 and over	%	29	0	5	60	5	0	2,558	930
Total	%	49	10	22	10	8	2	24,640	8,030
Total									
16-24	%	5	7	87	0	0	0	7,121	1,790
25-34	%	41	24	33	0	1	1	7,163	1,910
35-44	%	59	15	17	0	5	3	9,236	2,610
45-54	%	69	7	10	1	10	2	8,078	2,560
55-64	%	69	5	6	6	12	2	7,055	2,650
65-74	%	65	2	6	16	9	1	5,081	2,180
75 and over	%	42	1	5	47	4	1	4,332	1,630
Total	%	50	10	25	7	6	2	48,064	15,330

1 Results for 2009 include longitudinal data (see Appendix B).
2 Marital status as recorded at the beginning of the interview.
3 Married includes persons in a legally recognised Civil Partnership.
4 Total includes a very small number of same sex cohabitees.
5 All unweighted bases are rounded to the nearest 10.
* Information is suppressed for low cell count as a measure of disclosure control

Source: General Lifestyle Survey, Office for National Statistics

417

Table 5.3 Percentage currently cohabiting by sex and age

Men and women aged 16-59   *Great Britain: 2009[1]*

Age	All	Non-married[2]	Weighted base (000's) =100% [3]		Unweighted sample[3,4]	
			All	*Non-married[2]*	*All*	*Non-married[2]*
Men	Percentage cohabiting					
16-19	1	1	*1,106*	*1,106*	*290*	*290*
20-24	13	14	*1,218*	*1,117*	*280*	*260*
25-29	25	34	*1,366*	*983*	*310*	*220*
30-34	28	54	*1,447*	*745*	*370*	*180*
35-39	17	38	*1,863*	*822*	*490*	*200*
40-44	13	34	*1,898*	*703*	*500*	*170*
45-49	9	23	*1,729*	*661*	*520*	*180*
50-54	7	28	*1,579*	*395*	*490*	*120*
55-59	4	16	*1,451*	*395*	*520*	*120*
Total	13	26	*13,658*	*6,927*	*3,760*	*1,760*
Women						
16-19	3	3	*1,080*	*1,078*	*290*	*290*
20-24	20	23	*1,411*	*1,204*	*330*	*290*
25-29	28	48	*1,565*	*914*	*420*	*260*
30-34	23	51	*1,538*	*694*	*460*	*220*
35-39	17	40	*2,064*	*879*	*620*	*270*
40-44	13	32	*2,200*	*870*	*650*	*260*
45-49	8	21	*2,022*	*751*	*630*	*240*
50-54	4	15	*1,782*	*520*	*580*	*170*
55-59	5	15	*1,536*	*502*	*570*	*180*
Total	13	28	*15,198*	*7,411*	*4,530*	*2,160*

1 Results for 2009 include longitudinal data (see Appendix B).

2 Men and women describing themselves as 'separated' were in a legal sense still married. However, because the separated can cohabit, they have been included in the 'non-married' category.

3 Total includes a very small number of same sex cohabitees.

4 All unweighted bases are rounded to the nearest 10.

Source: General Lifestyle Survey, Office for National Statistics

Table 5.4   Percentage currently cohabiting by legal marital status and age

Men and women aged 16-59   *Great Britain: 2008[1] and 2009[1] combined*

Legal marital status[2]	16-24	25-34	35-49	50-59	Total	*Unweighted sample[3,5]*				
						16-24	*25-34*	*35-49*	*50-59*	*Total*
Men			Percentage cohabiting							
Married[4]	-	-	-	*	*	*30*	*540*	*1,940*	*1,540*	*4,040*
Non-married										
Single	8	44	36	21	26	*1,130*	*810*	*770*	*240*	*2,950*
Widowed	..	*	0	*	6	*0*	*0*	*10*	*30*	*40*
Divorced	..	67	40	25	35	*0*	*30*	*270*	*220*	*520*
Separated	..	*	9	11	10	*0*	*10*	*80*	*40*	*140*
(non-married subtotal)	8	44	35	21	27					
Total	8	27	14	6	14	*1,160*	*1,390*	*3,070*	*2,070*	*7,680*
Women										
Married[4]	-	*	-	-	*	*60*	*810*	*2,390*	*1,640*	*4,900*
Non-married										
Single	16	50	41	22	32	*1,180*	*930*	*840*	*190*	*3,130*
Widowed	..	..	17	*	6	*0*	*0*	*30*	*90*	*120*
Divorced	*	52	27	14	24	*0*	*60*	*520*	*370*	*960*
Separated	..	14	10	14	11	*0*	*40*	*180*	*70*	*290*
(non-married subtotal)	16	49	33	15	29					
Total	15	27	13	5	14	*1,250*	*1,840*	*3,960*	*2,350*	*9,400*

1 Results for 2008 & 2009 include longitudinal data (see Appendix B).

2 Men and women describing themselves as 'separated' were in a legal sense still married. However, because the separated can cohabit they have been included in the 'non-married' category.

3 Weighted bases not shown for combined data sets.

4 Married includes persons in a legally recognised Civil Partnership.

5 All unweighted bases are rounded to the nearest 10.

- No figures are available because there are no reporting respondents

.. Data are not available (base = 0).

Note: Shaded figures indicate the estimates are unreliable and any analysis using these figures may be invalid. Any use of these shaded figures must be accompanied by this disclaimer.

* Information is suppressed for low cell count as a measure of disclosure control

Source: General Lifestyle Survey, Office for National Statistics

Table 5.5   **Cohabitees: age by legal marital status**

Cohabiting persons aged 16-59   *Great Britain: 2008[1] and 2009[1] combined*

Legal marital status[2]	16-24	25-34	35-49	50-59	Total
	%	%	%	%	%
Men					
Married[3]	-	-	-	*	*
Non-married					
Single	100	95	74	46	82
Widowed	..	*	..	*	0
Divorced	..	4	25	49	16
Separated	..	*	2	4	1
Unweighted sample[4,5]	*90*	*400*	*460*	*140*	*1,090*
Women					
Married	-	*	-	-	*
Non-married					
Single	99	93	69	38	81
Widowed	..	..	1	*	0
Divorced	*	5	27	52	16
Separated	..	1	4	8	2
Unweighted sample[4,5]	*180*	*480*	*510*	*110*	*1,280*

1 Results for 2008 & 2009 include longitudinal data (see Appendix B).

2 Men and women describing themselves as 'separated' were in a legal sense still married. However, because the separated can cohabit they have been included in the 'non-married' category.

3 Married includes persons in a legally recognised Civil Partnership.

4 Weighted bases not shown for combined data sets.

5 All unweighted bases are rounded to the nearest 10.

 - No figures are available because there are no reporting respondents

* Information is suppressed for low cell count as a measure of disclosure control

.. No data available

Source: General Lifestyle Survey, Office for National Statistics

Table 5.6 Cohabitees: age by sex

Cohabiting persons aged 16-59   *Great Britain: 2009[1]*

Age	Men	Women
	%	%
16-19	0	2
20-24	9	14
25-29	19	21
30-34	22	17
35-39	18	17
40-44	14	14
45-49	9	8
50-54	6	4
55-59	4	4
Weighted base (000's) =100%	*1,776*	*2,047*
Unweighted sample[2]	*510*	*590*

1   Results for 2009 include longitudinal data (see Appendix B).

2   All unweighted bases are rounded to the nearest 10.

Source: General Lifestyle Survey, Office for National Statistics

Table 5.7 Legal marital status of women aged 18-49: 1979 to 2009

Women aged 18-49

Great Britain

Legal marital status[1]	Unweighted									Weighted										
	1979	1983	1985	1989	1991	1993	1995	1996	1998	1998	2000	2001	2002	2003	2004	2005[2]	2006[3]	2007[3]	2008[3]	2009[3]
	%	%	%	%	%	%	%	%	%	%	%	%	%	%	%	%	%	%	%	%
Married[4]	74	70	68	63	61	59	58	57	53	53	51	50	49	47	48	47	48	49	48	47
Non-married																				
Single	18	21	22	26	26	28	28	29	30	32	35	36	38	38	39	39	40	39	41	43
Widowed	1	1	1	1	1	1	1	1	1	1	0	1	0	1	1	1	1	1	0	0
Divorced	4	6	6	7	8	9	9	9	11	10	9	9	9	10	9	10	8	8	8	7
Separated	3	2	3	3	3	4	4	4	5	4	5	4	4	4	3	3	3	3	3	3
Weighted base (000's) =100%[5]										11,827	11,946	11,689	11,752	11,466	11,630	11,541	11,909	11,722	11,468	11,036
Unweighted sample[5,6]	6,010	5,290	5,360	5,480	5,360	5,170	4,950	4,700	4,180	4,180	3,980	4,330	4,090	4,820	4,140	5,870	4,450	4,000	3,640	3,160

1 Women describing themselves as 'separated' were in a legal sense still married. However, because the separated can cohabit they have been included in the 'non-married' category.
2 2005 data includes last quarter of 2004/05 data due to survey change from financial year to calendar year.
3 Results from 2006 onwards include longitudinal data (see Appendix B).
4 Married includes persons in a legally recognised Civil Partnership.
  Trend tables show unweighted and weighted figures for 1998 to give an indication of the effect of the weighting. For the weighted data (1998 and 2000 to 2009) the weighted base (000's) is the base for percentages.
5 Unweighted data (up to 1998) are based on the unweighted sample.
6 All unweighted bases are rounded to the nearest 10.

Source: General Lifestyle Survey, Office for National Statistics

Table 5.8 Percentage of women aged 18-49 cohabiting by legal marital status: 1979 to 2009

Women aged 18-49

Great Britain

Legal marital status[1]	Unweighted							Weighted										
	1979	1985	1991	1993	1995	1996	1998	1998	2000	2001	2002	2003	2004	2005[2]	2006[3]	2007[3]	2008[3]	2009[3]
Percentage cohabiting																		
Married[4]	..	..	..	..	..	..	..	..	..	..	..	..	..	..	..	..	..	..
Non-married	11	16	23	22	25	26	29	30	30	32	29	31	28	29	31	33	35	32
Single	8	14	23	23	26	28	31	32	31	35	31	33	29	31	33	36	37	35
Widowed	0	5	2	8	8	5	8	11	15	11	13	6	13	10	10	11	27	*
Divorced	20	21	30	25	27	31	31	32	35	33	32	35	32	31	31	30	33	26
Separated	17	20	13	11	11	7	12	12	11	14	15	14	9	10	12	11	12	10
Total	3	5	9	9	10	11	13	14	15	16	15	16	15	16	16	17	18	17
Weighted bases (000's) =100%[5]																		
Married[4]								6,212	6,051	5,899	5,727	5,445	5,540	5,430	5,760	5,730	5,488	5,133
Non-married																		
Single								3,760	4,176	4,155	4,458	4,331	4,580	4,539	4,748	4,622	4,657	4,703
Widowed								99	55	99	52	63	98	77	84	63	48	45
Divorced								1,229	1,120	1,023	1,029	1,171	1,060	1,097	972	918	912	814
Separated								528	544	513	486	456	353	397	341	388	348	334
Total								11,828	11,946	11,689	11,752	11,466	11,630	11,541	11,909	11,722	11,468	11,036
Unweighted sample[5,6]																		
Married[4]	4,460	3,650	3,270	3,050	2,860	2,680	2,230		2,030	2,180	2,050	2,400	2,040	2,920	2,230	2,020	1,800	1,490
Non-married																		
Single	1,060	1,180	1,420	1,430	1,410	1,360	1,270		1,340	1,520	1,490	1,720	1,560	2,170	1,680	1,490	1,390	1,270
Widowed	60	60	60	50	40	40	40		20	40	20	30	30	30	30	20	20	10
Divorced	260	340	450	450	440	420	440		390	390	360	480	380	550	370	340	320	270
Separated	170	140	180	190	210	190	200		190	200	170	190	130	200	130	140	120	110
Total	6,010	5,360	5,360	5,170	4,950	4,700	4,180		3,980	4,330	4,090	4,820	4,140	5,870	4,450	4,000	3,640	3,160

1 Men and women describing themselves as 'separated' were in a legal sense still married. However, because the separated can cohabit they have been included in the 'non-married' category.
2 2005 data includes last quarter of 2004/5 data due to survey change from financial year to calendar year.
3 Results from 2006 onwards include longitudinal data (see Appendix B).
4 Married includes persons in a legally recognised Civil Partnership.
5 Trend tables show unweighted and weighted figures for 1998 to give an indication of the effect of the weighting. For the weighted data (1998 and 2000 to 2009) the weighted base (000's) is the base for percentages. Unweighted data (up to 1998) are based on the unweighted sample.
6 All unweighted bases are rounded to the nearest 10.
Note: Shaded figures indicate the estimates are unreliable and any analysis using these figures may be invalid. Any use of these shaded figures must be accompanied by this disclaimer.
.. No data available
* Information is suppressed for low cell count as a measure of disclosure control

Source: *General Lifestyle Survey, Office for National Statistics*

Table 5.9   **Women aged 16-59:**
(a) Whether has dependent children in the household by marital status
(b) Marital status by whether has dependent children in the household

Women aged 16-59   *Great Britain: 2009[1]*

Marital status		Children			*Weighted base (000's) =100%*	*Unweighted sample[3]*
		Dependent children	Non-dependent children only	No children		
(a)						
Married[2]	%	55	16	29	*7,192*	*2,220*
Non-married						
Cohabiting	%	43	6	50	*2,251*	*660*
Single	%	19	2	79	*3,780*	*1,050*
Widowed	%	23	26	51	*159*	*50*
Divorced	%	35	25	41	*1,035*	*330*
Separated	%	61	14	26	*389*	*130*
Total	%	42	12	46	*14,814*	*4,440*
(b)		%	%	%	Total	
Married[2]		63	67	31	49	
Non-married						
Cohabiting		16	8	17	15	
Single		11	5	44	26	
Widowed		1	2	1	1	
Divorced		6	15	6	7	
Separated		4	3	1	3	
Weighted base (000's) =100%		*6,261*	*1,711*	*6,841*	*14,814*	
Unweighted sample[3]		*1,960*	*460*	*2,030*	*4,440*	

1 Results for 2009 include longitudinal data (see Appendix B).

2 Married includes persons in a legally recognised Civil Partnership.

3 All unweighted bases are rounded to the nearest 10.

Note: Shaded figures indicate the estimates are unreliable and any analysis using these figures may be invalid. Any use of these shaded figures must be accompanied by this disclaimer.

Source: General Lifestyle Survey, Office for National Statistics

Table 5.10 Women aged 16-59: percentage cohabiting by legal marital status and whether has dependent children in the household

Women aged 16-59 *Great Britain: 2009[1]*

Legal marital status	Percentage cohabiting			Weighted bases (000's) =100%			Unweighted sample[4]		
	Has dependent children	No dependent children	Total	Has dependent children	No dependent children	Total[2]	Has dependent children	No dependent children	Total[2]
Married[3]	-	-	-	3,937	3,272	7,269	1,200	1,030	2,240
Non-married	41	22	27						
Single	52	23	31	1,469	4,023	5,517	470	1,050	1,530
Widowed	0	*	*	37	127	164	10	40	50
Divorced	26	19	21	486	829	1,324	170	260	440
Separated	9	12	11	259	174	439	90	60	150
Total	15	13	14	6,195	8,425	14,720	1,930	2,450	4,410

1 Results for 2009 include longitudinal data (see Appendix B).

2 Totals include a small number of children for whom dependency could not be established.

3 Married includes persons in a legally recognised Civil Partnership.

4 All unweighted bases are rounded to the nearest 10.

Note: Shaded figures indicate the estimates are unreliable and any analysis using these figures may be invalid. Any use of these shaded figures must be accompanied by this disclaimer.

- No figures are available because there are no reporting respondents

* Information is suppressed for low cell count as a measure of disclosure control

Source: General Lifestyle Survey, Office for National Statistics

424

Table 5.11 Cohabiting women aged 16-59: whether has dependent children in the household by legal marital status

Cohabiting women aged 16-59			Great Britain: 2009[1]
Legal marital status	Has dependent children	No dependent children	Total[2]
	%	%	%
Non-married			
Single	84	88	84
Widowed	..	*	*
Divorced	14	10	14
Separated	2	2	2
Weighted base (000's) = 100%	919	1,007	2,041
Unweighted sample[3]	290	270	590

1 Results for 2009 include longitudinal data (see Appendix B).

2 Totals include a small number of children for whom dependency could not be established.

3 All unweighted bases are rounded to the nearest 10.

* Information is suppressed for low cell count as a measure of disclosure control

.. No data available

Source: General Lifestyle Survey, Office for National Statistics

Table 5.12   Number of past cohabitations not ending in marriage by sex and age

Men and women aged 16-59								Great Britain: 2009[1]
Age	Number of completed cohabitations[2]						Weighted base (000's) =100%	Unweighted sample[3]
		None	One	Two	Three or more	Total at least one		
Men								
16-19	%	99	*	..	..	*	739	190
20-24	%	93	6	1	*	7	1,027	250
25-29	%	88	9	3	*	12	1,297	290
30-34	%	74	17	7	2	26	1,374	350
35-39	%	76	16	4	4	24	1,720	460
40-44	%	76	15	4	4	24	1,731	460
45-49	%	80	11	5	4	20	1,616	490
50-54	%	87	7	2	3	13	1,467	460
55-59	%	90	6	3	2	10	1,381	500
Total	%	83	11	4	3	17	12,355	3,450
Women								
16-19	%	97	2	*	..	3	847	230
20-24	%	89	9	2	1	11	1,245	300
25-29	%	80	16	4	1	20	1,490	410
30-34	%	78	18	3	1	22	1,477	440
35-39	%	77	18	5	1	23	2,031	610
40-44	%	76	15	6	3	24	2,120	620
45-49	%	85	10	4	1	15	1,936	610
50-54	%	90	8	1	1	10	1,698	560
55-59	%	92	6	1	1	8	1,455	540
Total	%	83	12	3	1	17	14,300	4,310
All								
16-19	%	98	2	*	..	2	1,586	420
20-24	%	91	7	1	1	9	2,273	540
25-29	%	84	13	3	1	16	2,786	700
30-34	%	76	18	5	1	24	2,851	790
35-39	%	76	17	5	2	24	3,751	1,070
40-44	%	76	15	5	4	24	3,851	1,090
45-49	%	82	11	5	2	18	3,551	1,100
50-54	%	89	8	2	2	11	3,165	1,020
55-59	%	91	6	2	1	9	2,836	1,040
Total	%	83	11	4	2	17	26,655	7,760

1 Results for 2009 include longitudinal data (see Appendix B).

2 Excludes current cohabitations.

3 All unweighted bases are rounded to the nearest 10.

* Information is suppressed for low cell count as a measure of disclosure control

.. No data available

425

Source: General Lifestyle Survey, Office for National Statistics

Table 5.13   **Number of past cohabitations not ending in marriage by current marital status and sex**

Men and women aged 16-59   *Great Britain: 2009[1]*

Number of cohabitations[2]	Marital status						
	Married[3]	Non-married					
		Cohabiting	Single	Widowed	Divorced	Separated	Total[4]
	%	%	%	%	%	%	%
Men							
None	88	77	79	88	71	86	83
One	8	17	12	..	16	6	11
Two	3	4	5	*	6	*	4
Three or more	1	2	5	*	7	*	3
Total at least one	12	23	21	12	29	14	17
Weighted base (000's) =100%	*6,207*	*1,643*	*3,657*	*68*	*552*	*177*	*12,355*
Unweighted sample[5]	*1,880*	*470*	*870*	*20*	*150*	*50*	*3,450*
Women							
None	90	77	74	97	77	84	83
One	8	17	17	*	16	14	12
Two	1	5	7	..	5	*	3
Three or more	0	1	2	..	2	..	1
Total at least one	10	23	26	3	23	16	17
Weighted base (000's) =100%	*7,403*	*1,963*	*3,304*	*163*	*1,110*	*318*	*14,300*
Unweighted sample[5]	*2,270*	*570*	*940*	*60*	*350*	*110*	*4,310*

1   Results for 2009 include longitudinal data (see Appendix B).
2   Excludes current cohabitations.
3   Married includes persons in a legally recognised Civil Partnership.
4   Total includes a small number of same sex cohabitees.
5   All unweighted bases are rounded to the nearest 10.
Note: Shaded figures indicate the estimates are unreliable and any analysis using these figures may be invalid. Any use of these shaded figures must be accompanied by this disclaimer.
*   Information is suppressed for low cell count as a measure of disclosure control
.. No data available

Source: General Lifestyle Survey, Office for National Statistics

Table 5.14

Age at first cohabitation which did not end in marriage by year cohabitation began and sex

Persons aged 16-59 who have cohabited   *Great Britain: 2009[1]*

Age at first cohabitation	Year first cohabitation began			
	1960-1979	1980-1989	1990-2009	All
	%	%	%	%
Men				
16-19	31	17	18	19
20-24	59	49	38	41
25-29	10	27	23	23
30-34	..	7	10	9
35-59	..	*	11	8
Weighted base (000's) =100%	*82*	*363*	*1,283*	*1,729*
Unweighted sample[2]	*30*	*100*	*320*	*450*
Women				
16-19	47	39	27	31
20-24	44	44	36	39
25-29	10	8	18	16
30-34	..	6	9	8
35-59	..	1	10	7
Weighted base (000's) =100%	*818*	*500*	*1,425*	*2,007*
Unweighted sample[2]	*30*	*150*	*460*	*640*
All				
16-19	39	30	23	25
20-24	51	46	37	40
25-29	10	16	21	19
30-34	..	6	9	8
35-59	..	1	10	8
Weighted base (000's) =100%	*164*	*864*	*2,708*	*3,736*
Unweighted sample[2]	*60*	*250*	*780*	*1,090*

1 Results for 2009 include longitudinal data (see Appendix B).

2 All unweighted bases are rounded to the nearest 10.

Note: Shaded figures indicate the estimates are unreliable and any analysis using these figures may be invalid. Any use of these shaded figures must be accompanied by this disclaimer.

* Information is suppressed for low cell count as a measure of disclosure control

.. No data available

Source: General Lifestyle Survey, Office for National Statistics

Table 5.15 **Duration of past cohabitations which did not end in marriage by number of past cohabitations and sex**

Persons aged 16-59 who have cohabited[1]   *Great Britain: 2009[2]*

Duration of cohabitation	First cohabitation			Second cohabitation
	One only	One of two or more	All	All
	%	%	%	%
Men				
Less than 1 year	23	20	22	31
1 year, less than 2	21	21	21	24
2 years, less than 3	15	19	16	17
3 years, less than 5	17	14	16	15
5 years or more	24	25	24	14
Mean length in months	42	41	42	
Weighted base (000's) =100%	*1,138*	*586*	*1,724*	*598*
Unweighted sample[3]	*310*	*140*	*450*	*140*
Women				
Less than 1 year	16	12	15	17
1 year, less than 2	23	21	22	28
2 years, less than 3	14	19	15	14
3 years, less than 5	20	20	20	20
5 years or more	28	28	28	21
Mean length in months	47	45	46	
Weighted base (000's) =100%	*1,503*	*535*	*2,038*	*522*
Unweighted sample[3]	*490*	*160*	*650*	*160*
All persons				
Less than 1 year	19	16	18	24
1 year, less than 2	22	21	22	26
2 years, less than 3	14	19	16	16
3 years, less than 5	19	17	18	17
5 years or more	26	27	26	17
Mean length in months	45	43	44	
Weighted base (000's) =100%	*2,642*	*1,121*	*3,762*	*1,121*
Unweighted sample[3]	*790*	*300*	*1,100*	*300*

1   Includes current cohabitations.

2   Results for 2009 include longitudinal data (see Appendix B).

3   All unweighted bases are rounded to the nearest 10.

Source: General Lifestyle Survey, Office for National Statistics

Table 6.1   Current pension scheme membership by age and sex

Employees aged 16 and over excluding government schemes   *Great Britain: 2009[1]*

Pension scheme members	Age						
	16-17	18-24	25-34	35-44	45-54	55 and over	Total
				Percentages			
Men full time							
Occupational pension[2,3]	*	30	46	57	65	59	54
Personal pension[4]	0	4	13	24	28	29	21
Any pension	*	30	51	68	74	70	62
Women full time							
Occupational pension[2,3]	0	27	59	62	65	63	58
Personal pension[4]	0	3	14	18	18	21	16
Any pension	0	27	62	67	70	69	62
Women part time							
Occupational pension[2,3]	0	10	42	53	51	35	40
Personal pension[4]	0	2	6	17	13	13	11
Any pension	0	10	42	61	55	39	44
Weighted base (000's) =100%							
Men full time	*48*	*1,020*	*2,464*	*3,102*	*2,563*	*1,502*	*10,699*
Women full time	*29*	*858*	*1,695*	*1,833*	*1,829*	*859*	*7,103*
Women part time	*179*	*639*	*697*	*1,381*	*1,213*	*950*	*5,060*
Unweighted sample[5]							
Men full time	*10*	*250*	*600*	*850*	*800*	*570*	*3,080*
Women full time	*10*	*210*	*450*	*520*	*590*	*320*	*2,100*
Women part time	*50*	*150*	*220*	*430*	*390*	*380*	*1,610*

1 Results for 2009 include longitudinal data (see Appendix B).

2 Including a few people who were not sure if they were in a scheme but thought it possible.

3 Occupational pension schemes are schemes provided by employers. They do not include group personal pensions, group stakeholder pensions or group self-invested personal pensions.

4 Personal pensions include group personal pensions, group stakeholder pensions and may include group self-invested personal pensions.

5 All unweighted bases are rounded to the nearest 10

*   Information is suppressed for low cell count as a measure of disclosure control

Source: General Lifestyle Survey, Office for National Statistics

Table 6.2 **Membership of current employer's occupational pension scheme by sex and whether working full time or part time**

Employees aged 16 and over excluding government schemes   *Great Britain: 2009[1]*

Pension scheme coverage	Men			Women		
	Working full time	Working part time	Total	Working full time	Working part time	Total
	%	%	%	%	%	%
Current employer has a pension scheme						
Member[2]	54	17	50	58	40	50
Eligible but not a member	11 68	14 48	11 66	14 75	13 61	14 69
Not eligible to belong	3	17	5	4	7	5
Does not know if a member	0	*	0	0	*	0
Current employer does not have a pension scheme	31	51	33	24	38	30
Not known if employer has a pension scheme	1	1	1	0	1	1
Weighted base (000's) =100%	*10,660*	*1,367*	*12,027*	*7,099*	*5,053*	*12,151*
Unweighted sample[3]	*3,070*	*390*	*3,470*	*2,100*	*1,610*	*3,710*

1 Results for 2009 include longitudinal data (see Appendix B).

2 Including a few people who were not sure if they were in a scheme but thought it possible.

3 All unweighted bases are rounded to the nearest 10

* Information is suppressed for low cell count as a measure of disclosure control

Source: General Lifestyle Survey, Office for National Statistics

Table 6.3 Membership of current employer's occupational pension scheme by sex: 1983 to 2009

Employees aged 16 and over excluding government schemes[1]

Great Britain

Pension scheme coverage[2]	Unweighted								Weighted										
	1983	1987	1989	1991	1993	1995	1996	1998	1998	2000	2001	2002	2003	2004	2005[3]	2006[4]	2007[4]	2008[4]	2009[4]
	%	%	%	%	%	%	%	%	%	%	%	%	%	%	%	%	%	%	%
Men full time																			
Current employer has a pension scheme — Member[2]	66	63	64	61	60	58	58	57	55	54	54	55	55	53	54	53	53	54	54
Not a member	10	12	14	16	16	16	16	15	15	16	19	18	16	18	17	18	16	16	14
(has a scheme)	77	74	79	77	76	74	74	72	71	70	73	73	72	71	71	71	69	70	68
Does not know if a member	1	0	0	1	0	0	0	0	0	0	0	0	0	0	0	0	0	0	0
Current employer does not have a pension scheme	22	22	19	21	22	25	25	28	29	29	26	26	28	28	28	28	30	29	31
Not known if employer has a pension scheme	2	3	2	2	2	1	1	1	1	1	1	1	1	1	1	1	1	0	1
Weighted base (000's) =100%[5,6]	5,090	5,130	4,910	4,560	3,980	4,060	3,940	3,700	11,009	11,323	11,220	10,820	10,708	10,422	9,325	11,148	11,089	11,217	10,660
Unweighted sample[5,6]	2,260	2,560	2,600	2,480	2,240	2,330	2,140	2,240		3,560	3,880	3,710	4,430	3,650	4,680	4,090	3,790	3,570	3,070
Women full time																			
Current employer has a pension scheme — Member[2]	55	52	55	55	54	55	53	56	55	58	58	60	55	56	58	58	58	58	58
Not a member	17	16	21	21	22	20	20	17	18	17	20	18	20	19	20	19	17	17	17
(has a scheme)	72	68	76	77	76	75	73	73	73	75	78	78	76	76	78	77	75	75	75
Does not know if a member	0	1	0	0	0	0	0	0	0	0	0	0	0	0	0	0	0	0	0
Current employer does not have a pension scheme	24	28	21	20	22	24	26	26	27	25	21	21	24	23	21	22	24	24	24
Not known if employer has a pension scheme	4	4	3	3	2	1	1	0	0	1	1	1	1	1	1	1	1	1	0
Weighted base (000's) =100%[5,6]	2,260	2,560	2,600	2,480	2,240	2,330	2,140	2,240	6,429	6,353	6,465	6,362	6,554	6,601	6,099	7,152	7,331	7,439	7,099
Unweighted sample[5,6]										2,090	2,380	2,240	2,690	2,350	3,030	2,710	2,560	2,390	2,100
Women part time																			
Current employer has a pension scheme — Member[2]	13	11	15	17	19	24	26	27	26	31	33	33	33	34	37	36	39	39	40
Not a member	39	34	37	34	35	32	28	26	26	25	29	25	27	26	25	24	23	22	20
(has a scheme)	53	46	52	52	54	55	53	53	52	56	63	58	60	61	62	60	62	61	61
Does not know if a member	0	0	0	1	0	0	0	0	0	0	0	0	0	0	0	0	0	*	*
Current employer does not have a pension scheme	40	44	40	39	38	42	44	45	46	42	36	40	37	37	35	38	37	38	38
Not known if employer has a pension scheme	7	10	7	8	7	3	2	2	3	2	2	2	3	2	2	2	1	1	1
Weighted base (000's) =100%[5,6]	1,640	2,130	2,100	1,980	1,940	2,040	1,910	1,670	4,628	5,059	4,990	4,963	5,044	5,182	4,930	4,798	4,804	5,011	5,053
Unweighted sample[5,6]										1,730	1,880	1,800	2,180	1,900	2,600	1,910	1,790	1,780	1,610

1 Prior to 1985 full-time students are excluded. Figures since 1987 include full-time students who were working but exclude those on Government schemes.

2 Including a few people who were not sure if they were in a scheme but thought it possible.

3 2005 data includes last quarter of 2004/5 data due to survey change from financial to calendar year.

4 Results from 2006 onwards include longitudinal data (Appendix B).

5 Trend tables show unweighted and weighted figures for 1998 to give an indication of the effect of the weighting. For the weighted data (1998 and 2000 to 2009) the weighted base (000's) is the base for percentages. Unweighted data (up to 1998) are based on the unweighted sample.

6 All unweighted bases are rounded to the

* Information is suppressed for low cell count as a measure of disclosure control

Source: General Lifestyle Survey, Office for National Statistics

Table 6.4 Current pension scheme membership by sex and socio-economic classification

Employees aged 16 and over excluding government schemes   *Great Britain: 2009[1]*

Pension scheme members	Socio-economic classification			
	Managerial and professional	Intermediate	Routine and manual	Total[2]
	Percentages			
Men full time				
Occupational pension[3,4]	65	66	38	54
Personal pension[5]	23	24	17	21
Any pension	74	74	45	62
Women full time				
Occupational pension[3,4]	69	60	34	58
Personal pension[5]	18	15	11	16
Any pension	73	65	38	62
Women part time				
Occupational pension[3,4]	64	49	29	40
Personal pension[5]	20	15	7	11
Any pension	70	56	31	44
Weighted base (000's) =100%				
Men full time	*5,331*	*827*	*4,319*	*10,699*
Women full time	*3,713*	*1,389*	*1,785*	*7,103*
Women part time	*1,266*	*974*	*2,358*	*5,060*
Unweighted sample[6]				
Men full time	*1,540*	*230*	*1,250*	*3,080*
Women full time	*1,110*	*410*	*520*	*2,100*
Women part time	*420*	*310*	*760*	*1,610*

1 Results for 2009 include longitudinal data (see Appendix B).

2 Total includes a small number of employees for whom socio-economic classification could not be derived.

3 Including a few people who were not sure if they were in a scheme but thought it possible.

4 Occupational pension schemes are schemes provided by employers. They do not include group personal pensions, group stakeholder pensions or group self-invested personal pensions.

5 Personal pensions include group personal pensions, group stakeholder pensions and may include group self-invested personal pensions.

6 All unweighted bases are rounded to the nearest 10

Source: General Lifestyle Survey, Office for National Statistics

Table 6.5   Membership of current employer's occupational pension scheme by sex and socio-economic classification

Employees aged 16 and over excluding government schemes   *Great Britain: 2009[1]*

Pension scheme coverage	Socio-economic classification			
	Managerial and professional	Intermediate	Routine and manual	Total[2]
	%	%	%	%
Men full time				
Current employer has a pension scheme				
Member[3]	65 ⎤ 76	66 ⎤ 77	38 ⎤ 56	54 ⎤ 68
Not a member[4]	11 ⎦	11 ⎦	18 ⎦	14 ⎦
Current employer does not have a pension scheme	24	23	42	31
Not known if employer has a pension scheme	*	*	2	1
Weighted base (000's) =100%	*5,323*	*822*	*4,297*	*10,660*
Unweighted sample[5]	*1,540*	*230*	*1,250*	*3,070*
Women full time				
Current employer has a pension scheme				
Member[3]	69 ⎤ 82	60 ⎤ 81	34 ⎤ 56	58 ⎤ 75
Not a member[4]	13 ⎦	20 ⎦	23 ⎦	17 ⎦
Current employer does not have a pension scheme	18	19	43	24
Not known if employer has a pension scheme	0	1	1	0
Weighted base (000's) =100%	*3,711*	*1,389*	*1,782*	*7,099*
Unweighted sample[5]	*1,110*	*410*	*520*	*2,100*
Women part time				
Current employer has a pension scheme				
Member[3]	64 ⎤ 80	49 ⎤ 67	29 ⎤ 53	40 ⎤ 61
Not a member[4]	16 ⎦	18 ⎦	24 ⎦	20 ⎦
Current employer does not have a pension scheme	20	33	45	38
Not known if employer has a pension scheme	0	*	1	1
Weighted base (000's) =100%	*1,263*	*974*	*2,353*	*5,053*
Unweighted sample[5]	*420*	*310*	*750*	*1,610*

1 Results for 2009 include longitudinal data (see Appendix B).

2 Total includes a small number of employees for whom socio-economic classification could not be derived.

3 Including a few people who were not sure if they were in a scheme but thought it possible.

4 Including people who were not eligible and a few people who did not know if they were a member.

5 All unweighted bases are rounded to the nearest 10

* Information is suppressed for low cell count as a measure of disclosure control

Source: General Lifestyle Survey, Office for National Statistics

Table 6.6   **Current pension scheme membership by sex and usual gross weekly earnings**

Employees aged 16 and over excluding government schemes   *Great Britain: 2009[1]*

Pension scheme members	Usual gross weekly earnings (£)							
	0.01-100.00	100.01-200.00	200.01-300.00	300.01-400.00	400.01-500.00	500.01-600.00	600.01 or more	Total[2]
				Percentages				
Men full time								
Occupational pension[3,4]	27	10	28	42	52	63	71	54
Personal pension[5]	*	14	12	15	24	22	27	21
Any pension	29	20	33	49	63	69	81	62
Women full time								
Occupational pension[3,4]	35	17	36	56	73	70	83	58
Personal pension[5]	15	9	11	15	21	13	22	16
Any pension	36	23	40	60	77	76	88	62
Women part time								
Occupational pension[3,4]	16	35	62	74	88	85	65	40
Personal pension[5]	7	11	16	19	11	25	25	11
Any pension	19	39	66	80	88	90	79	44
Weighted base (000's) =100%								
Men full time	*85*	*261*	*1,342*	*1,643*	*1,770*	*1,317*	*3,532*	*10,699*
Women full time	*138*	*486*	*1,619*	*1,497*	*997*	*665*	*1,408*	*7,103*
Women part time	*1,517*	*1,775*	*824*	*391*	*166*	*97*	*96*	*5,060*
Unweighted sample[6]								
Men full time	*30*	*80*	*380*	*490*	*490*	*370*	*1,040*	*3,080*
Women full time	*40*	*130*	*480*	*440*	*280*	*200*	*420*	*2,100*
Women part time	*470*	*560*	*260*	*130*	*60*	*30*	*30*	*1,610*

1 Results for 2009 include longitudinal data (see Appendix B).

2 Totals include people whose income was not known.

3 Including a few people who were not sure if they were in a scheme but thought it possible.

4 Occupational pension schemes are schemes provided by employers. They do not include group personal pensions, group stakeholder pensions or group self-invested personal pensions.

5 Personal pensions include group personal pensions, group stakeholder pensions and may include group self-invested personal pensions.

6 All unweighted bases are rounded to the nearest 10

Note: Shaded figures indicate the estimates are unreliable and any analysis using these figures may be invalid. Any use of these shaded figures must be accompanied by this disclaimer.

* Information is suppressed for low cell count as a measure of disclosure control

Source: General Lifestyle Survey, Office for National Statistics

Table 6.7   Current pension scheme membership by sex and length of time with current employer, 2007[1]

Great Britain: 2007[2]

Pension scheme members	Length of time with current employer			
	Less than 2 years	2 years, but less than 5 years	5 years or more	Total[3]
	Percentages			
Men full time				
Occupational pension[4,5]	28	46	70	53
Personal pension[6]	19	23	29	23
Any pension	40	57	83	64
Women full time				
Occupational pension[4,5]	37	54	72	58
Personal pension[6]	14	17	20	16
Any pension	43	61	80	64
Women part time				
Occupational pension[4,5]	17	32	56	39
Personal pension[6]	7	9	16	11
Any pension	20	36	61	43
Weighted base (000's) =100%				
Men full time	*2,458*	*2,202*	*5,267*	*11,151*
Women full time	*1,940*	*1,611*	*3,332*	*7,359*
Women part time	*1,389*	*1,067*	*2,156*	*4,835*
Unweighted sample[7]				
Men full time	*810*	*720*	*1,880*	*3,810*
Women full time	*620*	*550*	*1,240*	*2,570*
Women part time	*480*	*390*	*840*	*1,800*

1 Data on the length of time with current employer were not collected in 2008 and 2009, therefore, the latest estimates are for 2007.

2 Results for 2007 include longitudinal data (see Appendix B).

3 Including a few where length of time in job was not known.

4 Including a few people who were not sure if they were in a scheme but thought it possible.

5 Occupational pension schemes are schemes provided by employers. They do not include group personal pensions, group stakeholder pensions or group self-invested personal pensions.

6 Personal pensions include group personal pensions, group stakeholder pensions and may include group self-invested personal pensions.

7 All unweighted bases are rounded to the nearest 10

Source: General Lifestyle Survey, Office for National Statistics

Table 6.8 **Whether or not current employer has a occupational pension scheme by sex and length of time with current employer, 2007[1]**

Employees aged 16 and over excluding government schemes   ***Great Britain: 2007[2]***

Pension scheme coverage	Length of time with current employer			
	Less than 2 years	2 years, but less than 5 years	5 years or more	Total[3]
	%	%	%	%
Men full time				
Current employer has a pension scheme				
Member[4]	28	46	70	53
Not a member[5]	17 56	18 66	8 79	12 69
Not eligible to belong	11	3	2	4
Current employer does not have a pension scheme	42	32	21	30
Not known if employer has a pension scheme	2	1	0	1
Weighted base (000's) =100%	*2,448*	*2,202*	*5,267*	*11,089*
Unweighted sample[6]	*810*	*720*	*1,880*	*3,790*
	%	%	%	%
Women full time				
Current employer has a pension scheme				
Member[4]	37	54	72	58
Not a member[5]	20 65	17 76	8 82	13 75
Not eligible to belong	9	4	2	4
Current employer does not have a pension scheme	33	24	18	24
Not known if employer has a pension scheme	2	0	0	1
Weighted base (000's) =100%	*1,938*	*1,611*	*3,331*	*7,331*
Unweighted sample[6]	*620*	*550*	*1,240*	*2,560*
	%	%	%	%
Women part time				
Current employer has a pension scheme				
Member[4]	17	32	56	39
Not a member[5]	13 42	19 57	14 77	15 62
Not eligible to belong	13	6	7	9
Current employer does not have a pension scheme	55	42	23	37
Not known if employer has a pension scheme	3	1	0	1
Weighted base (000's) =100%	*1,380*	*1,067*	*2,156*	*4,804*
Unweighted sample[6]	*480*	*390*	*840*	*1,790*

1 Data on the length of time with current employer were not collected in 2008 and 2009, therefore, the latest estimates are for 2007.

2 Results for 2007 include longitudinal data (see Appendix B).

3 Including a few whose length of time in job was not known.

4 Including a few people who were not sure if they were in a scheme but thought it possible.

5 Including a few people who did not know if they were a member.

6 All unweighted bases are rounded to the nearest 10

Source: General Lifestyle Survey, Office for National Statistics

Table 6.9   **Current pension scheme membership by sex and number of employees in the establishment**

Employees aged 16 and over excluding government schemes   *Great Britain: 2009[1]*

Pension scheme members	Number of employees at establishment					
	1-2	3-24	25-99	100-999	1000 or more	Total[2]
	Percentages					
Men full time						
Occupational pension[3,4]	39	24	52	69	86	54
Personal pension[5]	24	20	23	21	15	21
Any pension	53	38	62	74	87	62
Women full time						
Occupational pension[3,4]	29	36	53	72	83	58
Personal pension[5]	14	14	16	18	14	16
Any pension	36	42	58	75	84	62
Women part time						
Occupational pension[3,4]	13	26	44	55	84	40
Personal pension[5]	9	12	10	11	19	11
Any pension	18	31	47	59	85	44
Weighted base (000's) =100%						
Men full time	*460*	*2,769*	*2,425*	*3,801*	*1,139*	*10,699*
Women full time	*200*	*1,863*	*1,840*	*2,238*	*908*	*7,103*
Women part time	*306*	*1,967*	*1,227*	*1,188*	*337*	*5,060*
Unweighted sample[6]						
Men full time	*140*	*810*	*700*	*1090*	*320*	*3,080*
Women full time	*60*	*560*	*540*	*650*	*270*	*2,100*
Women part time	*100*	*620*	*400*	*370*	*110*	*1,610*

1 Results for 2009 include longitudinal data (see Appendix B).

2 Includes a few people for whom the number of employees at establishment was not known.

3 Including a few people who were not sure if they were in a scheme but thought it possible.

4 Occupational pension schemes are schemes provided by employers. They do not include group personal pensions, group stakeholder pensions or group self-invested personal pensions.

5 Personal pensions include group personal pensions, group stakeholder pensions and may include group self-invested personal pensions.

6 All unweighted bases are rounded to the nearest 10

Note: Shaded figures indicate the estimates are unreliable and any analysis using these figures may be invalid. Any use of these shaded figures must be accompanied by this disclaimer.

Source: General Lifestyle Survey, Office for National Statistics

Table 6.10 Membership of current employer's occupational pension scheme by sex and number of employees at the establishment

Employees aged 16 and over excluding government schemes   *Great Britain: 2009[1]*

Pension scheme coverage	Number of employees at establishment					
	1-2	3-24	25-99	100-999	1000 or more	Total[2]
	%	%	%	%	%	%
Men full time						
Current employer has a pension scheme						
Member[3]	39 ⎤ 48	24 ⎤ 36	52 ⎤ 68	69 ⎤ 85	86 ⎤ 94	54 ⎤ 68
Not a member[4]	10 ⎦	12 ⎦	16 ⎦	16 ⎦	9 ⎦	14 ⎦
Current employer does not have a pension scheme	52	62	31	14	6	31
Not known if employer has a pension scheme	0	2	1	1	0	1
Weighted base (000's) =100%	*460*	*2,761*	*2,422*	*3,776*	*1,139*	*10,660*
Unweighted sample[5]	*140*	*810*	*700*	*1,080*	*320*	*3,070*
	%	%	%	%	%	%
Women full time						
Current employer has a pension scheme						
Member[3]	29 ⎤ 40	36 ⎤ 54	53 ⎤ 72	72 ⎤ 90	83 ⎤ 96	58 ⎤ 75
Not a member[4]	12 ⎦	18 ⎦	19 ⎦	18 ⎦	13 ⎦	18 ⎦
Current employer does not have a pension scheme	58	46	27	9	4	24
Not known if employer has a pension scheme	*	1	1	0	0	0
Weighted base (000's) =100%	*200*	*1,863*	*1,840*	*2,238*	*908*	*7,099*
Unweighted sample[5]	*60*	*560*	*540*	*650*	*270*	*2,100*
	%	%	%	%	%	%
Women part time						
Current employer has a pension scheme						
Member[3]	13 ⎤ 25	26 ⎤ 43	44 ⎤ 70	55 ⎤ 82	84 ⎤ 92	40 ⎤ 61
Not a member[4]	12 ⎦	17 ⎦	26 ⎦	27 ⎦	8 ⎦	20 ⎦
Current employer does not have a pension scheme	71	56	27	17	8	38
Not known if employer has a pension scheme	*	1	2	*	0	1
Weighted base (000's) =100%	*303*	*1,967*	*1,223*	*1,188*	*337*	*5,053*
Unweighted sample[5]	*100*	*620*	*400*	*370*	*110*	*1,610*

1 Results for 2009 include longitudinal data (see Appendix B).

2 Includes a few people for whom the number of employees at establishment was not known

3 Including a few people who were not sure if they were in a scheme but thought it possible.

4 Including people who were not eligible and a few people who did not know if they were a member.

5 All unweighted bases are rounded to the nearest 10

* Information is suppressed for low cell count as a measure of disclosure control

Source: General Lifestyle Survey, Office for National Statistics

Table 6.11   Membership of current employer's occupational pension scheme by sex and industry group[1]

Employees aged 16 and over excluding government schemes   ***Great Britain: 2006[2], 2007[2] and 2008[2] combined***

Pension scheme members	Industry group[3]										
	Agriculture, forestry, fishing	Coal mining, energy and water supply	Mining (excl coal), manufact-ure of metals, minerals and chemicals	Metal goods, engineer-ing and vehicle	Other manufact-uring	Construc-tion	Distribu-tion, hotels, catering repairs	Transport and commun-ications	Banking, finance, insurance business services	Public and other personal services	Total
				Percentage with an occupational pension							
Men full time	19	70	55	55	51	38	30	56	51	78	54
Women full time	6	73	*	54	48	40	27	47	54	71	58
Women part time	16	32	*	34	27	24	15	43	35	52	38
Unweighted sample[4,5]											
Men full time	*130*	*270*	*30*	*1,360*	*1,150*	*1,230*	*1,610*	*1,110*	*2,000*	*2,550*	*11,430*
Women full time	*20*	*50*	***	*270*	*420*	*170*	*1,100*	*300*	*1,360*	*3,920*	*7,630*
Women part time	*30*	*10*	***	*80*	*130*	*80*	*1,520*	*130*	*620*	*2,860*	*5,460*

1 The Industry classification has been updated for the 2009 survey to the Standard Industrial Classification (SIC) 1997. As a consequence it has not been possible to produce this table for the 2009 results. The latest estimates are therefore for 2008 and use SIC 1992.

2 Results from 2006 onwards include longitudinal data (see Appendix B).

3 Standard Industrial Classification, 1992.

4 Weighted bases not shown for combined data sets.

5 All unweighted bases are rounded to the nearest 10

* Information is suppressed for unweighted sample sizes below 10 as a measure of disclosure control

Source: General Lifestyle Survey, Office for National Statistics

Table 6.12   Membership of personal pension scheme by sex and whether working full time or part time: self-employed persons

Self-employed persons aged 16 and over   ***Great Britain: 2009[2]***

Pension scheme coverage	Men			Women		
	Working full time	Working part time	Total	Working full time	Working part time	Total
	%	%	%	%	%	%
Informant belongs to a personal pension scheme	38	16	35	25	18	22
Informant no longer contributes to a personal pension scheme	23	40	26	22	19	20
Informant has never had a personal pension scheme	39	44	39	53	63	58
Weighted base (000's) =100%	*1,744*	*317*	*2,061*	*469*	*475*	*944*
Unweighted sample[3]	*520*	*120*	*640*	*150*	*160*	*300*

1 Results for 2009 include longitudinal data (see Appendix B).

2 All unweighted bases are rounded to the nearest 10

Source: General Lifestyle Survey, Office for National Statistics

Table 6.13 Membership of a personal pension scheme for self-employed men working full time: 1991 to 2009 [1]

Self-employed persons aged 16 and over   *Great Britain*

Pension scheme coverage	Unweighted							Weighted										
	1991	1992	1993	1994	1995	1996	1998	1998	2000	2001	2002	2003	2004	2005[2]	2006	2007	2008	2009
									Percentages									
Men working full time																		
Informant belongs to a personal pension scheme	66	65	67	60	61	64	65	64	54	54	52	49	49	45	45	42	45	38
Informant no longer contributes to a personal pension scheme	7	9	9	10	11	11	10	10	12	15	14	15	19	20	21	21	24	23
Informant has never had a personal pension scheme	27	26	24	30	28	25	26	27	34	32	34	36	33	35	34	37	32	39
Weighted base (000's) =100% [3,4]								*1,958*	*1,904*	*1,942*	*1,926*	*1,871*	*1,834*	*1,827*	*1,854*	*1,884*	*1,734*	*1,744*
Unweighted sample [3,4]	*930*	*870*	*850*	*840*	*880*	*700*	*680*		*630*	*700*	*700*	*780*	*640*	*960*	*720*	*660*	*600*	*520*

1 Results from 2006 include longitudinal data (see Appendix B).
2 2005 data includes last quarter of 2004/5 data due to survey change from financial year to calendar year.
3 Trend tables show unweighted and weighted figures for 1998 to give an indication of the effect of the weighting. For the weighted data (1998 and 2000 to 2007) the weighted base
  (000's) is the base for percentages. Unweighted data (up to 1998) are based on the unweighted sample.
4 All unweighted bases are rounded to the nearest 10

Source: General Lifestyle Survey, Office for National Statistics

Table 6.14   Membership of personal pension scheme by sex and length of time in self-employment, 2005-2007[1]

Self-employed persons aged 16 and over   ***Great Britain: 2005[2], 2006[2] and 2007[2] combined***

	Length of time in self-employment			
	Less than 2 years	2 years, but less than 5 years	5 years or more	Total[3]
	Percentage of self-employed who belong to a personal pension scheme			
Men full time	18	33	51	43
Women full time	10	24	38	30
Women part time	17	10	23	19
Unweighted sample [4,5]				
Men full time	*300*	*340*	*1,440*	*2,090*
Women full time	*100*	*110*	*360*	*570*
Women part time	*110*	*100*	*330*	*550*

1   Data on the length of time with current employer were not collected in 2008 and 2009, therefore, the latest estimates are for 2007.

2   2005 data includes last quarter of 204/5 data due to survey change from financial year to calendar year.

3   Results from 2006 include longitudinal data (see Appendix B).

4   Weighted bases not shown for combined data sets.

5   All unweighted bases are rounded to the nearest 10

Source: General Lifestyle Survey, Office for National Statistics

Table 7.1   Self perception of general health: 2005 to 2009

Persons aged 16 and over[1]   *Great Britain*

	2005[2,3]	2006[3,4]	2007[3,4]	2008[4]	2009[4]	Weighted base 2009 (000's) =100%	Unweighted sample[5]
	%	%	%	%	%		
Percentage who reported their general health was:							
Very Good	34	33	34	39	40	16,861	5,100
Good	41	43	43	40	39	16,250	5,320
Fair	18	17	17	16	15	6,485	2,240
Bad	6	5	5	4	5	1,945	670
Very Bad	1	1	1	1	1	433	160
Weighted base (000's) =100%	31,167	42,745	42,737	42,257	41,973		
Unweighted sample[5]	18,010	16,720	15,670	14,720	13,480		

1 This question was first introduced in April 2005 (see Appendix E for question wording).
2 2005 estimates are based on data collected from April to December. From 2006 estimates are based on the full calendar year.
3 There are potential exposure and order effects associated with the five-category general health question prior to 2008. Particular care should therefore be taken if drawing conclusions concerning the changes between 2007 and 2008.
4 Results from 2006 include longitudinal data (see Appendix B).
5 All unweighted bases are rounded to the nearest 10

Source: General Lifestyle Survey, Office for National Statistics

Table 7.2   Trends in self-reported sickness by sex and age, 1972 to 2009: percentage of persons who reported

(a) long-standing illness or disability
(b) limiting long-standing illness or disability
(c) restricted activity in the 14 days before interview due to illness or injury (acute sickness)

All persons   *Great Britain*

	Unweighted data								Weighted data											Weighted base 2009 (000's) =100%[3]	Unweighted sample 2009 [3,5]
	1972	1975	1981	1985	1991	1995	1996	1998	1998	2000	2001	2002	2003	2004	2005[1]	2006[2]	2007[2]	2008[2]	2009[2]		
Percentage who reported:																					
(a) long-standing illness or disability																					
Males																					
0-4	5	8	12	11	13	14	14	15	15	14	17	17	14	15	14	11	8	9	9	1,871	580
5-15[4]	9	11	17	18	17	20	19	21	21	23	20	21	18	19	19	17	17	15	14	3,883	1,310
16-44[4]	14	17	22	21	23	23	27	24	24	23	22	23	20	20	22	21	20	18	18	9,053	2,270
45-64	29	35	40	42	42	43	46	44	44	45	44	46	41	43	44	45	43	39	42	6,580	2,200
65-74	48	50	51	55	61	55	61	59	59	61	58	65	62	57	58	63	60	58	60	2,310	1,030
75 and over	54	63	60	58	63	56	64	68	68	63	64	71	61	63	65	70	66	64	64	1,719	680
Total	20	23	28	29	31	31	34	33	33	33	32	34	31	31	32	33	31	29	30	25,416	8,070
Females																					
0-4	3	6	7	9	10	11	13	15	15	13	12	12	10	11	10	10	11	7	7	1,746	540
5-15[4]	6	9	13	13	15	17	16	19	19	18	16	19	17	15	16	15	14	10	10	3,539	1,200
16-44[4]	13	16	21	22	23	22	27	23	23	22	21	25	22	22	24	23	22	20	20	10,062	2,820
45-64	31	33	41	43	41	39	47	43	43	42	42	44	41	42	43	44	41	38	39	7,243	2,550
65-74	48	54	58	56	55	54	58	59	59	54	56	61	59	55	61	63	56	53	56	2,557	1,060
75 and over	65	61	70	65	65	66	68	65	65	64	63	72	65	63	64	70	65	68	67	2,447	890
Total	21	25	30	31	32	31	35	34	34	32	31	35	32	32	33	34	32	30	31	27,595	9,040
All persons																					
0-4	4	7	10	10	12	13	13	15	15	14	14	15	12	13	12	11	10	8	8	3,617	1,120
5-15[4]	8	10	15	16	16	19	18	20	20	20	18	20	18	17	18	16	16	12	12	7,422	2,510
16-44[4]	13	16	21	22	23	23	27	24	24	22	22	24	21	21	23	22	21	19	19	19,115	5,080
45-64	30	34	41	43	41	41	47	44	44	44	43	45	41	43	43	45	42	39	40	13,823	4,740
65-74	48	52	55	56	58	55	59	59	59	57	57	63	60	56	60	63	58	56	58	4,867	2,090
75 and over	65	62	67	63	65	63	66	66	66	64	63	72	64	63	64	70	65	67	66	4,166	1,560
Total	21	24	29	30	31	31	35	33	33	32	32	35	31	31	33	33	31	30	30	53,011	17,110
Percentage who reported:																					
(b) limiting long-standing illness or disability																					
Males																					
0-4	::	3	3	4	4	5	4	4	4	4	5	5	4	4	5	3	2	2	3	1,871	580
5-15[4]	::	6	8	8	7	8	8	8	8	9	9	8	7	8	7	7	6	7	7	3,883	1,310
16-44[4]	::	9	10	10	10	12	14	12	12	11	10	12	10	10	11	10	11	9	9	9,050	2,270
45-64	::	24	26	27	25	28	31	28	28	27	28	28	24	26	26	23	25	22	25	6,577	2,190
65-74	::	36	35	38	40	37	42	36	36	38	36	43	37	33	36	37	37	33	36	2,310	1,030
75 and over	::	46	44	43	46	41	50	48	48	44	47	52	41	43	44	47	47	45	42	1,719	680
Total	::	14	16	16	17	18	21	19	19	18	18	20	17	17	18	17	18	16	17	25,410	8,060

443

Table 7.2

	Unweighted data								Weighted data											Weighted base 2009 (000's)³ =100%³	Unweighted sample 3,5 2009
	1972	1975	1981	1985	1991	1995	1996	1998	1998	2000	2001	2002	2003	2004	2005¹	2006²	2007²	2008²	2009²		2009
Females																					
0-4	..	2	3	3	3	3	4	5	5	4	4	3	4	4	3	3	3	3	3	1,746	540
5-15⁴	..	4	6	6	5	8	8	8	8	8	8	9	7	7	7	6	5	4	5	3,539	1,200
16-44⁴	..	9	11	11	11	13	16	13	13	11	12	14	11	12	13	12	12	11	11	10,062	2,820
45-64	..	22	26	26	25	26	32	29	29	27	26	28	25	24	26	27	25	23	23	7,240	2,550
65-74	..	39	41	38	34	37	40	39	39	35	37	39	37	33	39	39	36	34	35	2,557	1,060
75 and over	..	49	56	51	51	52	53	51	51	48	45	53	46	48	48	51	48	48	50	2,447	890
Total	..	16	19	18	18	20	23	21	21	19	19	22	19	19	20	20	19	18	19	27,592	9,040
All persons																					
0-4	..	2	3	3	4	4	4	4	4	4	4	4	4	4	4	3	3	3	3	3,617	1,120
5-15⁴	..	5	7	7	6	8	8	8	8	8	8	8	7	8	7	7	6	6	6	7,422	2,510
16-44⁴	..	9	11	10	10	12	15	13	13	11	11	13	11	11	12	11	11	10	10	19,112	5,080
45-64	..	23	26	26	25	27	32	28	28	27	27	28	24	25	26	25	25	23	24	13,817	4,740
65-74	..	38	38	38	37	37	41	38	37	37	36	41	37	33	37	38	37	33	36	4,867	2,090
75 and over	..	48	52	48	49	48	52	50	50	47	46	53	44	46	47	50	48	46	47	4,166	1,560
Total	..	15	17	17	18	19	22	20	20	19	19	21	18	18	19	19	18	17	18	53,002	17,110

1 2005 data includes last quarter of 2004/5 data due to survey change from financial year to calendar year
2 Results from 2006 include longitudinal data (see Appendix B).
3 Trend tables show unweighted and weighted figures for 1998 to give an indication of the effect of the weighting. Bases for earlier years can be found in GLF/GHS reports for each year.
4 These age-groups were 5-14 and 15-44 in 1972 to 1975
5 All unweighted bases are rounded to the nearest 10
.. Data are not available.

Source: General Lifestyle Survey, Office for National Statistics

444

Table 7.2 - continued

All persons

Percentage who reported:

(c) restricted activity in the 14 days before interview due to illness or injury (acute sickness)

	Unweighted data									Weighted data											Weighted base³ 2009 (000's) =100%	Unweighted sample³·⁵ 2009
	1972	1975	1981	1985	1991	1993	1995	1996	1998	1998	2000	2001	2002	2003	2004	2005¹	2006²	2007²	2008²	2009²		
Males																						
0-4	5	10	13	13	11	13	11	12	10	10	11	9	10	11	10	9	8	8	6	6	1,872	580
5-15⁴	6	9	12	11	11	11	10	10	9	9	10	9	9	8	10	9	7	7	6	5	3,883	1,310
16-44⁴	7	7	8	9	9	11	10	13	11	11	10	10	11	9	8	9	9	9	9	8	9,043	2,270
45-64	9	10	12	11	12	15	15	18	18	18	17	17	17	15	15	15	14	13	13	13	6,581	2,200
65-74	10	8	11	13	14	16	17	19	18	18	20	16	19	18	16	15	16	15	16	15	2,307	1,030
75 and over	10	12	15	17	18	17	20	23	24	24	23	23	24	20	20	18	19	16	17	17	1,715	680
Total	7	9	11	11	11	13	13	15	14	14	13	13	14	12	12	11	11	11	10	10	25,401	8,060
Females																						
0-4	6	8	12	13	10	10	11	9	8	8	7	8	10	9	11	9	7	7	7	7	1,746	540
5-15⁴	5	7	11	12	9	11	10	9	11	11	11	10	9	9	7	8	8	6	6	6	3,539	1,200
16-44⁴	8	10	11	13	12	13	13	15	13	13	12	12	13	12	12	13	11	11	10	11	10,049	2,810
45-64	9	10	13	14	13	17	17	22	20	20	19	18	19	19	18	17	17	16	15	14	7,239	2,550
65-74	10	12	17	18	16	19	20	21	23	23	21	21	20	22	20	21	21	17	20	17	2,557	1,060
75 and over	14	13	21	23	21	23	26	25	27	27	27	26	28	25	26	24	24	21	19	18	2,451	890
Total	8	10	13	14	13	15	15	17	16	16	15	15	16	15	14	15	14	13	12	12	27,581	9,040
All persons																						
0-4	6	9	13	13	11	11	11	10	9	9	9	9	10	10	10	9	8	7	7	6	3,619	1,120
5-15⁴	6	8	12	11	10	11	10	10	10	10	10	10	9	9	9	8	7	7	6	6	7,422	2,510
16-44⁴	8	9	10	11	10	12	12	14	12	12	11	11	12	11	10	11	10	10	9	9	19,092	5,080
45-64	9	10	12	12	13	16	16	20	19	19	18	17	18	17	16	16	15	15	14	13	13,819	4,740
65-74	10	11	14	16	15	18	19	20	21	21	21	19	20	20	18	18	19	16	18	16	4,864	2,090
75 and over	13	13	19	21	20	21	24	24	26	26	25	25	26	23	23	22	22	19	18	18	4,166	1,560
Total	8	9	12	12	12	14	14	16	15	15	14	14	15	14	13	13	13	12	12	11	52,981	17,110

1 Note: 2005 data includes last quarter of 2004/5 data due to survey change from financial year to calendar year.
2 Results from 2006 include longitudinal data (see Appendix B).
3 Trend tables show unweighted and weighted figures for 1998 to give an indication of the effect of the weighting. Bases for earlier years can be found in GLF/GHS reports for each year.
4 These age-groups were 5-14 and 15-44 in 1972 to 1975
5 All unweighted bases are rounded to the nearest 10

Source: General Lifestyle Survey, Office for National Statistics

Table 7.3   **Acute sickness: average number of restricted activity days per person per year due to illness or injury, by sex and age**

                                  Great Britain: 2009[1]

	Number of days			Weighted bases (000's) =100%			Unweighted sample[2]		
	Males	Females	Total	*Males*	*Females*	*Total*	*Males*	*Females*	*Total*
Age									
0- 4	7	9	8	*1,872*	*1,746*	*3,619*	*580*	*540*	*1,120*
5-15	8	7	8	*3,883*	*3,539*	*7,422*	*1,310*	*1,200*	*2,510*
16-44	15	21	18	*9,043*	*10,049*	*19,092*	*2,270*	*2,810*	*5,080*
45-64	30	30	30	*6,581*	*7,230*	*13,810*	*2,200*	*2,540*	*4,740*
65-74	34	41	38	*2,307*	*2,557*	*4,864*	*1,030*	*1,060*	*2,090*
75 and over	47	51	49	*1,715*	*2,451*	*4,166*	*680*	*890*	*1,560*
Total	21	25	23	*25,401*	*27,571*	*52,972*	*8,060*	*9,030*	*17,100*

1   Results for 2009 include longitudinal data (see Appendix B).

2   All unweighted bases are rounded to the nearest 10

Source: General Lifestyle Survey, Office for National Statistics

Table 7.4 Chronic sickness: prevalence of reported long-standing illness or disability by sex, age and socio-economic classification of household reference person

All persons   Great Britain: 2009[1]

Socio-economic classification of household reference person[2]	Males					Females				
	Age					Age				
	0-15	16-44	45-64	65 and over	Total	0-15	16-44	45-64	65 and over	Total

Percentage who reported long-standing illness or disability

	Males 0-15	16-44	45-64	65 and over	Total	Females 0-15	16-44	45-64	65 and over	Total
Large employers and higher managerial	10	12	30	52	22	8	12	23	44	16
Higher professional	7	15	34	58	24	8	16	29	49	22
Lower managerial and professional	13	17	37	60	28	10	21	38	62	31
[combined]	[11]	[16]	[35]	[58]	[26]	[9]	[18]	[34]	[58]	[26]
Intermediate	11	24	45	57	32	7	21	38	66	36
Small employers and own account	9	14	37	61	29	8	20	39	58	29
[combined]	[10]	[18]	[40]	[60]	[30]	[7]	[20]	[39]	[63]	[32]
Lower supervisory and technical	12	16	42	67	33	11	22	40	58	31
Semi-routine	13	23	53	62	33	13	21	45	65	35
Routine	17	23	54	69	40	8	24	51	65	37
[combined]	[14]	[21]	[49]	[66]	[35]	[11]	[22]	[45]	[63]	[35]
Never worked and long-term unemployed	12	22 *(shaded)*	50 *(shaded)*	54 *(shaded)*	30	12	32	63 *(shaded)*	59 *(shaded)*	38
All persons	12	18	42	62	30	9	20	39	62	31

Weighted bases (000's) =100%

	Males 0-15	16-44	45-64	65 and over	Total	Females 0-15	16-44	45-64	65 and over	Total
Large employers and higher managerial	423	604	448	232	1,707	493	694	490	148	1,825
Higher professional	581	1,017	725	349	2,672	380	955	625	213	2,173
Lower managerial and professional	1,429	2,403	1,700	887	6,419	1,164	2,598	1,998	1,084	6,844
Intermediate	348	608	456	228	1,640	388	750	729	702	2,569
Small employers and own account	455	757	724	431	2,366	498	815	661	383	2,358
Lower supervisory and technical	597	1,025	781	676	3,079	547	1,043	742	521	2,852
Semi-routine	843	1,108	686	456	3,093	721	1,388	960	873	3,942
Routine	575	816	750	571	2,712	626	925	720	744	3,015
Never worked and long-term unemployed	246	263	169	139	817	241	348	113	245	947
All persons	5,754	9,053	6,580	4,029	25,416	5,285	10,062	7,243	5,004	27,595

Unweighted sample[3]

	Males 0-15	16-44	45-64	65 and over	Total	Females 0-15	16-44	45-64	65 and over	Total
Large employers and higher managerial	140	160	160	100	570	160	200	180	60	600
Higher professional	190	240	240	150	820	130	270	220	100	720
Lower managerial and professional	460	610	600	380	2,040	390	740	710	430	2,270
Intermediate	130	150	150	90	520	130	210	250	250	840
Small employers and own account	140	190	230	190	750	150	220	230	160	760
Lower supervisory and technical	200	260	250	280	1,000	180	290	260	210	930
Semi-routine	280	280	220	200	970	250	380	330	330	1,290
Routine	190	210	250	240	880	200	260	250	280	990
Never worked and long-term unemployed	90	60	50	60	260	90	110	40	90	330
All persons	1,890	2,270	2,200	1,710	8,070	1,740	2,820	2,550	1,940	9,040

1 Results for 2009 include longitudinal data (see Appendix B).
2 Where the household reference person was a full-time student or had an inadequately described occupation these are not shown as separate categories but are included in the figure for all persons (see Appendix A).
3 All unweighted bases are rounded to the nearest 10

Note: Shaded figures indicate the estimates are unreliable and any analysis using these figures may be invalid. Any use of these shaded figures must be accompanied by this disclaimer.

Source: General Lifestyle Survey, Office for National Statistics

Table 7.5   Chronic sickness: prevalence of reported limiting long-standing illness or disability by sex, age and socio-economic classification of household reference person

All persons   *Great Britain: 2009[1]*

Percentage who reported limiting long-standing illness or disability

Socio-economic classification of household reference person[2]	Males 0-15	Males 16-44	Males 45-64	Males 65 and over	Males Total	Females 0-15	Females 16-44	Females 45-64	Females 65 and over	Females Total
Large employers and higher managerial	4	8	14	25	11	5	6	10	26	8
Higher professional	5	6	16	35	12	2	7	12	28	10
Lower managerial and professional	5	8	21	35	14	5	10	19	37	16
Intermediate	7	12	26	30	17	5	11	24	45	23
Small employers and own account	5	7	21	38	16	4	10	24	38	17
Lower supervisory and technical	6	8	24	44	20	5	12	22	42	19
Semi-routine	6	14	39	44	22	5	13	31	48	24
Routine	11	15	34	46	26	4	11	38	50	26
Never worked and long-term unemployed	8	10	38	29	19	5	27	52	42	28
All persons	6	9	25	39	17	4	11	23	42	19

Grouped (bracketed) combined figures:

Grouping	Males 0-15	Males 16-44	Males 45-64	Males 65 and over	Males Total	Females 0-15	Females 16-44	Females 45-64	Females 65 and over	Females Total
Large employers and higher managerial + Higher professional	5	7	19	34	13	4	9	16	35	14
Intermediate + Small employers and own account	6	9	23	35	16	4	11	24	43	20
Lower supervisory and technical + Semi-routine	7	12	32	45	22	4	13	30	47	23

Weighted bases (000's) = 100%

Socio-economic classification of household reference person[2]	Males 0-15	Males 16-44	Males 45-64	Males 65 and over	Males Total	Females 0-15	Females 16-44	Females 45-64	Females 65 and over	Females Total
Large employers and higher managerial	423	604	448	232	1,707	493	694	490	148	1,825
Higher professional	581	1,017	722	349	2,669	380	955	622	213	2,170
Lower managerial and professional	1,429	2,403	1,700	887	6,419	1,164	2,598	1,998	1,084	6,844
Intermediate	348	608	456	228	1,640	388	750	729	702	2,569
Small employers and own account	455	757	724	431	2,366	498	815	661	383	2,358
Lower supervisory and technical	597	1,025	781	676	3,079	547	1,043	742	521	2,852
Semi-routine	843	1,105	686	456	3,090	721	1,388	960	873	3,942
Routine	575	816	750	571	2,712	626	925	720	744	3,015
Never worked and long-term unemployed	246	263	169	139	817	241	348	113	245	947
All persons	5,754	9,050	6,577	4,029	25,410	5,285	10,062	7,240	5,004	27,592

Unweighted sample[3]

Socio-economic classification of household reference person[2]	Males 0-15	Males 16-44	Males 45-64	Males 65 and over	Males Total	Females 0-15	Females 16-44	Females 45-64	Females 65 and over	Females Total
Large employers and higher managerial	140	160	160	100	570	160	200	180	60	600
Higher professional	190	240	240	150	820	130	270	220	100	720
Lower managerial and professional	460	610	600	380	2,040	390	740	710	430	2,270
Intermediate	130	150	150	90	520	130	210	250	250	840
Small employers and own account	140	190	230	190	750	150	220	230	160	760
Lower supervisory and technical	200	260	250	280	1,000	180	290	260	210	930
Semi-routine	280	270	220	200	970	250	380	330	330	1,290
Routine	190	210	250	240	880	200	260	250	280	990
Never worked and long-term unemployed	90	60	50	60	260	90	110	40	90	330
All persons	1,890	2,270	2,190	1,710	8,060	1,740	2,820	2,550	1,940	9,040

1 Results for 2009 include longitudinal data (see Appendix B).
2 Where the household reference person was a full-time student or had an inadequately described occupation these are not shown as separate categories but are included in the figure for all persons (see Appendix A).
3 All unweighted bases are rounded to the nearest 10

Note: Shaded figures indicate the estimates are unreliable and any analysis using these figures may be invalid. Any use of these shaded figures must be accompanied by this disclaimer.

Source: General Lifestyle Survey, Office for National Statistics

Table 7.6 Acute sickness

(a) Prevalence of reported restricted activity in the 14 days before interview due to illness or injury, by sex, age, and socio-economic classification of household reference person

(b) Average number of restricted activity days per person per year due to illness or injury, by sex, age, and socio-economic classification of household reference person

All persons

Great Britain: 2009[1]

(a) Percentage who reported restricted activity in the 14 days before interview due to illness or injury

Socio-economic classification of household reference person[2]	Males 0-15	Males 16-44	Males 45-64	Males 65 and over	Males Total	Females 0-15	Females 16-44	Females 45-64	Females 65 and over	Females Total	All persons 0-15	All persons 16-44	All persons 45-64	All persons 65 and over	All persons Total
Large employers and higher managerial	4	6	7	8	6	6	9	7	16	6	5	8	7	16	8
Higher professional	7	6	9	15	8	4	15	13	8	8	7	9	13	8	12
Lower managerial and professional	5	10	13	16	11	8	10	16	16	11	5	10	16	16	12
Intermediate	4	9	12	15	10	11	9	16	18	10	7	11	12	18	14
Small employers and own account	7	5	10	15	9	8	11	10	18	9	5	10	10	18	11
Lower supervisory and technical	5	8	12	15	10	4	7	13	21	10	6	7	13	21	11
Semi-routine	7	7	18	19	11	7	12	14	19	11	4	12	14	19	13
Routine	6	8	13	16	11	4	9	15	20	11	7	9	15	20	12
Never worked and long-term unemployed	8	4	23	11	10	*	15	19	14	10	8	15	19	14	12
All persons	6	8	13	15	10	6	11	14	18	10	8	11	14	18	12

(b) Average number of restricted activity days per person per year due to illness or injury

Socio-economic classification of household reference person[2]	Males 0-15	Males 16-44	Males 45-64	Males 65 and over	Males Total	Females 0-15	Females 16-44	Females 45-64	Females 65 and over	Females Total	All persons 0-15	All persons 16-44	All persons 45-64	All persons 65 and over	All persons Total
Large employers and higher managerial	3	12	12	13	10	11	13	12	41	10	11	13	12	41	14
Higher professional	7	12	24	35	17	4	21	24	23	17	4	21	24	23	19
Lower managerial and professional	7	16	30	40	21	8	21	32	40	21	8	21	32	40	25
Intermediate	4	19	29	34	21	17	13	33	43	21	17	13	33	43	28
Small employers and own account	14	8	23	40	19	9	20	19	53	19	9	20	19	53	23
Lower supervisory and technical	5	16	31	44	24	3	19	29	46	24	3	19	29	46	23
Semi-routine	12	19	40	50	26	11	27	36	51	26	11	27	36	51	31
Routine	11	15	37	45	27	5	20	35	53	27	5	20	35	53	29
Never worked and long-term unemployed	9	9	68	35	25	3	30	48	41	25	8	30	48	41	28
All persons	8	15	30	40	21	8	21	30	45	21	8	21	30	45	25

Weighted bases (000's) = 100%

Socio-economic classification of household reference person	Males 0-15	Males 16-44	Males 45-64	Males 65 and over	Males Total	Females 0-15	Females 16-44	Females 45-64	Females 65 and over	Females Total	All persons Total
Large employers and higher managerial	423	604	448	148	1,707	493	694	490	232	570	1,825
Higher professional	581	1,017	726	213	2,670	380	955	622	347	820	2,170
Lower managerial and professional	1,429	2,400	1,702	1,084	6,419	1,164	2,598	2,000	887	2,040	6,846
Intermediate	348	609	456	702	1,640	388	750	729	228	520	2,569
Small employers and own account	455	757	722	383	2,364	498	813	661	431	1,000	2,355
Lower supervisory and technical	597	1,021	781	518	3,074	547	1,043	742	676	960	2,850
Semi-routine	843	1,105	686	873	3,086	721	1,382	956	452	880	3,933
Routine	575	816	750	748	2,712	626	923	720	571	260	3,017
Never worked and long-term unemployed	248	263	169	246	819	241	348	113	139		948
All persons	5,498	8,592	6,440	4,915	24,491	5,058	9,506	7,025	3,962	8,060	26,504

Unweighted sample[3]

Socio-economic classification of household reference person	Males 0-15	Males 16-44	Males 45-64								All persons Total
Large employers and higher managerial	140	160	160								600
Higher professional	190	240	240								720
Lower managerial and professional	460	600	600								2,270
Intermediate	130	150	150								840
Small employers and own account	140	190	230								760
Lower supervisory and technical	200	260	250								930
Semi-routine	280	270	220								990
Routine	190	210	250								1,280
Never worked and long-term unemployed	100	60	50								330
All persons	1,890	2,270	2,200								9,040

1 Results for 2009 include longitudinal data (see Appendix B)

2 Where the household reference person was a full-time student or had an inadequately described occupation these are not shown as separate categories but are included in the figure for all persons (see Appendix A).

3 All unweighted bases are rounded to the nearest 10

Note: Shaded figures indicate the estimates are unreliable and any analysis using these figures may be invalid. Any use of these shaded figures must be accompanied by this disclaimer.

* Information is suppressed for low cell count as a measure of disclosure control

Source: General Lifestyle Survey, Office for National Statistics

Table 7.7 Chronic sickness: prevalence of reported long-standing illness or disability by sex, age, and economic activity status

Persons aged 16 and over

Great Britain: 2009[1]

Economic activity status	Men				Women			
	16-44	45-64	65 and over	Total	16-44	45-64	65 and over	Total
Percentage who reported long-standing illness or disability								
Working	15	33	43	23	19	31	33	24
Unemployed	16	44	67	25	23	41	41	28
Economically inactive	35	68	64	59	24	58	64	52
Total[2]	18	42	62	35	21	39	62	36
Weighted bases (000's) =100%								
Working	*6,862*	*4,744*	*415*	*12,021*	*6,980*	*4,808*	*291*	*12,079*
Unemployed	*976*	*412*	*31*	*1,419*	*694*	*190*	*31*	*914*
Economically inactive	*1,203*	*1,424*	*3,583*	*6,210*	*2,381*	*2,245*	*4,683*	*9,309*
Total[2]	*9,044*	*6,580*	*4,029*	*19,653*	*10,059*	*7,243*	*5,004*	*22,307*
Unweighted sample[3]								
Working	*1,730*	*1,580*	*180*	*3,500*	*1,940*	*1,650*	*120*	*3,710*
Unemployed	*230*	*130*	*10*	*380*	*190*	*60*	*10*	*260*
Economically inactive	*300*	*480*	*1,520*	*2290*	*680*	*840*	*1,810*	*3,340*
Total[2]	*2,270*	*2,200*	*1,710*	*6170*	*2,820*	*2,550*	*1,940*	*7,300*

1 Results for 2009 include longitudinal data (see Appendix B)

2 Total includes a small number of people for whom economic activity status could not be derived

3 All unweighted bases are rounded to the nearest 10

Note: Shaded figures indicate the estimates are unreliable and any analysis using these figures may be invalid. Any use of these shaded figures must be accompanied by this disclaimer.

Source: General Lifestyle Survey, Office for National Statistics

Table 7.8   Chronic sickness: prevalence of reported limiting long-standing illness or disability by sex, age, and economic activity status

Persons aged 16 and over   *Great Britain: 2009[1]*

Economic activity status	Men				Women			
Age	16-44	45-64	65 and over	Total	16-44	45-64	65 and over	Total
Percentage who reported limiting long-standing illness or disability								
Working	6	14	14	10	9	13	15	11
Unemployed	10	27	56	16	11	27	*	14
Economically inactive	29	58	41	43	19	45	44	38
Total[2]	9	25	39	21	11	23	42	22
Weighted bases (000's) =100%								
Working	6,860	4,741	415	12,016	6,980	4,805	291	12,076
Unemployed	976	412	31	1,419	694	190	31	914
Economically inactive	1,203	1,424	3,583	6,210	2,381	2,245	4,683	9,309
Total[2]	9,041	6,577	4,029	19,647	10,059	7,240	5,004	22,304
Unweighted sample[3]								
Working	1,730	1,580	180	3,500	1,940	1,650	120	3,710
Unemployed	230	130	10	380	190	60	10	260
Economically inactive	300	480	1,520	2,290	680	840	1,810	3,340
Total[2]	2,260	2,190	1,710	6,170	2,820	2,550	1,940	7,300

1 Results for 2009 include longitudinal data (see Appendix B).

2 Total includes a small number of people for whom economic activity status could not be derived

3 All unweighted bases are rounded to the nearest 10

Note: Shaded figures indicate the estimates are unreliable and any analysis using these figures may be invalid. Any use of these shaded figures must be accompanied by this disclaimer.

* Information is suppressed for low cell count as a measure of disclosure control

Source: General Lifestyle Survey, Office for National Statistics

Table 7.9 **Acute sickness**
(a) Prevalence of reported restricted activity in the 14 days before interview due to illness or injury, by sex, age and economic activity status
(b) Average number of restricted activity days per person per year due to illness or injury, by sex, age, and economic activity status

Persons aged 16 and over   *Great Britain: 2009[1]*

Economic activity status	Age							
	Men				Women			
	16-44	45-64	65 and over	Total	16-44	45-64	65 and over	Total
(a) Percentage who reported restricted activity in the 14 days before interview due to illness or injury								
Working	7	8	12	8	10	9	9	10
Unemployed	4	13	0	6	8	18	0	10
Economically inactive	12	26	16	18	13	23	18	18
Total[2]	8	13	15	11	11	14	18	13
(b) Average number of restricted activity days per person per year due to illness or injury								
Working	14	19	24	16	19	15	19	17
Unemployed	3	30	0	11	18	39	0	22
Economically inactive	30	68	42	45	28	60	48	46
Total[2]	15	30	40	25	21	30	46	29
Weighted bases (000's) =100%								
Working	*6,855*	*4,744*	*412*	*12,012*	*6,971*	*4,803*	*291*	*12,065*
Unemployed	*973*	*412*	*31*	*1,415*	*694*	*190*	*31*	*914*
Economically inactive	*1,203*	*1,424*	*3,579*	*6,206*	*2,378*	*2,245*	*4,686*	*9,309*
Total[2]	*9,034*	*6,581*	*4,022*	*19,636*	*10,046*	*7,239*	*5,007*	*22,292*
Unweighted sample[3]								
Working	*1,730*	*1,580*	*180*	*3,500*	*1,940*	*1,650*	*120*	*3,700*
Unemployed	*230*	*130*	*10*	*380*	*190*	*60*	*10*	*260*
Economically inactive	*300*	*480*	*1,520*	*2,290*	*680*	*840*	*1,810*	*3,340*
Total[2]	*2,260*	*2,200*	*1,710*	*6,170*	*2,810*	*2,550*	*1,940*	*7,300*

1 Results for 2009 include longitudinal data (see Appendix B).
2 Total includes a small number of people for whom economic activity status could not be derived
3 All unweighted bases are rounded to the nearest 10

Note: Shaded figures indicate the estimates are unreliable and any analysis using these figures may be invalid. Any use of these shaded figures must be accompanied by this disclaimer.

Source: General Lifestyle Survey, Office for National Statistics

452

Table 7.10   **Self-reported sickness by sex and Government Office Region: percentage of persons who reported**

(a) long-standing illness or disability
(b) limiting long-standing illness or disability
(c) restricted activity in the 14 days before interview due to illness or injury (acute sickness)

All persons   *Great Britain: 2009[1]*

Government Office Region[2]	(a) Long-standing illness or disability	(b) Limiting long-standing illness or disability	(c) Restricted activity in the 14 days before interview	Weighted base (000's) =100%	Unweighted sample[3]
Males		Percentages			
England					
North East	36	21	8	857	310
North West	34	21	10	3,339	980
Yorkshire and the Humber	31	16	9	2,241	790
East Midlands	29	16	10	2,032	710
West Midlands	30	18	11	2,280	710
East of England	26	15	8	2,653	880
London	22	14	9	3,040	750
South East	30	16	9	3,622	1,090
South West	33	19	13	1,855	680
All England	30	17	10	21,920	6,880
Wales	29	17	11	1,337	480
Scotland	30	21	10	2,159	700
Great Britain	30	17	10	25,416	8,070
Females					
England					
North East	37	23	11	1,081	390
North West	34	20	14	3,318	1,040
Yorkshire and the Humber	33	20	11	2,421	880
East Midlands	30	19	13	2,063	750
West Midlands	32	19	10	2,526	790
East of England	27	16	12	2,702	920
London	26	17	14	3,404	830
South East	30	17	11	3,944	1,230
South West	33	22	13	2,257	870
All England	31	19	12	23,716	7,690
Wales	30	20	11	1,477	540
Scotland	30	18	12	2,401	810
Great Britain	31	19	12	27,595	9,040
All persons					
England					
North East	36	22	10	1,939	700
North West	34	20	12	6,657	2,010
Yorkshire and the Humber	32	18	10	4,661	1,670
East Midlands	30	17	11	4,095	1,450
West Midlands	31	19	11	4,806	1,500
East of England	27	15	10	5,355	1,800
London	24	15	11	6,444	1,580
South East	30	17	10	7,567	2,310
South West	33	21	13	4,113	1,550
All England	30	18	11	45,637	14,570
Wales	30	19	11	2,814	1,020
Scotland	30	19	11	4,560	1,510
Great Britain	30	18	11	53,011	17,110

1 Results for 2009 include longitudinal data (see Appendix B).

2 The data have not been standardised to take account of age or socio-economic group.

3 All unweighted bases are rounded to the nearest 10

Source: General Lifestyle Survey, Office for National Statistics

Table 7.11 Chronic sickness: rate per 1000 reporting long-standing condition groups, by sex

Persons aged 16 and over   *Great Britain: 2009[1]*

Condition group		Men	Women	Total
XIII	Musculoskeletal system	113	159	137
VII	Heart and circulatory system	114	95	104
VIII	Respiratory system	51	65	58
III	Endocrine and metabolic	55	62	58
IX	Digestive system	25	32	29
VI	Nervous system	31	28	29
V	Mental disorders	31	36	34
VI	Eye complaints	12	15	13
X	Genito-urinary system	15	11	13
VI	Ear complaints	14	13	13
II	Neoplasms and benign growths	12	15	14
XII	Skin complaints	8	7	8
IV	Blood and related organs	4	5	4
	Other complaints[2]	2	2	2
I	Infectious diseases	1	2	2
Average number of conditions reported by those with a longstanding illness		1.5	1.6	1.6
Weighted bases (000's) = 100%		*23,425*	*24,640*	*48,064*
Unweighted sample[3]		*7,290*	*8,030*	*15,330*

1 Results for 2009 include longitudinal data (see Appendix B).

2 Including general complaints such as insomnia, fainting, generally run down, old age and general infirmity and non-specific conditions such as war wounds or road accident injuries where no further details were given.

3 All unweighted bases are rounded to the nearest 10

Source: General Lifestyle Survey, Office for National Statistics

Table 7.12 Chronic sickness: rate per 1000 reporting long-standing condition groups, by age

Great Britain: 2009[1]

Condition group	16-44	45-64	65-74	75 and over
XIII Musculoskeletal system	51	168	269	339
VII Heart and circulatory system	16	123	290	300
VIII Respiratory system	42	59	93	98
III Endocrine and metabolic	19	81	126	116
IX Digestive system	18	34	40	57
VI Nervous system	21	36	41	40
V Mental disorders	33	37	27	30
VI Eye complaints	4	11	24	59
X Genito-urinary system	7	9	32	38
VI Ear complaints	6	17	18	40
II Neoplasms and benign growths	4	17	28	40
XII Skin complaints	6	8	9	12
IV Blood and related organs	2	3	12	13
Other complaints[2]	1	2	2	5
I Infectious diseases	1	2	4	2
Average number of conditions reported by those with a longstanding illness	1.3	1.5	1.7	1.8
Weighted bases (000's) =100%	*23,519*	*15,132*	*5,081*	*4,332*
Unweighted sample[3]	*6,310*	*5,210*	*2,180*	*1,630*

1 Results for 2009 include longitudinal data (see Appendix B).

2 Including general complaints such as insomnia, fainting, generally run down, old age and general infirmity and non-specific conditions such as war wounds or road accident injuries where no further details were given.

3 All unweighted bases are rounded to the nearest 10

Source: General Lifestyle Survey, Office for National Statistics

Table 7.13   Chronic sickness: rate per 1000 reporting selected long-standing condition groups, by age and sex

Persons aged 16 and over   *Great Britain: 2009[1]*

Condition group		16-44	45-64	65-74	75 and over	All ages
XIII Musculoskeletal system	Men	42	159	211	260	113
	Women	60	175	321	394	159
VII Heart and circulatory system	Men	16	149	322	337	114
	Women	17	98	262	275	95
VIII Respiratory system	Men	34	53	87	103	51
	Women	50	65	99	94	65
III Endocrine and metabolic	Men	15	79	136	107	55
	Women	24	82	117	121	62
IX Digestive system	Men	15	32	33	51	25
	Women	20	36	45	61	32
VI Nervous system	Men	22	38	43	41	31
	Women	19	34	39	40	28
Weighted bases (000's) =100%	*Men*	*11,807*	*7,427*	*2,417*	*1,774*	*23,425*
	Women	*11,713*	*7,705*	*2,664*	*2,558*	*24,640*
Unweighted sample[2]	*Men*	*3,010*	*2,500*	*1,080*	*700*	*7,290*
	Women	*3,300*	*2,710*	*1,100*	*930*	*8,030*

1   Results for 2009 include longitudinal data (see Appendix B).
2   All unweighted bases are rounded to the nearest 10

Source: General Lifestyle Survey, Office for National Statistics

Table 7.14　Chronic sickness: rate per 1000 reporting selected long-standing conditions, by sex and age

Persons aged 16 and over　　　　　　　　　　　　　　　　　　　　　　　　　　　　　*Great Britain: 2009[1]*

Condition	Men					Women				
	16-44	45-64	65-74	75 and over	All ages	16-44	45-64	65-74	75 and over	All ages
Musculoskeletal (XIII)										
Arthritis and rheumatism	9	69	104	145	48	16	98	214	252	87
Back problems	18	52	43	41	33	28	42	30	33	33
Other bone and joint problems	15	39	64	73	32	17	36	77	108	39
Heart and circulatory (VII)										
Hypertension	6	61	112	87	41	5	57	131	118	46
Heart attack	2	21	58	63	19	1	9	29	49	12
Stroke	*	8	23	31	7	1	4	13	21	5
Other heart complaints	5	47	106	120	38	5	23	64	69	24
Other blood vessel/embolic disorders	1	12	20	37	9	4	5	25	16	8
Respiratory (VIII)										
Asthma	28	31	35	41	31	45	52	68	55	51
Bronchitis and emphysema	0	7	20	25	6	*	6	16	17	6
Hay fever	3	2	*	0	2	1	*	*	0	1
Other respiratory complaints	3	13	32	37	12	3	6	12	23	7
Weighted bases (000's) =100%	*11,807*	*7,427*	*2,417*	*1,774*	*23,425*	*11,713*	*7,705*	*2,664*	*2,558*	*24,640*
Unweighted sample[2]	*3,010*	*2,500*	*1,080*	*700*	*7,290*	*3,300*	*2,710*	*1,100*	*930*	*8,030*

1 Results for 2009 include longitudinal data (see Appendix B).
2 All unweighted bases are rounded to the nearest 10
* Information is suppressed for low cell count as a measure of disclosure control

Source: General Lifestyle Survey, Office for National Statistics

457

Table 7.15   Chronic sickness: rate per 1000 reporting selected long-standing condition groups, by socio-economic classification of household reference person

Persons aged 16 and over   *Great Britain: 2009[1]*

Condition group		Managerial and professional	Intermediate	Small employers and own account	Lower supervisory and technical	Semi-routine and routine	Total[2]
XIII	Musculoskeletal system	103	149	125	156	191	137
VII	Heart and circulatory system	85	116	101	126	133	104
VIII	Respiratory system	46	49	59	64	80	58
III	Endocrine and metabolic	50	73	63	63	68	58
IX	Digestive system	19	43	26	31	41	29
VI	Nervous system	25	35	31	24	36	29
Average number of conditions reported by those with a longstanding illness		1.46	1.62	1.59	1.62	1.70	1.58
Weighted bases (000's) =100%		*19,710*	*3,978*	*4,479*	*5,365*	*11,224*	*48,064*
Unweighted sample[3]		*6,330*	*1,250*	*1,410*	*1,730*	*3,600*	*15,330*

1 Results for 2009 include longitudinal data (see Appendix B).

2 Where the household reference person was a full-time student, had an inadequately described occupation, had never worked or was long-term unemployed these are not shown as separate categories but are included in the figure for all persons (see Appendix A).

3 All unweighted bases are rounded to the nearest 10

Source: General Lifestyle Survey, Office for National Statistics

Table 7.16 Chronic sickness: rate per 1000 reporting selected long-standing condition groups, by sex and age and socio-economic classification of household reference person

Persons aged 16 and over   *Great Britain: 2009[1]*

Condition group	Men				Women				All aged 16 and over			
	16-44	45-64	65 and over	Total	16-44	45-64	65 and over	Total	16-44	45-64	65 and over	Total
XIII Musculoskeletal system												
Managerial and professional	43	109	189	87	55	135	290	119	49	122	240	103
Intermediate	34	145	230	105	47	156	370	164	40	151	317	136
Routine and manual	48	233	269	153	72	245	391	205	60	239	337	180
VII Heart and circulatory system												
Managerial and professional	14	131	325	100	12	73	247	70	13	101	286	85
Intermediate	7	140	309	104	22	91	290	112	14	115	297	108
Routine and manual	26	187	351	147	15	131	275	116	21	159	309	131
VIII Respiratory system												
Managerial and professional	34	43	75	43	39	51	74	49	37	47	75	46
Intermediate	36	56	91	52	49	53	74	57	42	55	80	54
Routine and manual	33	66	118	62	60	90	130	87	47	78	125	75
III Endocrine and metabolic												
Managerial and professional	11	66	117	45	18	80	119	55	14	73	118	50
Intermediate	30	89	134	68	24	65	142	67	27	76	139	68
Routine and manual	11	97	127	63	32	95	109	70	21	96	117	67
IX Digestive system												
Managerial and professional	7	26	39	18	13	29	29	21	10	27	34	19
Intermediate	24	38	51	33	17	27	75	35	21	32	66	34
Routine and manual	24	39	35	31	28	55	64	45	26	47	51	38
VI Nervous system												
Managerial and professional	19	30	39	26	17	28	39	24	18	29	39	25
Intermediate	14	43	63	32	28	34	42	33	20	38	50	33
Routine and manual	28	44	36	35	17	38	42	30	23	41	39	32
Weighted base (000's) =100%												
Managerial and professional	*5,127*	*3,214*	*1,524*	*9,865*	*4,950*	*3,342*	*1,552*	*9,845*	*10,077*	*6,556*	*3,077*	*19,710*
Intermediate	*1,966*	*1,351*	*693*	*4,009*	*1,858*	*1,469*	*1,122*	*4,449*	*3,823*	*2,820*	*1,815*	*8,457*
Routine and manual	*3,795*	*2,469*	*1,759*	*8,023*	*3,857*	*2,518*	*2,191*	*8,567*	*7,652*	*4,987*	*3,950*	*16,589*
Unweighted sample[2]												
Managerial and professional	*1,310*	*1,120*	*650*	*3,080*	*1,410*	*1,200*	*630*	*3,240*	*2,720*	*2,320*	*1,280*	*6,330*
Intermediate	*490*	*440*	*300*	*1,220*	*510*	*500*	*430*	*1,430*	*1,000*	*930*	*720*	*2,660*
Routine and manual	*980*	*810*	*740*	*2,530*	*1,080*	*880*	*840*	*2,800*	*2,070*	*1,690*	*1,580*	*5,340*

1 Results for 2009 include longitudinal data (see Appendix B).
2 All unweighted bases are rounded to the nearest 10

Source: General Lifestyle Survey, Office for National Statistics

459

Table 7.17   Trends in consultations with an NHS GP in the 14 days before interview by sex and age: 1972 to 2009

All persons   Great Britain

	Unweighted								Weighted											Weighted base 2009 (000's) =100% [3]	Unweighted sample [3,5] 2009
	1972	1975	1981	1985	1991	1995	1996	1998	1998	2000	2001	2002	2003	2004	2005[1]	2006[2]	2007[2]	2008[2]	2009[2]		
	Percentage consulting GP																				
Males																					
0-4	13	13	21	22	23	22	23	18	18	18	18	19	17	15	15	14	15	15	13	1,872	580
5-15 [4]	7	7	8	9	10	9	9	8	8	8	7	8	7	7	7	6	6	6	7	3,883	1,310
16-44 [4]	8	7	7	7	9	10	10	9	9	8	8	9	8	8	8	8	7	9	9	11,429	2,900
45-64	11	11	12	12	11	14	15	14	14	15	13	15	12	14	13	13	14	14	14	7,336	2,460
65-74	12	12	13	15	17	17	19	17	17	20	18	22	18	17	17	18	20	21	21	2,403	1,070
75 and over	19	20	17	19	21	22	21	21	21	20	22	21	21	21	21	24	21	23	25	1,766	700
Total	10	9	10	11	12	13	13	12	12	12	11	13	11	11	11	11	11	12	12	28,689	9,030
Females																					
0-4	15	13	17	21	21	21	20	18	18	14	18	14	14	17	15	15	15	16	12	1,746	540
5-15 [4]	6	7	9	11	11	13	9	10	10	9	9	8	7	7	6	6	6	7	7	3,539	1,200
16-44 [4]	15	13	15	17	17	18	20	17	17	16	15	18	15	16	17	15	16	17	17	11,437	3,210
45-64	12	12	13	15	17	17	19	18	18	17	18	17	17	17	17	15	16	17	18	7,636	2,690
65-74	15	16	16	17	19	23	21	19	19	22	18	21	22	21	21	22	17	21	23	2,654	1,090
75 and over	20	17	20	20	19	23	23	20	20	22	20	27	20	22	21	20	18	24	22	2,550	920
Total	13	12	14	16	17	18	19	17	17	16	16	17	16	16	16	15	15	17	17	29,563	9,660
All persons																					
0-4	14	13	19	21	22	21	22	18	18	16	18	17	16	16	15	15	15	15	13	3,619	1,120
5-15 [4]	7	7	9	10	10	11	9	9	9	8	8	8	7	7	7	6	6	6	7	7,422	2,510
16-44 [4]	12	10	11	12	13	14	15	13	13	12	11	14	12	12	12	12	12	13	13	22,866	6,120
45-64	12	11	12	14	14	16	17	16	16	16	16	16	15	15	15	14	15	16	16	14,972	5,150
65-74	14	14	15	16	18	20	20	18	18	21	18	22	20	19	19	20	19	21	22	5,057	2,160
75 and over	20	18	19	20	19	23	22	21	20	21	21	25	20	22	21	22	19	23	23	4,316	1,620
Total	12	11	12	14	14	16	16	14	14	14	13	15	13	14	14	13	13	14	15	58,252	18,680

1 2005 data includes last quarter of 2004/5 data due to survey change from financial year to calendar year.

2 Results from 2006 include longitudinal data (see Appendix B).

3 Trend tables show unweighted and weighted figures for 1998 to give an indication of the effect of the weighting. Bases for earlier years can be found in GLF/GHS reports for each year.

4 These age-groups were 5-14 and 15-44 in 1972 to 1975.

5 All unweighted bases are rounded to the nearest 10

Source: General Lifestyle Survey, Office for National Statistics

Table 7.18   Average number of NHS GP consultations per person per year by sex and age: 1972 to 2009

All persons [1]

Great Britain

	Unweighted								Weighted										
	1972[2]	1975	1981	1985	1991	1995	1996	1998	1998	2000	2001	2002	2003	2004	2005[3]	2006[4]	2007[4]	2008[4]	2009[4]
Males																			
0-4	4	4	7	7	7	7	8	6	6	6	6	7	6	5	5	4	5	5	4
5-15[5]	2	2	2	3	3	3	3	2	2	2	2	3	2	2	2	2	2	2	2
16-44[5]	3	2	2	2	3	3	3	3	3	3	3	3	3	3	3	2	2	3	3
45-64	4	4	4	4	4	4	5	4	4	5	4	5	4	4	4	4	4	4	5
65-74	4	4	4	5	5	5	6	5	5	6	5	7	6	5	5	6	7	7	7
75 and over	7	7	6	6	7	8	7	7	7	6	7	7	7	7	7	8	7	8	8
Total	3	3	3	3	4	4	4	4	4	4	4	4	3	3	4	3	4	4	4
Females																			
0-4	5	4	5	7	7	7	6	6	6	4	6	4	5	6	5	5	5	5	4
5-15[5]	2	2	3	3	3	4	3	3	3	3	3	2	2	2	2	2	2	2	2
16-44[5]	5	4	5	5	5	6	7	5	5	5	5	6	5	5	6	5	5	6	6
45-64	4	4	4	5	5	5	6	6	6	5	6	5	5	6	5	5	5	6	6
65-74	5	5	5	5	6	7	7	6	6	7	5	7	7	7	7	7	5	7	8
75 and over	7	6	6	7	6	7	7	6	6	7	6	9	6	7	7	7	6	7	7
Total	4	4	4	5	5	6	6	5	5	5	5	6	5	5	5	5	5	5	6
All persons																			
0-4	4	4	6	7	7	7	7	6	6	5	6	5	5	5	5	5	5	5	4
5-15[5]	2	2	3	3	3	3	3	3	3	2	3	2	2	2	2	2	2	2	2
16-44[5]	4	3	4	4	4	4	5	4	4	4	4	4	4	4	4	4	4	4	4
45-64	4	4	4	4	4	5	5	5	5	5	5	5	5	5	5	5	5	5	5
65-74	5	4	5	5	6	6	6	6	6	6	5	7	6	6	6	7	6	7	7
75 and over	7	7	6	6	6	7	7	6	6	7	6	8	7	7	7	7	6	8	8
Total	4	4	4	4	5	5	5	4	4	4	4	5	4	4	4	4	4	5	5

1 Trend tables show unweighted and weighted figures for 1998 to give an indication of the effect of weighting. Bases for 2009 are shown in table 7.17. Bases for earlier years can be found in GHS reports for each year.
2 1972 figures relate to England and Wales.
3 2005 data includes last quarter of 2004/5 data due to survey change from financial year to calendar year.
4 Results from 2006 include longitudinal data (see Appendix B).
5 These age-groups were 5-14 and 15-44 in 1972 to 1975.

Source: General Lifestyle Survey, Office for National Statistics

Table 7.19 NHS GP consultations: trends in site of consultations: 1971 to 2009

Consultations in the 14 days before interview   *Great Britain*

Site of consultation	Unweighted								Weighted										
	1971	1975	1981	1985	1991	1995	1996	1998	1998	2000	2001	2002	2003	2004	2005[1]	2006[2]	2007[2]	2008[2]	2009[2]
	%	%	%	%	%	%	%	%	%	%	%	%	%	%	%	%	%	%	%
Surgery[3]	73	78	79	79	81	84	84	84	84	86	85	86	86	87	87	87	88	86	86
Home	22	19	14	14	11	9	8	6	6	5	5	5	4	4	3	4	3	3	2
Telephone	4	3	7	7	8	7	8	10	10	10	10	9	10	9	10	10	10	11	11
Weighted bases (000's) =100% [4]									*9,658*	*9,744*	*9,161*	*10,284*	*9,165*	*9,379*	*9,316*	*9,265*	*9,344*	*10,300*	*10,654*
Unweighted sample [4,5]	*5,030*	*4,460*	*4,700*	*4,120*	*4,230*	*4,390*	*4,340*	*3,500*	*3,500*	*3,290*	*3,420*	*3,660*	*3,980*	*3,380*	*4,940*	*3,680*	*3,490*	*3,620*	*3,550*

1 2005 data includes last quarter of 2004/5 data due to survey change from financial year to calendar year.

2 Results from 2006 include longitudinal data (see Appendix B).

3 Includes consultations with a GP at a health centre and those who had answered 'elsewhere'.

4 Trend tables show unweighted and weighted figures for 1998 to give an indication of the effect of the weighting. For the weighted data (1998 and 2000 to 2009) the weighted base (000's) is the base for percentages. Unweighted data (up to 1998) are based on the unweighted sample.

5 All unweighted bases are rounded to the nearest 10

Source: General Lifestyle Survey, Office for National Statistics

462

Table 7.20 Percentage of persons who consulted an NHS GP in the 14 days before interview by sex and site of consultation, and by age and site of consultation

Persons who consulted in the 14 days before interview *Great Britain: 2009[1]*

Site of consultation[2]	Total	Males	Females	Age[3]					
				0-4	5-15	16-44	45-64	65-74	75 and over
	%	%	%	%	%	%	%	%	%
Surgery	88	89	88	92	88	90	89	88	80
At home	2	2	2	*	*	1	1	2	10
Telephone	12	11	12	9	12	12	13	13	11
Weighted base (000's) =100%	*8,621*	*3,581*	*5,039*	*458*	*536*	*3,038*	*2,456*	*1,125*	*1,009*
Unweighted sample[4]	*2,890*	*1,210*	*1,680*	*150*	*190*	*850*	*850*	*470*	*390*

1 Results for 2009 include longitudinal data (see Appendix B).

2 Percentages add to more than 100 because some people consulted at more than one site during the reference period.

3 Consultation might have been made on behalf of the person

4 All unweighted bases are rounded to the nearest 10

* Information is suppressed for low cell count as a measure of disclosure control

Source: General Lifestyle Survey, Office for National Statistics

Table 7.21 **NHS GP consultations**
(a) Percentage of persons who consulted a doctor in the 14 days before interview, by sex, age, and economic activity status
(b) Average number of consultations per person per year, by sex, age, and economic activity status

Persons aged 16 and over   *Great Britain: 2009[1]*

Economic activity status	Age							
	Men				Women			
	16-44	45-64	65 and over	Total	16-44	45-64	65 and over	Total
(a) Percentage who consulted a GP in the 14 days before interview								
Working	9	12	17	11	17	16	13	17
Unemployed	6	11	24	8	16	18	26	16
Economically inactive	11	26	24	21	20	24	23	22
Total	9	15	23	13	18	19	23	19
(b) Average number of consultations per person per year								
Working	3	4	4	3	6	5	4	5
Unemployed	2	4	11	3	5	5	10	5
Economically inactive	4	9	8	7	7	8	8	7
Total	3	5	8	4	6	6	7	6
Weighted bases (000's) =100%								
Working	6,883	4,728	402	12,014	7,006	4,788	276	12,069
Unemployed	1,165	427	31	1,623	772	196	31	999
Economically inactive	1,678	1,468	3,681	6,827	2,820	2,371	4,857	10,048
Total	9,726	6,624	4,114	20,464	10,597	7,355	5,164	23,116
Unweighted sample[2]								
Working	1,740	1,580	180	3,490	1,950	1,640	110	3,700
Unemployed	280	140	10	430	210	60	10	280
Economically inactive	430	500	1,560	2,480	820	880	1,880	3,580
Total	2,440	2,210	1,750	6,400	2,980	2,580	2,000	7,560

1 Results for 2009 include longitudinal data (see Appendix B).
2 All unweighted bases are rounded to the nearest 10
Note: Shaded figures indicate the estimates are unreliable and any analysis using these figures may be invalid. Any use of these shaded figures must be accompanied by this disclaimer.

Source: General Lifestyle Survey, Office for National Statistics

Table 7.22 **Percentage of persons consulting an NHS GP in the 14 days before interview who obtained a prescription from the doctor, by sex, age and socio-economic classification of household reference person**

Persons who consulted in the 14 days before interview

Great Britain: 2009[1]

Socio-economic classification of household reference person[2]	Males					Females				
	Age					Age				
	0-15	16-44	45-64	65 and over	Total	0-15	16-44	45-64	65 and over	Total
	Percentage consulting who obtained a prescription									
Managerial and professional	53	56	59	63	58	51	61	60	64	60
Intermediate	51	54	63	60	58	66	57	71	66	65
Routine and manual	63	59	62	70	64	49	63	71	76	68
All persons consulting	56	56	61	66	60	54	60	66	71	64
Weighted bases (000's) =100%										
Managerial and professional	198	419	400	335	1,352	195	781	558	297	1,830
Intermediate	60	178	156	153	547	95	289	279	268	931
Routine and manual	216	387	464	409	1,476	153	691	518	548	1,909
All persons consulting	521	1,059	1,051	950	3,581	473	1,979	1,405	1,183	5,039
Unweighted sample[3]										
Managerial and professional	70	120	140	150	470	60	220	200	130	600
Intermediate	20	50	50	70	180	30	80	100	100	310
Routine and manual	70	100	150	160	490	50	210	190	210	650
All persons consulting	180	280	350	400	1,210	150	560	500	460	1,680

1 Results for 2009 include longitudinal data (see Appendix B).
2 Where the household reference person was a full-time student, had an inadequately described occupation, had never worked or was long term unemployed these are not shown as separate categories, but are included in the figure for all persons (see Appendix A
3 All unweighted bases are rounded to the nearest 10
Note: Shaded figures indicate the estimates are unreliable and any analysis using these figures may be invalid. Any use of these shaded figures must be accompanied by this disclaimer.

Source: General Lifestyle Survey, Office for National Statistics

Table 7.23 **GP consultations: consultations with a doctor in the 14 days before interview by sex of person consulting and whether consultation was NHS or private**

Consultations in the 14 days before interview   *Great Britain: 2009[1]*

Type of consultation	Consultations made by males	Consultations made by females	All persons
	%	%	%
NHS	97	97	97
Private	3	3	3
Weighted base (000's) =100%	*5,199*	*7,171*	*12,369*
Unweighted sample[2]	*1,750*	*2,360*	*4,110*

1 Results for 2009 include longitudinal data (see Appendix B).
2 All unweighted bases are rounded to the nearest 10

Source: General Lifestyle Survey, Office for National Statistics

Table 7.24 Trends in reported consultations with a practice nurse by sex and age: 2000 to 2009
(a) percentage consulting a practice nurse in the 14 days before interview
(b) average number of consultations with a practice nurse per person per year

All persons | Great Britain

	(a) percentage consulting a practice nurse										(b) average number of consultations with a practice nurse per person per year										Weighted base 2009 (000's) = 100%[2]	Unweighted sample[3] 2009
	2000	2001	2002	2003	2004	2005	2006	2007	2008	2009	2000	2001	2002	2003	2004	2005[1]	2006[2]	2007[2]	2008[2]	2009[2]		
Males																						
0-4	4	3	4	5	5	5	3	4	5	4	1	1	1	1	1	1	1	1	1	1	1,872	580
5-15	2	2	2	1	2	2	2	2	2	2	0	1	0	0	1	1	1	0	1	0	3,883	1,310
16-44	2	2	3	2	2	2	2	3	3	2	1	1	1	1	1	1	1	1	1	1	11,433	2,910
45-64	5	6	6	5	6	7	7	7	7	6	1	2	2	2	2	2	2	2	2	2	7,334	2,460
65-74	10	12	13	13	11	13	11	13	15	15	3	4	4	4	3	4	4	4	5	5	2,403	1,070
75 and over	8	13	11	10	14	15	15	15	15	16	3	4	3	3	4	5	5	4	4	5	1,766	700
Total	4	5	5	4	5	5	5	5	4	5	1	1	1	1	1	1	1	2	2	2	28,692	9,030
Females																						
0-4	5	3	5	6	3	4	3	4	4	5	1	1	1	2	1	1	1	1	1	2	1,746	540
5-15	1	1	1	1	1	2	2	1	2	1	0	0	0	0	0	0	1	0	0	0	3,539	1,200
16-44	5	5	6	5	6	7	6	5	6	6	1	1	2	2	2	2	2	2	2	2	11,437	3,210
45-64	6	7	7	7	7	7	6	9	8	8	2	2	2	2	2	2	2	3	3	2	7,639	2,690
65-74	10	11	11	14	12	14	12	12	13	13	3	4	3	4	4	4	4	3	4	4	2,656	1,090
75 and over	9	12	12	14	12	14	12	13	14	15	3	4	4	4	4	4	4	5	5	5	2,550	920
Total	5	6	7	7	6	7	6	7	7	7	2	2	2	2	2	2	2	2	2	2	29,568	9,660
All persons																						
0-4	4	3	4	6	4	5	3	4	4	4	1	1	1	2	1	1	1	1	1	1	3,619	1,120
5-15	1	2	1	1	1	2	2	2	2	2	0	1	0	0	0	0	0	0	0	0	7,422	2,510
16-44	3	4	4	4	4	5	4	4	5	4	1	1	1	1	1	1	1	1	1	1	22,870	6,120
45-64	6	6	7	6	6	7	7	8	7	6	2	2	2	2	2	2	2	2	2	2	14,973	5,150
65-74	10	12	12	14	12	13	12	12	14	14	3	4	4	4	3	4	4	4	4	5	5,059	2,170
75 and over	9	12	12	12	13	14	13	14	14	15	3	4	4	4	4	5	4	5	5	5	4,316	1,620
Total	5	5	6	6	6	6	6	6	6	6	1	2	2	2	2	2	2	2	2	2	58,259	18,690

1 2005 data includes last quarter of 2004/5 data due to survey change from financial year to calendar year.
2 Results from 2006 include longitudinal data (see Appendix B).
3 All unweighted bases are rounded to the nearest 10

Source: General Lifestyle Survey, Office for National Statistics

467

Table 7.25   Percentage of children using health services other than a doctor in the 14 days before interview

All persons aged under 16

	Male			Female			Total		
	0-4	5-15	Total	0-4	5-15	Total	0-4	5-15	Total
Percentage who reported:[2]									
Seeing a practice nurse at the GP surgery	4	2	3	6	2	3	5	2	3
Seeing a health visitor at the GP surgery	3	0	1	5	0	2	4	0	2
Going to a child health clinic	5	1	2	5	1	2	5	1	2
Going to a child welfare clinic	0	0	0	*	*	0	0	0	0
None of the above	89	97	95	86	97	94	88	97	94
Weighted base (000's) =100%	1,872	3,883	5,755	1,746	3,539	5,285	3,619	7,422	11,041
Unweighted sample[3]	580	1,310	1,890	540	1,200	1,740	1,120	2,510	3,630

1 Results for 2009 include longitudinal data (see Appendix B).
2 Percentages may sum to greater than 100 as respondents could give more than one answer
3 All unweighted bases are rounded to the nearest 10
* Information is suppressed for low cell count as a measure of disclosure control

Source: General Lifestyle Survey, Office for National Statistics

Table 7.26   Trends in percentages of persons who reported attending an outpatient or casualty department in the 3 months before interview by sex and age: 1972 to 2009

All persons[1]

Percentages

	Unweighted								Weighted										
	1972[2]	1975	1981	1985	1991	1995	1996	1998	1998	2000	2001	2002	2003	2004	2005[3]	2006[4]	2007[4]	2008[4]	2009[4]
Males																			
0-4	8	9	12	13	14	12	13	16	16	14	16	17	13	14	15	15	12	13	13
5-15[5]	9	8	11	12	11	11	12	12	12	11	10	11	10	11	10	11	10	11	9
16-44[5]	11	9	11	12	11	12	13	13	13	12	11	11	11	10	10	10	11	9	9
45-64	11	10	12	16	15	16	16	17	17	16	16	15	16	17	16	15	13	16	14
65-74	10	11	14	16	18	21	20	25	25	24	22	24	21	24	22	21	21	24	24
75 and over	10	12	14	15	22	26	25	29	29	26	31	26	24	26	26	27	23	25	26
Total	10	10	11	13	13	14	15	16	16	15	14	14	14	14	14	13	13	14	13
Females																			
0-4	6	8	9	11	11	12	9	13	13	10	11	12	11	11	12	12	10	12	10
5-15[5]	6	6	8	9	8	9	10	11	11	8	8	9	9	8	9	8	8	6	8
16-44[5]	9	9	11	12	12	12	13	13	13	13	12	12	13	12	12	12	13	13	11
45-64	11	10	13	15	16	17	18	18	18	16	18	16	18	18	16	18	16	16	15
65-74	12	12	16	17	18	21	22	21	21	21	21	20	20	21	21	22	20	22	19
75 and over	13	10	16	17	20	22	24	26	26	24	23	25	22	22	24	27	20	24	24
Total	10	9	12	13	14	14	15	16	16	15	14	14	15	15	15	15	14	14	14
All persons																			
0-4	7	8	10	12	13	12	11	14	15	12	13	14	12	13	13	13	11	12	11
5-15[5]	8	7	10	10	10	10	11	11	11	10	9	10	10	10	9	10	9	9	8
16-44[5]	10	9	11	12	12	12	13	13	13	13	12	12	12	11	11	11	12	11	10
45-64	11	10	13	15	16	16	17	18	18	16	17	15	17	18	16	17	15	16	15
65-74	11	11	15	17	18	21	21	23	23	22	21	22	21	24	21	22	20	23	21
75 and over	12	10	15	16	21	24	24	27	27	25	26	25	23	24	25	27	22	25	25
Total	10	9	12	13	13	14	15	16	16	15	14	14	14	14	14	14	14	14	13

1 Trend tables show unweighted and weighted figures for 1998 to give an indication of the effect of the weighting. Bases for 2009 are shown in Table 7.2. Bases for earlier years can be found in GLF/GHS reports for each year.

2 1972 figures relate to England and Wales.

3 2005 data includes last quarter of 2004/5 data due to survey change from financial year to calendar year.

4 Results from 2006 include longitudinal data (see Appendix B).

5 These age groups were 5-14 and 15-44 in 1972 to 1975.

Source: General Lifestyle Survey, Office for National Statistics

Table 7.27   Trends in day-patient treatment in the 12 months before interview by sex and age, 1992 to 2009

All persons / Great Britain

Percentage receiving day-patient treatment

	Unweighted					Weighted											Weighted base 2009 (000's) =100%[3]	Unweighted sample[3,4] 2009
	1992	1994	1995	1996	1998	1998	2000	2001	2002	2003	2004	2005[1]	2006[2]	2007[2]	2008[2]	2009[2]		
Males																		
0-4	4	4	4	5	6	6	6	7	8	7	6	6	6	6	4	8	1,872	580
5-15	2	3	3	3	4	4	5	4	5	4	4	4	4	4	4	4	3,883	1,310
16-44	4	5	6	5	6	6	6	7	7	7	7	6	5	5	6	6	11,433	2,910
45-64	4	5	7	6	7	7	8	8	8	8	9	10	7	7	9	9	7,337	2,460
65-74	5	6	6	7	6	6	10	8	11	10	12	12	9	10	12	13	2,403	1,070
75 and over	4	5	5	6	12	11	7	10	12	12	13	10	8	11	11	12	1,766	700
Total	4	5	5	5	6	6	7	7	8	7	8	7	6	6	7	7	28,694	9,030
Females																		
0-4	2	3	3	3	5	4	6	4	5	6	5	5	4	3	4	4	1,746	540
5-15	2	3	2	4	4	4	3	3	4	4	4	4	3	3	3	4	3,539	1,200
16-44	5	7	6	7	8	8	8	8	9	8	8	8	7	8	9	8	11,444	3,210
45-64	5	5	7	8	8	8	9	8	8	9	10	9	8	8	8	9	7,641	2,690
65-74	4	5	5	6	6	6	12	8	10	9	10	10	9	11	11	11	2,656	1,090
75 and over	3	5	5	7	8	8	8	8	10	11	9	9	9	11	12	11	2,550	920
Total	4	5	5	6	7	7	8	7	8	8	8	8	7	8	8	8	29,577	9,660
All persons																		
0-4	3	3	3	4	5	5	6	5	6	6	6	6	5	4	4	6	3,619	1,120
5-15	2	3	3	3	4	4	4	4	4	4	4	4	3	3	3	4	7,422	2,510
16-44	4	6	6	6	7	7	7	7	8	7	7	7	6	6	7	7	22,877	6,120
45-64	5	5	7	7	8	8	8	8	8	8	9	9	7	8	8	9	14,978	5,150
65-74	4	5	6	7	6	6	11	8	10	9	11	11	9	10	12	12	5,059	2,170
75 and over	3	5	5	6	9	9	8	9	11	12	11	10	9	11	12	11	4,316	1,620
Total	4	5	5	6	7	7	7	7	8	8	8	8	7	7	8	8	58,271	18,690

1 2005 data includes last quarter of 2004/5 data due to survey change from financial year to calendar year
2 Results from 2006 include longitudinal data (see Appendix B).
3 Trend tables show unweighted and weighted figures for 1998 to give an indication of the effect of the weighting. Bases for earlier years can be found in GHS reports for each year.
4 All unweighted bases are rounded to the nearest 10

Source: General Lifestyle Survey, Office for National Statistics

Table 7.28 Trends in inpatient stays in the 12 months before interview by sex and age, 1982 to 2009

All persons   Great Britain

Percentage with inpatient stay

	Unweighted						Weighted												Weighted base 2009 (000's) =100%[3]	Unweighted sample[3,4] 2009
	1982	1985	1991	1995	1996	1998	1998	2000	2001	2002	2003	2004	2005[1]	2006[2]	2007[2]	2008[2]	2009[2]		
Males																			
0-4	14	12	10	9	9	9	9	8	11	11	8	8	8	7	4	5	6	1,872	580
5-15	6	8	6	5	5	5	5	5	4	4	3	3	3	2	2	3	2	3,883	1,310
16-44	5	6	6	5	5	5	5	4	5	5	4	4	4	4	4	3	4	11,433	2,910
45-64	8	8	8	9	8	8	8	8	8	8	8	7	7	7	6	8	7	7,337	2,460
65-74	12	13	13	15	13	15	15	13	12	15	13	11	12	11	12	12	12	2,403	1,070
75 and over	14	17	20	21	18	21	21	18	19	18	16	17	19	17	16	15	16	1,766	700
Total	7	8	8	8	7	8	8	7	7	7	7	6	7	6	6	6	6	28,694	9,030
Females																			
0-4	12	8	8	8	7	10	10	6	6	7	5	6	6	5	4	6	6	1,746	540
5-15	4	5	4	4	4	4	4	3	3	2	4	3	3	3	3	2	2	3,539	1,200
16-44	15	16	15	12	12	11	11	10	9	9	9	10	8	8	9	9	8	11,447	3,210
45-64	8	8	9	8	10	8	9	7	8	8	7	9	6	6	7	7	7	7,641	2,690
65-74	8	18	11	11	12	10	10	13	10	8	10	11	11	11	12	12	11	2,656	1,090
75 and over	12	13	16	20	16	15	15	18	15	16	14	15	17	15	15	17	14	2,552	920
Total	11	11	11	10	10	10	10	9	8	8	8	9	8	8	8	9	7	29,582	9,660
All persons																			
0-4	13	10	9	9	8	9	9	7	9	9	7	7	7	6	4	6	6	3,619	1,120
5-15	5	6	5	4	4	5	5	4	4	3	3	3	3	3	3	3	2	7,422	2,510
16-44	10	11	10	8	9	8	8	7	7	7	7	7	6	6	6	6	6	22,880	6,120
45-64	8	8	8	8	9	8	8	8	8	8	7	8	7	7	7	7	7	14,978	5,150
65-74	10	10	12	13	12	12	12	13	11	11	12	11	11	12	12	12	11	5,059	2,170
75 and over	13	15	18	20	17	17	17	18	17	17	15	16	17	15	15	16	15	4,318	1,620
Total	9	10	10	9	9	9	9	8	8	8	7	8	8	7	7	7	7	58,275	18,690

1 2005 data includes last quarter of 2004/5 data due to survey change from financial year to calendar year.

2 Results from 2006 include longitudinal data (see Appendix B).

3 Trend tables show unweighted and weighted figures for 1998 to give an indication of the effect of the weighting. Bases for earlier years can be found in GLF/GHS reports for each year.

4 All unweighted bases are rounded to the nearest 10

Source: General Lifestyle Survey, Office for National Statistics

Table 7.29 **Average number of nights spent in hospital as an inpatient during the 12 months before interview, by sex and age**

All inpatients

Great Britain: 2009[1]

Age	Average number of nights			Weighted base (all inpatients) (000's) =100%			Unweighted sample[2]		
	Male	Female	Total	Male	Female	Total	Male	Female	Total
0-4	6	7	6	105	98	203	40	30	60
5-15	3	4	4	74	66	140	30	20	50
16-44	6	3	4	432	867	1,298	110	280	390
45-64	8	6	7	495	530	1,025	170	190	360
65-74	7	8	8	281	280	561	130	110	240
75 and over	13	12	12	289	345	634	120	120	240
All persons	8	6	7	1,676	2,187	3,863	580	750	1,340

1 Results for 2009 include longitudinal data (see Appendix B).
2 All unweighted bases are rounded to the nearest 10

Source: General Lifestyle Survey, Office for National Statistics

Table 7.30 **Inpatient stays and outpatient attendances**
  (a) **Average number of inpatient stays per 100 persons in a 12 month reference period, by sex and age**
  (b) **Average number of outpatient attendances per 100 persons per year, by sex and age**

All persons

Great Britain: 2009[1]

Age	(a) Average number of inpatient stays per 100 persons during the 12 months before interview			(b) Average number of outpatient attendances per 100 persons per year			Weighted bases (000's) =100%			Unweighted sample[2]		
	Males	Females	Total	Males	Females	Total	Males	Females	Total	Males	Females	Total
0-4	7	9	8	81	62	72	1,872	1,746	3,619	580	540	1,120
5-15	2	3	3	57	54	56	3,883	3,539	7,422	1,310	1,200	2,510
16-44	5	6	6	64	92	78	11,433	11,447	22,880	2,910	3,210	6,120
45-64	10	9	9	119	139	129	7,337	7,641	14,978	2,460	2,690	5,150
65-74	17	13	15	263	168	213	2,403	2,656	5,059	1,070	1,090	2,170
75 and over	21	18	19	206	228	219	1,766	2,552	4,318	700	920	1,620
Total	8	8	8	104	117	110	28,694	29,582	58,275	9,030	9,660	18,690

1 Results for 2009 include longitudinal data (see Appendix B).
2 All unweighted bases are rounded to the nearest 10

Source: General Lifestyle Survey, Office for National Statistics